INDIAN ROCK ART AND ITS GLOBAL CONTEXT

• Kalyan Kumar Chakravarty •
• Robert G. Bednarik •

INDIAN ROCK ART
AND ITS GLOBAL CONTEXT

• Kalyan Kumar Chakravarty •
• Robert G. Bednarik •

MOTILAL BANARSIDASS PUBLISHERS PRIVATE LIMITED, DELHI, INDIA
INDIRA GANDHI RASHTRIYA MANAV SANGRAHALAYA, BHOPAL, INDIA

First Edition: Delhi, India 1997

ISBN : 81-208-1464-9

Price : Rs.1700.00

Also available at:
MOTILAL BANARSIDASS
- 41 U.A. Bungalow Road, Jawahar Nagar, Delhi - 110 007
- 8 Mahalaxmi Chamber, Warden Road, Mumbai 400 026
- 120 Royapettah High Road, Mylapore, Chennai 600 004
- Sanas Plaza, Subhash Nagar, Pune 411 002
- 16 St. Mark's Road, Bangalore 560 001
- 8 Camac Street, Calcutta 700 017
- Ashok Rajpath, Patna 800 004
- Chowk, Varanasi 221 001

PUBLISHED BY NARENDRA PRAKASH JAIN
FOR MOTILAL BANARSIDASS PUBLISHERS PRIVATE LIMITED,
BUNGALOW ROAD, DELHI 110 007 &
CO-PUBLISHED BY DIRECTOR,
INDIRA GANDHI RASHTRIYA MANAV SANGRAHALAYA, BHOPAL, INDIA

PRINTED IN INDIA
BY JAINENDRA PRAKASH JAIN AT SHRI JAINENDRA PRESS,
A-45 NARAINA, PHASE I, NEW DELHI 110 028

Composing, Art work, Layout designing, Laser Typesetting by: K. Seshadri, IGRMS, Bhopal.
Photo Typeset printing at:Tara Chand Sons, New Delhi.

CONTENTS

• ACKNOWLEDGEMENTS •

ACKNOWLEDGEMENTS

The photographs on Indian Rock Art are mostly from the Archive of Indira Gandhi Rashtriya Manav Sangrahalaya. Photographic work had been undertaken by Naval Jaiswal, Assistant Curator, Devendra Kumar Jain, Assistant Keeper and Ravi Shrivas, Senior Photographer, in the IGRMS. The photographs of Kumaon Himalayas and Manipur have been taken from the Archive of Indira Gandhi National Centre of Arts, New Delhi. Photographs of several regions are contributed by individual scholars engaged in the study and documentation of rock art. The names of the scholars are: Shankar Tiwari, Bhopal; V. H. Sonawane, Vadodarā; Giriraj Kumar, RASI, Agra; Rakesh Tewari, Lucknow; P. P. Shirodkar, Goa; Pradeep Shukla, Sagar and Maheshwari, Hoshangabad. Our gratitudes are due to all of them. Thanks are also due to G. Jayaprakasan, K. Seshadri, Santosh Pandey and Rachna Mathur for Scanning/typesetting the script and to Pratibha Nigam and her staff for library assistance.

K. K. Chakravarty, Director, IGRMS and his staff gratefully acknowledge the unstinted help and involvement of IFRAO/ R. G. Bednarik without which this project would not have have come through.

Most of the non-Indian illustrations in this volume are from the archive of the International Federation of Rock Art Organisations in Melbourne, and the majority of these were provided by R. G. Bednarik. However, his material has been supplemented by photographs from several leading rock art researchers from around the world. We express our utmost gratitude to the following scholars for contributing some of the best photographic material from their respective research regions: J. Mikilani Ho (U.S.A.), Dr Majeed Khan (Saudi Arabia), Dr Georgia Lee (U.S.A.), Howard P. McNickle (New Zealand), Gerhard Milstreu (Denmark), Professor William Breen Murray (Mexico), Alfred Muzzolini (France), Linda O'Connor and the Ontario Ministry of Natural Resources (Canada), Masaru Ogawa (Japan), Dr María Onetto and María Mercedes Podestá (Argentina), Tang Huisheng (China), H. C. (Bert) Woodhouse (South Africa). Their valuable contributions have helped shape this collection into the representative sample we have tried to present.

Finally, R. G. Bednarik acknowledges the generous support of the Australia-India Council in Canberra, Australia, for underwriting his travel expenses to India as well as costs of preparing the exhibits of the WAC exhibition. Similarly, he thanks the Indira Gandhi Rashtriya Manav Sangrahalaya for the generous hospitality extended to him while in India, and for its support of his research in Bhopal in late 1994.

• INTRODUCTION •

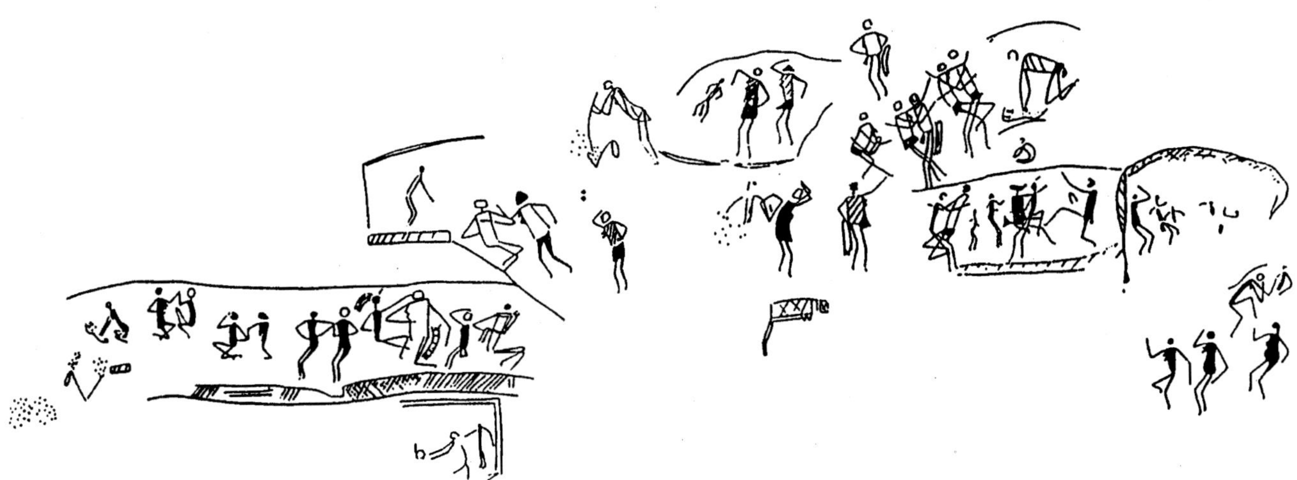

INTRODUCTION

Prehistoric rock art represents by far the largest body of evidence we possess of humanity's artistic, cognitive and cultural beginnings. It occurs in most countries of the world, having served as an almost universal expression and communication of human thought since the dawn of humanity. Through its relative permanence, rock art has profoundly influenced the beliefs and artistic conventions of subsequent societies to the present day; it is an integral part of humanity's collective memory. It is one of our greatest surviving art treasures.

Nevertheless, rock art is very unevenly distributed in the world, and India is fortunate in possessing one of the three largest concentrations of this world heritage; the two others are those of South Africa and Australia. This volume endeavours, for the first time ever, to place this rich body of Indian rock art into its global setting. A representative sample of world rock art thus provides a fitting background for one of this global body's most stunning regional components.

Many tens of millions of figures or motifs of rock art have been found world-wide, and many more are being discovered by researchers each year. While it is impossible to show an exhaustive sample of all the art traditions and regions of the world, this catalogue does attempt to be as representative as it is possible within the constraints of present knowledge. Most examples selected are probably fairly typical for particular major corpora. Moreover, some attempt has been made to allow size or significance of art traditions to be reflected in the number of illustrations included on these pages.

In India, rock art occurs in many regions, from the Himalayas to the tip of the subcontinent. The largest concentrations, however, are found in the country's central sandstone regions, particularly in Madhya Pradesh, Uttar Pradesh and Rajasthan. Rock painting traditions of great diversity in motif range, technique and style provide an incredibly rich array of visual information about the lives, technologies, beliefs and preoccupations of the peoples of the country's distant past.

While in India the most spectacular rock art consists usually of pigmented pictures or paintings, in the rest of the world paintings and petroglyphs (or engravings) are fairly equally represented overall. The choice of technique is often related to the type of rock being used as a canvas. Rock art is found in deep caves as well as on high mountains, from the tropics to the arctic regions. Some traditions, such as some of those found among the illustrations from Australia, are known to be well over 40,000 years old; others from that very same continent were created only a few decades ago. Together, this incredibly rich and ancient tapestry of artistic and aesthetic sophistication provides but an inkling of the complexity of the societies it records.

This catalogue is therefore no more than a most humble effort to pay homage to the prehistoric and tribal artists of India and of the world. It is dedicated to the nameless masters of humanity's earliest artistic past - the creators of what we believe is the greatest art ever produced. ❐

• ABOUT ROCK ART •

ABOUT ROCK ART

This volume is not intended as an explicitly scholarly work, but it still attempts to present the subject in a reasonably balanced fashion; it is also intended to be in complete accordance with all the present scientific knowledge we possess in this area of academic research, including that which has been acquired only most recently. As the volume addresses not only the academic reader but also the interested general public, it is requisite to begin with certain introductory considerations.

With the exception of a handful of countries (particularly in Europe) where no rock art has been reported so far, this form of human expression occurs universally around the earth. However, it is found in a very great variety of forms and shapes. But there are also significant consistencies, both in the technological sense (the methods used in its production) and in the graphic repertoire ethnically unrelated peoples have used. There is a strong suggestion that such identical techniques and graphic forms were re-invented many times, by many peoples and in different eras. Such uniformities are perhaps expressions of the ultimate unity and uniformity of human modes of expression, and much less commonly of processes of diffusion. This general impression differs entirely from models of diffusion, which so much dominated academic thought under the shadow of past colonialism. Art itself, we believe today, was not 'invented' in a particular world region, nor even in a particular era

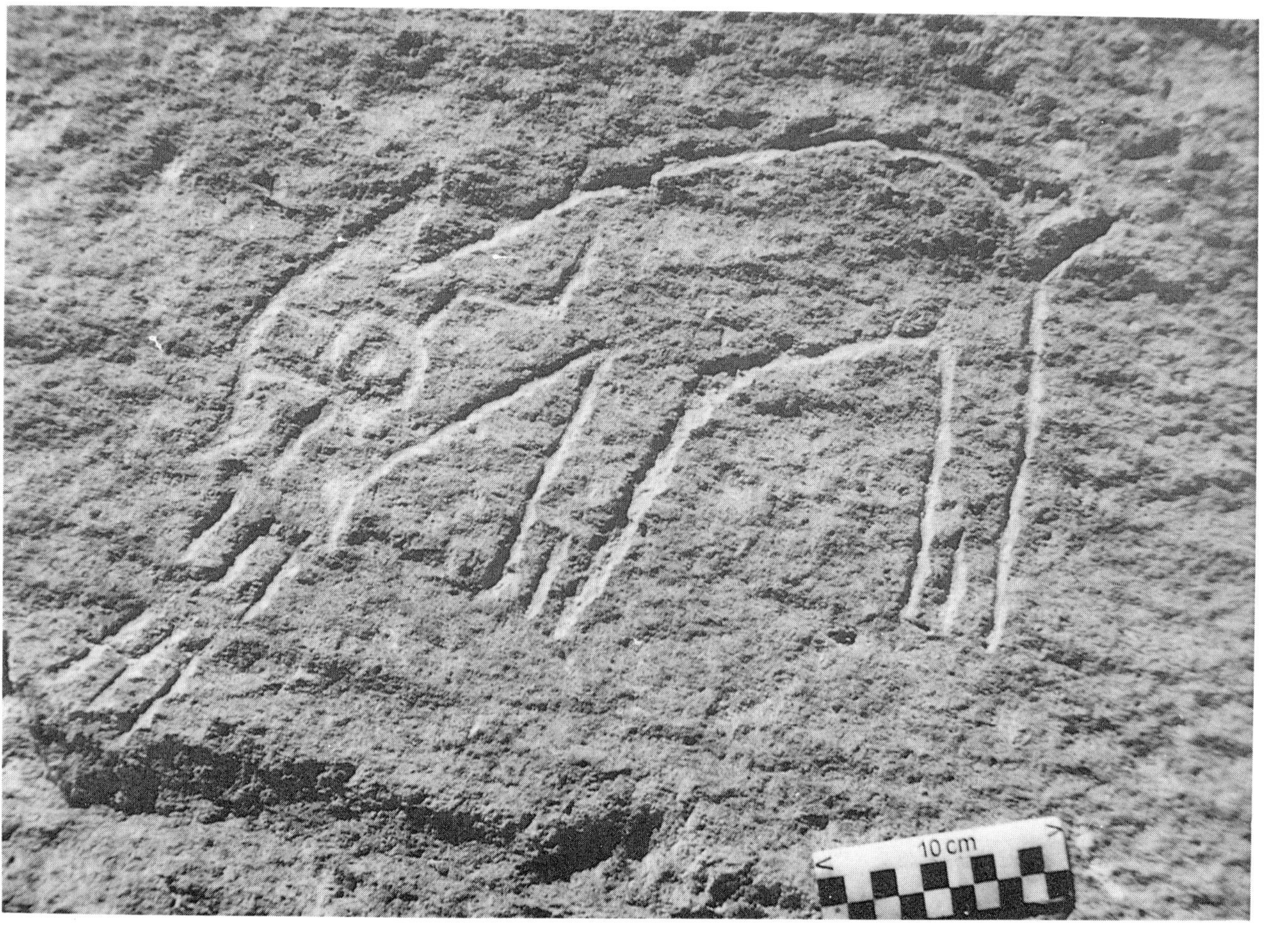

Figure 1. Petroglyph of an animal, with sound apparently depicted at mouth. Toro Muerto site complex, Aplao, Arequipa, Peru.

of prehistory. Rather it evolved concurrent with various other developments pertaining to culture: with language, symbolism, concepts of the self, concepts of external reality, developed human cognition - in short, as part of a process of culture-forming, consciousness-forming processes, in human societies as well as in the neural evolution of our species as a whole. It is almost certainly futile to try to pinpoint where or when art first developed: there is probably no such place or time. There is perhaps not even a hard and fast division between art and art-like productions and activities.

Fortunately for the rock art scientist, the many uniformities we see in global world rock art have been a great help in creating some level of order and system in this enormously complex evidence which collectively we call rock art. Scientists always have a penchant for order, for creating taxonomies, and rock art has not escaped their endeavours. At the most fundamental level, the rock art of the world has been divided into two main categories: the first, petroglyphs, are figures or motifs that were created by a reductive process, by removing some

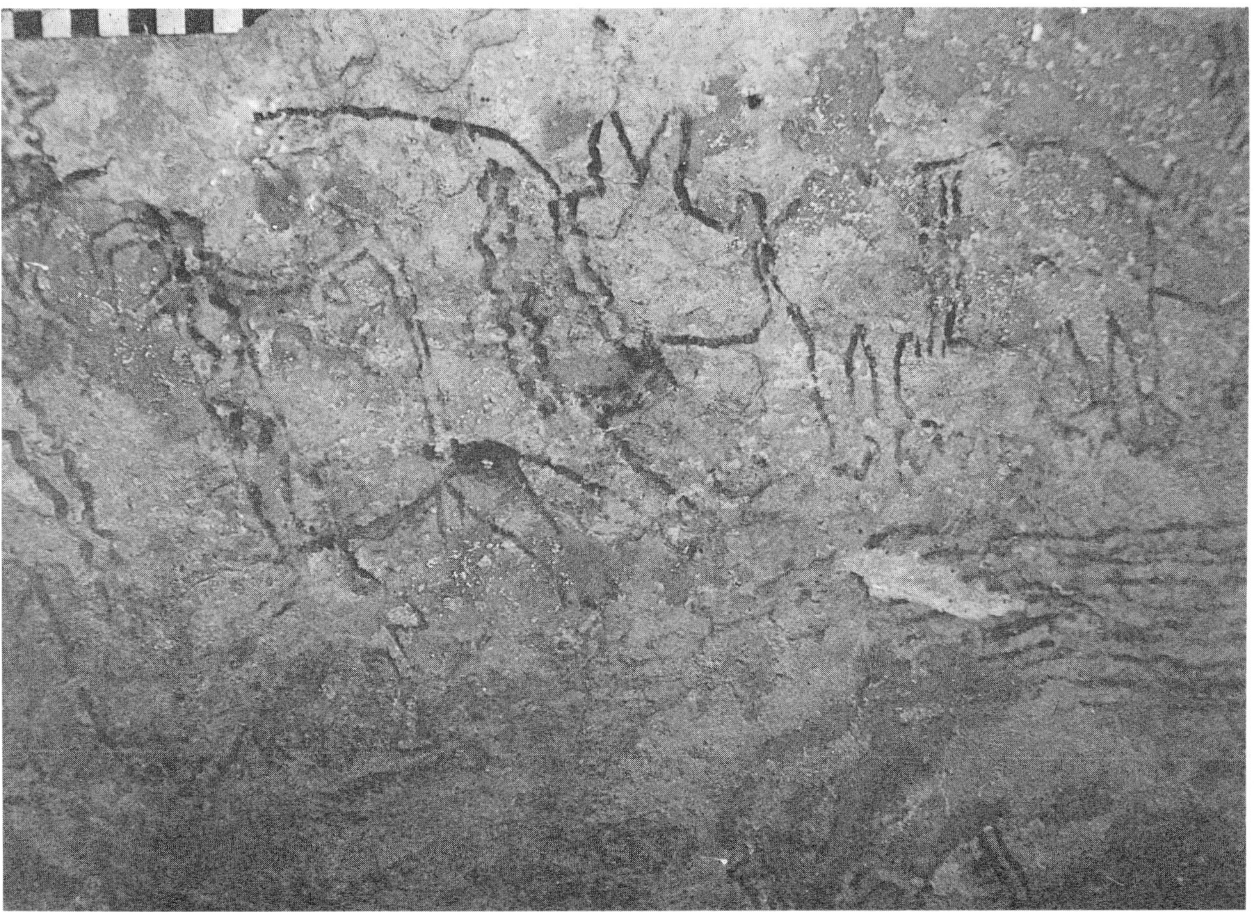

Figure 2. Rock paintings of two rhinoceroses and human figures, Chaturbhujnāth Nālā, Chambal Valley, Madhya Pradesh, India.

substance from the rock surface. This resulted either in a colour difference, because the rock bore a thin crust of distinctive colour which was removed; or it resulted in a somewhat deeper mark, rendered visible by its relief. Petroglyphs were created by hammering, chiselling, abrading, engraving, boring or etching the intended design into the rock. There are even examples of rock art on soft cave deposits which were simply made by marking such deposits with the fingers (Figure 1).

In the second class of rock art, something has typically been added to the rock surface. Such an additive is almost invariably either a paint, which is applied wet, or a pigment that was applied dry. There are some rare exceptions, where the applied substance was not a paint or a pigment, but some other substançe such as beeswax. In general, however, additive processes of rock art production result in rock paintings, and these have been preserved in a great variety of colours around the world (Figure 2).

The choice of method was usually related to factors such as the rock type available, the type of sites available, and the cultural conventions of the societies producing these arts. In the majority of cases, either petroglyph or painting was the preferred art form of societies, but there are also a number of traditions which seem to have been using both methods with equal enthusiasm. Generally, petroglyphs have better chances of survival, and since a great deal of rock art has been lost, we must assume that the total number of paintings was significantly greater than the total number of petroglyphs ever made. It is also noticeable that there tends to be a predominance of petroglyphs, so older an art corpus is. Again, this is perhaps the result of natural selection: the paintings deteriorated faster, and survived less often.

We have even observed selective processes relating to the colour of paintings: certain colours tend to survive much longer than others, and some paint pigments are known to change their colours consistently with time. Ochres, for instance, which may be found in a great range of yellows, browns, oranges and reds, age consistently towards a deep-red colour, particularly in the hot and dry climates of deserts. These chemical ageing processes are well understood and we know therefore that paintings were not necessarily applied in the colours in which they appear today.

One of the greatest problems in the scientific study of rock art has been the question of how to determine the age of the art. People have been occupied with this topic for centuries, and for the past hundred years, archaeologists have tried various approaches to solve this question. Their work resulted in very little reliable information about antiquity, and many of the chronological models researchers have presented are based on rather desperate methods. They are not reliable, and not widely accepted by rigorous scientists. In particular, the common-sense idea that different ethnic groups used different styles in rock art, and that these styles can be reliably detected by a researcher, is not accepted by science. This is not to say that such claims are necessarily invalid. What it does mean is that such claims of age are based on several deductive ideas which we cannot check. For instance, the names that archaeology has invented for all the periods and stone tool industries of early prehistory don't refer to real ethnic groups, to tribes, nations or other distinctive and real cultural entities. They refer merely to technological pigeonholes of archaeologists, to tool types they believe define particular tool traditions. Even the tool types themselves are subjective designations, there is no proof that the prehistoric users of stone tools used these same designations and taxonomies. But perhaps more importantly, tool assemblages or traditions do not necessarily equate with ethnic groups, nor with cultures. Arts, among other things, define cultures, but in the case of very ancient arts, only those on rocks survived consistently (and not those created on perishable surfaces). This brings us to the main problem. If we don't know what the age of the rock art is, we also cannot know to which tool tradition (or archaeological pigeonhole) the art belongs.

Our dilemma is well illustrated by these considerations: we know that arts are a part of real cultures, but without knowing their ages we have no time framework for these traditions, and we cannot relate them to archaeological ideas of past 'cultures'. The latter we can date, and have been doing so for a long time. This is because the archaeological finds always include some that consist of materials the age of which may be determined. Even the soil layer in which these finds were buried can be dated, by a great variety of methods. In rock art, however, until a few years ago no materials had been found in adequate quantities that could have been dated with the methods available to us. And this is why scholars have resorted to numerous speculations, inventing styles of rock art as they perceived them, identifying animals and other objects as they perceived them, and attributing these 'identified' animals and objects to particular periods.

We know today that most of these speculations were unwarranted, and did not lead to any sound knowledge. Disillusioned with archaeological 'dating' of rock art, some researchers began turning to the alternative approach of 'direct dating' during the past fifteen years. In this new approach it is attempted to secure some physical or chemical quantification of the age of a material or other feature that is in some direct and irrefutable physical relationship with rock art, and that is either older, younger or the same age as the art. The material or feature may be a mineral deposit, or the paint itself, or perhaps some geochemical or geomorphological feature directly related to the art. Such results then provide us with a maximum, minimum or true age respectively, and they can be checked by repeating the test. Repeatability, of course, is a principal requirement of a method that claims scientific status.

These new methods of direct dating of rock art have found wide use only in the last five years, therefore very few such dates are available at this stage. Several such methods were pioneered in Australia, a few in the U.S.A., and many more are in the process of being developed now. At the present time, secure dating of rock art is available for only a few figures in about seven countries, but more will be produced shortly as the methods proliferate and are eagerly adopted by researchers around the world. ❐

• A CATALOGUE OF ROCK ART •

A CATALOGUE OF ROCK ART

All of this helps to explain certain features of this catalogue. The assumed ages of rock art examples are very rarely stated in it, which is in stark contrast to many earlier publications on rock art that made so many claims concerning antiquity. Those we list here are very sparse, and they are the ones we believe are secure enough to find mention. Even in the case of the celebrated and much discussed cave art of western Europe, which has been so 'securely' dated by stylistic speculation to the various phases of the Upper Palaeolithic (the last division of the Older Stone Age, roughly from 35,000 to 10,000 years ago), we refrain from attributing them to these specific phases. This may seem a little over-judicious, but the recent revisions made on the basis of direct dating results amply justify such restraint. We like to think that most datings of that particular rock art corpus are correct, but before adopting them we would still prefer to see them tested in a scientific fashion. Recent results in other countries have also shown that the greatest care must be taken in separating fact from fiction in archaeology. Examples of recent major revisions to rock art age estimates come from Spain and the Sahara.

Secondly, the reader will notice in this catalogue that there is very limited identification of what the depicted art is supposed to illustrate. Again, the reason is that we feel only reliable, or at least scientifically responsible captions of this type should be featured in a publication of this type. We can all look at the glorious rock art, admire the often incredible artistic maturity, the confidence and the competence of the artists. Inevitably we ourselves are tempted to identify the motifs, recognise the animals, the objects humans seem to hold in their hands, and many other features. We are tempted to interpret what we think the artists tried to convey, the meaning of scenes, the attitudes of individual figures, the activities they are engaged in. It is quite possible that our subjective identifications are correct, and they may even be correct in the majority of cases.

But there are two factors we need to consider here. Firstly, however convincing our own identifications and interpretations may appear to us, and however certain we may be of their validity, they do not tell us how the ancient artist and his or her contemporaries saw the art. Their ways of seeing art, their ways of expressing ideas in art, their conventions of depicting specific motifs may have differed significantly from our ways. In fact they are likely to have differed quite dramatically. We have no way of checking this, no way at all, therefore the scientist has no choice but to ignore these 'identifications' we make intuitively. They don't tell him/her anything at all about what was depicted in the rock art, they only tell one how the modern observer reacts to the forms and colours remaining on the rock, and how he or she makes sense of them. Hence such identifications are very interesting in terms of how modern humans think and perceive, but they are of no help in telling us about the perception of the artists. In effect, our identifications of rock art motifs are not part of scientific considerations of rock art, they belong into the field of psychology of contemporary perception. Not surprisingly, eminent psychologists have already begun to take a special interest in ancient rock arts. But their interest has little to do with the ancient artists or societies, it is much more directed at universals in human perception.

From this, the second reason for omitting most interpretative commentary (however much we may be tempted to impose our own versions) already becomes apparent. It concerns the question of proof. If we identified objects according to our own criteria, how would we prove such identifications? It is at once clear that such proof will never be scientific, whatever we care to submit as evidence. In science, the question of proof is not even paramount, rather it is the question of refutation, or falsification of propositions. So in order to render a proposition - any proposition - scientific we need to specify the conditions under which it can be refuted. This is yet another fundamental tenet of rigorous science, posed in recognition of the ultimate subjectivity of all human knowledge.

As in archaeology generally, such refutation is not really possible in propositions of rock art motif identification. We don't expect to ever find a message from the rock artist telling us whether our speculation was right. We have never found a prehistoric picture with a neat label, 'I painted this picture and it is the picture of a horse'. Hence we have no scientific means of testing our identifications in nearly all cases.

Except in one. Almost forty years ago, a professor of anatomy studied a rock art site in Australia, and he did what we have so often done: he identified all the animal pictures the best he could. Being an anatomist, Professor Macintosh's identifications would seem to be about as sound as science can ever hope to do this. Many years later he discovered, to his great surprise, that a few of the artists who had created this art, or the traditional tribal custodians of the site who knew the true meaning of the figures, were still alive. Realising what a unique experiment he could conduct, he took these knowledgeable people to the site and asked them to identify each animal figure he himself had identified earlier. This was a controlled experiment, and the only one of this kind science has ever been able to conduct. The professor reported the outcome in 1977: in ninety per cent of all his identifications, he had been wrong! In a scientific sense, our identifications of animal species (and presumably any other object) are simply idle speculation. If a professor of anatomy cannot achieve a better success rate than ten per cent correct identification, surely the speculations of lesser 'qualified' people are not very relevant. They are no more than interesting responses of 'amateur' observers, irrespective of whether they are the speculations of artists, children, tribal people, academics or scientists.

These are some of the reasons why the present catalogue of Indian and world rock art keeps well clear of subjective identification, presenting only apparently factual information, just as in the case of the age of the art. One of the most secure forms of information about rock art is its location, and this is provided herein. Where the general attribution to an archaeological period is considered sufficiently secure, it is also provided. We hope that the reader appreciates this restraint and severity on our part; we don't believe in disseminating information haphazardly, only to find that some years later it will be refuted by new evidence. We believe that the reader prefers sound information to a wealth of colourful embellishment about what this art means or conveys. The artist, the poet, the dreamer, moved by the beauty and power of rock art may still use this book in any way desired, but we feel that we owe it to the readers to reserve them that option, and to present the facts and not our interpretations of them. Indeed, the interpretations of the readers may be more correct than our own! We, very simply, do not claim the privilege of knowing the meaning of the world's greatest art. But we find that it is stunning enough in all its mystique, its visual splendour, its often incredible antiquity, and in its powerful message of ancient artistic sophistication that it can stand without interpretation. To us, our interpretation almost seems like an infringement. We feel barely entitled to provide some small footnotes to these achievements of artistic greatness, so that their appreciation may be facilitated. But we feel not justified in creating, and presenting here, our own interpretations.

Guided by our convictions as they are implied above, we have organised this catalogue of Indian and world rock art along geographical divisions, rather than temporal, interpretational or any other. Some comment needs to be made also about the selection of illustrations. Almost all previous attempts to summarise the rock art of the world reflected the priorities of their authors or editors. Indeed, the first serious attempts of presenting world rock art in anything resembling a geographically, thematically or temporally balanced fashion only appeared in the last few years. Usually, European rock art, and most specifically Upper Palaeolithic rock art of France and Spain (the so-called cave art), had been given an amount of attention that was entirely disproportionate to the relative size or importance of this rather small corpus. At the present time, Upper Palaeolithic rock art in Europe is claimed to occur in 294 caves, the vast majority of which occur in just two countries. Bearing in mind that even the more conservative estimates of global rock art would be in the order of over a million sites of rock art, it is evident that this European tradition is very small indeed. Moreover, the actual number of motifs at its sites is in most cases quite small. One may argue that the main significance of the 'Franco-Cantabrian cave art', as it is called, lies in its antiquity, being older than other rock art. This, however, is also a misconception. We only need to consider Australia to see this. The number of sites there remains unknown, but the most knowledgeable people have generated rough estimates ranging from 100,000 sites to perhaps several times that many. It is further not entirely unreasonable to suggest that perhaps fifteen or twenty per cent of these sites possess Ice Age art (over 10,000 years old). Whatever the true numbers may be, it seems that the number of Australian Ice Age rock art sites exceeds that of Europe by a factor in the order of one hundred or so times.

Moreover, we already know that a part of this Australian Ice Age art is older than the Upper Palaeolithic, which began about 35,000 years ago: minimum radiocarbon dating of Australian rock art of well over 40,000 years has been reported, and still older dates are anticipated. Consequently neither age nor quantity provide a justification for the massive over-representation of European Palaeolithic rock art in publications pretending to present a balanced picture of the subject.

In this volume we find an over-representation of Indian rock art, for which we make no apology. As the title states, the catalogue explores the place of Indian rock art in the global perspective, therefore it is most appropriate that Indian rock art should be the volume's main feature. Other than that qualification, we have attempted to achieve a selection of illustrations that to some degree resembles the size of regional rock art corpora, as well as their significance, representativeness, and science's knowledge about them. Several regional rock art traditions or corpora are not represented at all here, or perhaps by only one example. Of others we offer several examples, because these are of huge bodies of art, and their mere size needs to be reflected accordingly. Overall, and with perhaps a few exceptions, we have assembled as representative a sample as we can reasonably expect to obtain of global rock art - bearing in mind various limitations: this enormous body remains inadequately explored, studied and documented.

In the following chapters we present brief regional descriptions, continent by continent, each time offering an outline of the rock art traditions best known. This may include some comments on the history of their exploration, the types of rock art found, together with detail of what else we might know about the art. But before we begin the actual catalogue, there is one more specific subject we should like to present, however briefly, because we believe that it is of particular importance in appreciating the significance of the most ancient art: its role in understanding the human being and the conceptual constructs created by it. The beginnings of art, it seems, have been a crucial factor in the humanisation of our species. We have already noted above that they were intricately connected with the beginnings of all the traits we regard as distinctively human: conscious perception of reality (at the level humans are capable of), the exploitation of iconicity (the property of an object to resemble or represent another object) to create the possibility of symbolism, the beginnings of language, the discovery of the human self (as evidenced by the beginnings of body decoration), and perhaps even the origins of the human propensity of creating taxonomies (binary or other) through the conscious discrimination of opposites. All these faculties and achievements are closely intertwined with the origins of modern human cognition, the development of our ontology. Their significance to understanding ourselves as an intelligent species is absolutely profound. It is suggested that, of all the possible forms of evidence that may have conceivably survived to document these extremely important developments, only one is found in quantity: the earliest art. It is our only remaining evidence, however tenuous, of the humanisation of our species, of how our hominid forebears created the conceptual construct we call reality.

The ultimate significance of this evidence we call palaeoart, then, is philosophical. It is not equalled by any other scientific or philosophical endeavour, because its role is to define human (anthropocentric) reality and its origins. It qualifies all human knowledge. Or as the scientist would say: all human knowledge is a function of the cognitive processes apparently documented in palaeoart. Rock art accounts for nearly all surviving palaeoart (which defines ancient art which is beyond ethnological explanation) in the world. Therein lies its true significance. ❐

• THE ANTIQUITY OF ART •

THE ANTIQUITY OF ART

We have already mentioned the distortion in the published record of ancient art, particularly the over- representation of Upper Palaeolithic European art. This emphasis has led to another distortion, the widespread belief that this Upper Palaeolithic art is in fact the oldest art we have found. This is a significant error. We have ample evidence now of much earlier art or art-like productions, of archaeological finds suggestive of some symbolic function. They are not necessarily of rock art, and they are not necessarily from Europe. A great deal of such evidence is from Asia and Africa. Indeed, if it is our intention to explore the beginnings of art, this evidence is not just crucial; it is all-important.

The traditional explanation of artistic beginnings assumes, essentially, that all art and art-related activities began with the advent of the Aurignacian in western Europe, about 33,000 to 35,000 years ago. These beginnings were said to coincide with certain technological innovations, as well as the appearance of beads and pendants, portable art objects, and even the appearance of modern humans. This version includes many misconceptions. To begin with, essentially modern humans appear very much earlier in other parts of the world. The oldest fossil finds of *Homo sapiens sapiens* we have today are from southern Africa and south-western Asia. They are in the order of 100,000 years old.

Small perforated objects such as teeth and bone fragments are thought to be beads or pendants. It is reasonable to assume that they served for decorating

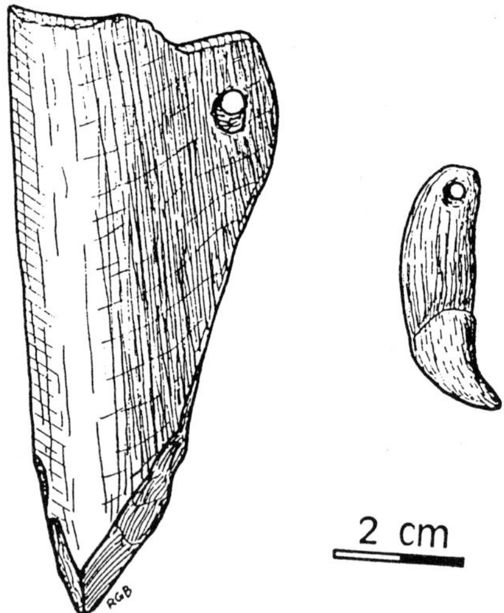

Figure 3. Flaked bone point and wolf incisor, both perforated. Lower or Middle Palaeolithic, Repolust Cave, Austria, thought to be almost 300,000 years old.

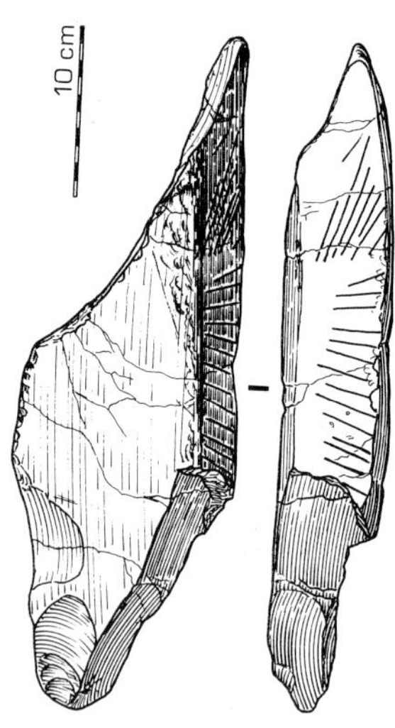

Figure 4. Engraved bone fragment of an extinct forest elephant, Lower Palaeolithic, Germany, from the Mindel/Riss interglacial, 250,000 - 350,000 years old.

the human body, therefore they would imply the human faculty of self-awareness, of being aware of one's own existence in some conscious fashion. Such drilled or perforated objects must have been threaded onto strings, which implies the use of knots. Without tying the ends of a string it cannot serve any useful purpose, so several technological capabilities are strongly implied by such perforated objects. It is then relevant to ask at what time such objects first appear in the archaeological record. The answer is: we have over 200 perforated objects that are significantly older than 35,000 years, and the oldest seem to be almost 300,000 years old (Figure 3).

Clearly, then, such practices began very much earlier than our traditional model of artistic beginnings tends to imply. And this is so even without considering that body decoration is not very likely to have begun with beads and pendants. Body painting, tattoos and many other forms of decoration are likely to have appeared much earlier. Indeed, we have evidence of much earlier use of red paint, including in India, and although the use to which this paint may have been put still eludes us, there is always the possibility that it was used for body painting. Moreover, perishable beads may have been used before non-perishable materials were introduced for such purposes. It is therefore quite naive to assume that the earliest finds of beads even relate to the earliest use of body decoration. Such practices are much more likely to have begun significantly earlier. Common logic tells us so.

Much the same applies to early art. Portable objects with simple geometric engravings, series of notches and other such modifications first appear on the present archaeological record perhaps around 300,000 years ago, although

Figure 5. Engravings of the Middle Palaeolithic: from Prolom II, Crimea, Ukraine, on a phalange (a), a bone splinter (b) and a horse canine (c); engraved fossil (nummulite) from Tata, Hungary (d); engraved parallel lines on bone from La Ferrassie, France (e); and zigzags on bone fragment from Bacho Kiro, Bulgaria (f).

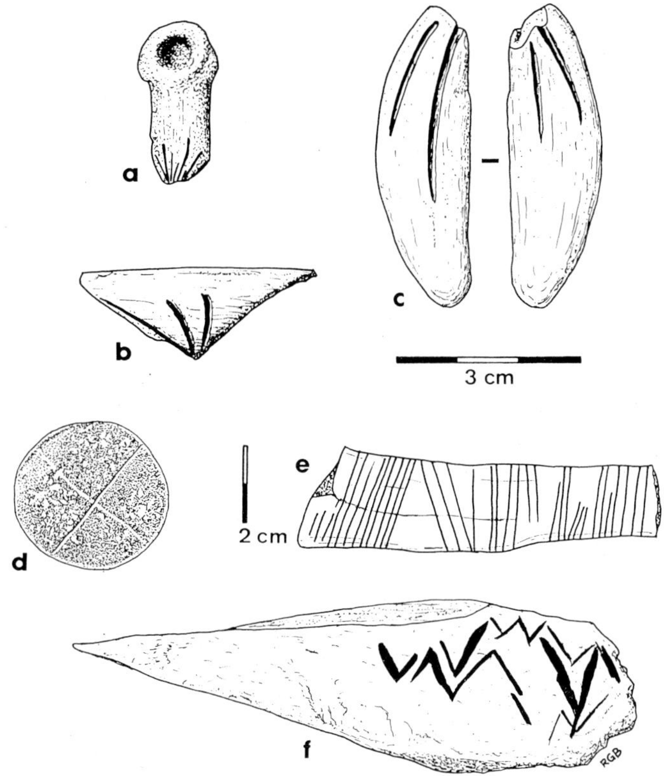

Figure 6. Scoria pebble with engraved lines from Berekhat Ram, Israel, Lower Palaeolithic, more than 233,000 years old.

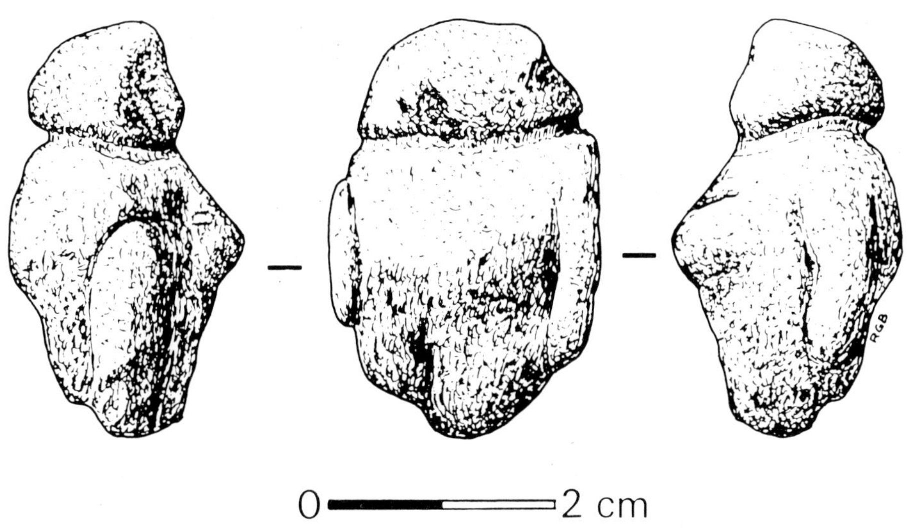

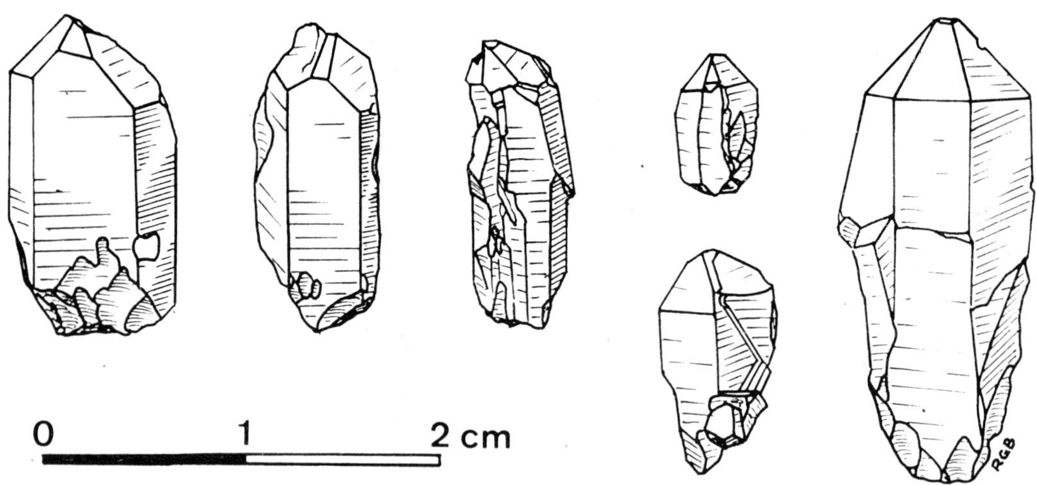

Figure 7. Tiny quartz crystals from an occupation site in Karnataka, India collected by early humans several hundred thousand years ago.

very rarely (Figure 4). They become a little more frequent around perhaps 100,000 years ago, by which time they are found in western Europe, central Europe and the Ukraine (Figure 5). The oldest presently known 'proto-sculpture', from Israel, is safely dated to more than 233,000 years; it consists of a naturally shaped scoria pebble resembling a female human figure, and this resemblance has been emphasised by several engraved lines (Figure 6). This important find, of a period archaeologists call the Acheulian, suggests that the hominids concerned already possessed the ability of recognising a resemblance of form between two otherwise unrelated objects. This suggests a rather more developed cognitive sophistication than one would perceive on the basis of purely technological evidence, such as stone tools. But then, one should never rely on such technological indices to infer cognitive, intellectual or cultural abilities. We even know from modern societies that such judgments may be fundamentally false: some cultures are spiritually very rich and sophisticated, but have a simple technology, while others (such as Western civilization) combine the greatest technological sophistication with a distinct spiritual poverty. It is therefore rash to deduce the cognitive capacity of very ancient societies from such largely irrelevant information as the kinds of stone tools they used. Often we lack even information about their wooden and other tools, which would be required to permit informed judgments about such material cultures.

Rock art probably appeared around the same time as the introduction of pigment use, artistic modification of natural objects, collection of tiny quartz crystals (Figure 7) and fossil casts, and similar cognitive developments pointing

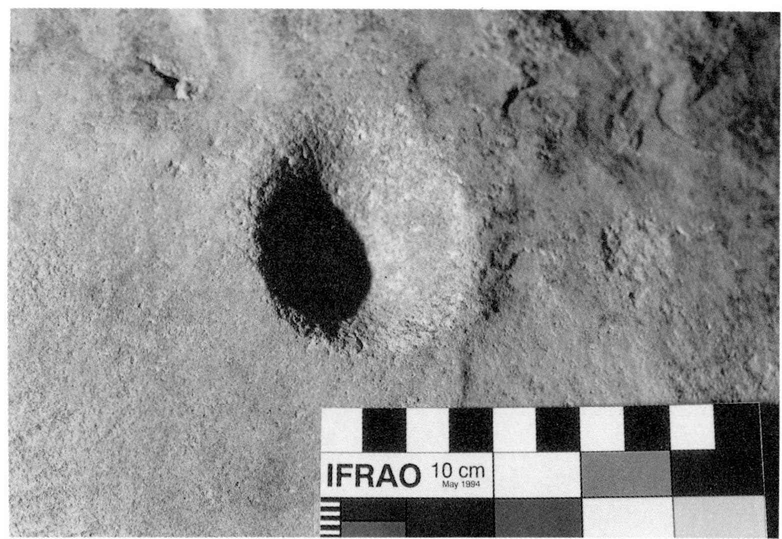

Figure 8. Cupule or cup mark made in the Acheulian, possibly 200,000 or 300.000 years ago. in a cave in Madhya Pradesh, India.

These faculties can be traced back several hundred thousand years in Africa, Asia and Europe, and it is in this context that the beginnings of rock art should be expected to have occurred. Haematite pebbles, the oldest known source of red pigment, have been excavated, bearing markings indicating that they were rubbed against hard rock surfaces in this same period, the Acheulian - including in India (in Karnataka). We cannot know what these rock markings looked like, if indeed they had any form or structure. None have been found, and none are likely to be ever found; the likelihood of their survival over such an immense time span is practically nil. But we do have some petroglyphs (rock carvings) from the same period, at a site in Madhya Pradesh, and they are the earliest presently known rock art in the world (Figure 8). They are very similar to more recent petroglyphs in a cave in France (still

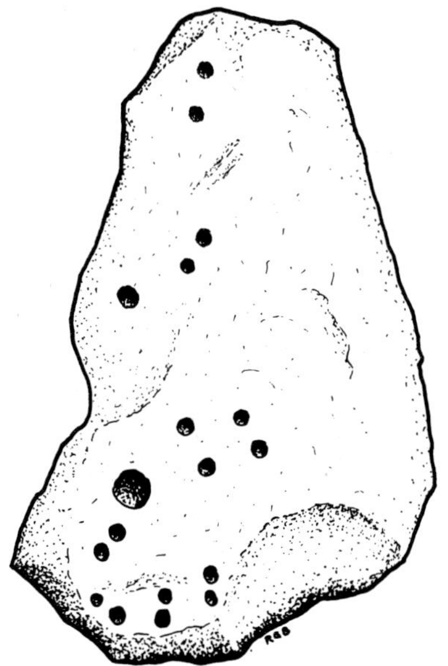

Figure 9. Pattern of cup marks found on the underside of a stone slab placed over the grave of a Neanderthal child in a French cave, Middle Palaeolithic.

much older than 40,000 years; Figure 9), and also to the oldest rock art in the Americas and to some of the oldest known in Australia.

After the first known ocean navigators in human history - the people who ultimately succeeded in reaching Australia perhaps 60,000 years ago by crossing several stretches of open sea - settled that continent, such petroglyphs begin to become quite common there, still well before the French Aurignacian. Rock art production proliferated probably not just in Australia during that period, but also in many other centres around the world, during the late stages of the Ice Ages. It is against this background that the position of the Upper Palaeolithic rock art and portable art of Europe, which commences perhaps around 33,000 to 35,000 years ago, must be seen, if it is to be seen in its true context.

In the present volume, however, we are primarily concerned with seeing the Indian rock art in its context - its context of world rock art. To do that we will now travel across the width and breadth of the Indian subcontinent, then the rest of Asia, and finally the rest of the world. ❒

• THE ROCK ART OF INDIA: A SYNOPSIS •

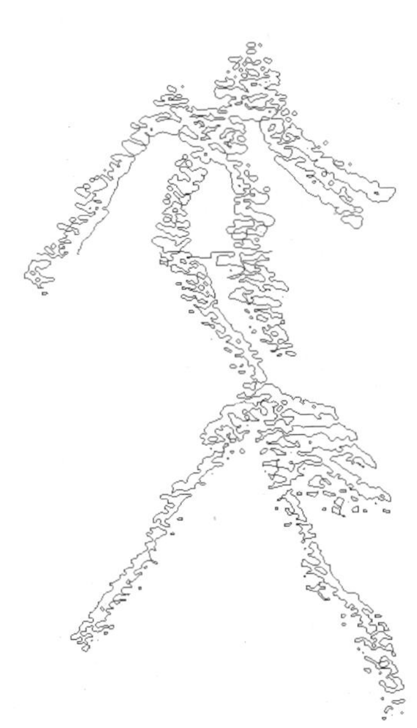

THE ROCK ART OF INDIA: A SYNOPSIS

Background

India is fortunate in possessing one of the three largest concentrations of the world heritage of rock art, the two others being in South Africa and Australia. The first petroglyphs were reported from Almora in India as early as 1856 (W.G. Henwood, *Edinburgh New Philosophical Journal,* 1856: 204-5). The first reported discovery of rock art in India was made by Archibald Carlleyle, First Assistant in the Archaeological Office, at Sohāgi Ghāt in Mirzāpur district in the present state of Uttar Pradesh in 1867-68, 12 years before the discovery of Altamira in Spain by Marcelino De Sautuola in 1879. Carlleyle's notes were published later by V.S. Smith in 1986. (Smith, *Indian Antiquary* 6, 1986:87). Carlleyle collected 1200 microliths, charcoal and haematite pieces from the undisturbed floor layers of two shelters and associated them with ancient stone chippers. The oldest currently known Stone Age walls and rock art have also been reported recently by R.G. Bednarik from the so-called 'Auditorium Rock' in the massive quartzite sandstone complex of Bhīmbetkā in central India. (Bednarik, *The Artefact* 15:39; 16:60; 17:76). Indian rock art research and exploration is more than a century old, in which a series of landmark publications in the nature of surveys have been brought out by some of the greatest explorers in the world since the first scientific paper was published on a rock art site of Mirzāpur district in Uttar Pradesh by John Cockburn, an officer in the Opium Department of the British Government. Both rock paintings and petroglyphs have been found and dis-

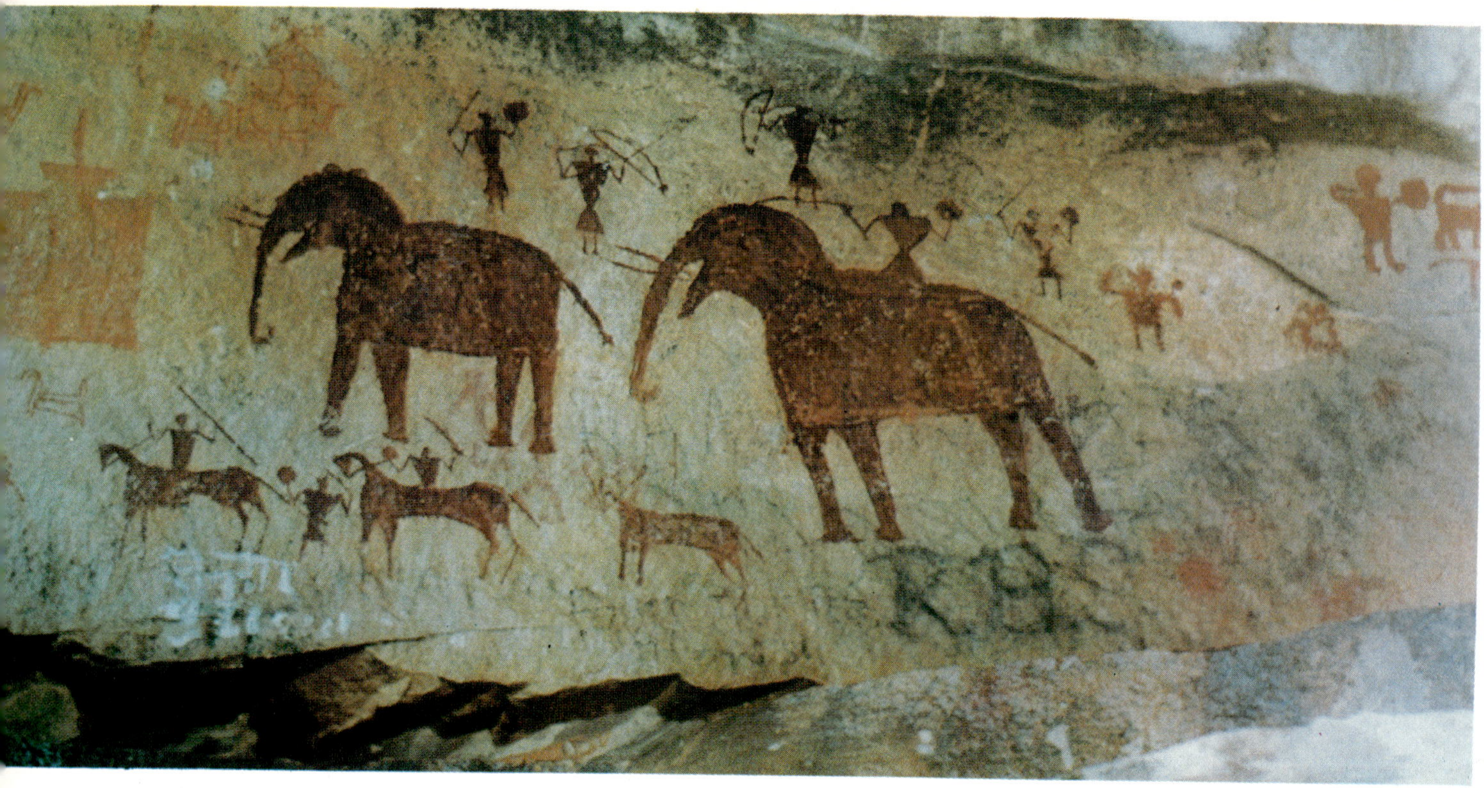

Figure 10. Cavalry, Likhniyādari, Mirzāpur, Uttar Pradesh, Northern India

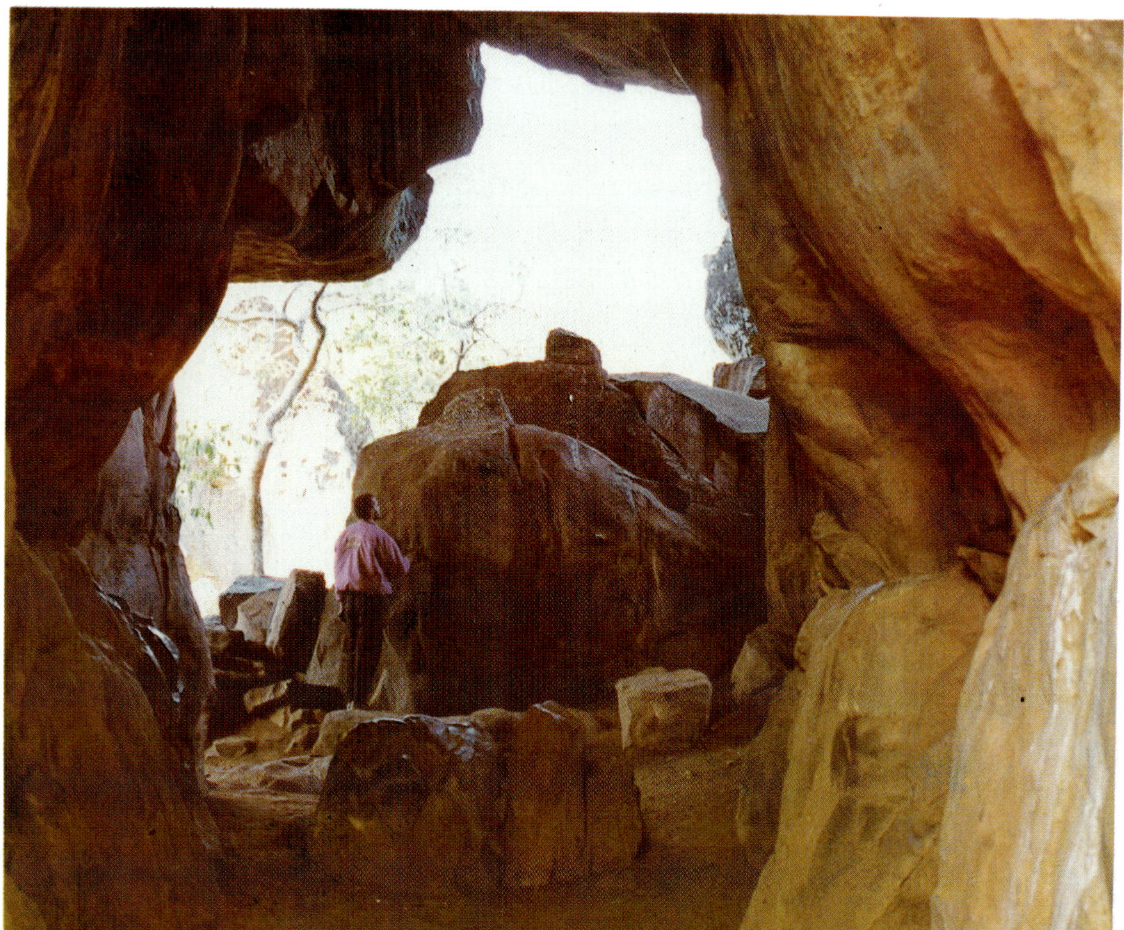

Figure 11.'Auditorium Rock', Bhīmbetkā, Rāisen, Madhya Pradesh, Central India.

cussed from the length and breadth of the sub-continent, from all geological and ecological regions.

In spite of this, very little of Indian rock art is firmly dated. The temporal and spatial location of rock art, or, for that matter, any other art, has not been a besetting concern of Indian artists in the pre-colonial period because they appear to have seen their art as a collective rather than an individual signature, and the use and beauty of this signature as two sides of the same coin. No distinction seems to have been made between art and craft and the nature of reality does not appear to have been generally perceived as anthropocentric. Ever since chronology has become a preoccupation of rock art research in India in colonial days, it has remained tied to older archaeological methods of trying to establish a correlation between the rock art and the tool assemblages and artefacts found in excavation in or near the shelters in the prehistoric period, and with the rare inscribed noting on the rock surface in the historic period. Where the painting itself has been studied, dates and sequences have been derived from the uncertain evidence of superimposition of the different layers of painting, colours, motifs or themes which supposedly indicate the cultural behaviour of hunters and gatherers, pastoral or agricultural populations. Such attempts to recognise the physical shape, meaning and theme of motifs have to be *ipso facto* subjective in the case of rock art because of the vast span of time that separates the contemporary interpreter from the artist. Unlike in Australia, traditions of this art are not continuous in India, and even in Australia, the reinterpretation is implicit in retouch (*AURA Occasional publication* 5 on retouch, 1992). Ethnographic parallels are also occasionally drawn from folk and tribal art in a doubtful exercise to explain this art. Ambiguity and polysemy characterise the various corpus of mythology and symbolism in vogue among the same tribal and folk groups. Nor do such groups associate themselves with such art in their areas emotionally or physically, except to explain it as the work of evil spirits or epic heroes, and, to either avoid such sites or convert their environs to use as denominational temples or monastic habitations.

Introduction

Understanding of Indian rock art has been often marred by positivist, empiricist and teleological assumptions about cognitive constants in style, material, techniques, tools, motifs and patterns, in which the Franco-Cantabrian cave art tradition has been put at the head of all developments in rock art in the world. In these oecumenical assumptions of European or Judeo-Christian Telos, rock art in other parts of the world, including India, has been seen to be coming out or deviating from the aesthetic, plastic, naturalistic, Palaeolithic cave art of Europe. This assumption has been shown to be incorrect. It is born out of the accident that cultural and technological evidence of rock art has survived in deep lime stone caves in which the diurnal and seasonal variations of temperature and humidity have not affected the lithology and speleo-climate in the radical manner in which human intrusion, pH conditions, climatic, geological and pedological changes have affected the environment and preservation of the open non-European rock shelters in most of the countries including India. Such cognitive colonialism has, on the other hand, generated an extreme atomism of ethnocentric, nuclear local models, officiated by extreme postulates of polygenetic relativism, and chauvinistic claims of seperior antiquity, aesthetic quality or symboling capacity.

However, the problem of understanding Indian rock art as part of the cognitive beginning of the human language can not be ignored. For this, differentiation of human from natural markings, or identification of the temporal location or spatial composition of the support, pigment, encrustation, precipitate or any other deposit in such human markings are as important as any attempt

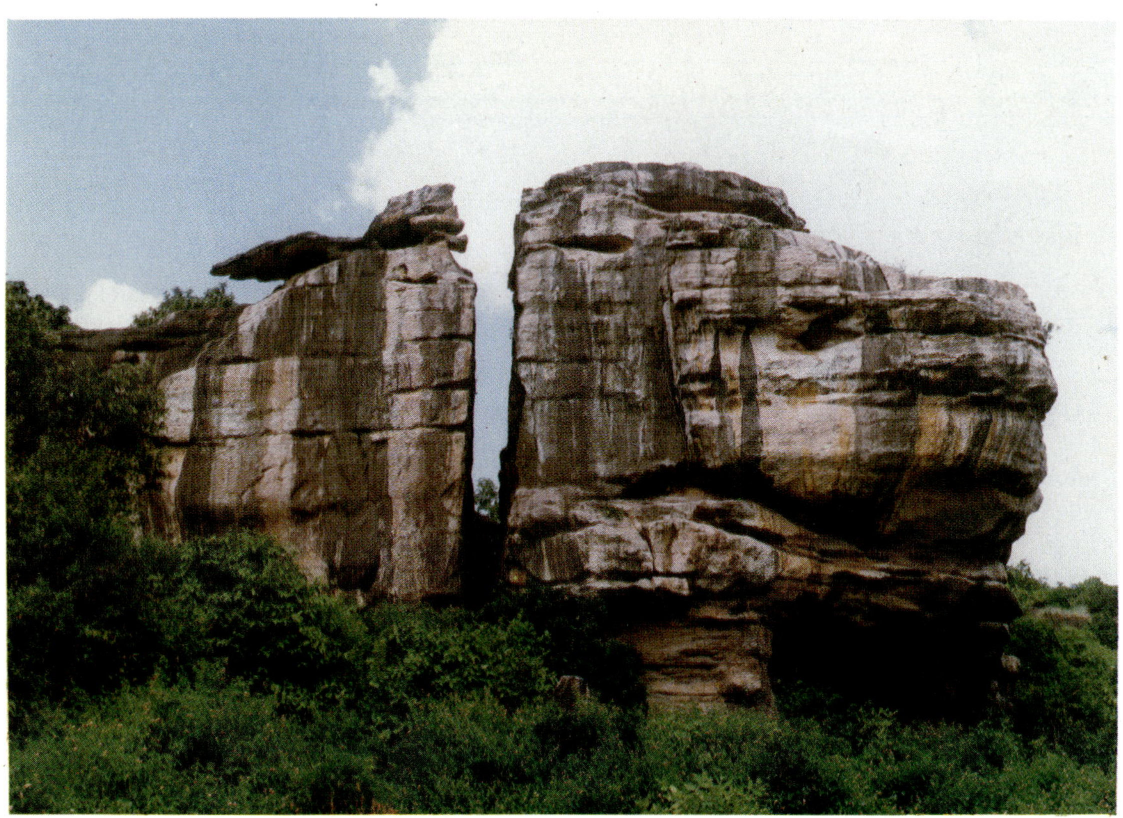

Figure 12. General view of rock shelters, Rāmchhajjā, Rāisen, Madhya Pradesh, Central India.

to understand their graphic and iconic pattern or pristine intentions, by using testable, confirmable and falsifiable data and methods.

Geology and Conservation

The largest accumulation of Indian rock paintings, nearly two thirds, are located in the quartzitic, sandstone belt of central India, mainly in the Vindhyas and also in the Sātpurās and Kaimur, principally in the present state of Madhya Pradesh and also in the states of Rajasthan and Uttar Pradesh, between the rivers Narmadā in the south and Gangā-Yamunā in the north. The typical Vindhyan chains resist erosion by weathering and project out into hogbacks, mesas, buttes and questas. Locally called a *dant* or tooth, these hills rise gently to circumscribed summits and plunge suddenly into precipitous scarps, or canyon like gorges between vertical walls abutting rivulets, in which the softer underlying layers of sandstone, shale or limestone are differentially eroded by water and wind into hollowed shelters. Some of the major complexes found in this area of about 40,000 square miles are of about 457 painted rock shelters in a continuous chain of 31 hills in the Betwa source region (Shankar Tiwari, in K.K. Chakravarty ed., *Rock Art in India* : 228-40); about 754 rock shelters with over 500 painted shelters at Bhīmbetkā (V.S. Wakankar *Painted Rock Shelters.* Ph.D. thesis 1973; Wakankar & Brooks, *Stone Age Painting in India* 1976); nearly 250 such shelters in Mirzāpur, U.P. (R.K. Varma, *Stone Age Cultures of Mirzapur.* Ph.D. thesis 1964); about 650 shelters in 63 complexes in the Chambal Valley (G.Kumar et al., *Purakala* 3.1-2, 1992:13-67). River Chambal, a tributary of Yamunā, forms its shelters along its own bank and on the bank of its tributaries in the sandstone, limestone and laterite of Rajasthan in Kotā, Jhālwār, Bhilwādā, Sirohi and Chittorgarh districts; Gwālior, Morenā districts in Madhya Pradesh. The sandstone shelters in Rajasthan are found in an area bounded by the Sawāi Mādhopur hills in the north, Mukandarā hills in the south, Ārāvalli hills in the west and Shāhābād and Vindhya hills in the east. The Mirzāpur rock shelters are found in indurated sandstone of the Vindhyan Super group and the southern scarp of the Kaimur overhanging the Son valley. Of the different groups of Mirzāpur shelters, Likhaniyā, Kohbār and Bhaldariā lie north of Kaimur range and Maharāriā and Vijaygarh in south.

The rock art sites from Orissa are concentrated in the western districts of Sambalpur, Sundergarh, Mayūrbhanj and Kālāhāndi, which geologically form an extension of the Chhotānagpur plateau and Chhattisgarh basin. The geological system is an extension of the easily weathered sandstone of central India with the usual accretions of shale, grit

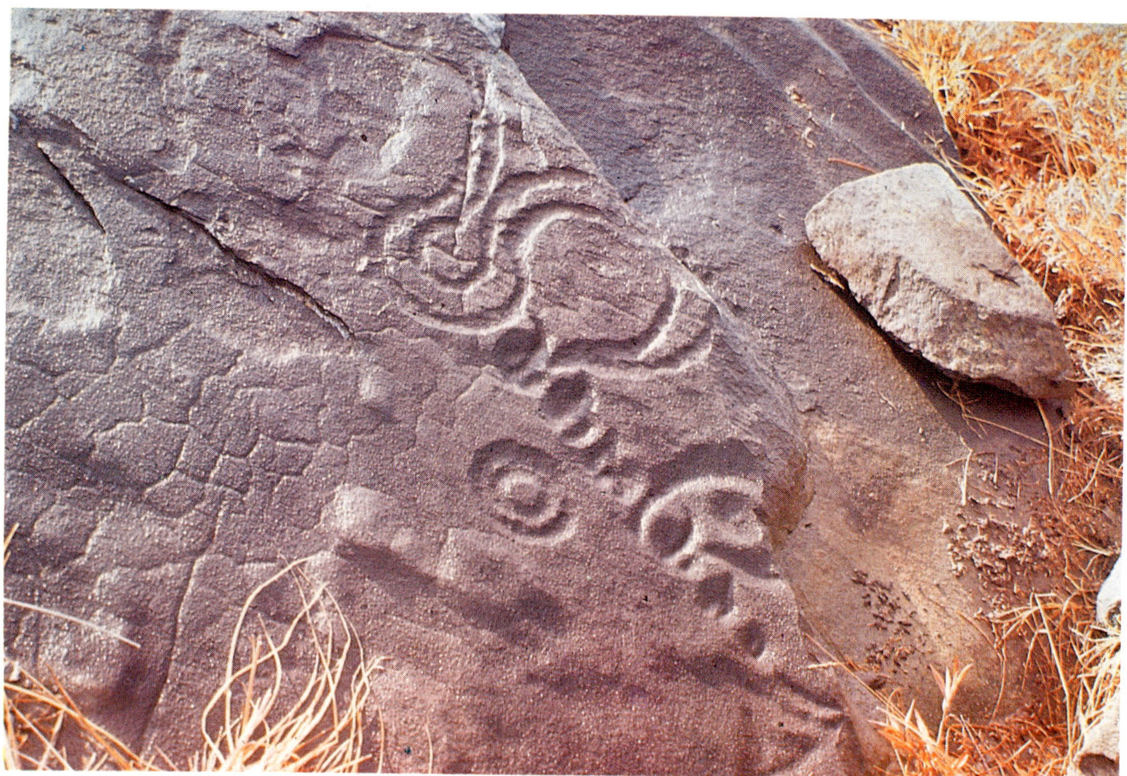

Figure 13. Petroglyphs, Muuiya ki dhāi, Uttarākhand, Uttar Pradesh, Northern India.

and silt. The largest concentration, almost three fourths of the shelters, are situated in Sundergarh. These western uplands of Orissa flank river Mahānadī flowing east to west and politically form part of the ancient Mahākāntāra and Dakshina Koshala, part of which is recognised today as Chhattisgarh in eastern Madhya Pradesh. In Bihar, rock paintings have been reported in the Kaimur range at Makwā, Patesar, Jhaniā Pāhār and Dughdha Hāthiādah, and rock engravings have been recorded from Ghātshilā in Singhbhum district (Mitra, *Prehistoric India* 1923:149). The rock art sites of the state of Gujarat in western India, unlike the central Indian rock art sites, are mostly situated in colossal round granite boulders, arrayed in tiers, one above the other, in Pānchmahal, Sabarkanthā, Barodā, Bhāvnagar district, on the ridges, which, together, constitute a southern intrusion of the Āravalli range, and also in the isolated Thāngarh granite hills in Surendranagar district of the peninsula of Saurāshtra. Rock engravings have been found on lateritic platforms and granite boulders from Usgalimal and Kajur near the west-flowing Kushāvatī river in the south-western belt of the Indian peninsula (P.P. Shirodkar, in article presented in *World Archaeological Congress-3* 1994). Rock art is also reported in the north-eastern belt from the Gāro hills of Assam, Bengal, Manipur (*Indian Archaeology Review* 3, 1982:104; 4, 1983:59-60) and in the west, from Ināmgāon, Chandrapur and Nāsik in Maharashtra.

The extreme north, north-west and the Deccan as well as the extreme south seem to have a dominant tradition of rock engraving. Petroglyphs have been found at an altitude of 4000 m or thereabout at fords, passes and pastures of steppes of Thikshe, She, Nurlā, Mulbekh, Leh, Kārgil, Drās in Lādākh, (Francfort et al., *Arts Asiatique* 45:5-27: 1992) in in the Himalayas (Mathpal, *Rock Art in Kumaon Himalayas,* IGNCA 1995). Paintings and petroglyphs have been found in the Himalayas in stratified belts of sandstone, limestone, slate as well as in the crystalline belts of granite, gneiss and

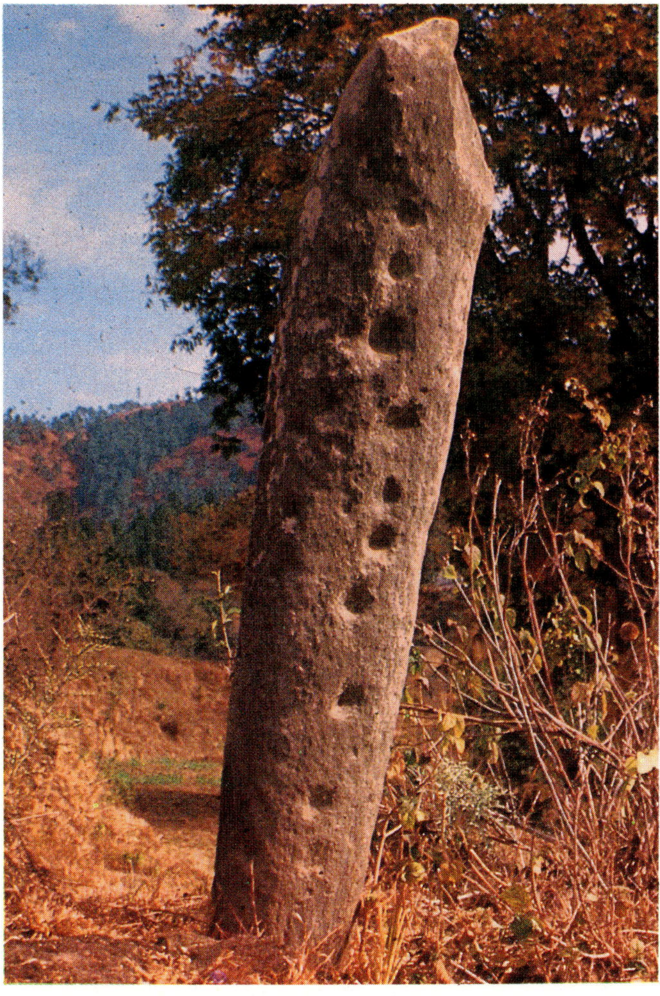

Figure 14. Cup marks on pillar, Kafada-Nangāon, Uttarākhand, Uttar Pradesh, Northern India

Zānskār and western Tibet in the upper Indus Valley, at Burzāhom in Kashmir, near Tābo monastery in Spiti valley in Himachal Pradesh, and also in the eight districts of Almorā, Kumāon and Gārhwāl schist. At least, sixty-eight sites have been recorded in the Kumāon-Gārhwāl region, the largest concentration being found in the valley of Suyāl river, a tributary of river Kośi. Petroglyphs have been found

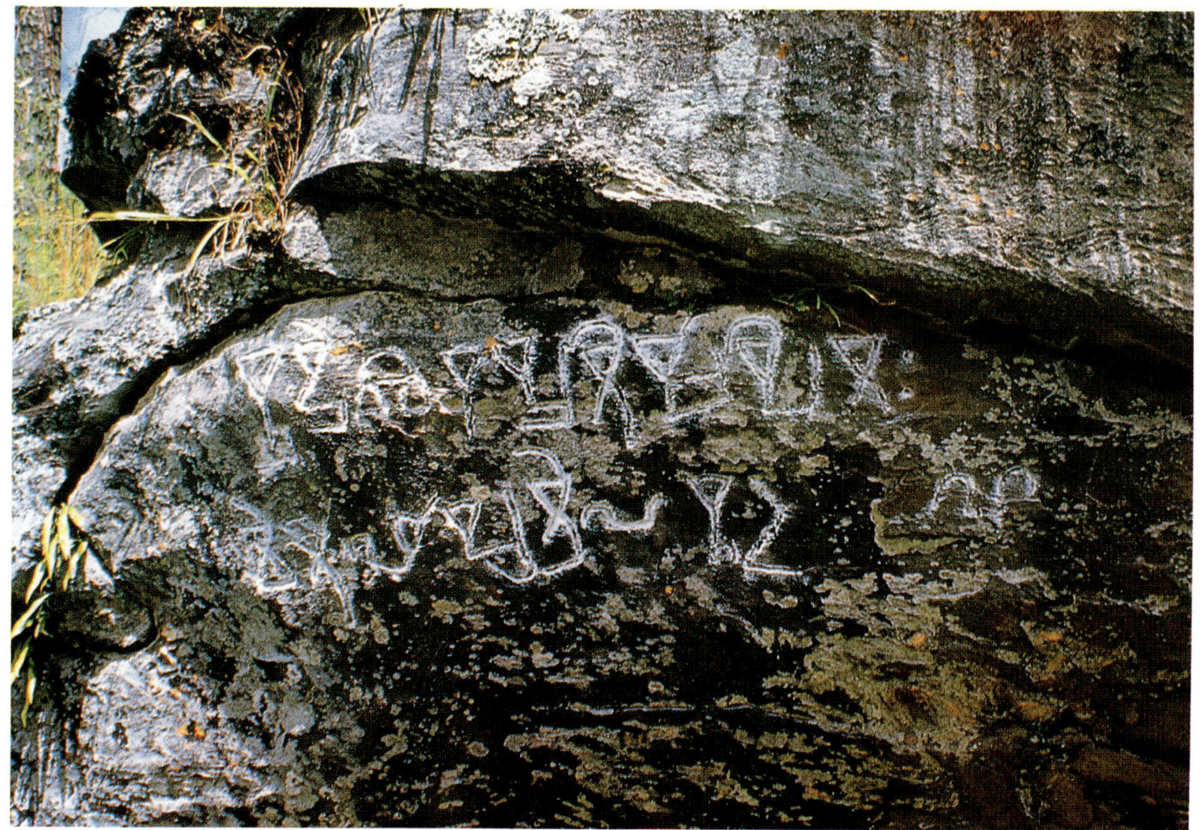

Figure 15. Geometrical/pictographic design, Kāsar devi, Uttarākhand, Uttar Pradesh, Northern India.

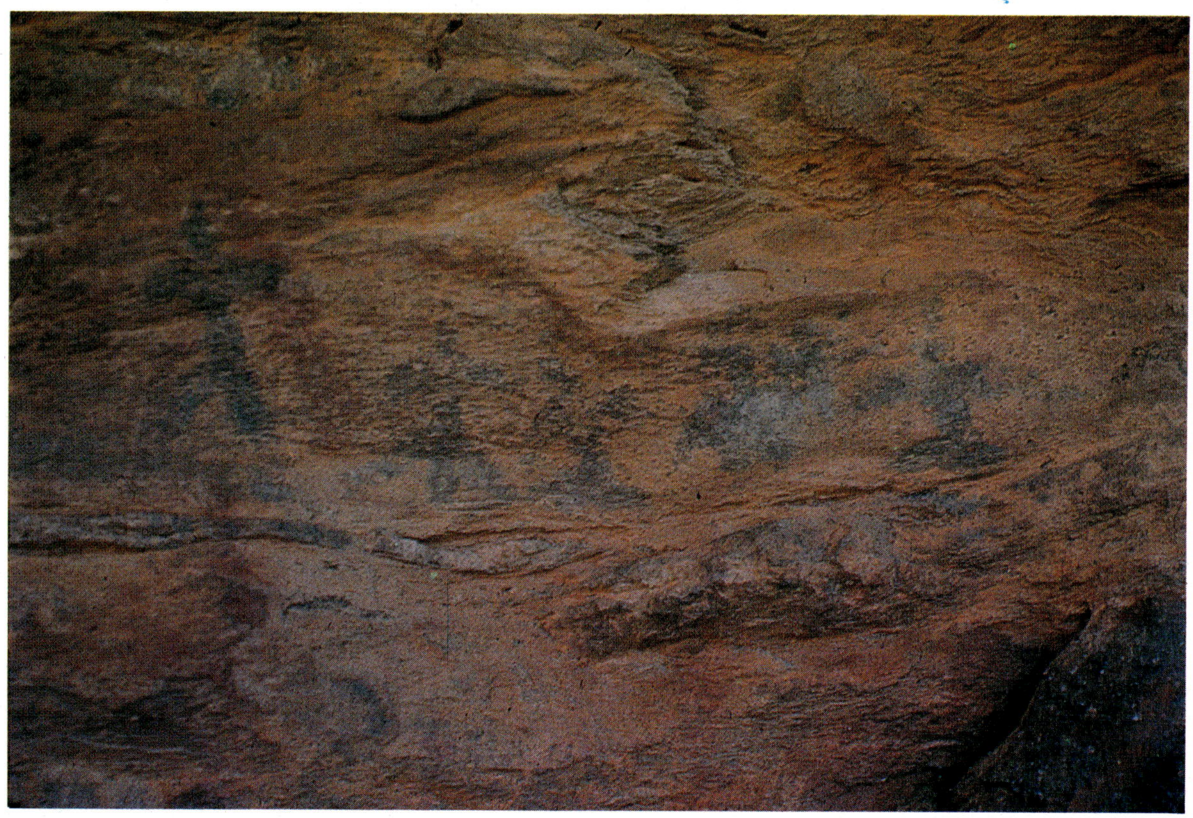

Figure 16. Human figures, Lakhu-Udyār, Uttarākhand, Uttar Pradesh, Northern India.

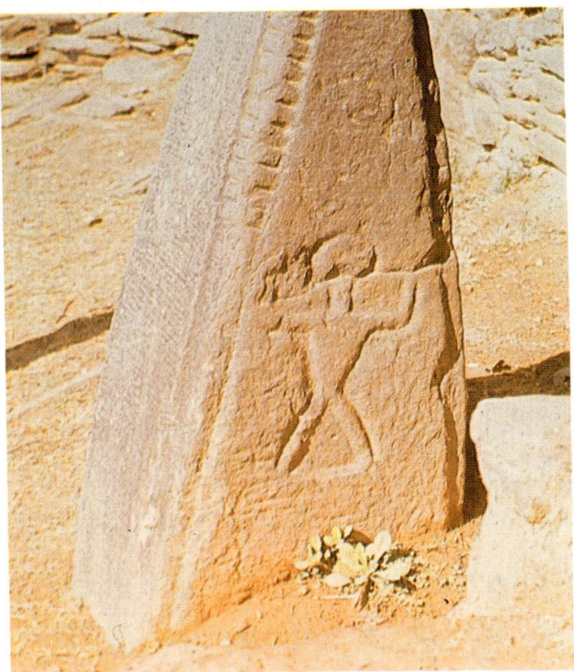

Figure 17. Human figure, engraving on pillar, Sarāi Khet, Uttarākhand, Uttar Pradesh, Northern India.

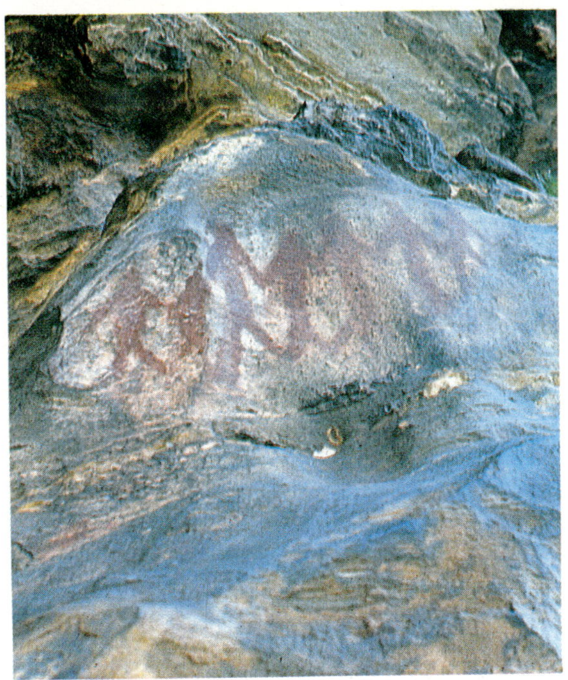

Figure 18. Dancers, Lakhu-Udyār, Ālmorā, Uttarākhand, Uttar Pradesh, Northern India.

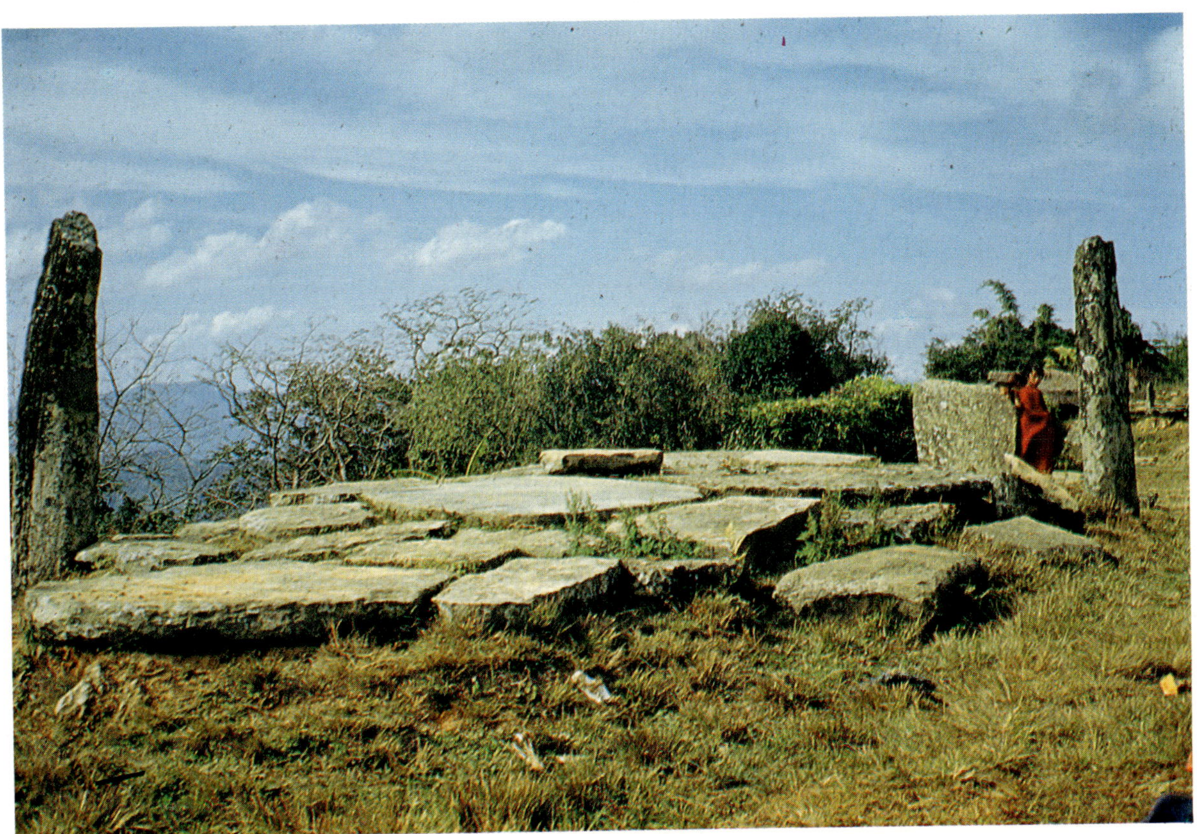

Figure 19. Open air site rock engraving, Matuā museum, Manipur, North eastern India.

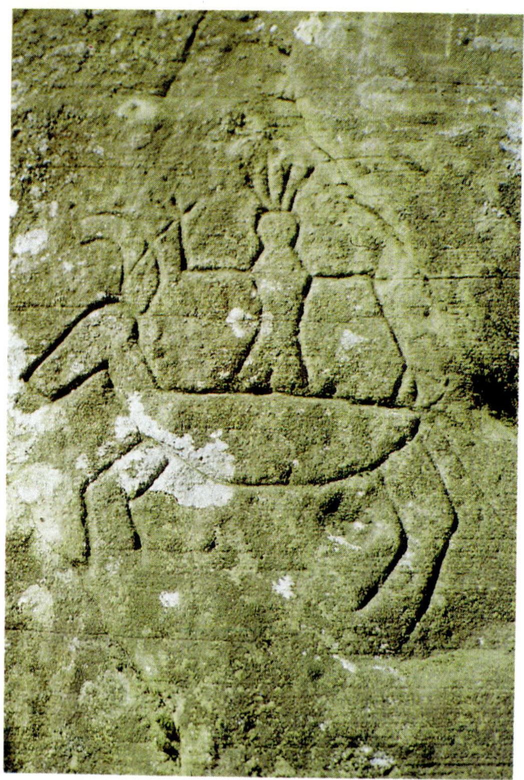

Figure 20. Deer and Hunter, Matuā Museum, Manipur, North eastern India.

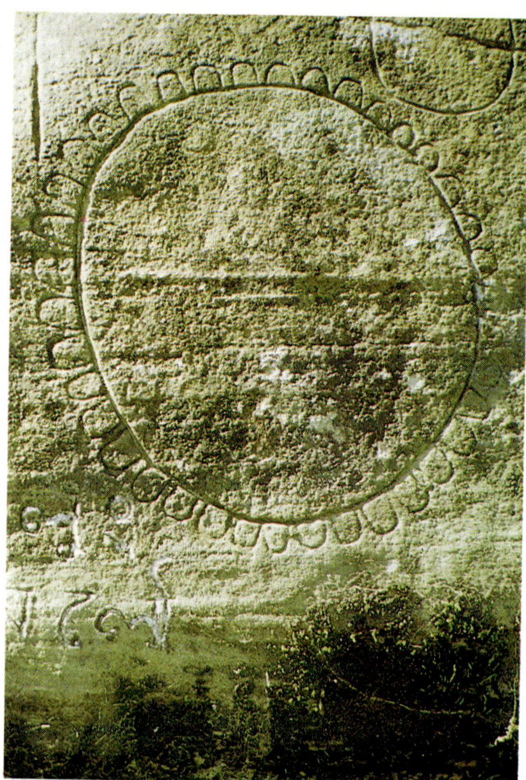

Figure 21. Circullar petalled design, Matuā museum, Manipur, North eastern India.

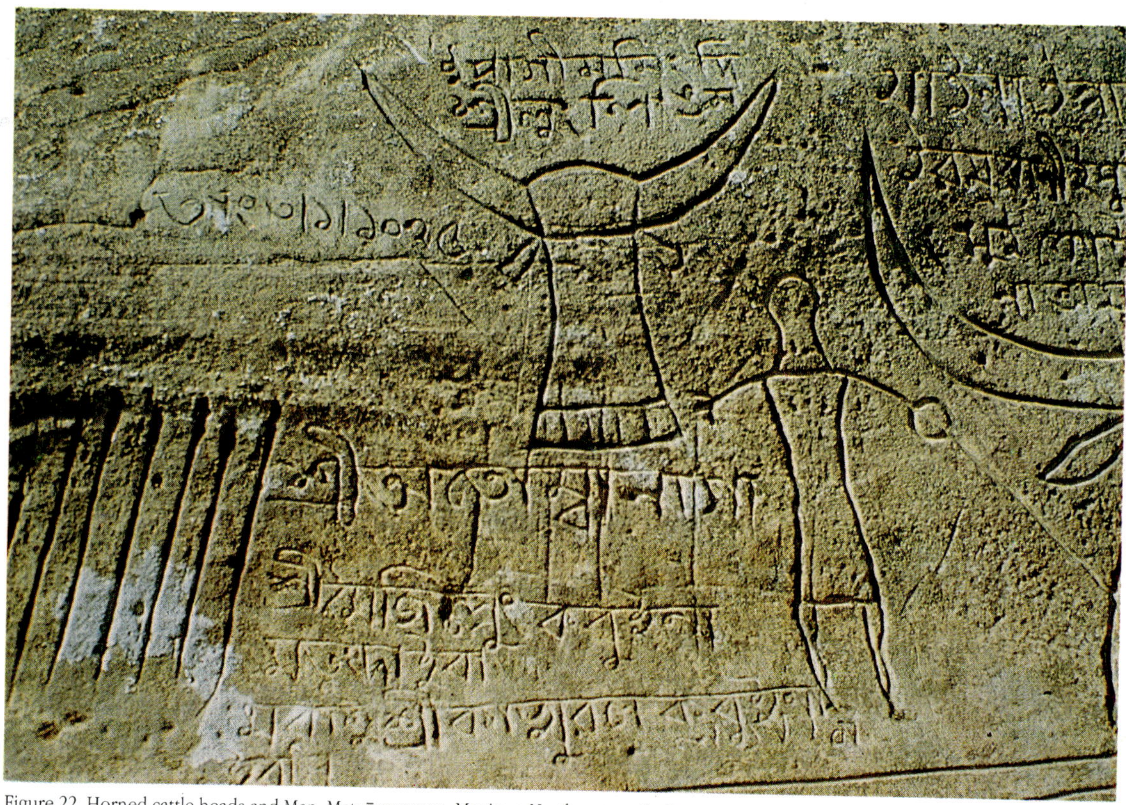

Figure 22. Horned cattle heads and Man, Matuā museum, Manipur, North eastern India.

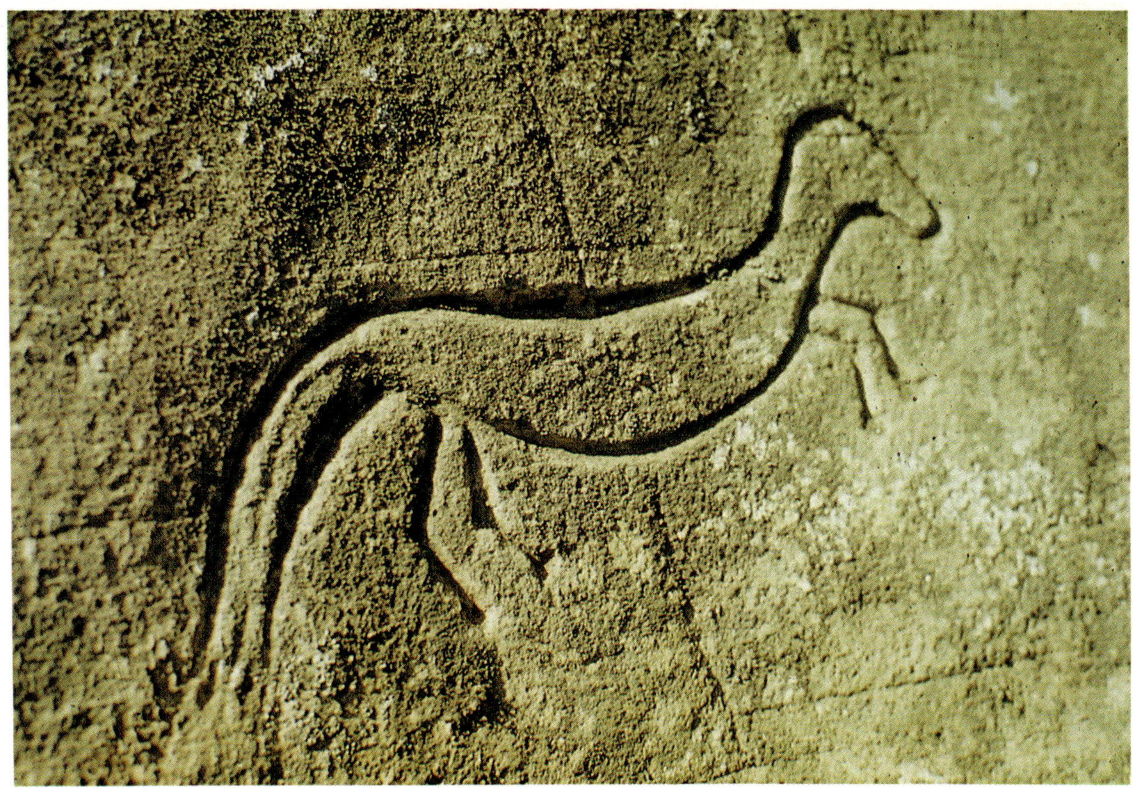

Figure 23. Elongated animal figure, Matuā museum, Manipur, North eastern India.

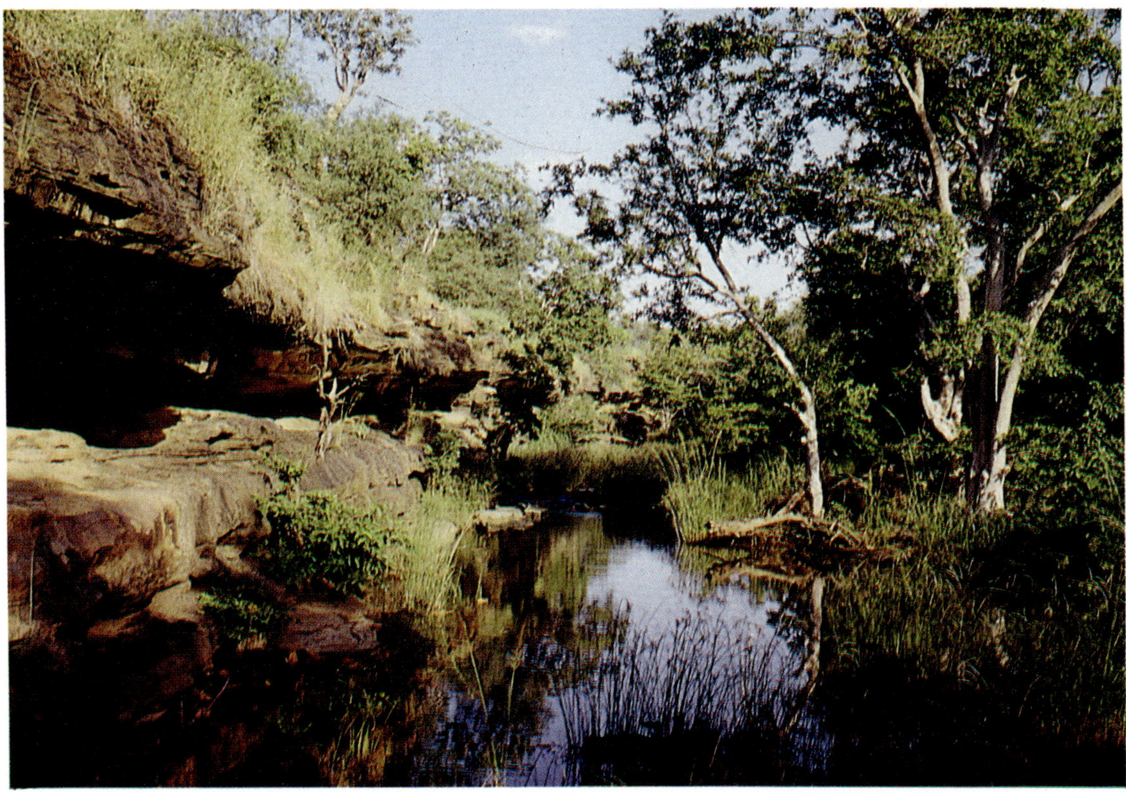

Figure 24. General view of shelter, Chaturbhujnāth Nālā (stream), Māndāsor, Madhya Pradesh, Central India.

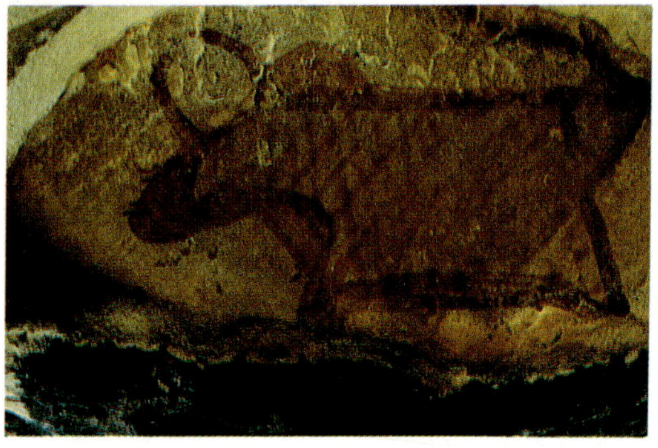

Figure 25. Bull, Chaturbhujnāth Nālā, Chambal Valley, Māndāsor, Madhya Pradesh, Central India.

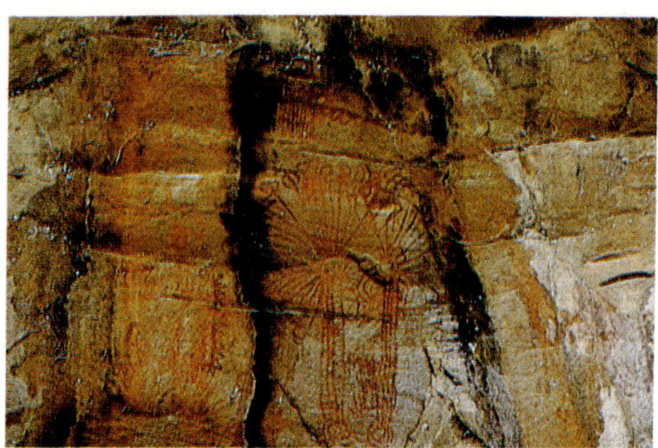

Figure 26. Flowering trees, Modi, Chambal Valley, Māndāsor, Madhya Pradesh, Central India.

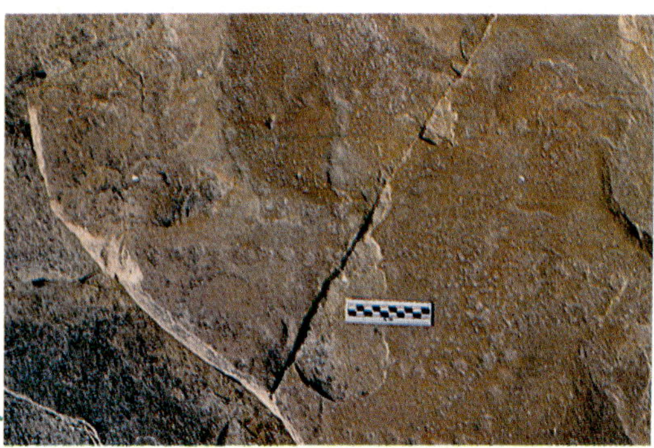

Figure 27. Petroglyphs, Chattaneshewar, Kotā, Rajasthan, Central India.

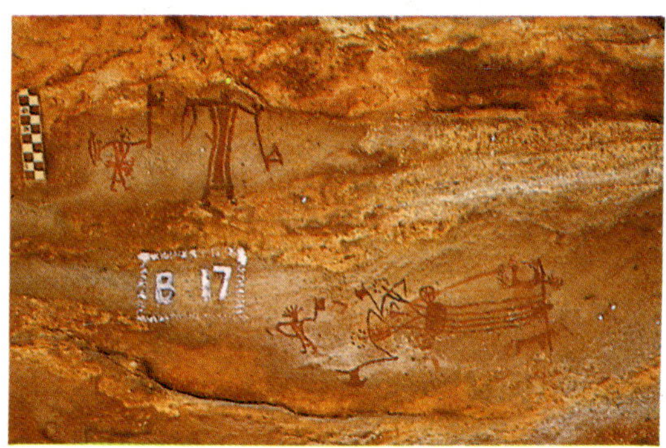

Figure 28. Axe men and Charioteer, Chaturbhujnāth Nālā, Māndāsor, Madhya Pradesh, Central India.

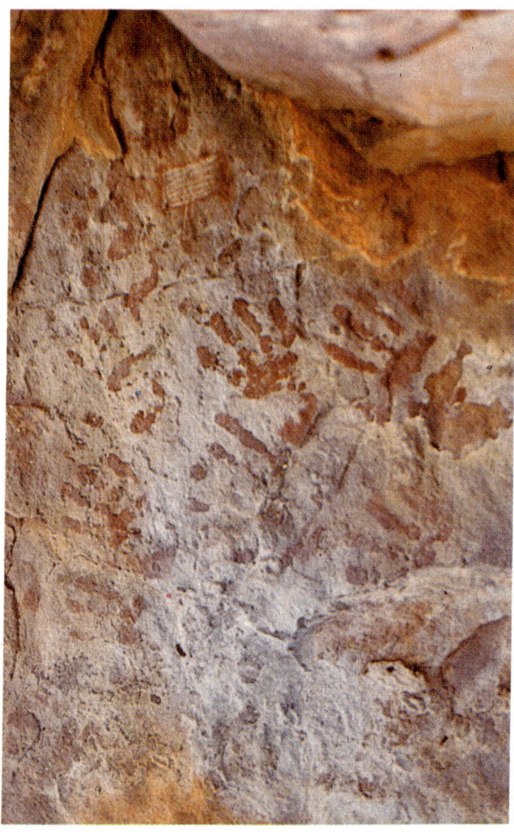

Figure 29. Hand prints, Kanyādeh, Kotā, Rajasthan, Central India.

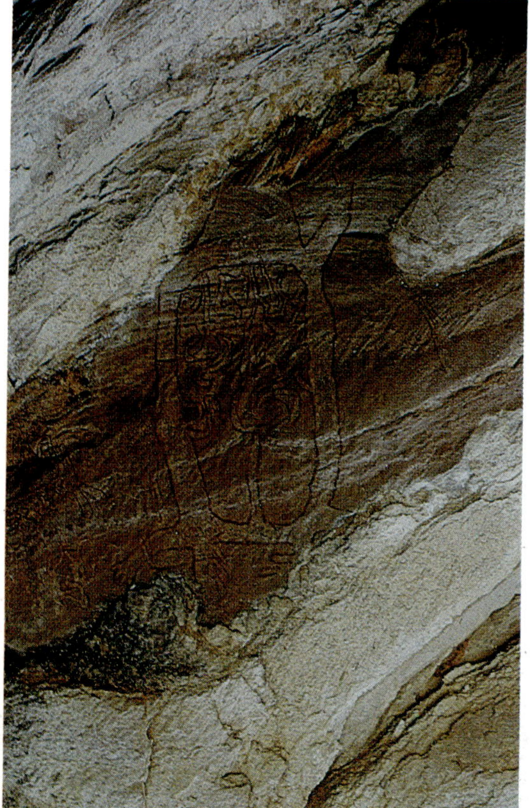

Figure 30. Dissected reptile, Gāndhi Sāgar, Chambal Valley, Māndāsor, Madhya Pradesh, Central India.

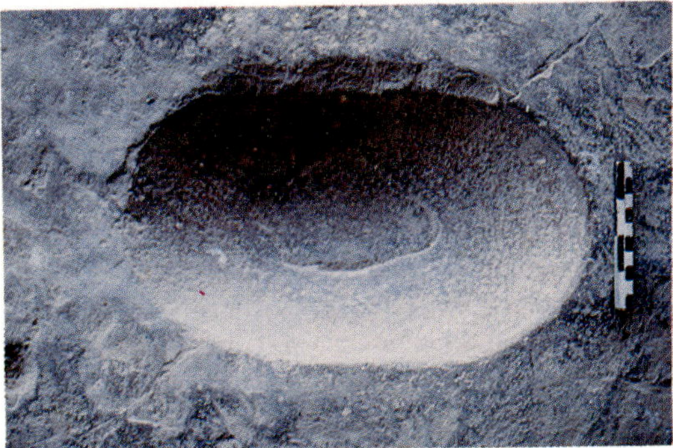

Figure 31. Petroglyphs, Chattaneshewar, Kotā, Rajasthan, Central India.

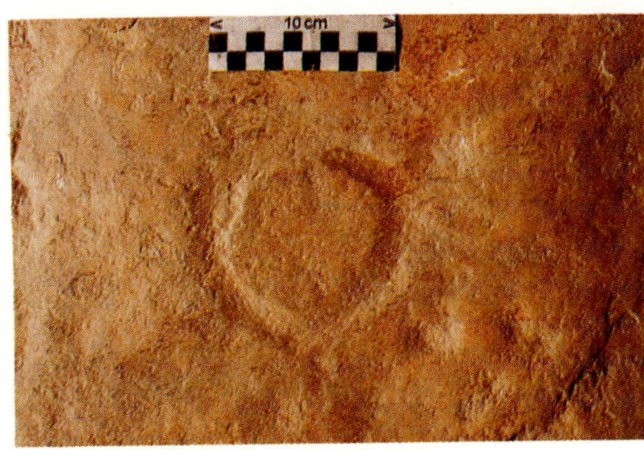

Figure 32. Petroglyphs, Chattaneshewar, Kotā, Rajasthan, Central India.

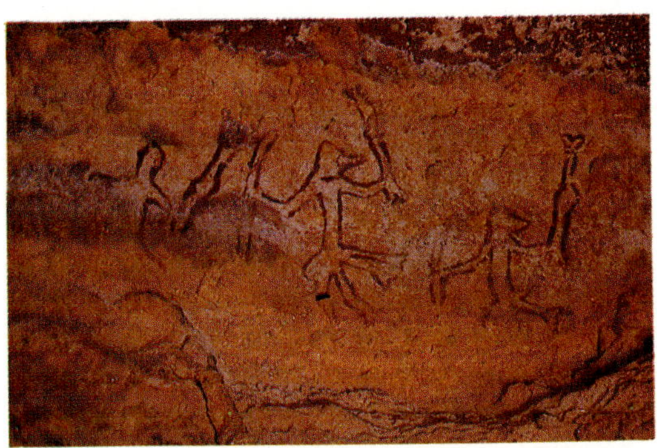

Figure 33. Archers, Chaturbhujnāth Nālā, Māndāsor, Madhya Pradesh, Central India.

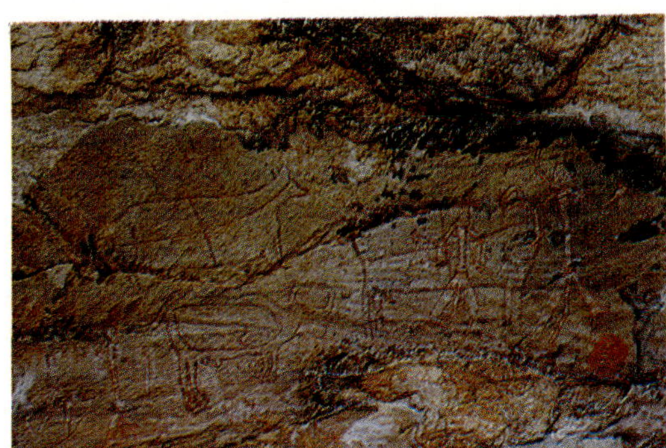

Figure 34. Cattle and men, Modi, Māndāsor, Madhya Pradesh, Central India.

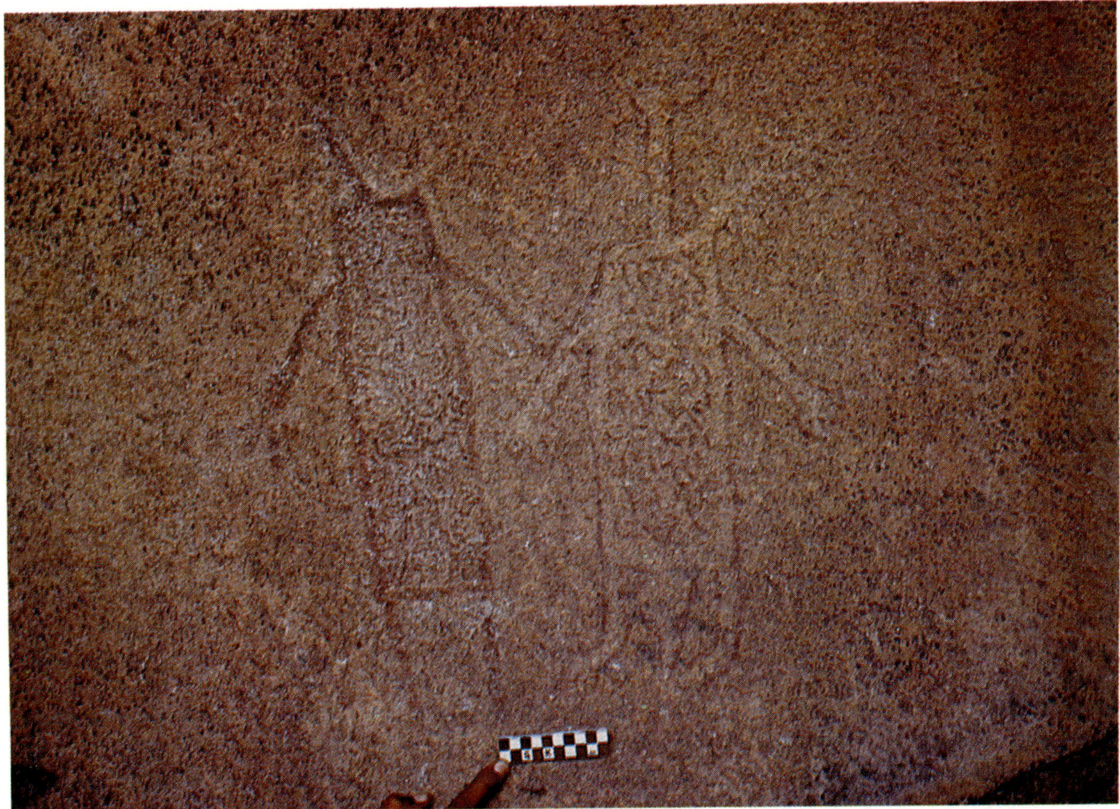

Figure 35. Twin Humans, Chaturbhujnāth Nālā, Chambal Valley, Māndāsor, Madhya Pradesh, Central India.

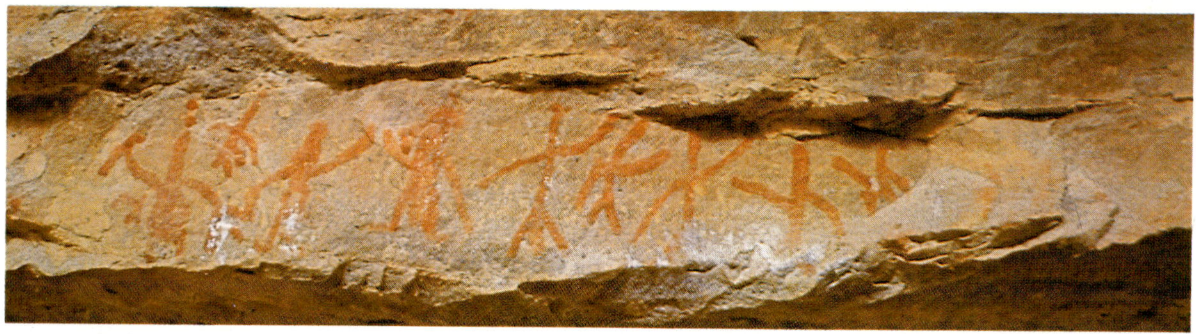

Figure 36. Human figures brandishing arms, Chaturbhujnāth Nālā, Māndāsor, Madhya Pradesh, Central India.

in coastal Mālnād, the peninsular gneissic complex of northern Karnataka, while rock paintings of Karnataka have been found in the sandstone hills of the Kālādgi group at Rāmdūrga in Belgāon district, Bādāmi (Areguddā and Hireguddā), Pattadakal, Āihole, Kutakanakari. Line engravings and bruisings have been reported in the plains of Benākal forest at Piklihāl and Māski in Rāichur, Chitradūrga, Hāmpi, Korugodu and Koppugāllu, Sangankāllu in Bellāry district. Much of the Karnataka rock art is confined to the Krishnā Tungabhadrā valley (A. Sundara in Chakravarty ed., *Rock Art of India*:137-48; *Prehistoric Art in Karnataka* in Kannada 1985, 1994). Rock paintings in Andhra Pradesh have been found in Ketāvaram in Kurnool, Chinnānur and Chintākuntā in Cuddapāh, and rock bruisings have come to light in the saddle plateaus of granite hills at Vīrpalli Mallasamudram, Sanganunpalli in

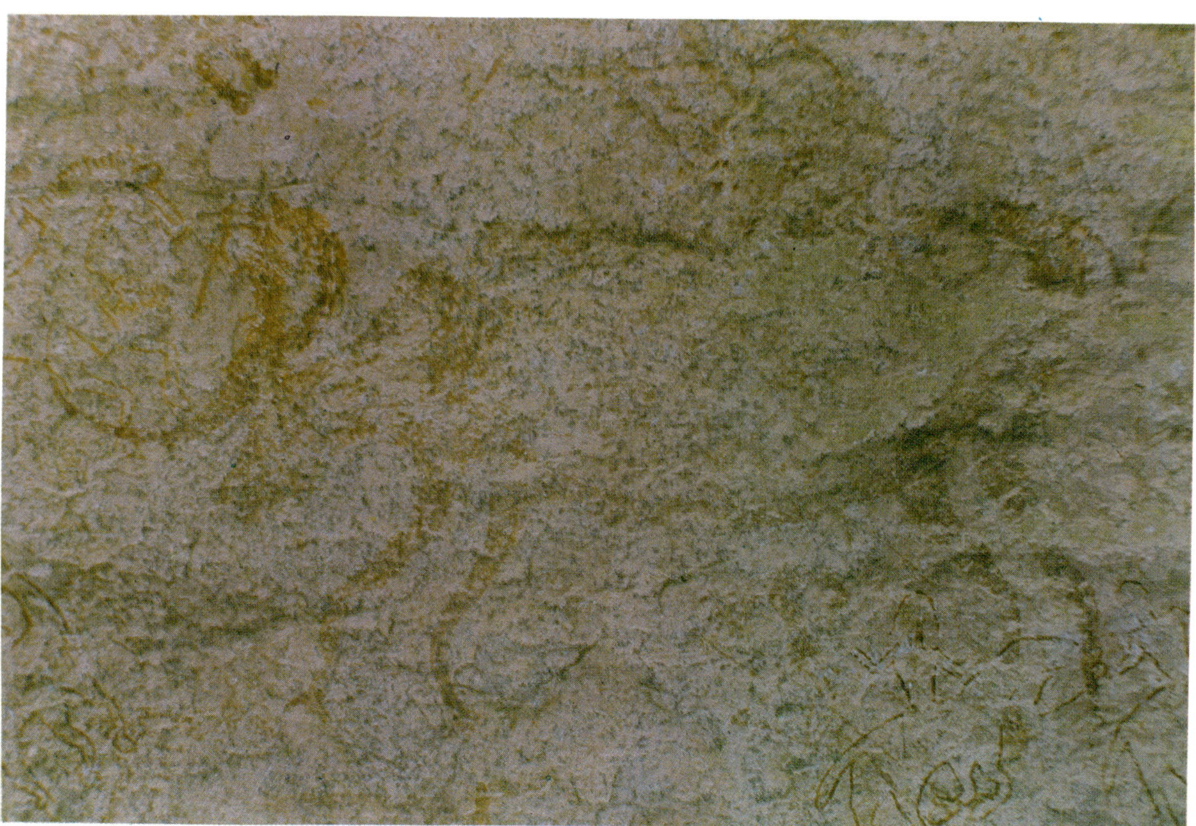

Figure 37. Buffalo, Ādamgarh, Hoshāngābād, Madhya Pradesh, Central India

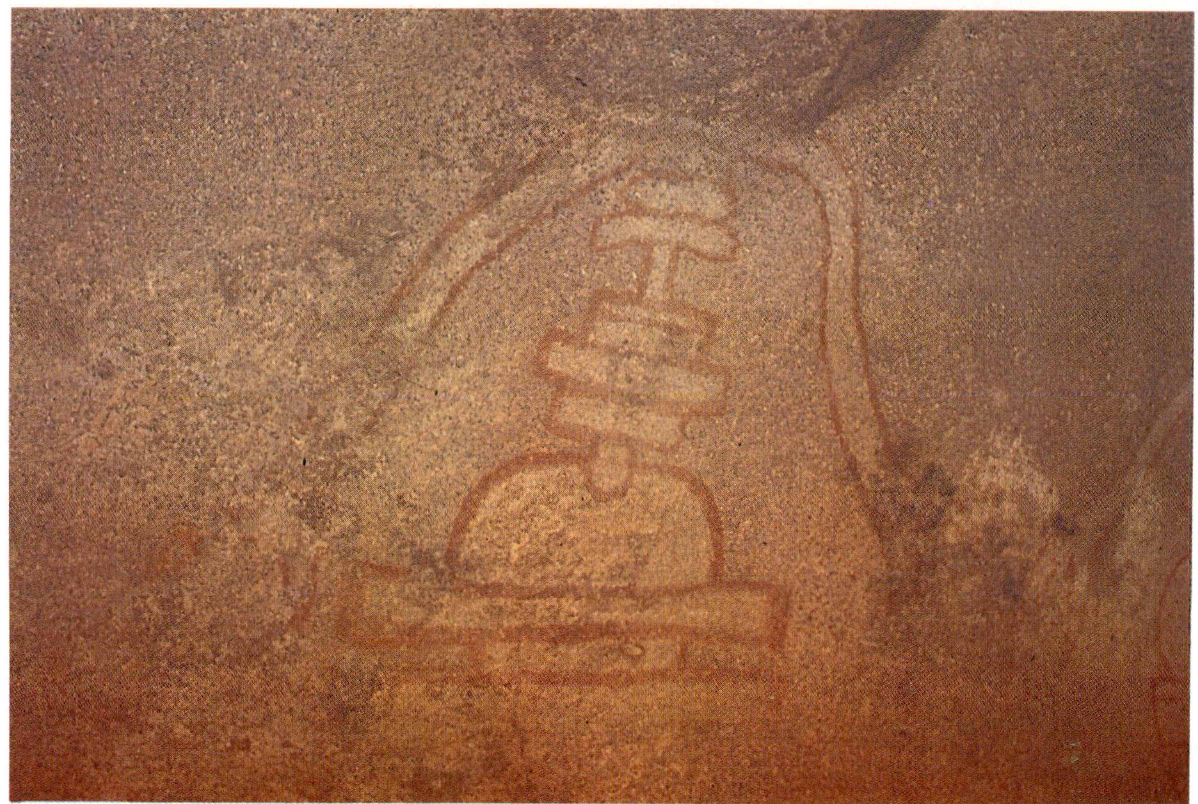

Figure 38. Stupa, Idar, Sabarkanthā, Gujarat, Western India.

Mehboob Nagar, and in Lankāpally reserve forest in Kāmmām district (Mathpal, *Dinman*, Sept 21-27, 1980; 10-1, Neumayer, *Lines on stone* 1993). Rock paintings have been also found at Iduhātti in the Nilgiris, Mādurāi, and the south and north Ārcot districts of Tamilnadu. Finally, hundreds of paintings have been found in Edakkal in Kozhikode district, in the Mārāiyur region in Anjunād valley, in Idukki district, and at Attalā, Kavilkādāvu, Tenmālāi, Thovarymālā and

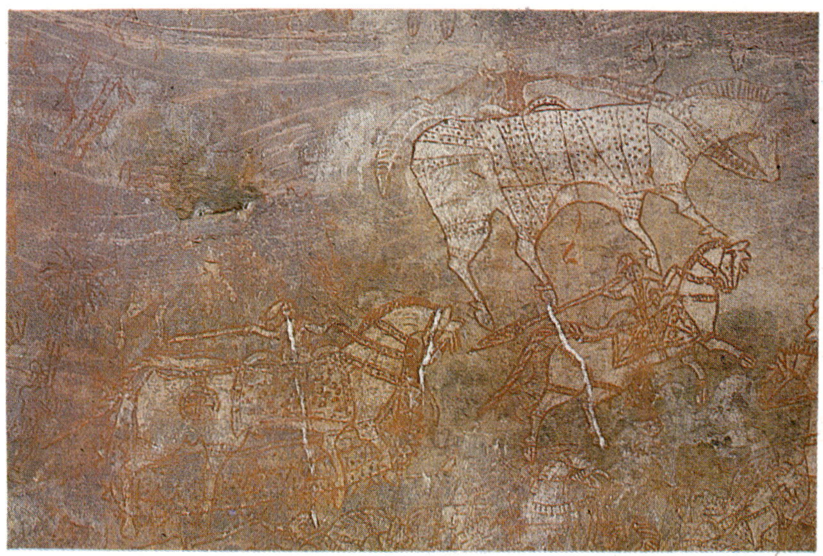

Figure 39. Decorated horses with riders, Lādi Ki Karār, Sehore, Madhya Pradesh, Central India.

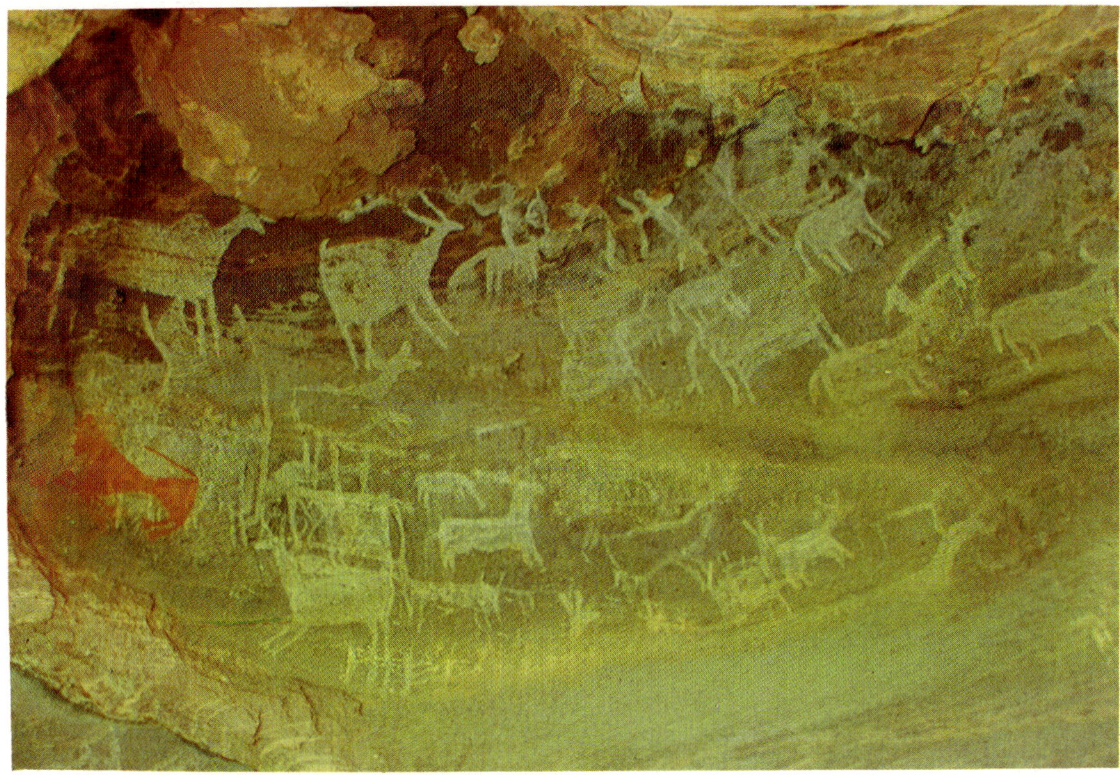

Figure 40. Decorated Animals, Lādi Ki Karār, Sehore, Madhya Pradesh, Central India.

Perumkādāvil in Kerala (S.P. Thampi *BDCRI* 35, 3-4, 1976:37-44).

Needless to say, this is an illustrative rather than an exhaustive list of the principal regions and sites of India, wherefrom rock art is reported and published. Thousands of rock art sites known to the local populations remain to be 'discovered' and published. Major problems are the inaccessible locations of many of the sites in hills and forests, and the dearth of researchers equipped with adequate knowledge of recording techniques or with investigative tools and laboratory facilities, including those for differentiating natural from human markings, or for direct dating.

There appears to be greater similarity between problems of rock art deterioration in the several climatic zones and geological regions of Australia, America, Africa and Asia, including India, than between these regions and the lime stone cave environment of temperate Europe. However, the relative exposure of different sections of rock, causing different rates of erosion, patination or flaking, the difference in the depth of penetration of paints due to the variation in rock porosity, humidity, viscosity of paint or size and shape of pigment grains, have accounted for different degrees of preservation and recognition even in these non-European environments. The rock art sites of central India, are found both in hard, silicified as well as softer sandstone. The sand stone surface is impoverished by bio-degradable debris left by visitors, feeding micro-organisms. The non-homogeneous, honeycombed structure of the sand stone helps in preferential condensation in small depressions, water seepage into interstitial pores between the constituent grains of

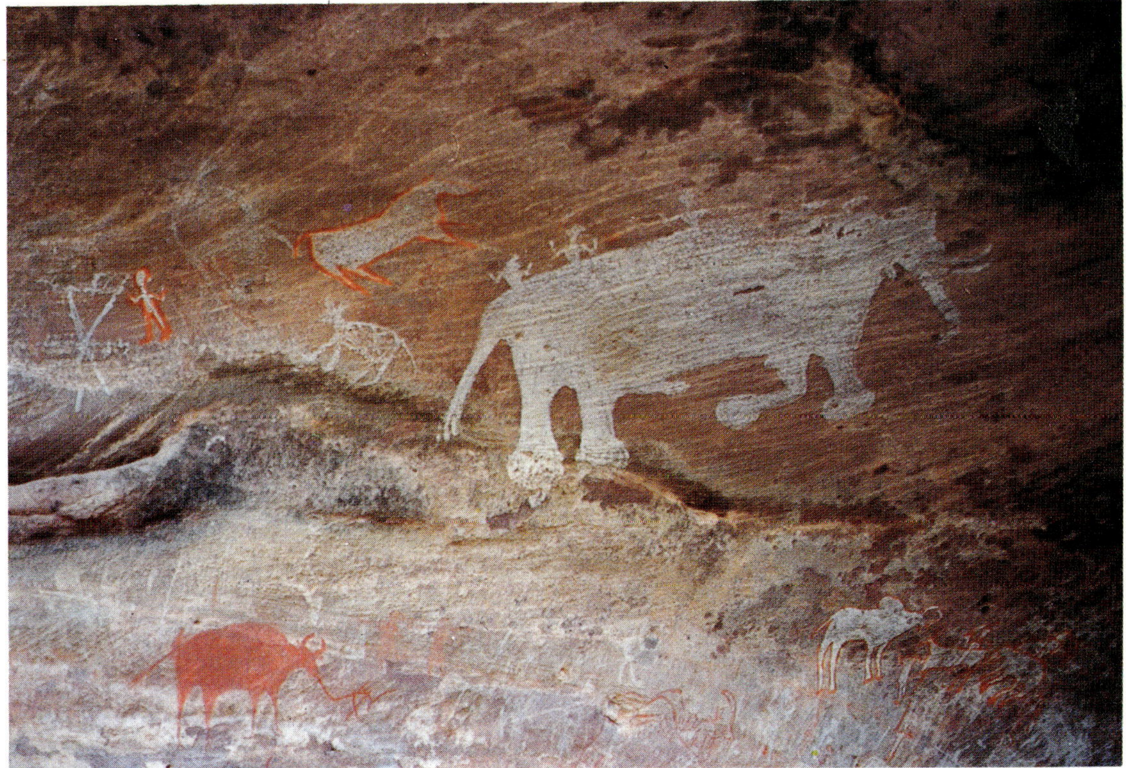

Figure 41. Animals, Lādi Ki Karār, Sehore, Madhya Pradesh, Central India.

rock, exfoliation through thermal gradients caused in bush fires, salt efflorsence and cryptogamic growth, occasioned by capillary flow of water through fissures in the rock fabric. In siliceous sandstone, a crypto-crystalline and amorphous silica skin is formed through a bonding of pigment with iron oxide, manganese and titanium which protects the art but also contributes to its fading by choking off the light. In arid regions of western Australia, north Africa, USA, and central and western India with conditions of less than 250 mm mean annual precipitation, a non-autochthonous, dark brownish black, glossy skin of desert varnish consisting of clay, iron and manganese oxide, deriving from the desert dust storms, tends to form on the rock art. This acts as a protective patina.

At least in India, an ecological rather than structural or chemical conservation may prove useful in view of most of the rock art sites being still protected

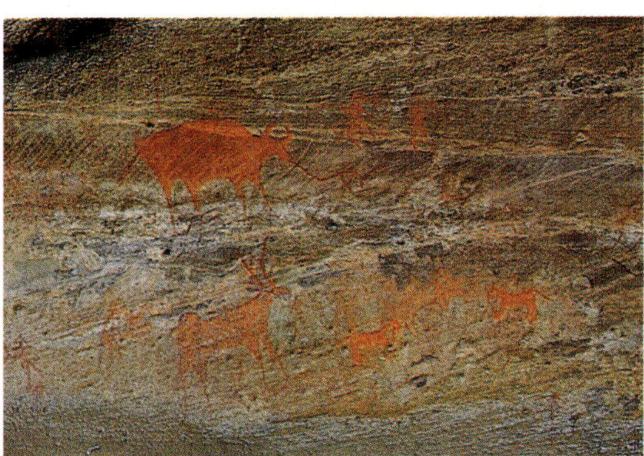

Figure 42. Elephant with riders and animals, Lādi Ki Karār, Sehore, Madhya Pradesh, Central India.

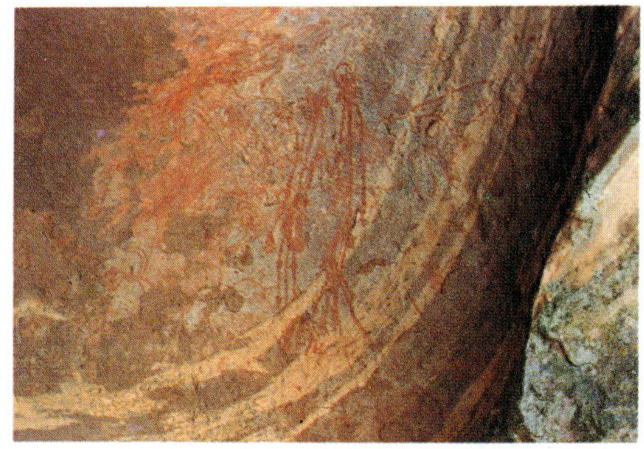

Figure 43. Stylized human figures, IGRMS (Indira Gandhi Rāshtriya Mānav Sangrahālaya or National Museum of Man)premises, Shāmlā hills, Bhopal, Madhya Pradesh, Central India.

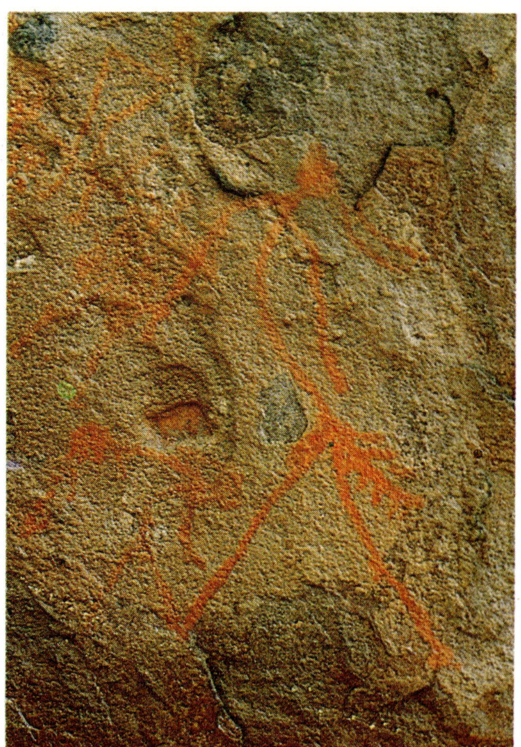

Figure 44. Stylized stick shaped human figure, IGRMS premises, Shāmlā hills, Bhopal, Madhya Pradesh, Central India. Compare Fig. 104., from France on page 83.

by thick forests and inaccessible terrains. Vegetation barriers, diversion of water, regulation of access can still prove useful. Rock art sites like those in the Betwā source region and Narmadā valley, consisting of thousands of painted shelters and traces of pre-historic human settlements, should be protected as world heritage parks in the same way as the Tongariro national park in New Zealand or Kakadu national park or Uluru(Ayer's Rock) in Australia, sacred to peoples like the Maori or the Anangu, or protected as part of a natural sanctury like the Tonskyya Pisanista rock art sites in Siberia. The dogged and successful attempts by activists in Portugal in saving the Côa valley rock art from destruction in mega-developmental activities provide a lesson in awareness for the Indians about the need for combative strategies for protection of the hot spot areas of Indian rock art.

Materials, Techniques and Chronological Tools

Though about 21 colours have been detected at rock art sites like Bhīmbetkā, the Indian tradition of rock painting would seem, rather incorrectly, at first sight, to be overwhelmingly monochrome with a predominant use of red of various shades derived from ochre or haematite containing iron oxide, and secondarily, of white, derived from lime, and rarely, of green and yellow derived from copper minerals, or blue or coal black obtained from manganese or charcoal. Differential quality of shading using different colours of pigments to model the shapes, to indicate volume, to suggest overlapping and foreshortening, evident in San rock art of South Africa, is not paralleled in India. The painting, as it survives today, appears to have been done by rubbing the colour nodule dry, or with water without any visible use of organic binding material, using finger tips, twigs, hair brush or by spraying with the mouth (Mathpal, *Prehistoric Rock Paintings of Bhimbetka* 1984: 187-97; Neumayer 1993:293-95). The paintings are usually outlined once or sometimes twice in red with red infill, and occasionally in white, with red or white infill varied by alternation of yellow, green and red. However, what survive in case of the older paintings are the shadows of oxidation covered by a transparent patina of silica or water soluble, opaque patina of

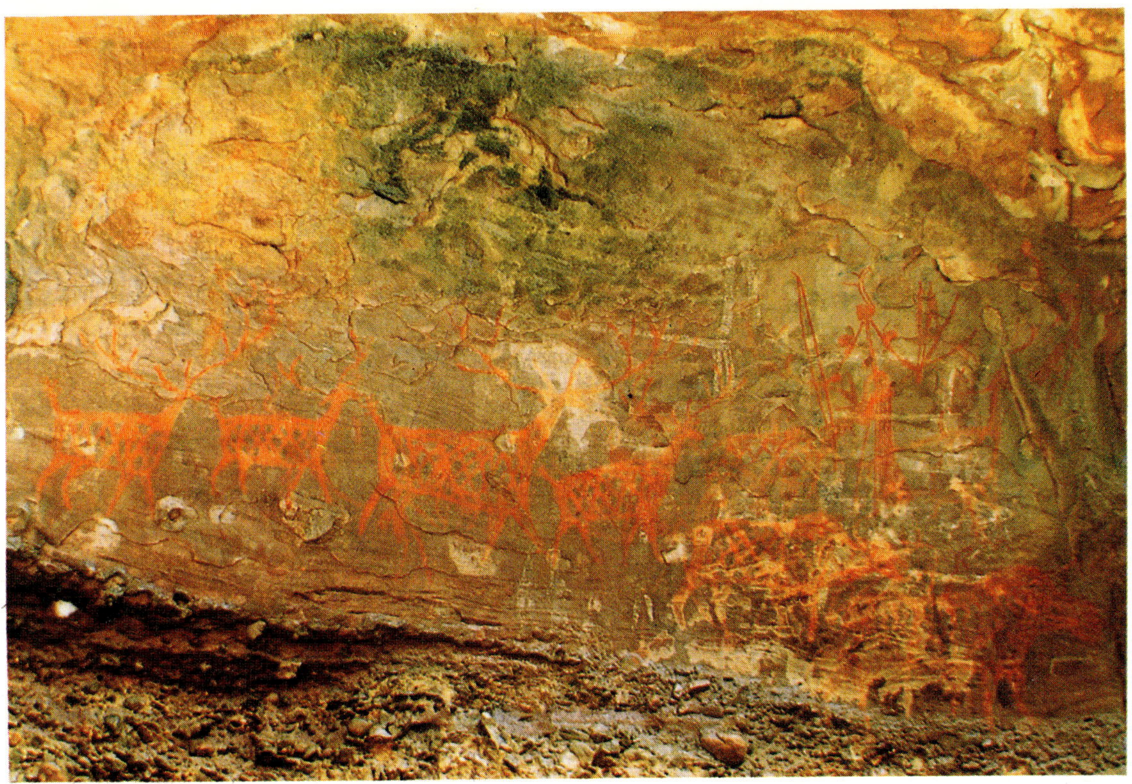

Figure 45. Deers and hunters, IGRMS premises, Shāmlā hills, Bhopal, Madhya Pradesh, Central India.

dust or mineral precipitate. The pigments or the techniques used in India have been used in other parts of the world, and the oldest open air paintings have been found to be of a dark red colour, in the warm and dry regions of Mexico, north-east Brazil, south-east USA, Australia, Sahara and central India. The attempt to use colours, their brightness, their combinations or their statistical indices as indicators of patterns, styles, age, sequence, spatial distribution or even meaning in India have come to grief, because these have been shown to be subject to transformation in taphonomic processes. Iron oxide is a metastable mineral and its reflective properties vary with post-depositional alterations due to different moisture regimes, and degrees of solar exposure, which accompany seasonal and diurnal fluctuations in temperature and relative humidity, due to the nature of rock support or grain size. Thus, the dark red painting might have been initially made in orange and yellow. The white pigment is very transient compared with red and, at the painted rock shelters at Jāorā in Madhya Pradesh, the white paint has changed to black. In the red and white bichrome art of India as well as Sahara, South Africa or Kimberley in Australia, the white has disappeared altogether, leaving the red alone (Bednarik *Antiquity* 68, 1994: 70-71). Water seepage has been a corrosive and highly misleading agent as at Sātkuṇḍā in central India, where the older paintings in white appear to be brighter and fresher than the nebulous white paintings of the later, historic period which overlie them (Neumayer 1993: 28).

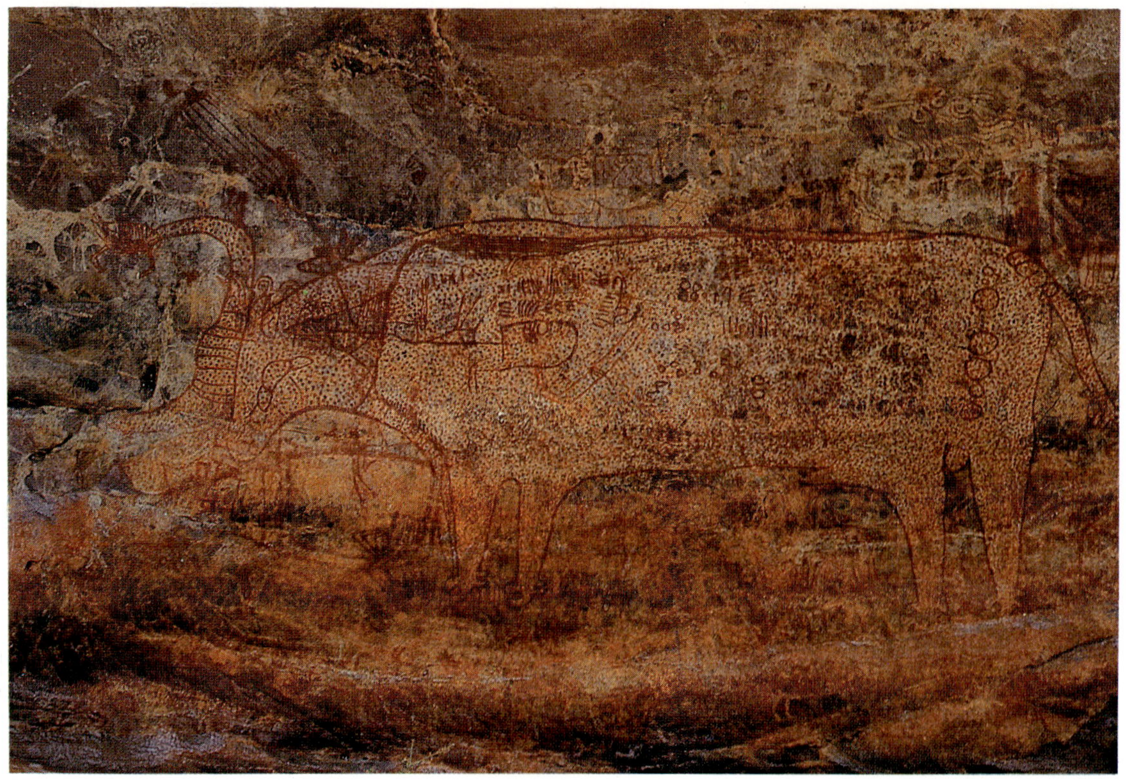

Figure 46. Mythical bull, Jāorā, Rāisen, Madhya Pradesh, Central India.

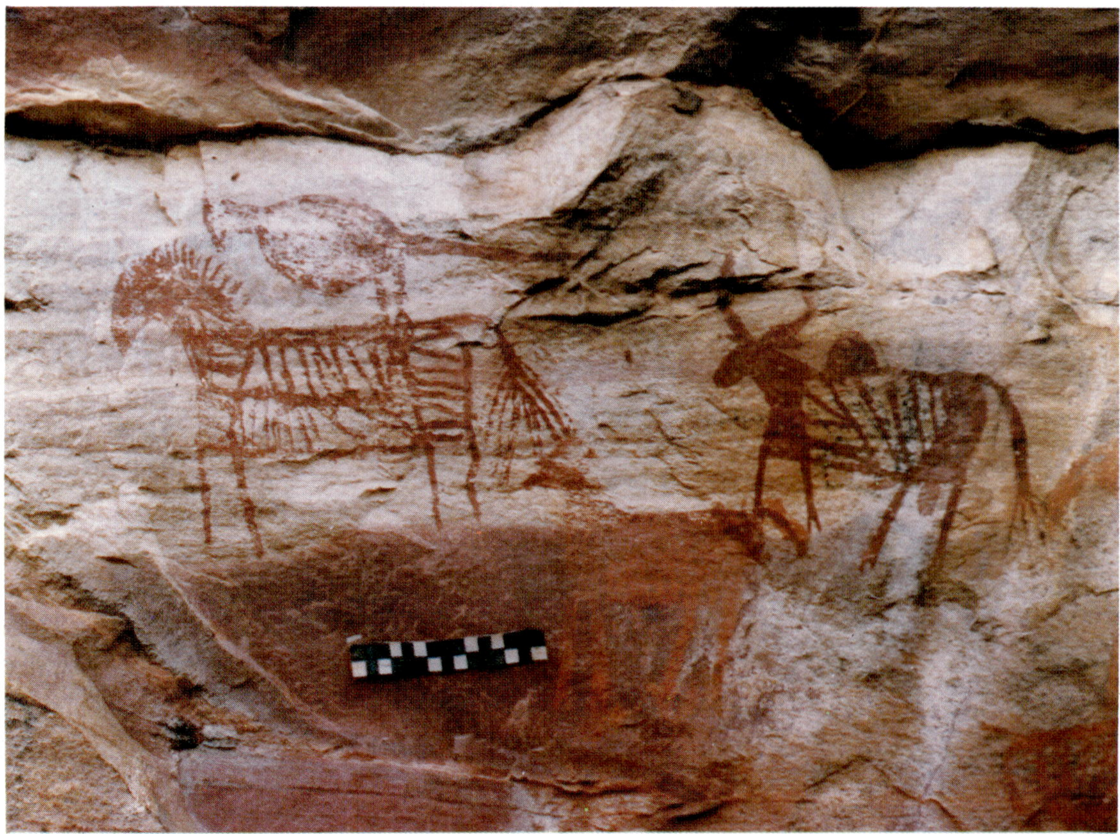

Figure 47. Bird, horses and bull, Putalikarār, Rāisen, Madhya Pradesh, Central India.

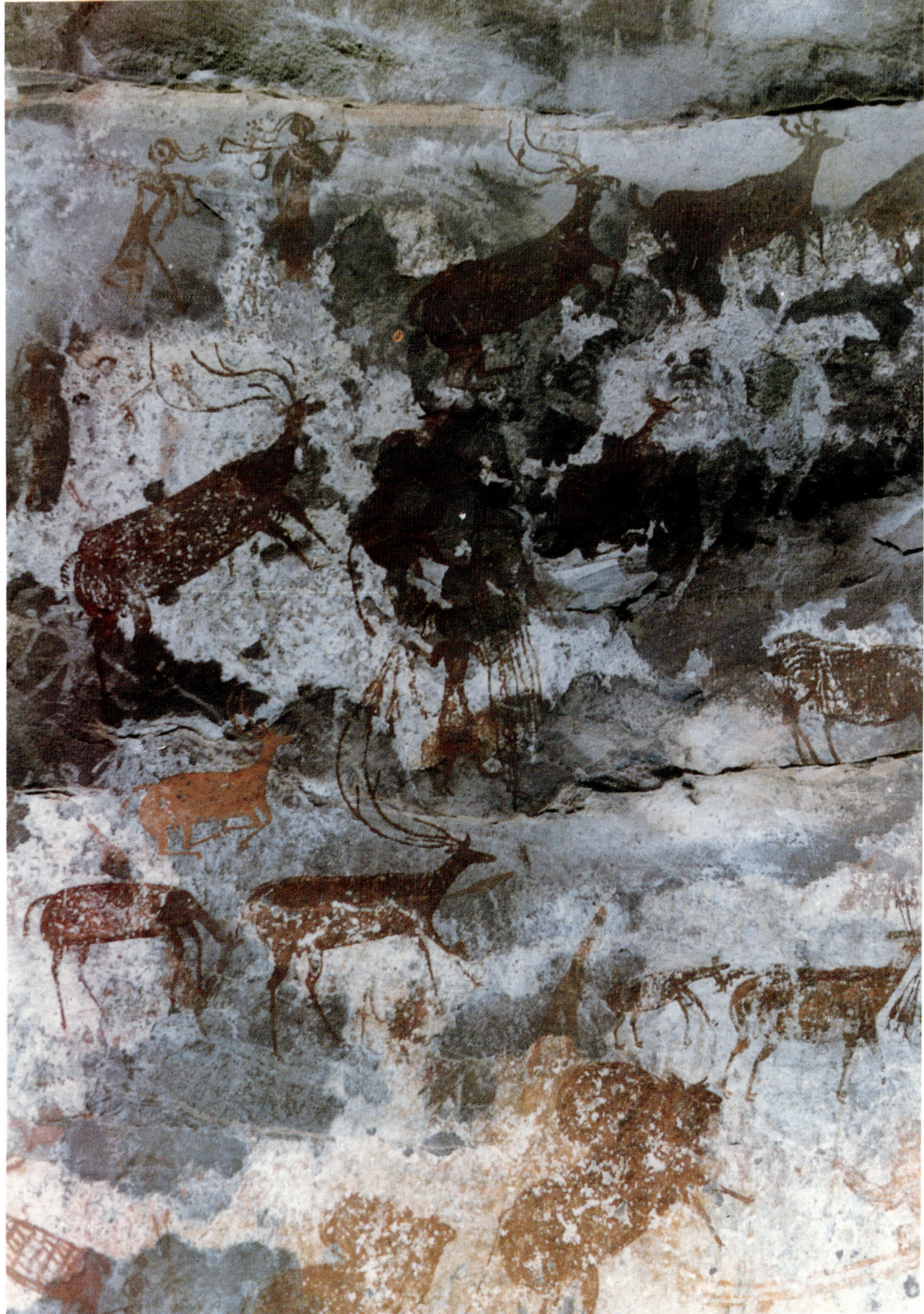

Figure 48. Deers, humped bulls and humans, Sātkuṇḍā, Rāisen, Madhya Pradesh, Central India.

The petroglyphs are mostly in the nature of bruisings rubbed with stone on granite in southern Deccan, and are found rarely on the hard quartzite rocks at Bādāmi in Karnataka and in Chintākuntā in Andhra Pradesh. In the Himalayas these include dots, holes, conical, U-shaped cup marks, large pits, foot prints, ostensibly done by hammering and drilling, probably with metal tools. Both in the Kumāon Gārhwāl region as also in Karnataka, these petroglyphs appear to be physically associated with the remains of a megalithic necropolis. Except for the Himalayan petroglyphs, the Indian tradition of petroglyphs is largely figural. Most of the s'graffito, scratched or engraved on the open rock shelters of India, are not patinated like most of the world's petroglyphs in arid or semi-arid regions. The dark-brown rock varnish which provides the lamina for such art is usually very thin, and on hard rocks shallow petroglyphs become difficult to detect if they are repatinated. It is possible that the older petroglyphs in India, made outside speleo-environment, remain to be recognised by careful survey. On the other hand, a proper analysis needs to be undertaken to distinguish natural marking generated by distinctive variations, xenolithic inclusions, tesselation in rock structures due to selective crystallisation, weathering, chemical solution, exfoliation, kinetic plant marks, animal scratches or utilitarian anthropic marks (Bednarik *RAR* 11.1, 1994: 23-44). That this kind of misidentification has taken place in relation to Indian rock art, has been demonstrated in relation to markings on ostrich egg shell fragments found in India (Bednarik, *The Artefact* 13.3, 1992: 233-240). Being caused, like the entire world, by non-random processes, the natural markings mimic artificial markings, and have been misread as intentional (A. Marschack, *RAR* 8.2, 1991: 82-93; 9.1, 1992: 37-64; T.Lenssen Erz, *RAR* 9.2, 1992: 87-105; Bednarik, *RAR* 11.1, 1994: 33-44).

Though the Indian rock paintings, like similar paintings in the rest of the world, can be presumed to have been done in an additive manner, more or less at the same time as the paint was prepared, the age of the organic component of the paint is not always coterminous with the age of the paint or of its application. The date of the charcoal which precedes its use in pigment, indicates the approximate time when the tree that provided the carbonised wood lived, and not the time when the painting was done. However, organic pigments have been identified in different parts of the world, including at least three cases in India (Bednarik, *RAR* 10.1, 1993:49), and carbon dating in such cases is possible. Many paintings in India are found encapsulated in a finely laminated series of silica skins formed by dust, salt and other carbon bearing substances. Silicification of sand stone, which is not a rare phenomenon in the Indian sand stone belts, is no necessary indication of great antiquity of rock art as is evidenced in case of siliceous skins on European inscriptions in the central Queensland highlands of Australia.

Microchronostratigraphic sequences of such laminations have been determined from bottom to top in a cross section through A.M.S. ^{14}C (Alan Watchman, *The Artefact* 16, 1993: 40-41) While it is possible to use the FLECS (Focused Laser Extraction of Carbon-bearing Substances) AMS (Accelerator Mass Spectrometry) to date carbonate precipitate, rock varnish or oxalate skin covering petroglyphs, the dating can not be absolutely correct. Being produced reductively, the petroglyphs can, through the AMS process, provide only minimum dates from the encrustation which cover and postdate them. It has been found difficult to establish a reliable calibration curve from dates derived from rock varnish, in which the rate of leaching of mobile cations is affected by several environmental factors.

Use of features related to the material of rock art, which either date (e.g. Pigment), predate (e.g. the rock art medium of surface) or post-date it (e.g. later cracks dissecting a motif or precipitates deposited over it), to determine chronology of the rock art, has run into insuperable problems in different parts of the world. The direct dating methods use rate processes which are not constant in the rate of change and have to be calibrated by one another. Whether one uses ratios of carbon or counts the decay in carbon, radio-carbon dating is possible only when organic material exists in adequate quantity in the paint, which is rare, when the carbon in such material has not been exchanged with older or younger carbon, and when the collection of sample is done by careful inter-disciplinary team work without incurring contamination. The older the date, smaller the sample, the greater the possibility of contamination and error. Apart from the fact that detached, painted rock fragments, stratified in datable segments of an excavated site are found most rarely, the correlation of pigments stratified in rock shelter floors with the micronano stratigraphy of the painted crusts on rock is hardly substantiated by convincing chemical data. Even when all these difficulties are overcome, which is virtually impossible in the Indian situation, in view of the near absence of evidence of organic pigments or glue, lack of comprehensive statistical indices and laboratory limitations, only the minimum and maximum date of the pigments is obtained, not the time of execution of the painting, nor of the portion of the rock below or varnish above the engraving, nor of the engraving itself.

The direct dating studies have often tended to be integrated into archaeological confirmationism and traditional uniformitarianism which are not

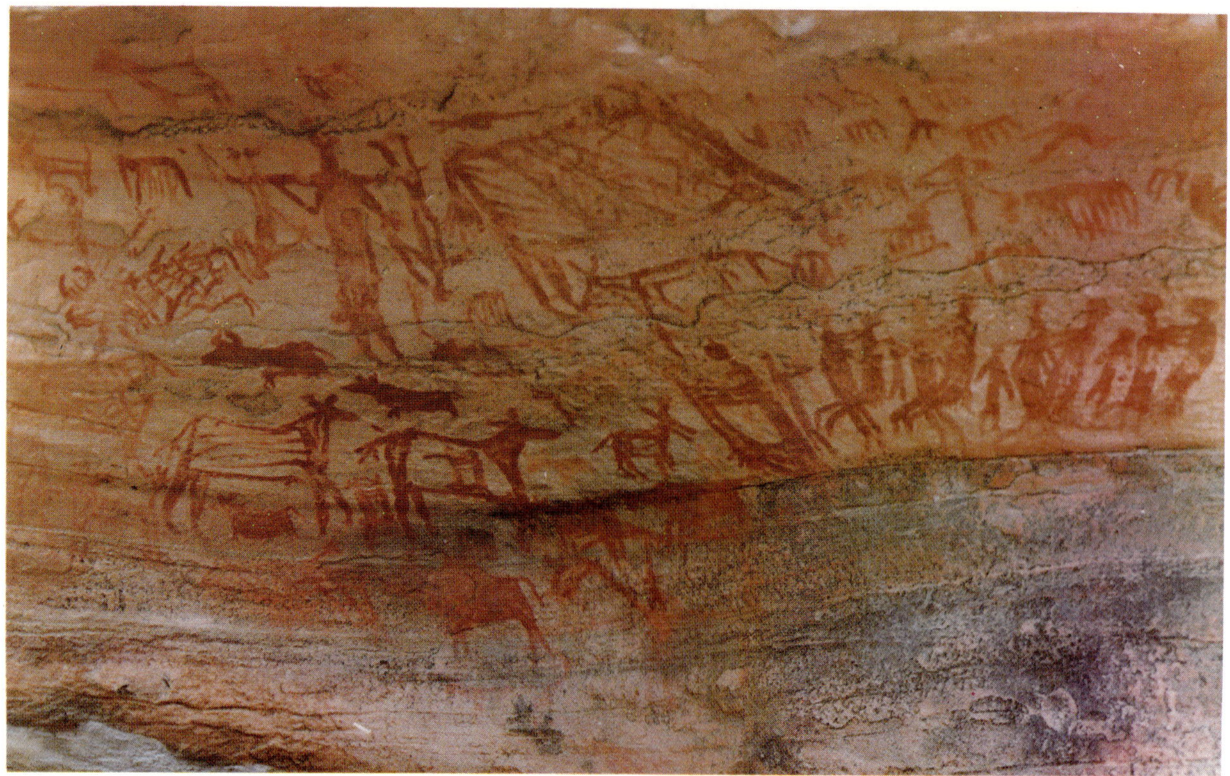

Figure 49. Human activities and animals, Pengavān, Rāisen, Madhya Pradesh, Central India.

falsifiable, and offer a key to the date of encrustations and modifications on or in the rock rather than to the date of the painting or the engraving itself. And yet, direct dating methods, being reinforcive of the exaggerated claims of antiquity, have tended to widen the gap between the scientific haves and have nots, creating a neo-colonialist cultural hegemony of technological advanced nations. Microerosion dating has been suggested as a more direct and non-destructive method for making a calibrated quantitative assessment of microscopic modifications to crystalline and fractured edges of the petroglyphs. Application of microerosion dating methods to the petroglyphs in the granite regions of India and Egypt and other suitable rock-types has been suggested as a low cost non-laboratory oriented approach, which can free Indian rock art research from the neo-colonialist effect of scientific progress. Unlike AMS dating, it does not involve any extraction of rock samples. And yet, even this process can not provide precise results since it involves examination of many complex geological, geochemical and geomorphological events and processes to which the petroglyphs have been subjected over time (Bednarik *AURA Occasional publi.* 8, 1993: 64-66).

Palaeolithic Context

Recognition of the earliest phase of Indian rock art has been hindered by the long standing presumption that the earliest rock art of the world is found only in deep limestone caves of Europe. However, this presumption has been changed after the discovery of

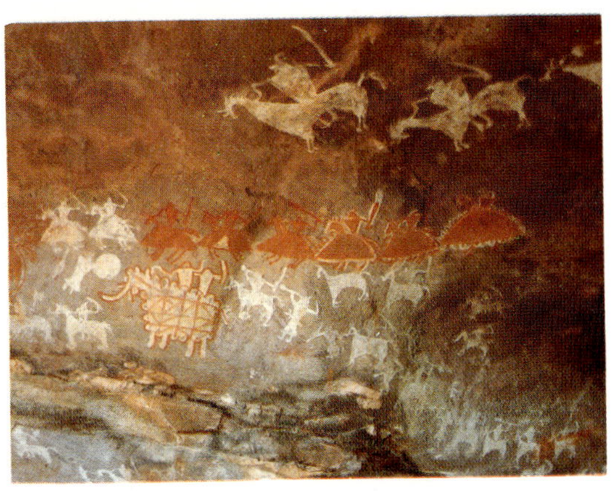

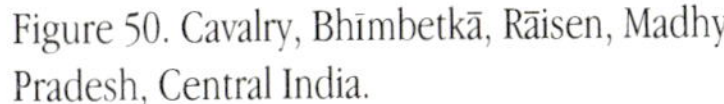

Figure 50. Cavalry, Bhīmbetkā, Rāisen, Madhya Pradesh, Central India.

Palaeolithic rock art of Pleistocene age at open sites of Spain and Portugal in Europe itself and in other continents outside Europe since 1980s (Paul G. Bahn and Jean Vartut, *Images of the Ice Age* 1988: 26-40). It would appear that very little of the Upper Palaeolithic Art has survived even in Europe, and that it represents a much larger body of Art, however minuscule its surviving evidence may be because of taphonomic changes. The acceptance of the presence of such early art from India has also been made difficult by the fact that in spite of the much vaster rock art production found outside Europe, there was no clear-cut surviving evidence of Palaeolithic rock art in Asia with the probable exception of petroglyphs in Mount Carmel caves in Israel. The method of research has also come in the way of the recognition of the claim of the Upper Palaeolithic antiquity for Indian rock art to be stretching back to 40 thousand years. The suggestion of such antiquity has been made on the presumption that the earliest phase of this art is one of dynamic figures executed in green pigment, associated with the *terra verta* or green earth nodules excavated from the Upper Palaeolithic layer of Bhīmbetkā shelter III A-28 (Wakankar, *Science Today* 20, 1993: 43-48; 1987, *Collected Works*: 168-84). However, the suggestion has been rejected by a further demonstration that, where they occur together, the 'S' type green dynamic figures postdate intricate decorative patterns (G.S. Tyagi in Michael Lorblanchet ed., *Rock Art in the Old World,* 1992:303-17). Needless to say that further investigations may further change this latter conclusion.

Inspite of the fact that 97% of the Pleistocene parietal and portable art in Eurasia is non-iconic, the possibility that the Upper Palaeolithic art in India could also well be non-iconic has not found acceptance. It would appear that the small percentage of iconic content in Franco-Cantabrian Cave Art has come in the way of the belated recognition of this possibility. Despite the small number of geometric art motifs on portable Pleistocene objects in Asia and Africa in general, or in India in particular, it is likely that further research will yield, taphonomic changes apart, many more such objects. About 46 and more marked ostrich eggshell fragments, principally found from Bhīmbetkā, Rāmnagar and Chandreśāl, have been assigned to a period ranging between 25,000 to about 39,000 years B.P. (Kumar et al. *RAR* 19, 1988: 43-53; *Rock Art in the Old World* 1993: 193-202). Out of all these, only one fragment, from Pātne, radio-carbon dated to about 25,000 years B.P., has been found to possess a deliberately made anthropic marking, which bears some resemblance to the engraving on a limestone cobble from Urkan E-Rub in Israel from about 19,000 to 14,000 years B.P. and to an engraving on a Palaeolithic antler fragment from China. The engraving on the Pātne specimen comprises two cross-hatched bands, one complete and the other truncated, with grooves scored by a stone burin mechanically, in straight lines and in fairly uniform depth. Unlike these, the other specimens are rounded in section, and possess meandering lines of varying depths, which appear to have been produced by a chemical solution process without any recognisable pattern. Some of these ostrich eggshell objects are associated with an Upper Palaeolithic industry, while the ostrich itself is known to have been extinct by the early Holocene period in India. Though pre-existing human markings on the other fragments have not been completely ruled out, the markings made on any of these objects may often be much younger than the object itself, and any resemblance between such markings and Indian rock art may be purely accidental. This would be true also about the four perforated ostrich eggshell beads reported from the Upper Palaeolithic horizon in India, of which two are from Pātne and two from Bhīmbetkā. The Palaeolithic use of ostrich eggshells as containers and as ornament has been reported from southern Africa, Sahara and China as well (R.G.

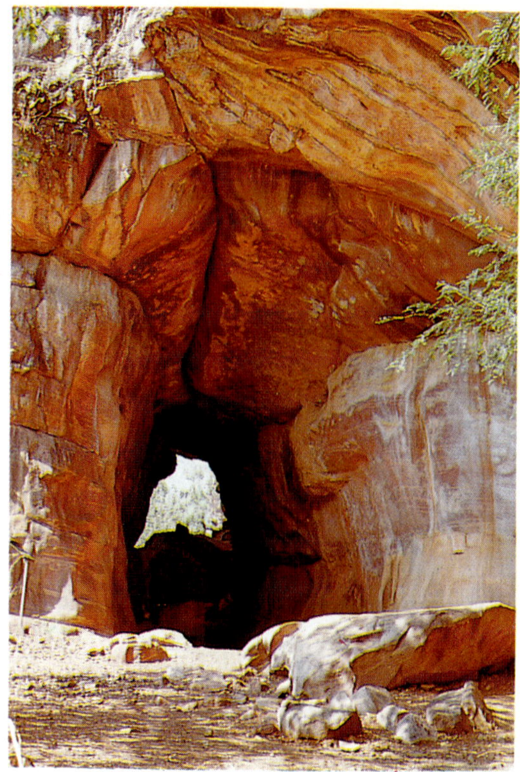

Figure 51. General view of rock shelters, Bhīmbetkā, Rāisen, Madhya Pradesh, Central India.

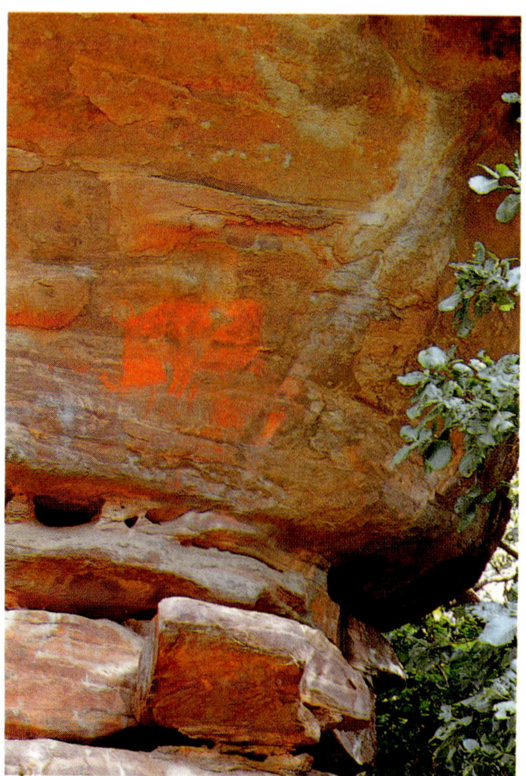

Figure 52. Mythical boar, Bhīmbetkā, Rāisen, Madhya Pradesh, Central India.

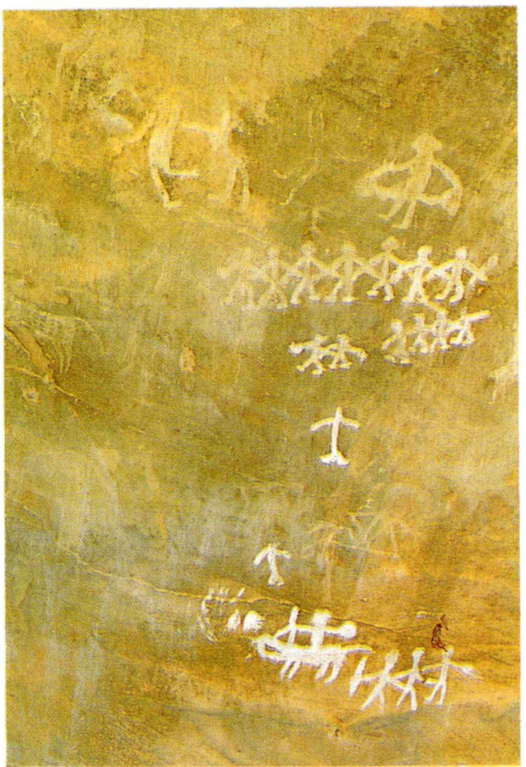

Figure 53. Groups of dancers, Bhīmbetkā, Rāisen, Madhya Pradesh, Central India.

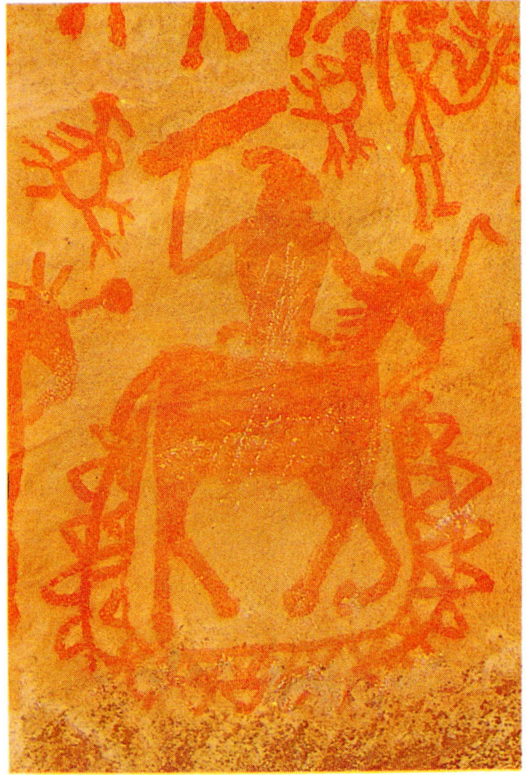

Figure 54. Horse riders, Bhīmbetkā, Rāisen, Madhya Pradesh, Central India.

Bednarik, *Anthropologie* 30.3, 1992: 234-36; *IPPA Bulletin* 13, 1993: 34-43).

Among other Palaeolithic objects are reported a very small number of Upper Palaeolithic beads, perforated or grooved, including Acheulian stone discs from Bhīmbetkā and Maihār and bovid teeth from Kurnool caves in Andhra Pradesh. Such finds are parallelled by the large-scale occurrence of pendants in teeth, ivory, bones, fossils and shells from Palaeolithic deposits from Europe (Murty and Reddy, *Asian Perspectives* 18.2, 1975:214-26; Bednarik, *Man & Environment* 18.2, 1993: 34-5). A T.L. date of c. 19,000 B.P. has been obtained from the Upper Palaeolithic cave site of Muchchatalā Chintāmanu Gāvi where one such bone bead has been found (M.L.K. Murti, *Proceedings of the American Philosophical Society*, 118. 2: 196-230). A carved Upper Palaeolithic bone object has been excavated from Belān gravel III in association with a shell sample, and a blade and burin industry assigned to a period between 19,715 ± 340 B.P. and 25,790 ± 830 B.P. (G.R. Sharma, *Indian Archaeology, A Review;* V.D. Mishra, *Some Aspects of Indian Archaeology*, 1977). Identified earlier as a female figurine and a mother goddess, it has been found to possess seven areas of fracture, and, to be a harpoon which was originally much longer before being damaged (Bednarik, *Man & Environment* 18.2, 1993: 34-35). It is not only parallelled by an Upper Palaeolithic bone

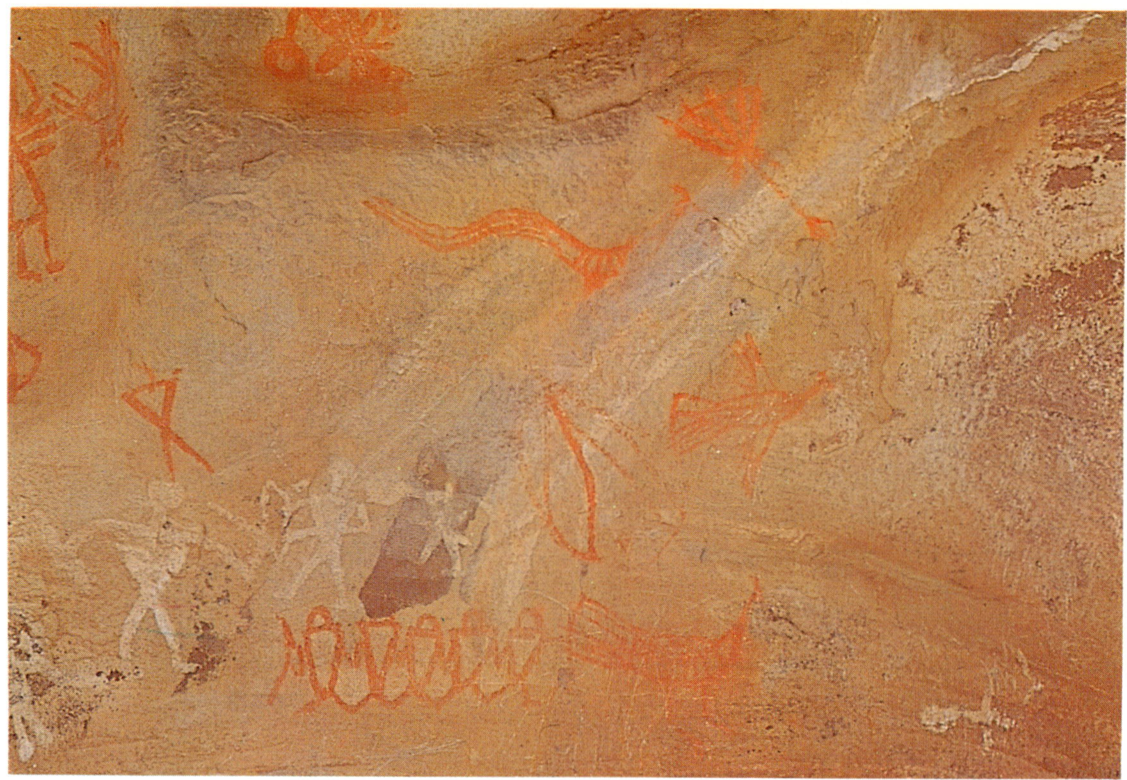

Figure 55. Groups of dancers, Bhīmbetkā, Rāisen, Madhya Pradesh, Central India.

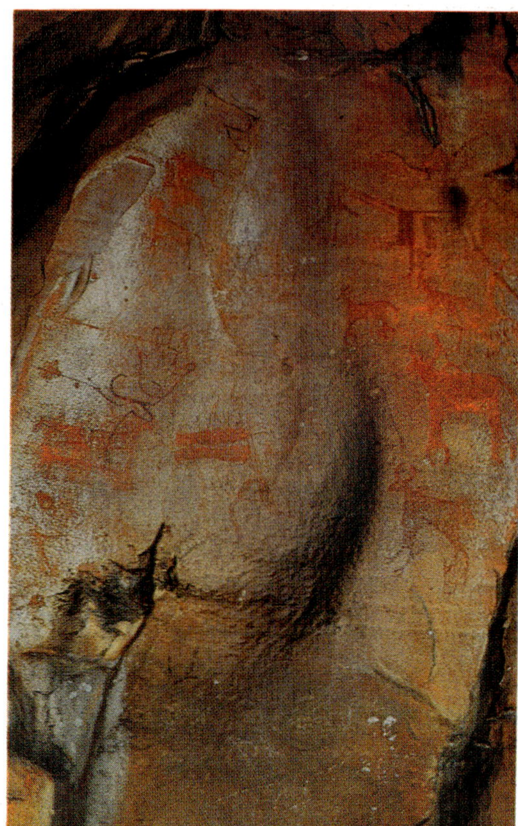

Figure 56. A group of animals, Bhīmbetkā, Rāisen, Madhya Pradesh, Central India.

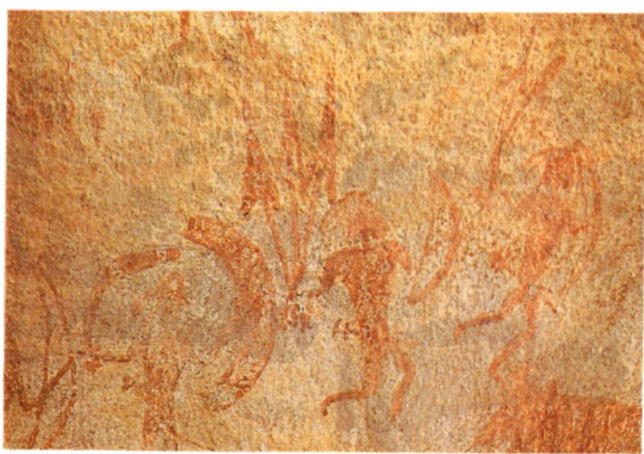

Figure 57. Horse riders, archers and a feline, Bhīmbetkā, Rāisen, Madhya Pradesh, Central India.

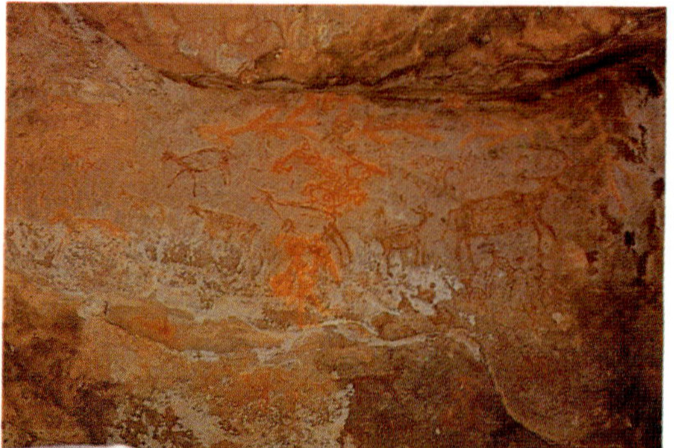

Figure 58. A group of animals, Bhīmbetkā, Rāisen, Madhya Pradesh, Central India.

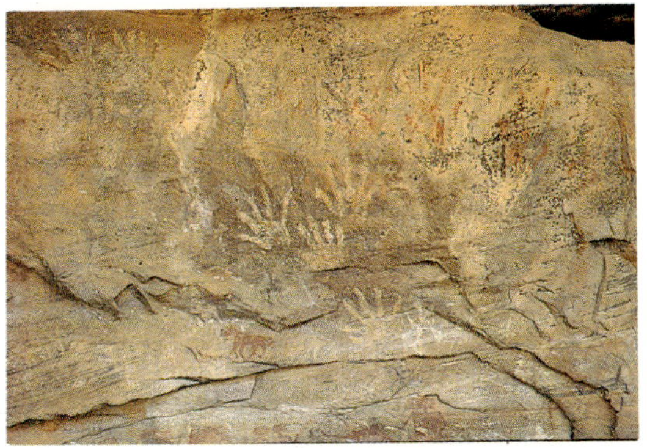

Figure 59. Hand prints, Bhīmbetkā, Rāisen, Madhya Pradesh, Central India.

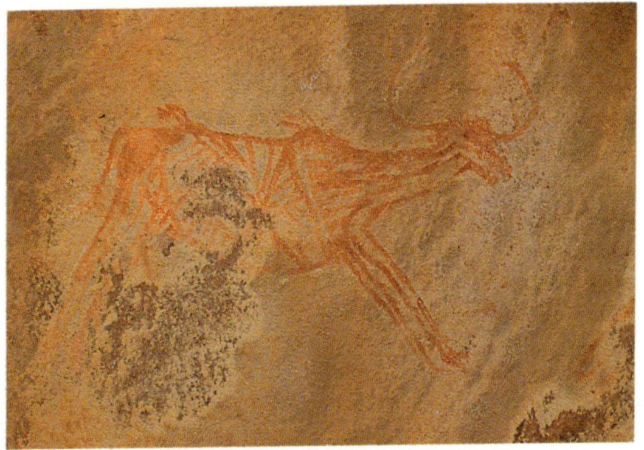

Figure 60. Cattle, Bhīmbetkā, Rāisen, Madhya Pradesh, Central India.

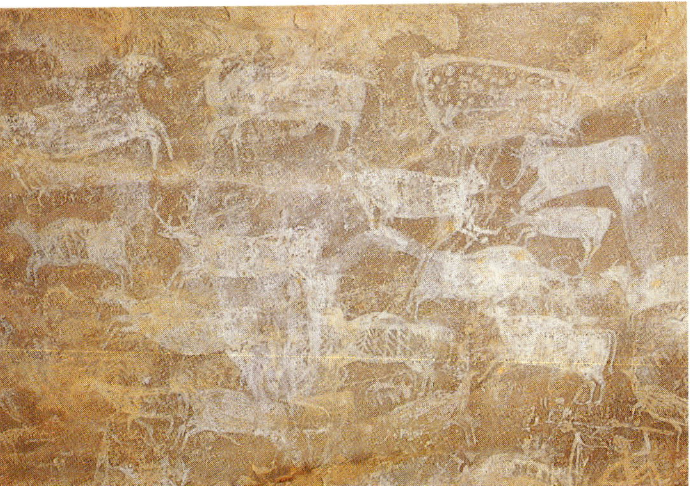

Figure 61. A group of animals, Bhīmbetkā, Rāisen, Madhya Pradesh, Central India.

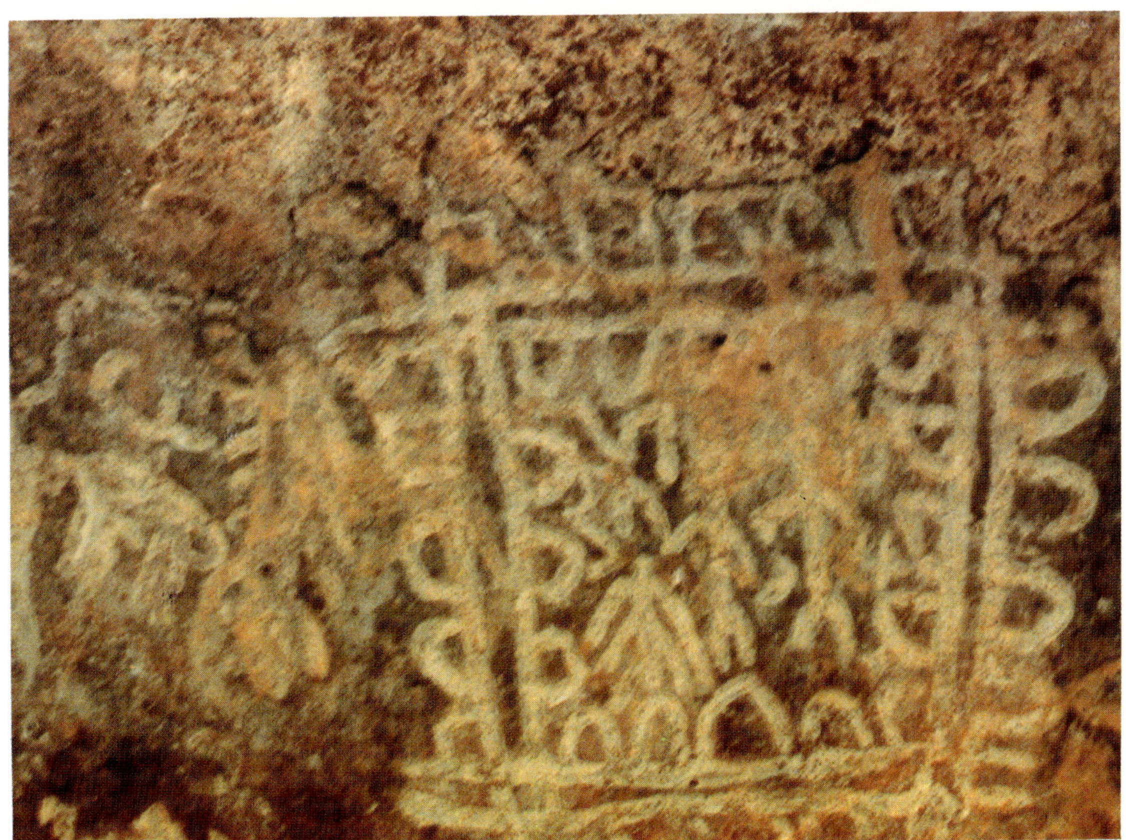

Figure 62. Chowk (Square), Bhīmbetkā, Rāisen, Madhya Pradesh, Central India. Compare squares from Indian and Bolivian figures on pages 76, 81, 83, 86.

harpoon from Pratāpgarh (Wakankar, *Prachya Pratibha* 3.2: 7-29), but also by similar early bone harpoons in Africa and the Ngandong deposit on the Solo river, Java, which suggests knowledge of the technology of a bone harpoon before it is known to have been introduced in northern Asia and Europe (Bednarik, *Man & Environment* 18.2, 1993:35). Six quartz crystals, too small to be used as stone tools and only one of them showing any microflaking at the edge, have been found at the base of the lower Acheulian site of Singi Tālāv in Rajasthan (D' Errico, Gaillard and Mishra, *Hominidae. Proceedings of the Second International Congress of Human Palaeontology* 1989: 237-39), and similar finds have been made in the Acheulian layers in Austria, Israel, China and South Africa. While there is no exact dating for the the Acheulian at Singi Tālāv, at the adjacent site of Didwānā, the Acheulian is more than 390,000 years old (Raghavan, Rajaguru and Mishra, *Man & Environment* 13, 1989: 19-22). A triangular sandstone piece with concentric triangular laminations has been found on a raised circular rubble platform at Bāghor I in the Son Valley in Madhya Pradesh, which is identified as a Palaeolithic shrine from around 8000 B.C. for the worship of female energy. Whatever the authenticity of the interpretation, the arrangement of the platform appears to be deliberate and not accidental (Kenoyer, Clark, Pal and Sharma, *Antiquity* L VII, 1983:88-94). All such evidence, however circumstantial in nature, points to a considerable body of Palaeolithic art, which remains to be excavated, and which proves the existence of a non-iconic artistic sense, not so different from ours today.

However, evidence for what may be the oldest rock art and stone walls in the world, has been offered on the basis of an examination of the so called 'Chief's Rock' at Bhīmbetkā. The 'Chief's Rock' has a flat vertical wall facing the longer passage of a tunnel ending in a hall of rocks with three other openings. While many stone walls have been reported from European Upper and Middle Palaeolithic sites, the two stone walls at Bhīmbetkā were found in the Middle Palaeolithic occupation layer of shelter III F-24 and in an older adjacent shelter III A-30 in association with some 80 Acheulian stone tools, including bifacial handaxes lying between the two walls. Though the Bhīmbetkā walls are undated, the Indian Middle Palaeolithic goes back to around 170,000 years B.P. while the older European stone walls, found so far, are Mousterian (Bednarik, the *Artefact* 16, 1993:60). Ten petroglyphs in the shape of what are considered to be Acheulian cupules or cup marks and a long wandering line, have been found here. Nine of these cupules have been found above the ground level on the vertical wall. These are extremely weathered, stretch up to 16.8 mm depth and appear to precede the 14-20 mm deep cutaneous layer, which is exfoliating probably due to subcutaneous deposition of salt from capillary moisture. The eighth cupule has been found at the base of the pit excavated by Wakankar in 1972, on a large boulder, close to the vertical panel, on the sloping surface, over 1.5 m below the surface, along with a pecked line which meanders down to the cupule, accompanies it and then moves off to the right. These artificial markings (since reburied by the Archaeological Survey of India) on the boulder have been found below a Middle Palaeolithic occupation deposit, near its interface with the upper of two Acheulian layers. The deposit itself is densely cemented by a calcite-encrusted breccia, about 60 cm deep, which suggests wet climatic conditions as against the drier conditions indicated by the upper layers, which are not cemented by carbonate precipitation. The cementing excludes the possibility of post-depositional stratigraphic disturbance. Below the Acheulian red clay at the Auditorium Cave have been found a non-occupational Pisolithic layer, overlying a pebble tool industry, and this Pisolithic layer possesses early Acheulian tools and Lavallois cores at other excavated sites of Bhīmbetkā (Bednarik, *Man & Environment* 18.2, 1993: 35-36; *RAR* 10.2, 1993: 138-39).

The cupules are the oldest surviving rock art known in the world. The oldest cupules found so far in the Americas, Africa, Australia, Canada and Europe stretch up to the Mousterian at La Ferrassie in France and to about 50,000 years B.P. in Australia. The cupules found at Bhīmbetkā appear to be much older, because the Indian Acheulian has been shown, through the thorium-uranium dating method, to be generally beyond the limit of that method, which is around 350,000 B.P. (S. Mishra, *Current Anthropology* 33, 1992: 325-28; Bednarik, *Oxford Journal of Archaeology*,12.1,1993: 1-8; *Anthropos* 89: 169-80). In the absence of a microerosion calibration curve for the region and extensive weathering, the microerosion study of the cupules has been useful only in yielding a minimum relative age for cupule number 5 as being probably well above 100,000 years and being located in the Middle and Lower rather than the Upper Palaeolithic period (Bednarik, *Puratan,* Issue on Rock Art,1996, in press). While petroglyphs have been reported from India as early as 1856, they were not recognised as cupules till 1990. The vertical rock panel with nine cupules was misidentified as a musical stone or lithophone (V.S. Wakankar in K.K. Chakravarty ed. *Rock Art of India*, 1984: 196-200), and the patination was not seen as a viable datable factor. Identification of cupules or cup marks in the Himalayas or in south African or western north American sites as fossils of acoustic events in Palaeolithic art have been difficult to sustain in the absence of any

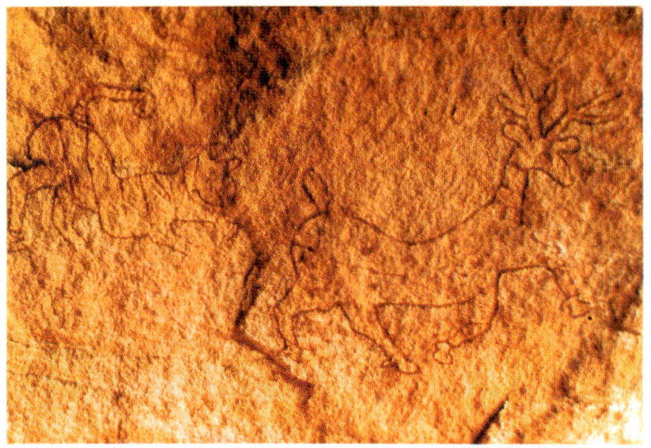

Figure 63. Composite animal and fighter, Churṇā Gundi, Mahādeo hills, Hoshāngābād, Madhya Pradesh, Central India.

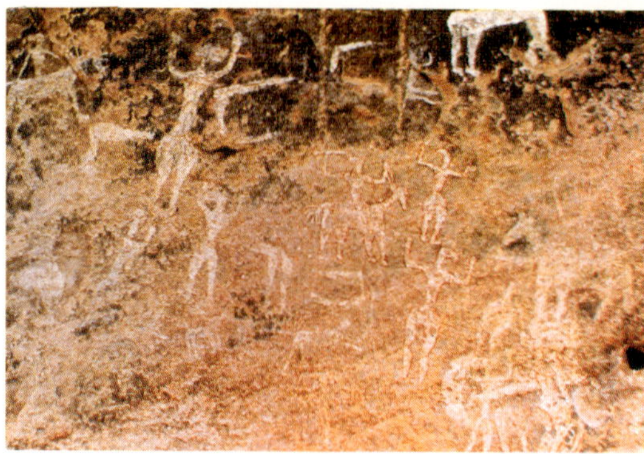

Figure 64. Human figures, Mahādeo hills, Hoshāngābād, Madhya Pradesh, Central India.

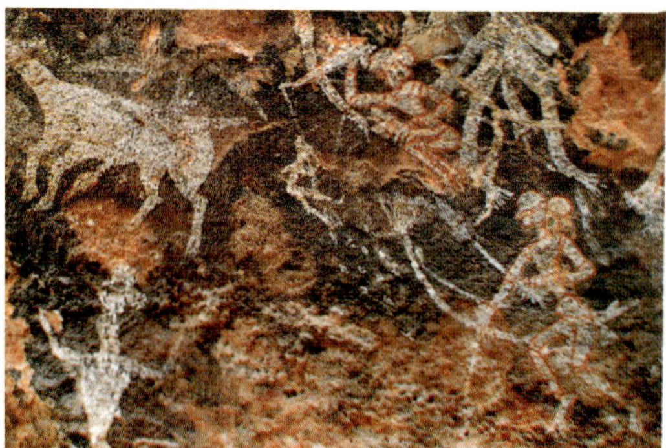

Figure 65. Archers, Churṇā Gundi, Mahādeo hills, Hoshāngābād, Madhya Pradesh, Central India.

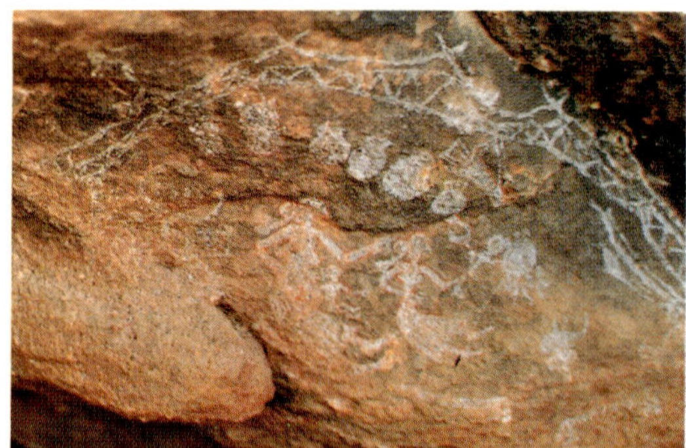

Figure 66. Family at work on ritual in enclosure, Mahādeo hills, Hoshāngābād, Madhya Pradesh, Central India.

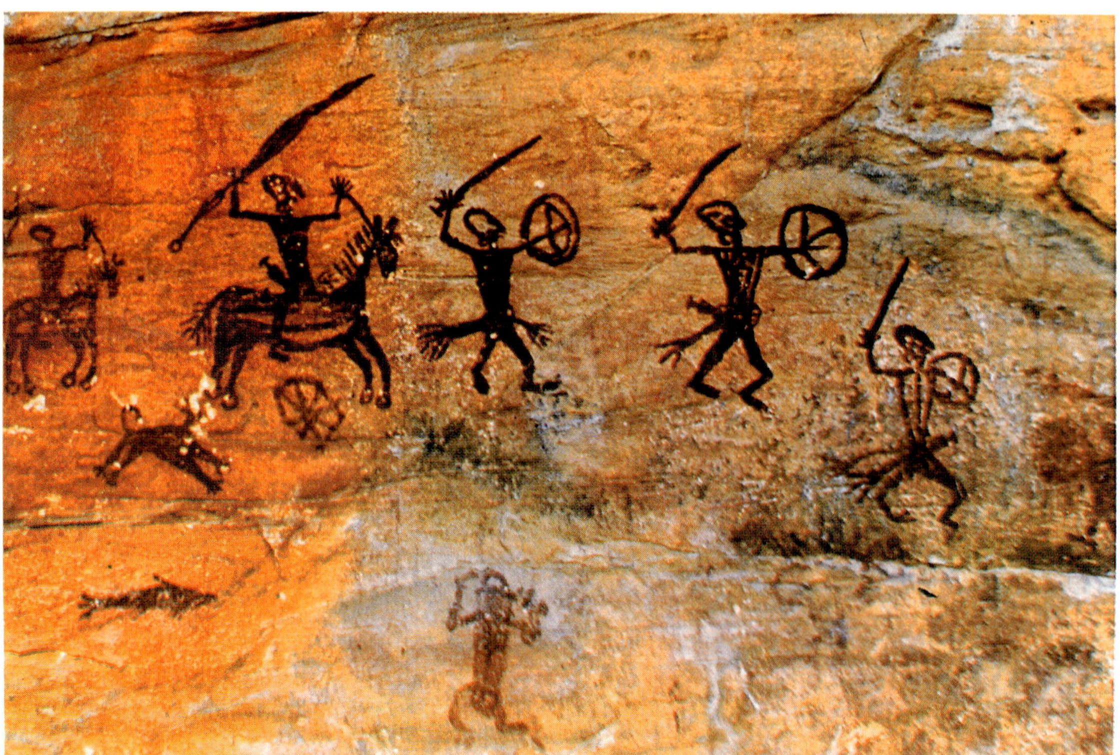

Figure 67. Cavalry and Infantry, Mahādeo hills, Hoshāngābād, Madhya Pradesh, Central India.

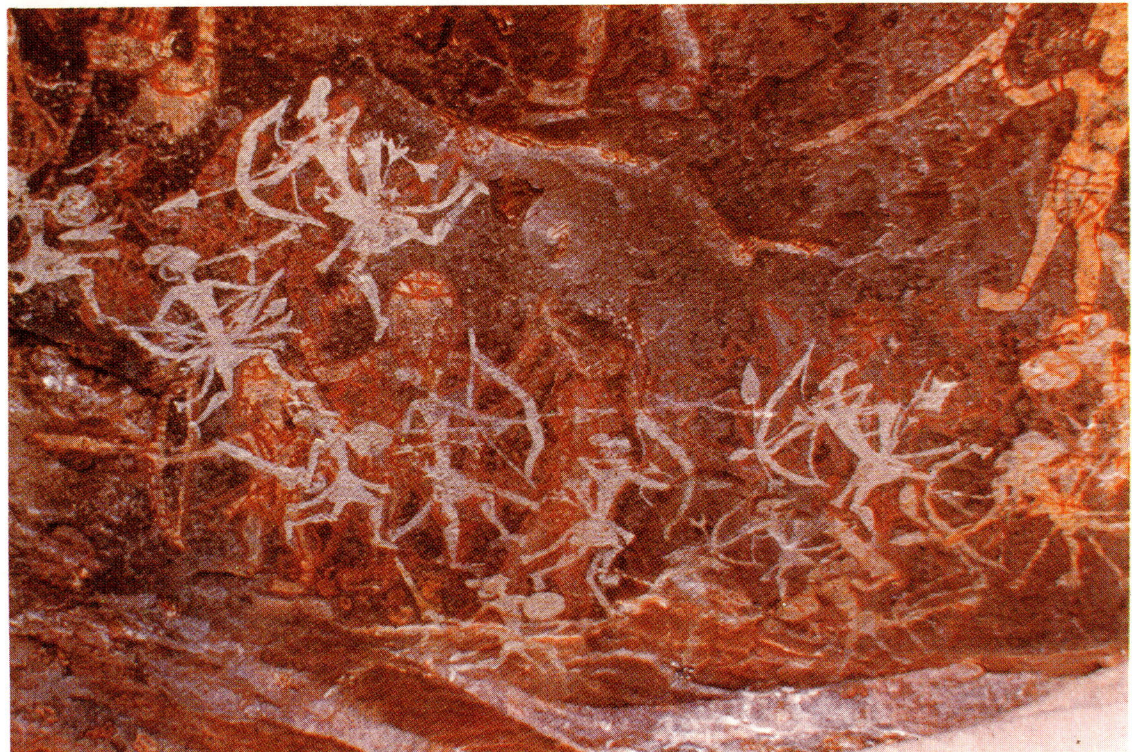

Figure 68. Battle scene, Mahādeo hills, Hoshāngābād, Madhya Pradesh, Central India.

evidence of understanding among Palaeolithic men of the nature of percussion or sound reflection. In 1990 a circle with several hundred deeply pounded impact marks, attached lines formed by similar marks, and one or two adjacent cupules, have been found patinated to a glazed light-brown on a sloping quartzite floor panel at the Hāthitol rock shelter in Rāisen district of Madhya Pradesh. Pounded and patinated cupule grooves covered by mineral deposit have been found also at Kanyādeh near Kotā in Rajasthan. The cupules found at Chintākuntā, Andhra Pradesh, Chhattaneshwar, Chambal or Vidarbha, Maharashtra or the Himalayas appear to be composed of patterns preceding patination and exfoliation and hence much younger. It is quite likely that many Palaeolithic cupules remain to be recognised and once this is done, this will remove the wrong impression of the Indian rock art traditions being limited to the Holocene and indicate their Pleistocene component (Bednarik, Kumar and Tyagi, *Purakala* 2.1,1991: 24-27).

A further evidence of Acheulian art activity in India has been found at Hunsgi in Karnataka where a faceted and striated haematite pebble has been found among many iron hydroxide and haematite pebbles in the Acheulian deposit at locality V (K. Paddayya, *Acheulian Culture of Hunsgi Valley* 1982). Such iron pigments have been reported from different parts of the world and the oldest red ochre fragments, going back to 800,000 to 900,000 years, occur along with quartz crystals, and coloured river pebbles in the early Acheulian Wonderwork Cave site of South Africa (Bednarik, *The Artefact* 16, 1993: 61).

The Holocene context

The overwhelming body of Indian Rock art has been attributed to a Mesolithic society of hunters and gatherers and this art has been distinguished from the art of agriculturists and animal keepers in the Neolithic or the Chalcolithic period. While this art is iconographically rich and various, the distinction of periods made on the basis of iconography has been misleading. It has been pointed out that the sequence of Saharan and eastern Spanish rock art traditions, among others, has been similarly and inaccurately assessed on the ground of iconographic themes, styles and superimpositions. Many thoroughgoing hunting and gathering peoples like those of the Bradshaw tradition in the Kimberley, Australia, lack hunting and foraging scenes, while many Neolithic rock art traditions like those of Scandinavia, Karelia and Sahara are full of hunting motifs (Bednarik, *A Global Perspective of Indian Palaeoart,* submitted for W.A.C-3, 1994). To this date in India, Stone Age hunters and gatherers can be found among the Cholānāiks of Kerala; slash and burn agriculturists among the Māriā Gonds of Bastār; nomadic pastoralists among the Bhotiyās of the Himalayas and the Bāvlis of Western Ghat hill tracts; and subsistence agriculture of the dry Deccan co-exists with commercial agriculture in Sutlej-Godāvarī deltas.

The attempt to differentiate such periods by evidence drawn from archaeologicial excavations has also not been very successful in the absence of clear-cut association of the painting with the excavated finds. A series of excavations conducted in and around the rockshelters at Modi, Ādamgarh, Hoshāngābād, Pāchmārhi and Bhīmbetkā in Madhya Pradesh, Mirzāpur in Uttar Pradesh, Bāgor in Rajasthan, Lānghnāj in Gujarat have yielded haematite from layers of Epi-Palaeolithic and Mesolithic periods, radiocarbon-dated from about 7500 to 4000 BP. (V.D. Mishra, *Some Aspects of Indian Archaeology* 1977). These and other excavations have also yielded Microlithic artefacts, deer and rhino bones from Mesolithic levels, and also Neolithic and Chalcolithic ware

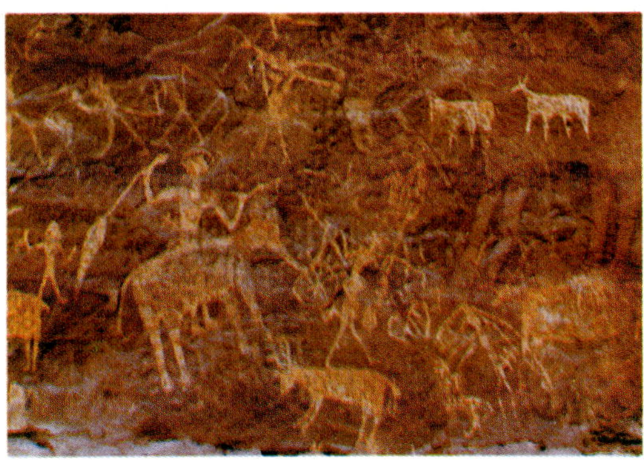

Figure 69. Elephant rider, human and animal figures, Mahādeo hills, Hoshāngābād, Madhya Pradesh, Central India.

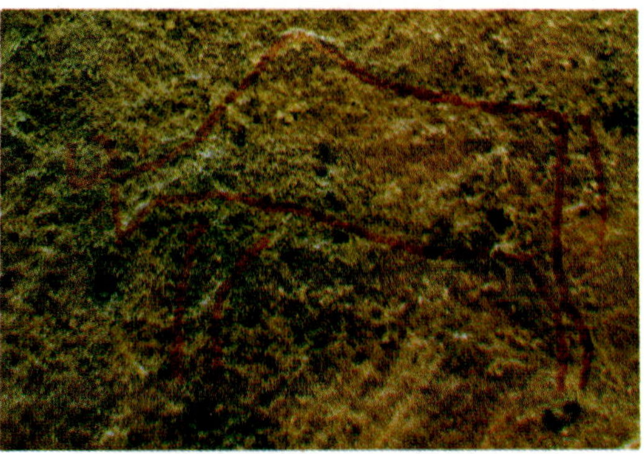

Figure 70. Bull, Kathotiyā, Sehore, Madhya Pradesh, Central India.

(*Indian Archaeololgy, A Review*, 1957-58: 26; 1958-59: 28; 1960-61:13; R.K. Varma, *Stone age Cultures of Mirzapur* 1964, unpublished thesis; V.S. Wakankar, *Prachya Pratibha* 3.2, 1975: 7-29; V.N. Misra and P. Bellwood ed. *Recent Advances in Indo-Pacific Prehistory* 1985: 119-20; Rakesh Tiwari, *Rock Paintings of Mirzapur* 1990). The few examples of portable Mesolithic art are a fluted chert core from Chandrāvatī in Rajasthan, engraved with a cross hatched diamond-shaped design on its flat patinated cortex (V.H. Sonawane, in Pande and Chattopadhyaya ed. *Archaeology and History* 1987: 53-56), and a few engraved tooth and bone objects (Bednarik, *Man and Environment* 18.2, 1993: 33-40. However, the comparison of the design on the Chandrāvatī core with the concentric or voluted geometric in-fill designs in the bodies of animals and birds, or the suggestion that the core is a symbolic expression of the hunting gathering ritual (Kenoyer, *Paper at 16th Annual Conference on South Asia* 1987), can neither be substantiated nor refuted. Extensive comparisons have been made between designs on Chalcolithic as well as late and pre-Harappan pottery and the paintings in Malwa region of central India. Even the occurrence of straight, convex, poised, out-turned and forward bent horns in the rock art of the coastal Mālnād region

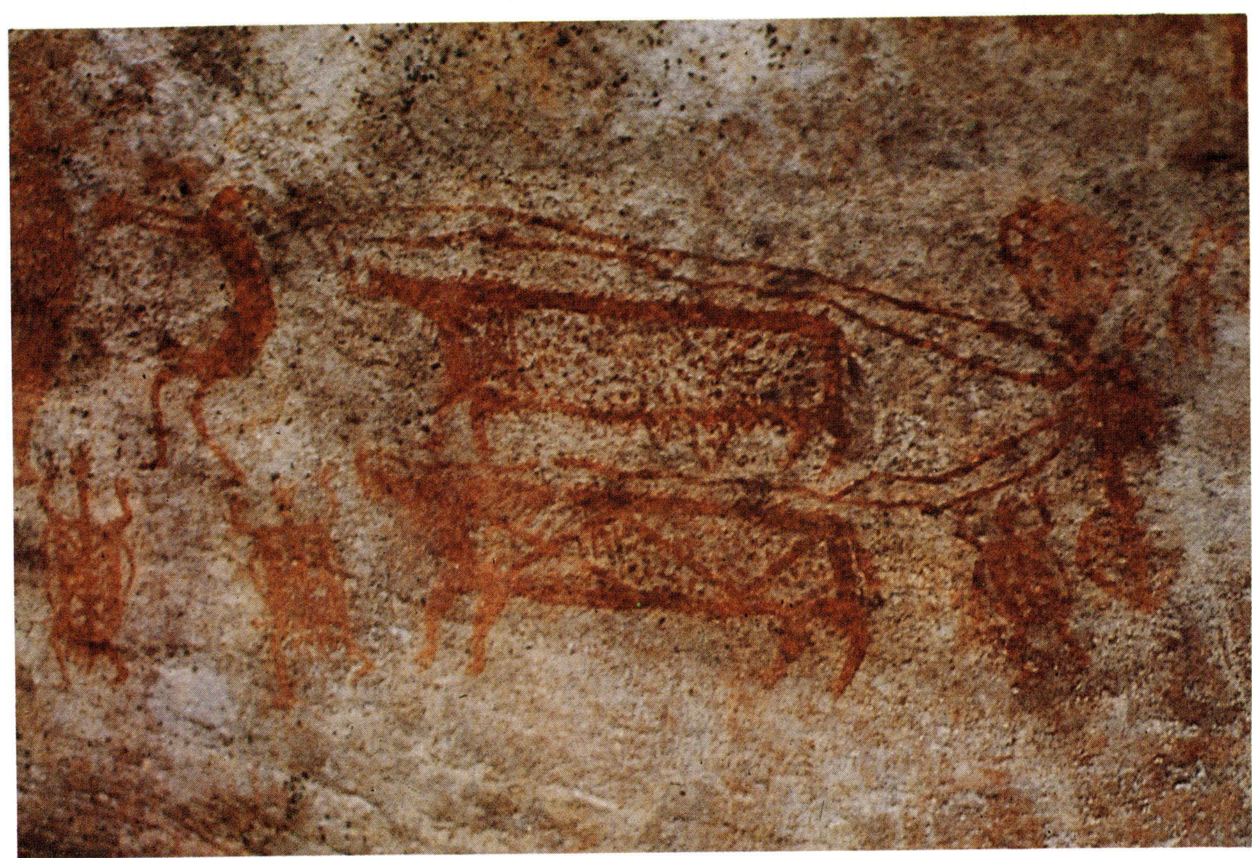

Figure 71. Bullock cart, Kathotiyā, Sehore, Madhya Pradesh, Central India.

of Karnataka has been compared with designs on Chalcolithic Deccan pottery (Wakankar, *Painted Rock Shelters of India*, thesis, 1973: 358-59; A. Sundara, *Journal of Karnataka University 6 & 7*, 1970 & 71). Such visual comparisons between designs found outside similar stratigraphic context tend to be unreliable. Moreover, once a comprehensive amount of material has been studied, such designs are found not only to pertain to different periods and areas with remarkable consistency and continuity, but also to simultaneously undergo subtle variations which may not be possible to assess visually. Most of these designs being part of a common human cognitive repertoire, are cognate and parallel developments rather than the result of any human migration or cultural diffusion.

Sequence and Content

Analysis of Mesolithic or Chalcolithic rock art in India has been afflicted by other subjective suggestions of an artificial sequence of styles. Some of these suggestions are that the non-iconic precedes the iconic; geometric patterns are Epi-Palaeolithic and geometric infill designs are Mesolithic; the dynamic S-type human figures precede static squarish figures or the more 'anatomical' precedes the less 'anatomical'; naturalism is followed by geometrisation and abstraction, just as non-geometric Upper Palaeolithic Microliths without pottery are followed by Mesolithic geometric microliths and pottery; the degree of realism and dynamism diminishes from the Mesolithic to the Chalcolithic drawings; free use of space in Mesolithic period gives way to linearism in the Chalcolithic; the dichotomy and physical contact between sexes, accent on man rather than animal, on weapons and implements are later events. The entire approach of seeing a growing complexity or simplicity in rock art is a negation of the entire history of the arts in which the rigorous and the free, simple and complex, closed or open styles have always co-existed; the collective style has always contained elements that belong to differ-

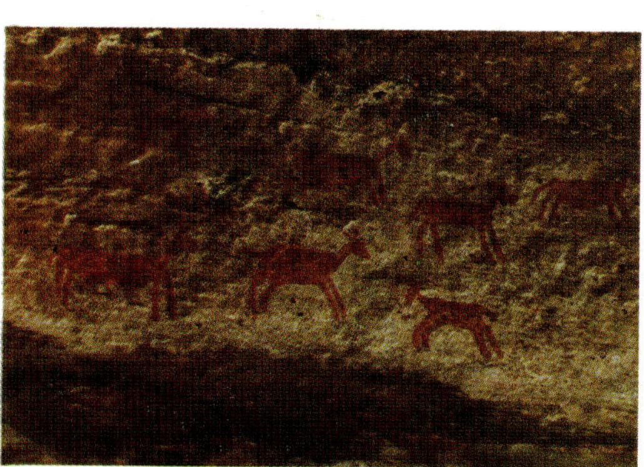

Figure 72. Animals, Kathotiyā, Sehore, Madhya Pradesh, Central India.

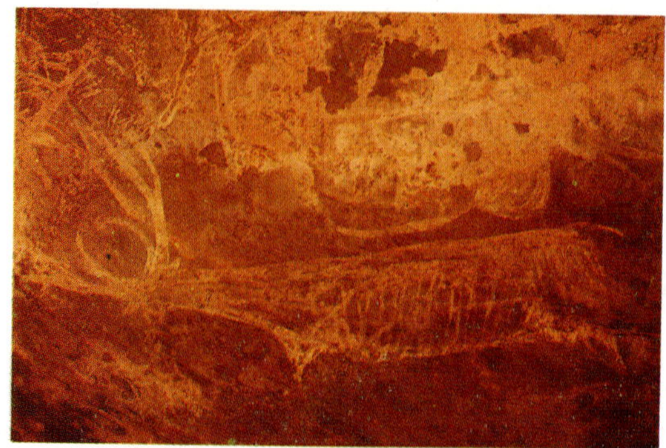

Figure 73. Deer, Kathotiyā, Sehore, Madhya Pradesh, Central India.

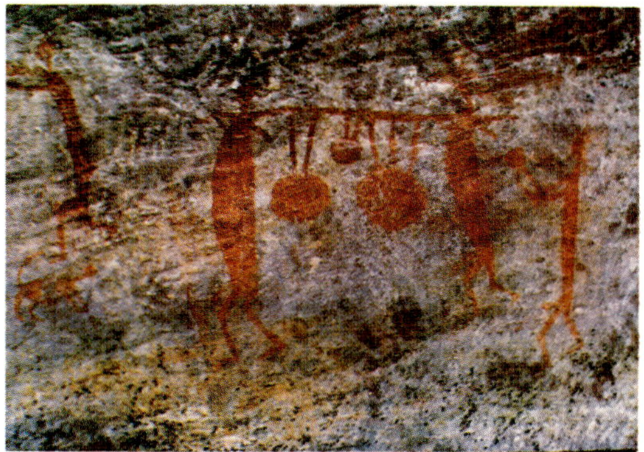
Figure 74. Men carrying material slung on pole, Kathotiyā, Sehore, Madhya Pradesh, Central India.

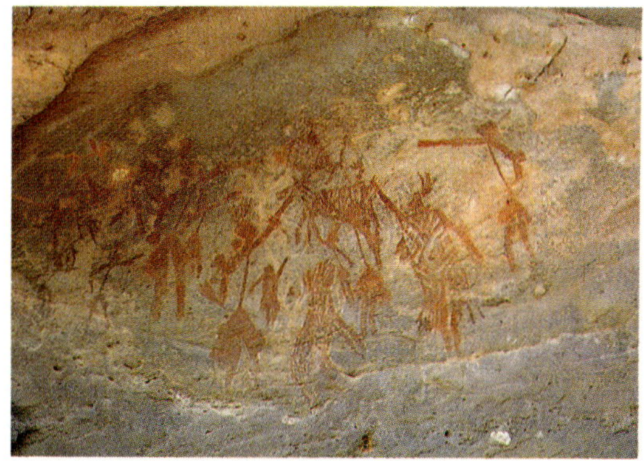
Figure 75. Ritual gathering, Kathotiyā, Sehore, Madhya Pradesh, Central India.

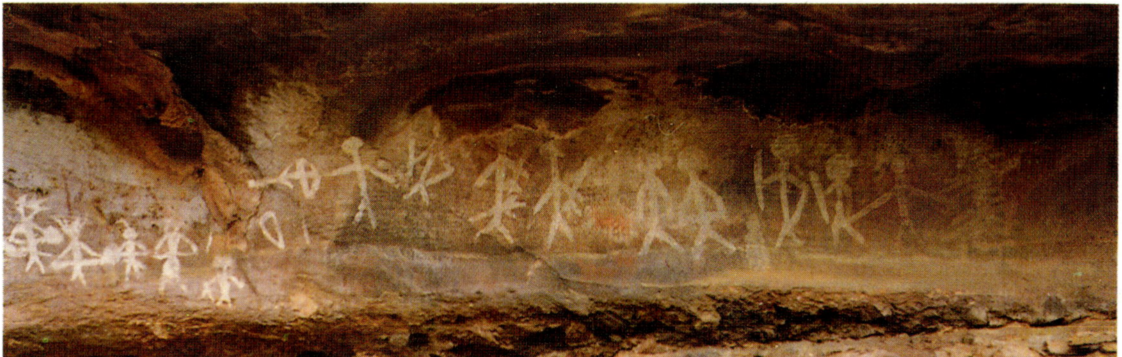
Figure 76. Humans arrayed in dance or battle, Sātkunḍā, Rāisen, Madhya Pradesh, Central India.

ent historical strata, as in a language; and the dominant style has never affected the arts of different regions in the same degree, creating a large variation of styles in the same period. To a great extent, such perceptions stem from an organic conception of cyclic, biological analogies in the growth of forms, which is not borne out in the actual history of creative human expression (Meyer Schapiro in *Anthropology Today*, 1952: 287-312).

The differentiation of the Palaeolithic and Mesolithic from Neolithic and Chalcolithic traditions, which has been made by many rock art researchers, is based primarily on the distinctions drawn between motifs associated with hunting gathering cultures on the one hand, and agricultural and animal keeping cultures on the other. Attempts have been made often to fit the available evidence of superimpositions or style selectively into this straitjacket pattern. There are, of course, many scenes of honey gathering (in Pāchmārhi, Madhya Pradesh; Lankāpalli, Andhra Pradesh), foraging for small game or fish (at Jāorā, Lākhājuār, or Kathotiyā in Madhya Pradesh and Kerwāghāt, Mirzāpur in Uttar Pradesh), men carrying yokes, pouches and loads to scaffoldings (at Urden and Lakhājuār in Rāisen), animal hunt at sites all over India (including engraving at Usgalimal in Goa), display of animals of all kinds including what are identified as pangolin or porcupine

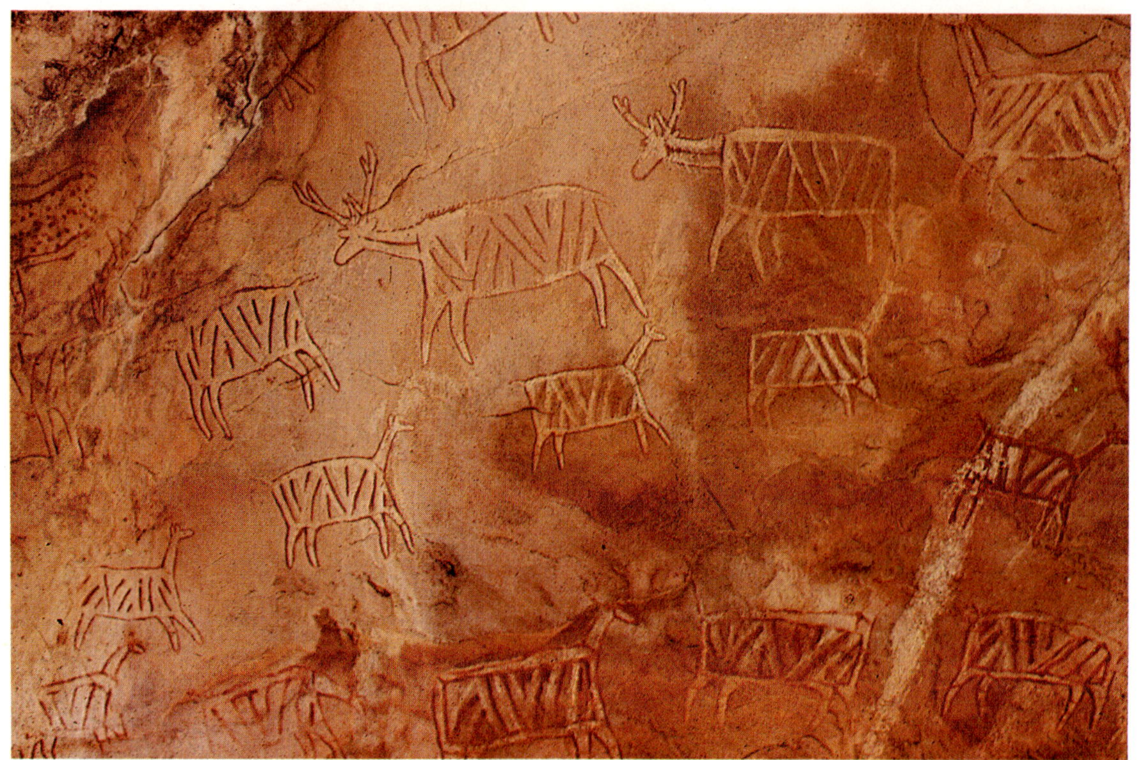

Figure 77. Deers and other animals, Bhīmbetkā, Rāisen, Madhya Pradesh, Central India.

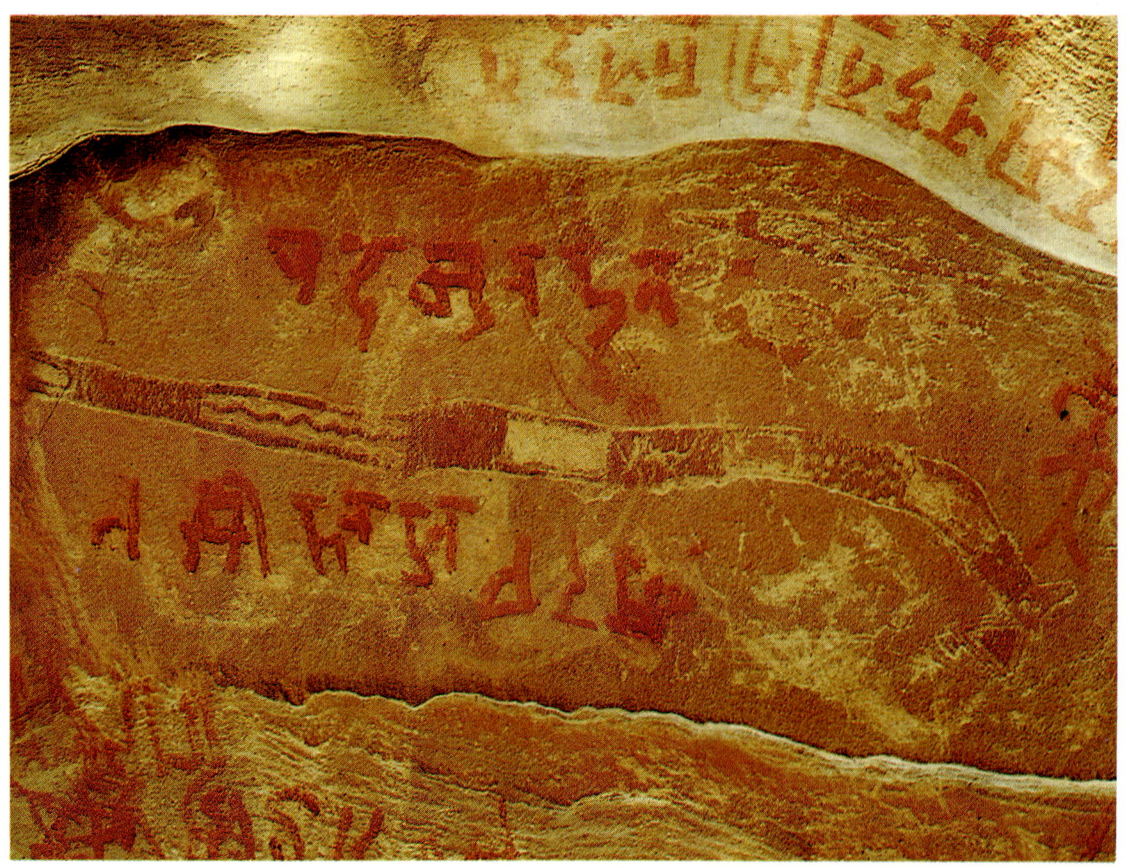

Figure 78. Decorated snake and scripts, Kathotiyā, Sehore, Madhya Pradesh, Central India.

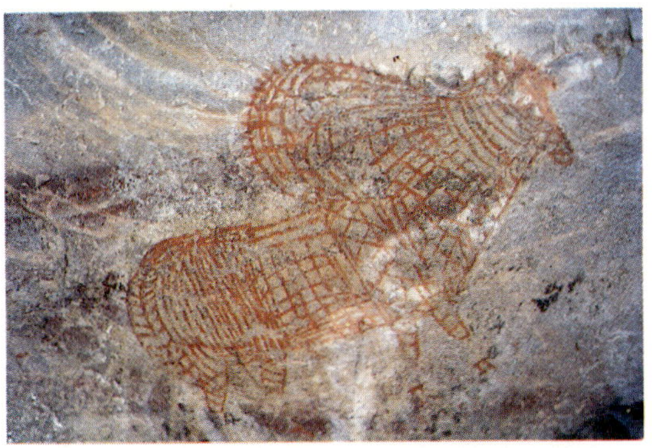

Figure 79. Humped bull, Firangi, Sehore, Madhya Pradesh, Central India.

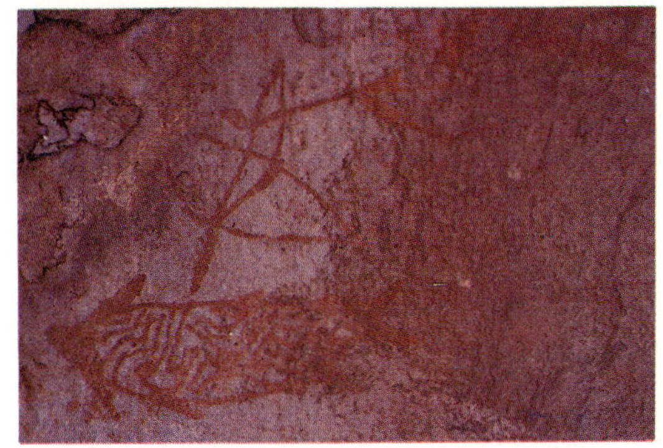

Figure 80. Fish, Jāorā, Rāisen, Madhya Pradesh, Central India.

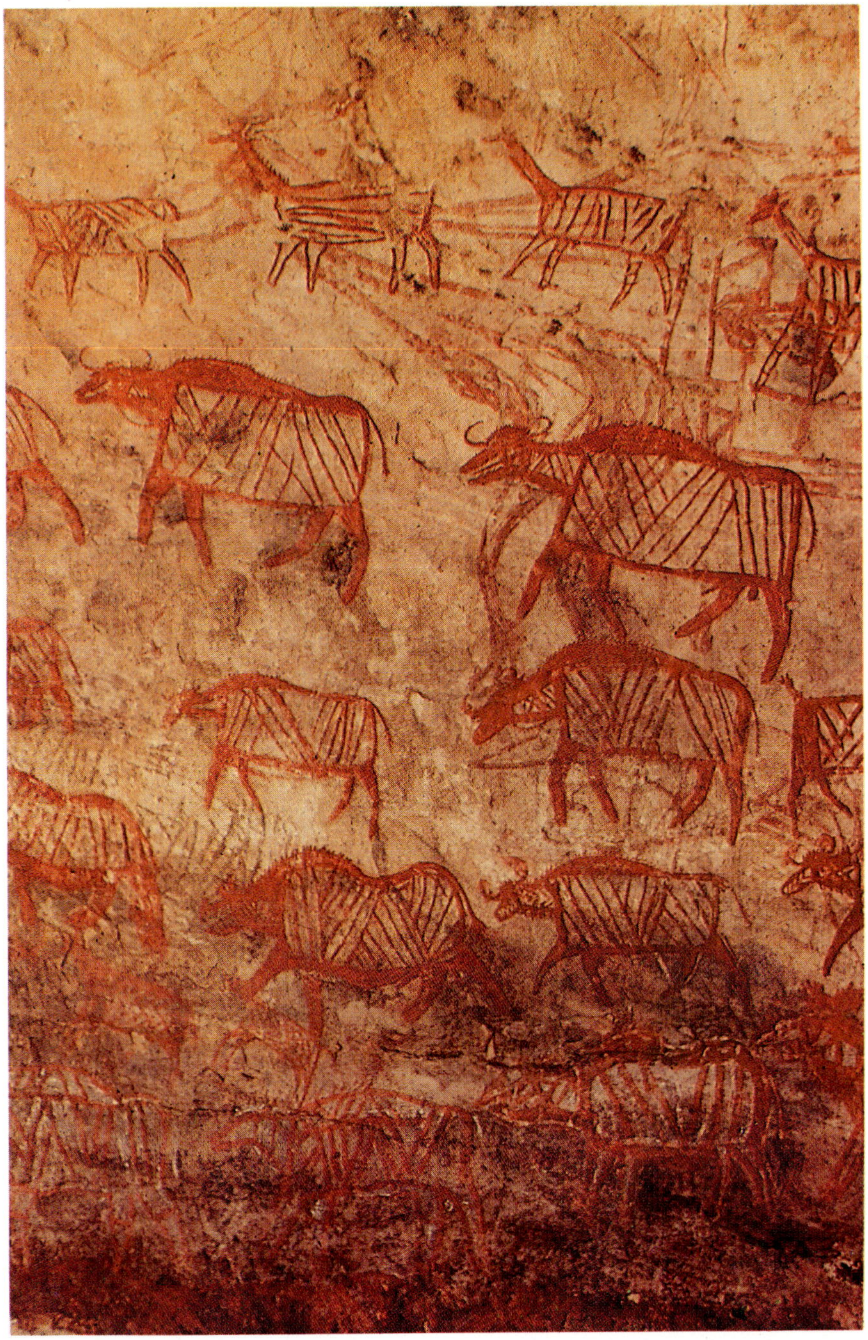

Figure 81. Buffalos, felines and other animals, Rāmchhajjā, Rāisen, Madhya Pradesh, Central India.

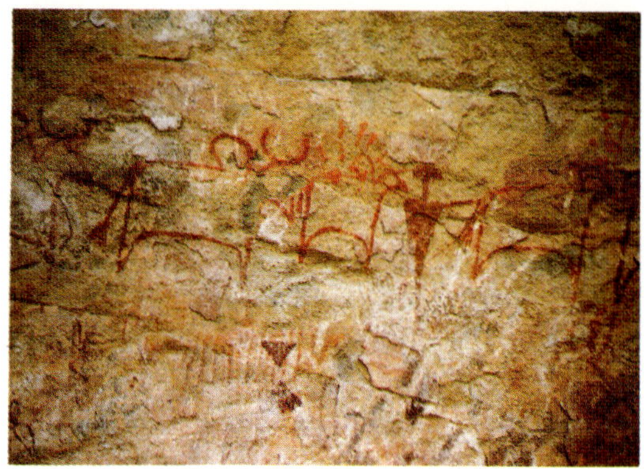

Figure 82. Humped bulls and a human figure, Ekatāl, Rāigarh, Madhya Pradesh, Central India.

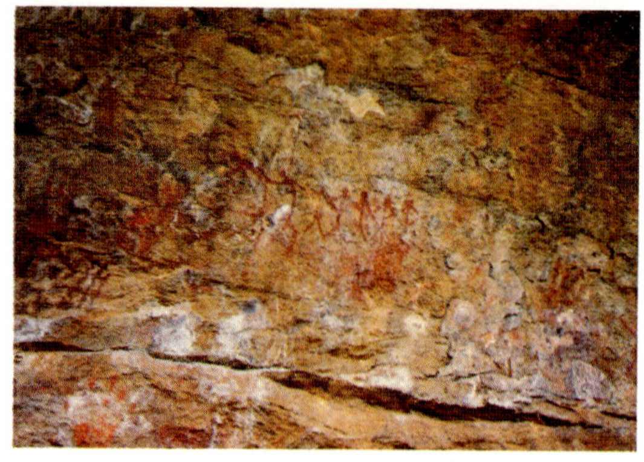

Figure 83. Dancing scene, Ekatāl, Rāigarh, Madhya Pradesh, Central India.

(Hāthitol in Rāisen), sarus crane or ostrich (at Kathotiyā), a tiger mauling a man (Chibbarnālā, Māndāsor). Huge boars and bulls dominate the scene, and at Bhīmbetkā the boar drives a puny human being before it with a crab standing by, provoking speculation about a struggle between a crab and a bull tribe. The bodies of animals may be filled with geometric designs or shown with foetus and innards in x-ray style. Antlers are found all over, including the Himalayas where they prompted thinking on the probability of Bonism infecting Buddhism, like in Tibet. Animals are seen as being driven into traps, bamboo splinters or pit-falls (Lākhājuār, Urden, Bhīmbetkā). At Jāorā an entire cosmology of the universe is seen in what are identified as fish among reeds, lotus stems, flying birds and a square marked in strips with a central circle.

Domestication of cattle is seen in the art of sites like Chaturbhujnāth Nālā, Narsinghgarh in Madhya Pradesh, at Yogimath in Orissa, accompanied by bullock-carts or chariots at places like Chibbarnālā, Pāhārgarh, Dekan, Gelpur in Madhya Pradesh. Men are supposed to be driving and herding animals or gathering the harvest of the day at Pāchmārhi and Sātkuṇḍā, also in Madhya Pradesh. Sometimes, as at Piklihāl, Rāichur, Karnataka, the animals are seen alone. With this goes identification of ithyphallic, megalophallic, pederastic, copulating males at shelters like Sātkuṇḍā, Chaturbhujnāth Nālā, Kathotiyā, Firingi, Urden, Lākhājuār in central India and also at Koppagallu, Bellāry, Karnataka. Fabulous creatures, masked men and demons, courting men and women, fighting men and men in war or in ceremonial procession are supposed to have become common. Comparisons are made between bulls in the Rock Art of Piklihāl and Māski and drawings on Chalcolithic pottery from Karnataka, to reinforce the chronological conclusion.

This artificial distinction of periods breaks down in the illustrations given by different researchers. The animals, the stick-men, the hunting gathering or herding activities appear impartially in different periods. Use of ethno-zoology as a stylistic and chronological marker in Indian rock art has proved to be as problematic as in Saharan rock art because, variations in the evolution of domestic animals have obscured their independent history in time and space, and made it difficult to either link their distant animal populations genetically, derive them from one another or to extract a sequence of man-animal relationship from certain trends (A. Gautier, *RAR* 7.5, 1990: 102). The linear, triangular, square, rectangular and cylindrical men appear everywhere, and the anatomical style seems to spill over into non-anatomical pigeon holes. The phallic accent or pronounced sexuality seems to be often derived from hand drawn accentuations of the genitalia and photographic distortions which tend to be accepted as true to the original. Inspite of this, the rock art of this period has certain common elements. It is overwhelmingly a tradition in which the animal looms larger than life and is rendered with great sensitivity to contour and, sometimes, to the volume. The human figures, inspite of their pervasive role, are shadow-graphs or a few sweeping lines, rendered with swift and deft strokes. Even the weapons they hold are sometimes bigger than them, like the shields at Firingi. The landscape is never prominent, and the trees or the meadow described at Jāorā, Sātkuṇḍā, Vangāonā generally partake of the minimalism and the geometrisation reserved for the depiction of the human beings. There are exceptions as in the manneristically rendered elegant figures of Mahādev hills at Pāchmārhi or the occasional horse-riders, who become one with horses in the finicky decorative designs at Gelpur. The sense of rhythm is never missing with the figures of men and animals being arrayed at regular intervals, and the human figures being sometimes linked up in an undulating, all over line as at Urden. The stick-men facing one another at Firingi are marvels of curvilinear fluency and are vibrant with arrested motion. Inspite of the varying stylistic configurations, this body of art is coherent and homogeneous. The spatial and temporal variations in this art can be grasped only after the entire body of material available on the ground has been properly recorded and mastered.

Megalithic Associations

Comparisons have been made between engraving of a human figure on an orthostat in an Iron Age burial at Chinnānur, Mehboobnagar, Andhra Pradesh, figures of horse riders at Kilvelay and Sundarajanapatti and some paintings at Bīrpalli Mallasamudram in Tamilnadu. Graffito at Kilvelay have been compared with potters' marks on megalithic black and red ware. While use of superimposed triangles to form human figures is a feature found at many places and in different times, the comparison of such figures as similar in the present instance, ignores emphatic stylistic variations among them. The script-like alignment and formation of the human

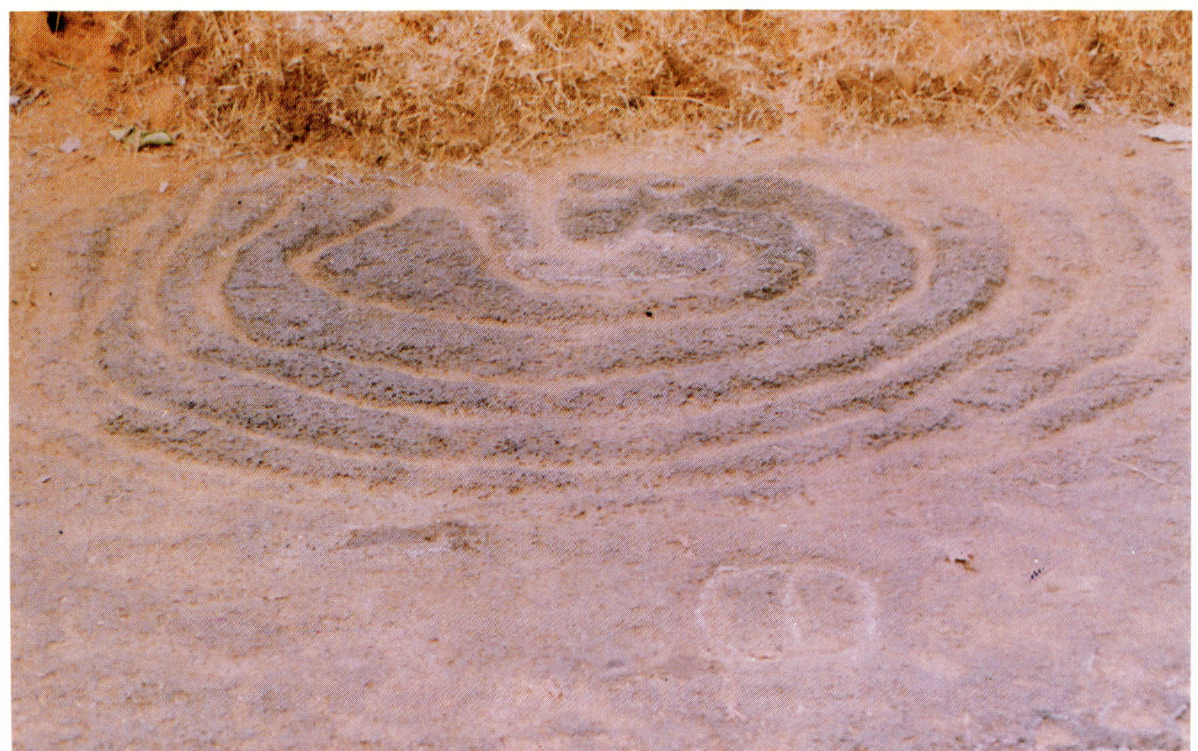

Figure 84. Labyrinth, engraving, Usgalimal, Goa, Southern India.

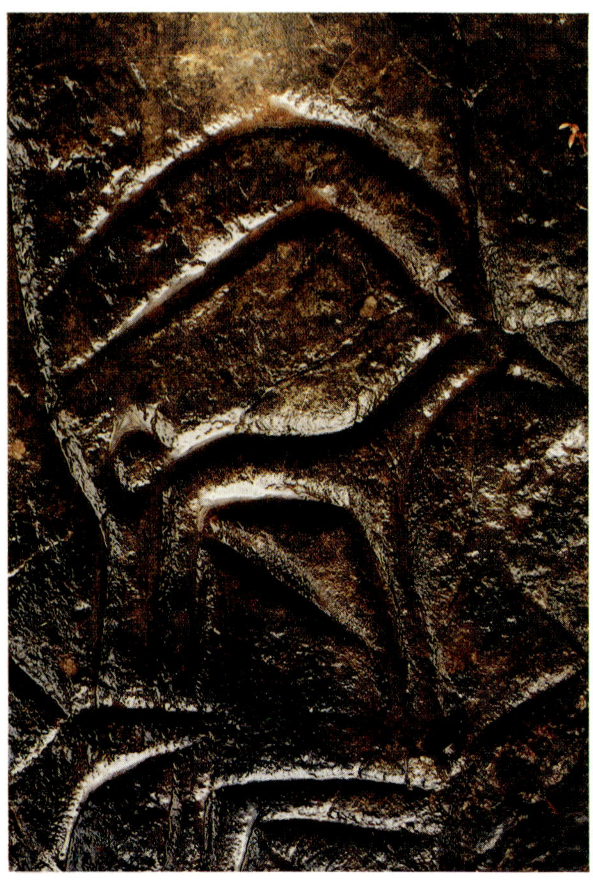

Figure 85. Deer, engraving, Kajur, Goa, Southern India.

and geometric designs are not even visually comparable. None of the paintings at Bīrpalli was recorded from a chamber grave in a controlled archaeological operation (Neumayer 1993: 199-200, Figs. 532-38). The rock carvings of animals, tectiforms and other designs on the granite slabs at Kajur in Goa have been associated with what is considered to be a megalithic stone circle with a round granite stone in the centre (Shirodkar, Article read in World Archaeological Congress-3, 1994). Suggestions have also been made about diffusion of designs of ritualistic post-firing grafitti on megalithic white-painted white and red pottery from Harappa and Dholāvīrā, and of double-line knotted geometrical designs from Harappan copper tablets in Gujarat, to megalithic engraving sites of Belgāun, Gāvāli, Hirebenkal and other sites in Krishnā-

Tungabhadrā valley of Karnataka (A. Sundara, *Prehistoric Art in Karnataka* in Kannada, 1994). While lateritic stone enclosures of chamber tombs have been found in areas adjacent to the rock art sites, possible association between the art and the burial sites has not been possible to establish on such grounds alone. Many megalithic dolmens have been reported in association with sites showing navigation in boats in Pallanād in Kerala (S.P. Thampi, *BDCRI* 35, 3-4:37-44). At the Putli Karār rock art site in Rāisen in central India, a dressed stone boundary wall has been found enclosing a massive stone slab on standing stone slab pillars. In the Kumāon Himalayas, boulders with cup marks and pits have been mostly found in association with what are assumed to be early Medieval monoliths used as boundary posts, and also with cylindrical granite monoliths or triangular stones with human figures carved on them (Mathpal,1995). While the megalithic chronology of the rock art has been inferred circumstantially, a greater analysis of the evidence is required to establish the art firmly as a ritualistic death rite activity, associated with megalithic grave sites.

Protohistoric/Historic

The chronological markers become much sharper with the use of Kharoshthi, Brāhmī, Nāgari and Shaṅkha-lipi (conchshell script) and early Tamil inscription in association with or proximity to rock art. A common Euro-Asiatic bronze age animal style accompanied by inscriptions in Brāhmī, Kharoshthi and Chinese with rock engravings of Ibex, goats, horse-riders can be discerned in Kashmir valley in Lādākh, Mulbekh, Kārgil, Thickshe, Jānskār-Lādākh, Spiti and also along the Karakorum high way in north Pakistan or in the Kumāon hills and even in China and Central Asia (Mathpal,1995; Chen Zhaofu, 'Discovery of Rock Art in China', in *Rock Art in the Old World, ed,* M. Lorblanchet 1992:361-71 figs. 2,3 and 5). The discovery of motifs of hunting ibex or gazelle, depiction of wild yak, horses poised on hoof tips in the Lādākh, western Tibetan and Chinese areas suggest a diffusion of a central Asian steppe animal style culture in this area. Costumes and trappings of war, denominational iconographic cognizances of Hinduism, Buddhism, Jainism, chariots, caparisoned horses, extensive archaeological finds, occasionally associated with the occupation of the painted rock shelters, and certain contemporary myths, beliefs and rituals, have tended to suggest tenuous links between the painted traditions and prevalent folk ways.

However, even in this period, hasty assumptions have sometimes been made by dating the art directly to the date of the script of the inscription on the rock surface; or by putting dynastic nomenclatures like Maurya, Gupta, Kshatrapa, Kushāṇa, Katyūrī etc. on sartorial or ornamental motifs and patterns. The emergence of a cultic activity has often been gratuitously associated with the meaning of the motifs in the rock art without comprehending that boundaries between these cults in India have never been emphatically sharp, and most of the motifs have been shared by them in common for their art and ritual. Such forced associations ignore the fact that in this period, with the flowering of iconographic conventions, the alphabet of art, like that of the inscriptions, which are dated in many unknown regnal eras in India, differs with different territories and periods, and not with diverse religious or sectarian denominations or dynastic inspiration. Thus the Kushāṇa-style costume has been detected at Shahad Karār, and also at Mori, Mārodeo, Āgamdwār in Hoshāngābād, central India (Neumayer, 1993). Figures dancing away with a sword and decapitated head at Rajatprabhāt, Kitescrag, Āgamdwār have been identified as head hunters (Meenakshi Dube 'Rock Paintings in Pāchmārhi Hills' in *Rock Art in the Old World, 1992*: 131-45). In certain sites like Kālājikui near Mukandarā hills, or at shelters near Virātnagar, in Rajasthan; Chhibadnālā in Māndāsor, Kotrāvihār near Narsinghgarh, Gufāmāser near Sānchi and Sauro Mauro in Sehore in Madhya Padesh, Brāhmī inscriptions are

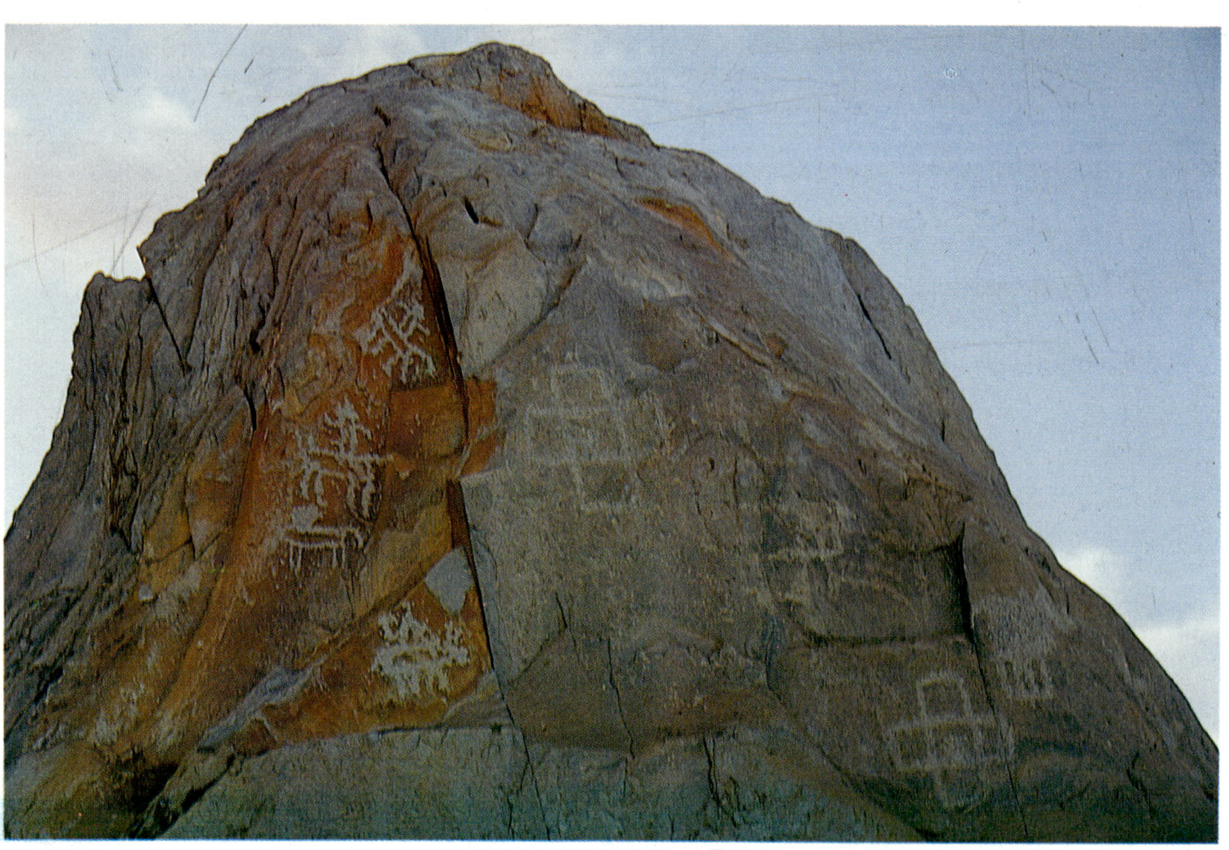

Figure 86. A view of engraved boulders, Mārkāmpurā, Andhra Pradesh, Southern India.

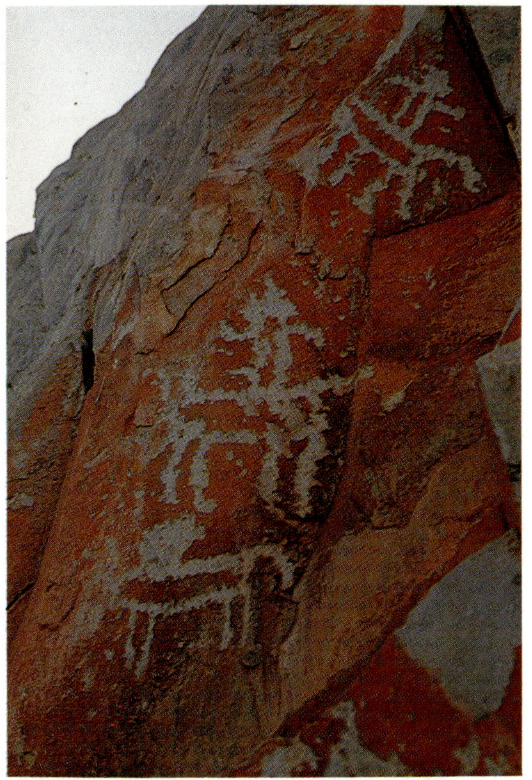

Figure 87. Horse riders, petroglyphs, Mārkāmpurā, Andhra Pradesh, Southern India.

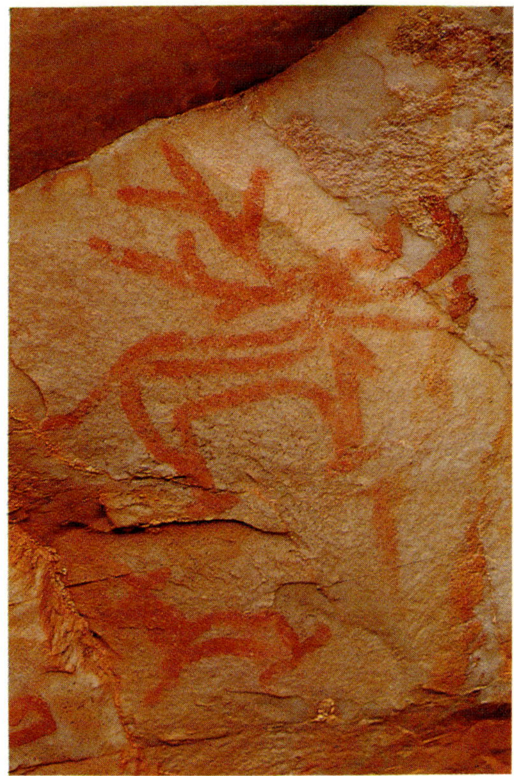

Figure 88. Antelope, Ketāvaram, Kurnool, Andhra Pradesh, Southern India.

more reasonably associated with Buddhist stupas, *dharmachakras* (wheel of order), *bodhi* trees, *triratna* (taurine). The Mauryan Brāhmī inscriptions near Mukandarā mention seven artists and refer to King Kalapi who imposed discipline on the Buddhist *saṁgha* (congregation), which may indeed be an allusion to emperor Ashoka's intervention in calling the second Buddhist council to end dissension. Buddhist stupas are also found in the paintings in the rock shelters of Sabarkanthā in Gujarat and can well be associated with the strong Buddhist traditions in the locality embodied in the Devnimori stupa from the 5th century A.D. (Sonawane, *Puratattva* 23, 1993: 66-69). However, mere find of a taurine or a tree motif would not justify casually made suggestions of Buddhist inspiration. Similarly, Krishnā-Balarāmā has been identified at Tikula, Gwalior; Ganesha at Bhīmbetkā; Lajjā Gaurī, a mother goddess exposing her pudendum at Chintākuntā, Andhra Pradesh; the folk hero Loric holding and trampling elephants at Kawār Khoh, Mirzāpur, without the benefit of inscriptions. While some of these identifications may be correct, they do not offer any chronological clue to the sequence in the religious history of the area.

Ethnography, Meaning and Shape

Hundreds of inscriptions have also been found in different scripts at Kharwai, Sītākhardi, Bhīmbetkā, Kankālitilā, Pāchmārhi in central India; at Mirzāpur in Uttar Pradesh; in the Pāchmahal district and Sabarkanthāh in Gujarat; Bādāmi,

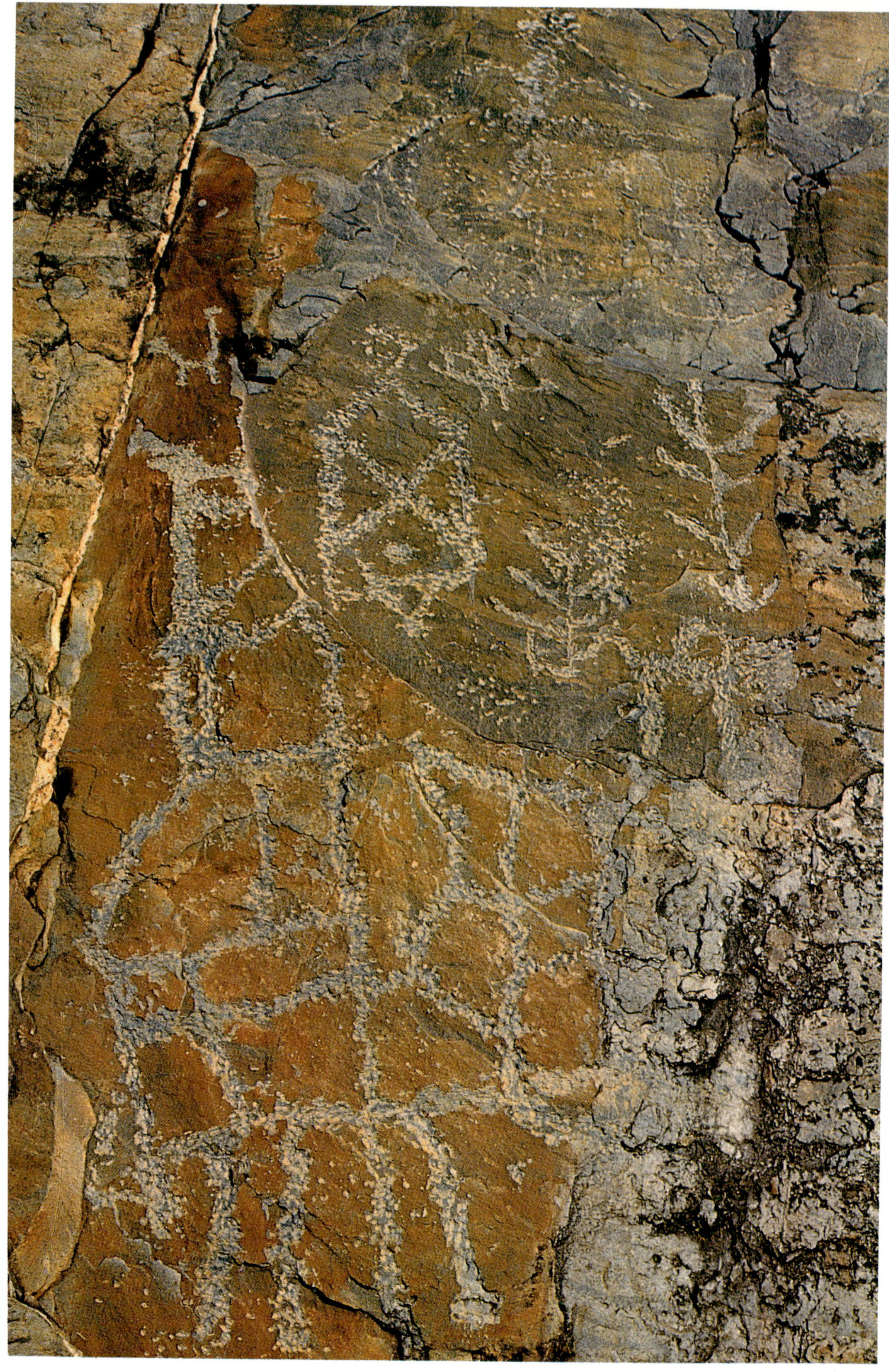

Figure 89. Trees and geometric patterns, petroglyphs, Mārkāmpurā, Andhra Pradesh, Southern India.

Sidalpadi in Karnataka; at Thāḍuṅgā, Hunḍuli in Kumāon-Ālmorā hills; in Ārcot districts of Tamilnadu, and even on the remote bank of Indus near Chilas (Pakistan) or Mānḍori near Attock. They record events like making and donation of a shelter by one Dambuka at Ādamgarh, a gift to Jaina monks at Sundarajanapaṭṭi near Mādurai in Tamilnadu, a pilgrimage to a Buddhist centre in an inscription near Chilas, propagation of the Kutumbi family by Vishnuvarman, at Edakkal Cave in Kerala, visit or residence of people at sites like Bādāmi and other places in Karnataka, an incantation in multiple repetitive letters at Dorothy Deep, Pāchmārhi. They certainly do not either refer to the rock art at the site, or to the painter, patron or occasion of such art. While the Shaṅkha-lipi inscriptions remain to be correctly read, there is also frequent confusion about whether certain dots, loops and dashes as at Vikramkhol or Ushākothi rock shelters are proto-Brāhmī inscriptions, slightly later ritualistic writings or geometric non-iconic patterns.

On the other hand, efforts to read different kinds of marks as visual notations for encoding information or of solving problems have been scarcely attempted in India. Such attempts are bound to suffer from arithemetical imprecision, and from the defect of ignoring non-notational traditions or notations, which look like notations, but are not. Attempts to see clues in rock art for demographic movements, mnemonic metaphors for initiation, cohesion, networking, astronomical or mathematical formula, organised in terms of periodicity and regularity, have been *non sequiter* in the global as well as the Indian context. In any case, such analysis has not moved beyond surface information to offer any clue to sequence or meaning. (F. D'Errico, *RAR* 8.2., 1991: 83-93; 9.1, 1992: 37-64).

Detailed typological analysis has been attempted of the chariots. Long-stemmed sailing boats (*Kotiyās*) and other boats in rock art of Gujarat have been associated with the maritime traditions of the Vallabhi Maitraka dynastic capital of Saurashtra near Ghogābandar, while corollary depictions at Pāllānād, Kerala have been connected with the navigational traditions of Kerala. The grooves on the slab at Kajur in Goa have been identified as indicating lunar rotations; rayed circles at the same site as solar symbols or omphalos, Buddha's navel. Ethnographic analogies with forms in the rock art have been drawn from contemporary beliefs, folk dance forms (Sudha Malaiya, *AURA Occasional Publication* 5, 61-66) and musical instruments (Neumeyer, 1993). Lithopones at rock art sites in India (Neumeyer 1993:30) have been taken to suggest hierophany in older days, with some reason, in the use of ringing rocks for art production, in the context of such locations and beliefs in

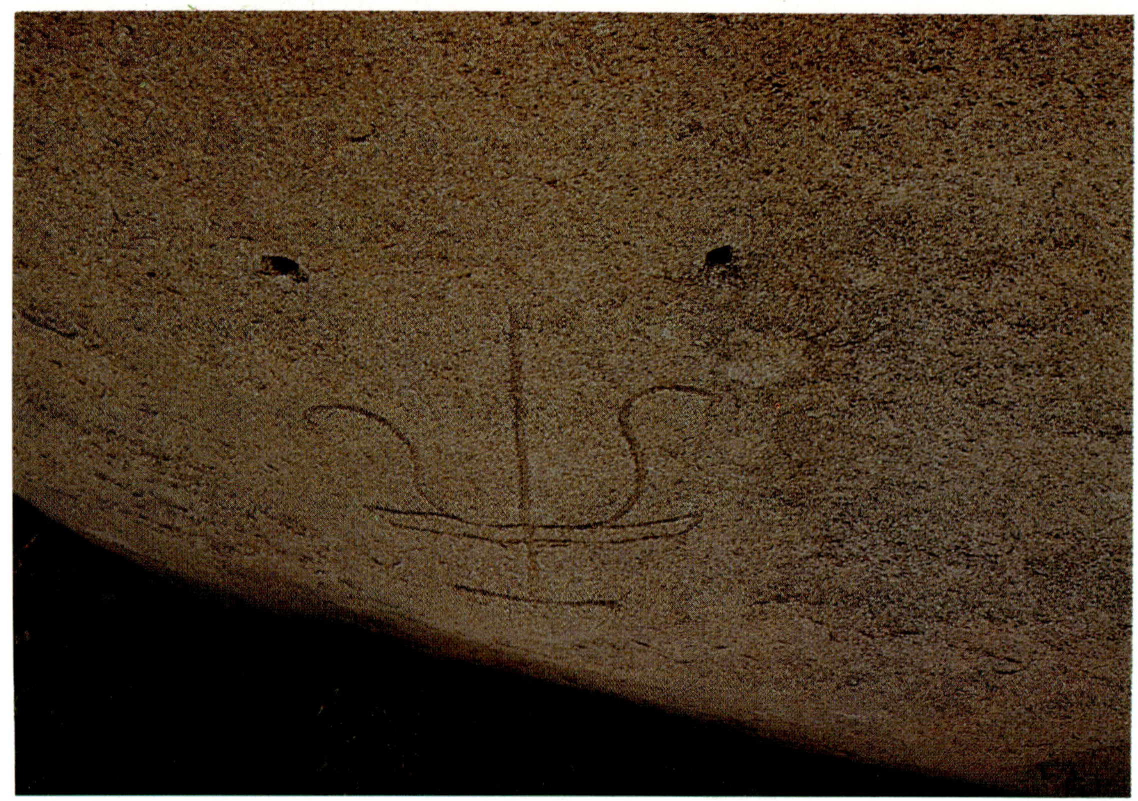

…gure 90. Trident, engraving, Ketāvaram, Kurnool, Andhra Pradesh, Southern India.

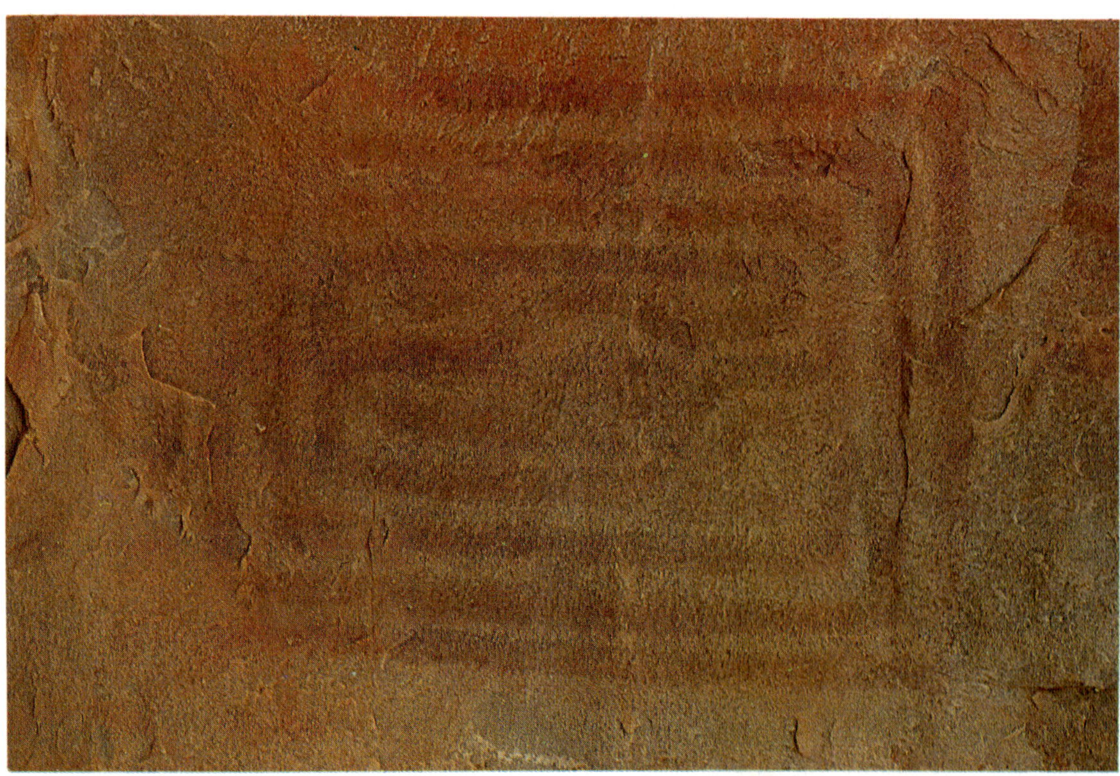

Figure 91. Design, Ketāvaram, Kurnool, Andhra Pradesh, Southern India.

other parts of the world (Ken Hodges, *AURA Occasional Publication 8;* 1993:121-27).

Comparisons have been made between Orissan and central Indian rock art and Sāorā , Kond, Sānthāl, Wārli and Gond wall paintings to suggest similar motivation to promote fertility of land and women and to exorcise calamities, diseases and evil spirits. Similar comparisons have been made with Pithorā paintings of Rāthwās and paintings of Nāiks of Barodā and Pāchmahal districts of Gujarat. The local beliefs in Bundelkhand of Madhya Pradesh have been quoted that the rock paintings are *putariā* (Sanskrit: *puttalikā* or dolls) painted by witches in the dark nights of *Diwāli* (Sans. *Deepāvāli* or the lamp lighting festival) as part of a ritual celebration after rains; or are depiction of the battle between Rāmā and Rāvana, described in the epic Rāmāyaṇa, or of the marriage procession of kings (S.K. Pandey, *Indian Rock Art* 1994: 28-29). The hand-prints in rock art have been seen, on the current analogy of decorating cows and gate-walls with hand-prints, as apotropaic designs to nullify evil spirits at auspicious occasions like birth and marriage. Such suggestions remain speculative. Since the body and foot size of Palaeolithic man is mostly unknown, attempts to use hand prints or finger flutings, to determine age and suggest initiation rituals have proved abortive in European cave art also. At Lakhudyār in district Ālmorā, the paintings, engravings and carved boulders are identified by local people as finger-prints, baking plates, discs and ladles of Bhīmsen or as game-boards of the Pāṇḍavas, epic heroes of the Mahābhārata; as signs made by Gorkhā soldiers from Nepal; as *pitharkhāni* or *pitharkudi* or ancestral places; or as bloody imprints from the remnants of a pyrrhic battle between two marriage parties (one rock art site is Lwethā which literally means blood imprints). The monoliths are called *brikhām* or hero-stones, and some grooves are identified as foot-prints of lord Rāmā. The dancing figures in the rock art are compared with performers of the contemporary *Jhorā* dance and their drums, large and small, with contemporary counterparts. These are associated with community pounding festivals in Kumāon hills of Uttar Pradesh Himalayas, like *bāgwāl*, using mortars (Mathpal, 1995). The Edakkal, in Kerala, on the other hand, was seen as the home of the minor local imp, Kuttichāthān, and the paddy field with a long stone at the foot of Edakalmālā was known as Ambukuttyvāyāl or the swamp, where Kutty's arrows struck (Fawcett, *Indian Antiquary* 1901: 409).

Many of these parallels between contemporary and old folk beliefs, rituals, exorcisms, incantations, dances, instruments, game boards, totems have emerged from selective preservation or reporting, by artificially relating small samples of rock art to excerpts of ethnological information, selected from a wide variety of ornament, equipment, gestures, postures, reduction and shaping processes, used within the same group of contemporary performers or artists. Such heterogeneity of practices cannot be used as a common denominator for extrapolation or parallels between contemporary and older art. Different functional contexts are associated even today among different modern primitive groups with different kinds of social organisation, economy or ideology. It has not proved possible to prove the identity of objects in India or elsewhere by looking at the interplay of organisms with the environment in contemporary terms.

Sympathetic, homeopathic, fertility, hunting, rain making or evil-negating magic, totemic worship of animals and ancestors has been implicit in explanations of the Indian rock art as in rock art elsewhere in the world. But attempts to invest iconic types like tectiforms, scutiforms or pediforms with properties of totemistic, homeopathic or fetishistic magic, or with sexual differentiation or interaction, have proved no more useful in Indian rock art than in the binary division of European cave art, on sexual or other lines, because of the interchangeability, complementarity, and equivalence of such representations.

The socio-cultural analogies from contemporary ethnography have been reinforced by psycho-biological models.

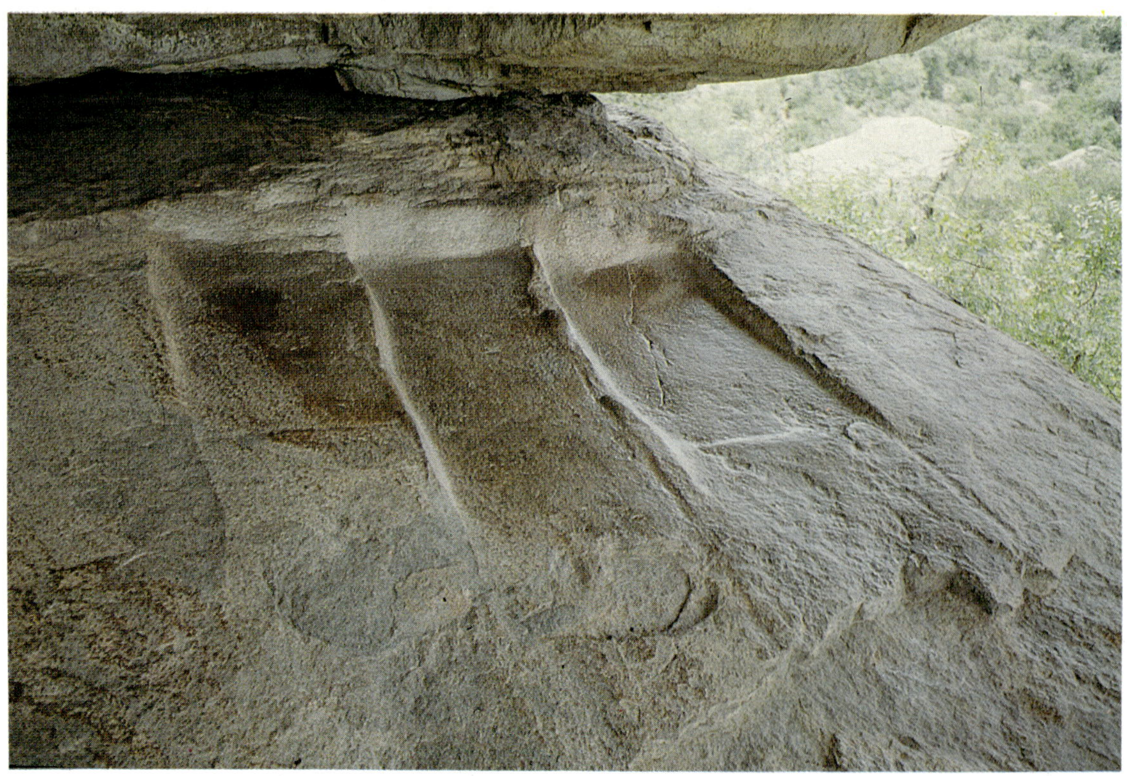

Figure 92. General view of shelter, North Ārcot, Tamilnadu, Southern India.

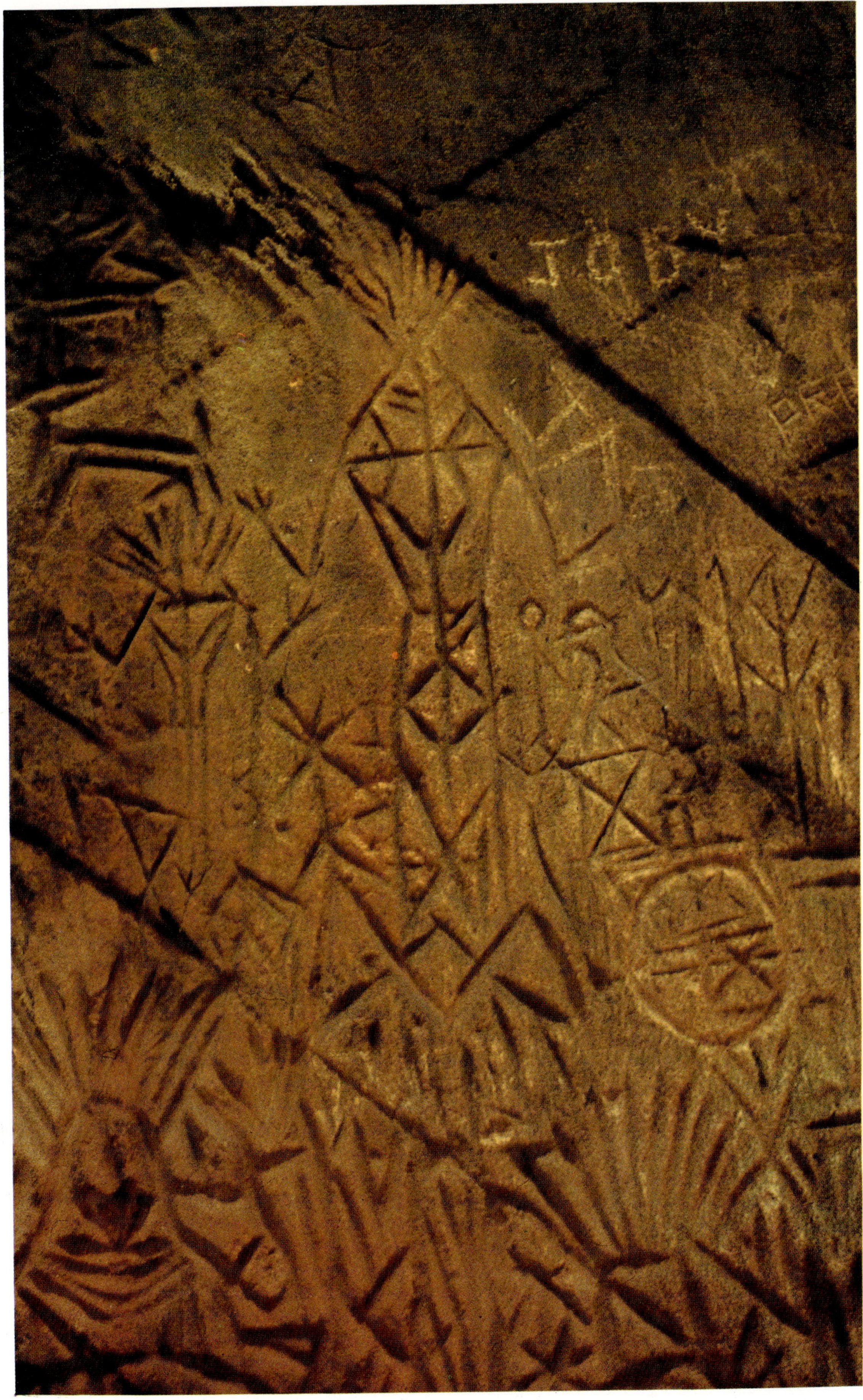

Figure 93. Engraving, Edakkal, Kozikhode, Kerala, Southern India.

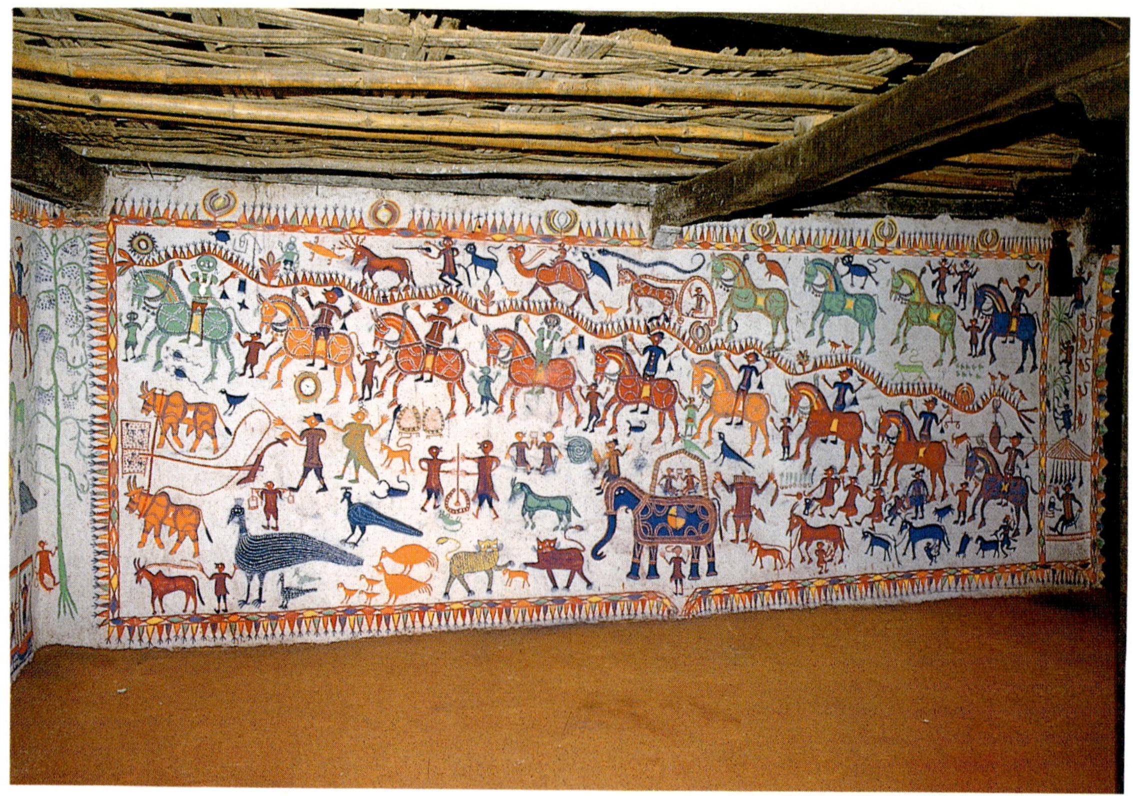

Figure 94. Pithorā Wall painting of Rāthwā tribe, Gujarat, in IGRMS premises, Shāmlā hills, Bhopal, Madhya Pradesh, Central India.

Elsewhere in the world, recurrent, elemental geometric forms have been seen to enter the graphic depiction in rock art as entoptic constants projected neurologically in an artificially induced, altered state of consciousness (Lewis Williams and Dowson, *Current Anthropology* 29, 2: 201-45). These have also been alternatively seen as phosphene types, which project mental images externally, and which possess phylogenetic longevity (*The Artefact* 8, 1984:27-32; *Anthropos* 89:169-80). The dots, zig-zags, arcs, grids, concentric circles, sets of meandering and parallel lines, ovals, triangles, nested catenary curves, spirals and serpentine forms are supposed to be images found in all arts, which can be explained by such excitation.

However, bio-neurological suggestions about the rock art being generated by a state of mind altered by isolation, hallucination, de-hydration, deprivation of sleep, hypnagogic and hypnopompic situation induced by self hypnosis, intense rhythmic movement and hyper ventilation through drugs and other toxic pharmacological agents, would hardly justify a suggestion that the non-iconic marks in rock art were generated by the aberrant mental state of the ancestor of a trance-dancer or medicineman, who is still found in Namibia, Botswana, or among the Baigās or Guniās in the highlands of central India, or that the wall painting of Sāorās of Orissa, Wārlis of Maharashtra or Rāthwās of Gujarat, or the rock art of the San people of south Africa, Algonqians of Canada, Bedouins of the near east, the Warlpiris of Australia was driven by identical goals. Such images can be experienced by human beings independently in different parts of the

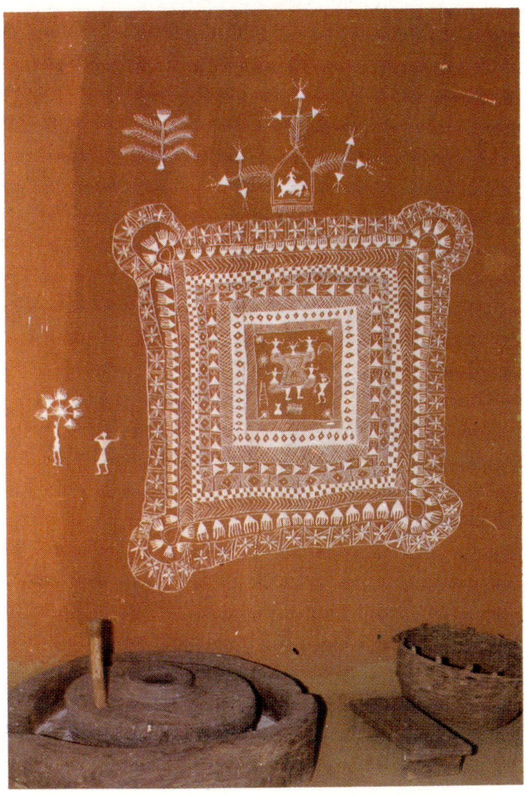

Figure 95. Wall painting of Wārli tribe, Thāne, Maharashtra, in IGRMS premises, Shāmlā hills, Bhopal, Madhya Pradesh, Central India.

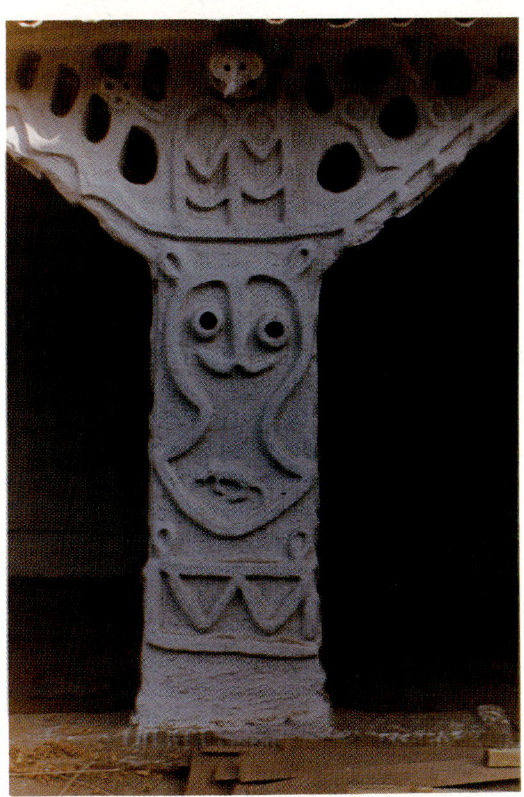

Figure 96. Decorative clay relief work on pillar prepared by Gond artist from Māndlā district of Madhya Pradesh in IGRMS premises, Shāmlā hills, Bhopal, Madhya Pradesh, Central India.

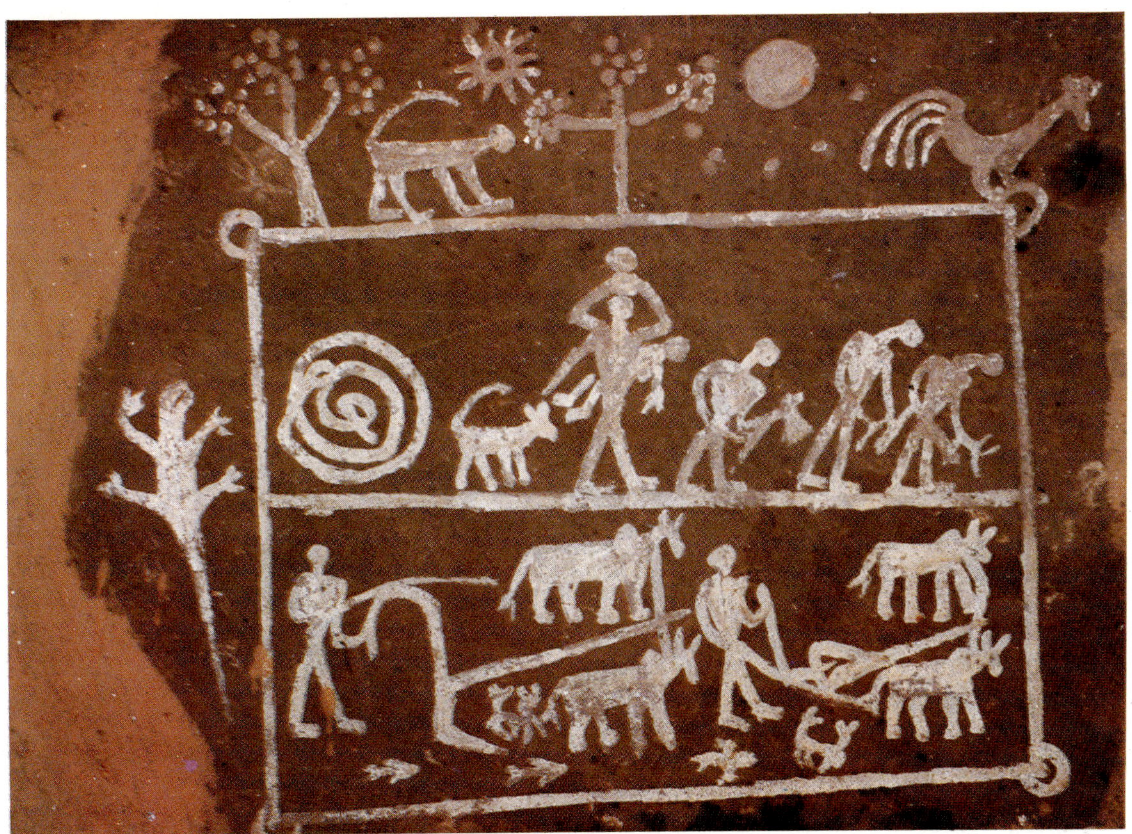

Figure 97. Wall painting of Sāorā tribe, Ganjām, Orissa, Eastern India.

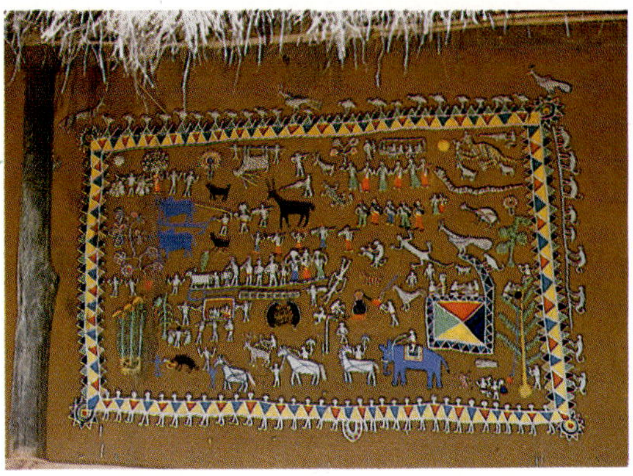

Figure 98. Wall painting of Kutiākond, Orissa, in IGRMS premises, Shāmlā hills, Bhopal, Madhya Pradesh, Central India.

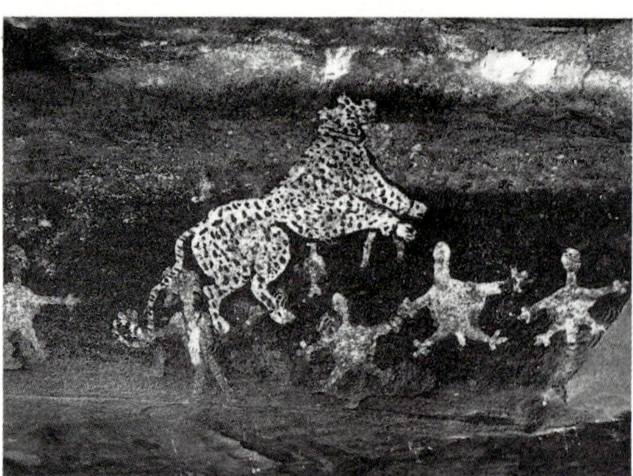

Figure 99. Leopard and men, Churnā Gundi rock shelter, Hoshāngābād, Madhya Pradesh, Central India

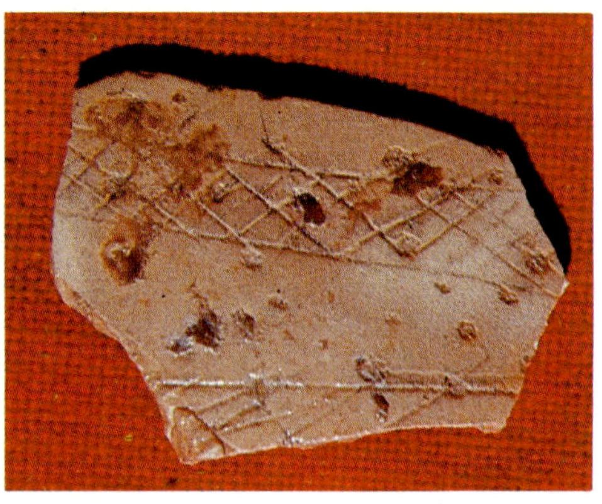

Figure 100. Palaeolithic ostrich eggshell fragment from Pātne, Jalgāon, Maharashtra, Central India.

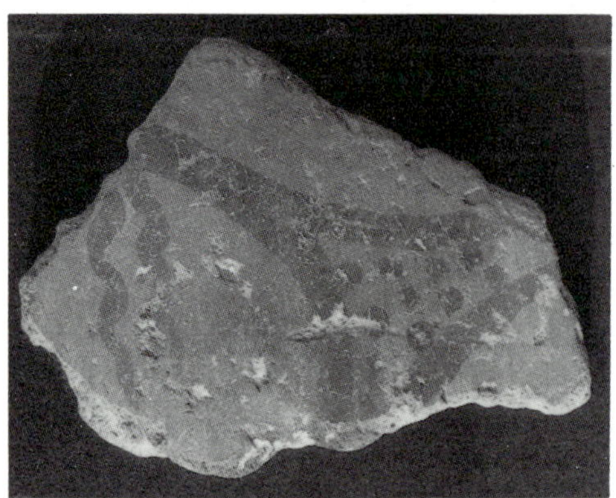

Figure 101. Mālwā ware, Āwrā, Māndāsor, Madhya Pradesh, Central India

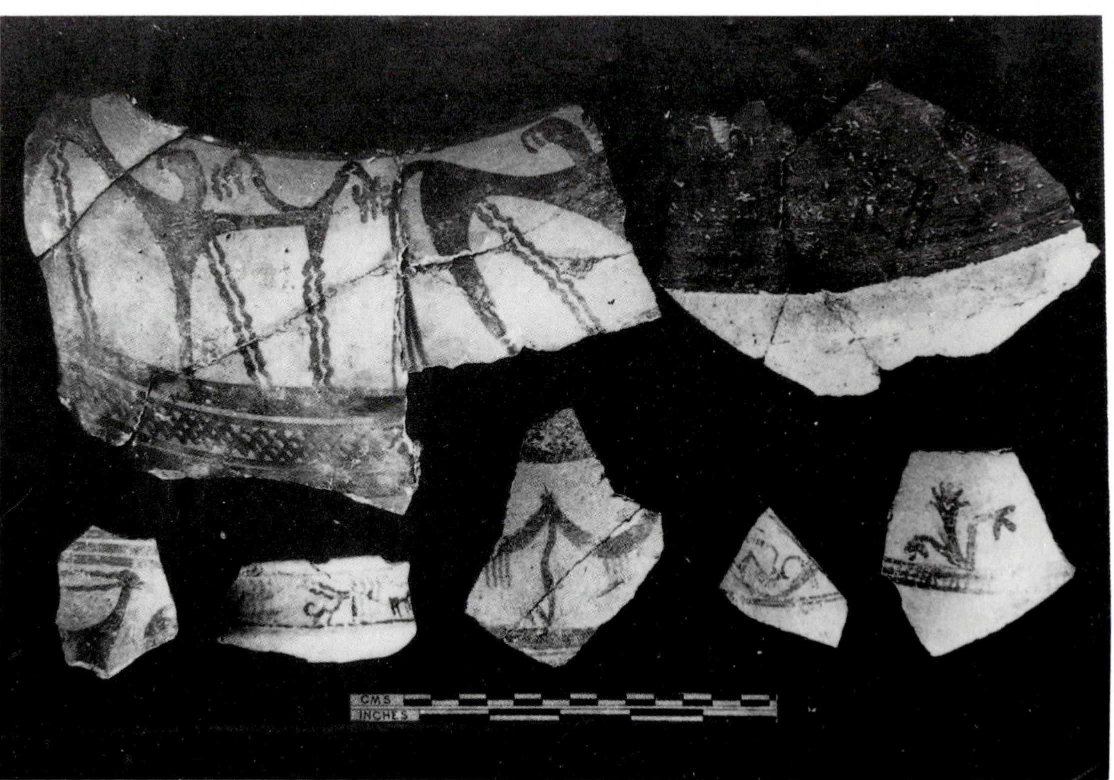

Figure 102. Mālwā ware, Dāngwādā, Ujjain, Madhya Pradesh, Central India.

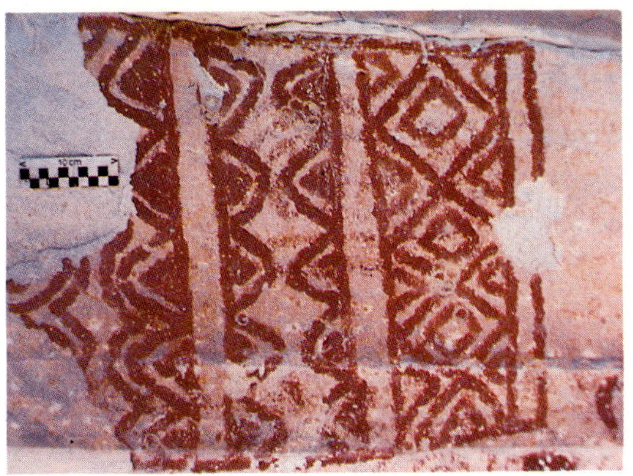

Figure 103. Geometric motif on sandstone, El Buey, Bolivia, South America.

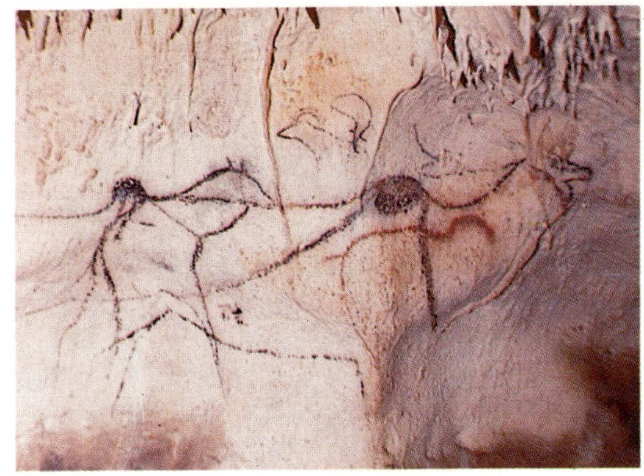

Figure 104. Animal paintings in limestone cave, Upper Palaeolithic period, Cougnac cave, Lot, France.

world in different periods. Cognitive and neurological queries should not ignore the universal and continuing human capacity for making such images, whatever the location and time-specific symboling may have been. They may also be markings of participatory rituals rather than hallucinations (Alexander Marshack *RAR* 6.1, 1989: 17-31), but one does not exclude the other. The processes of replication, fragmentation, integration, superpositioning, juxtapositioning, reduplication and rotation, which have been identified as processes for generating entoptic forms, or the processes generating phosphene images, should be common to the ordering human mind and vision everywhere in every period. Even the figural art in India or elsewhere, which is mostly an art of outline, formed into different combinations of basic geometric shapes, should not be considered to be outside the range of such bioneurological bridges, and hence geometricity should not be considered exclusively pertinent to any particular period or rock art. Psychograms, ideograms and pictograms are some of the archetypes suggested alternatively as heuristic methods to emancipate us from the naturalistic geometric dichotomy (Emmanuel Anati, *Felsbilder* etc. 1991, reviewed by Bednarik in *RAR*, 10.1, 1993: 70-71).

Inspite of their defects, such methods, to the extent they concentrate on the study of the art itself, remain useful in liberating Indian rock art studies from the cyclic, organic theories of biological evolution. Indeed, in most of earlier Indian art, the figural art, which appears tactile (haptic in Riegel's term), and distinct from the graphic art at close quarters, assumes optic qualities at distance and merges in the graphic art, as part of the same ornamental patterns. In Indian aesthetic theory formulated in the historic period, ornament (Sanskrit, *alaṁkāra,* making of sufficiency or bounty) embraces both graphic and figural arts.

Comparisons

Iconographic and iconological comparisons have been made to integrate European and Indian rock art as part of a common body of Indo-European or Indo-Germanic traditions. Shamanistic ideas of cosmic trees with honey combs and Germanic mead trees, death boats for

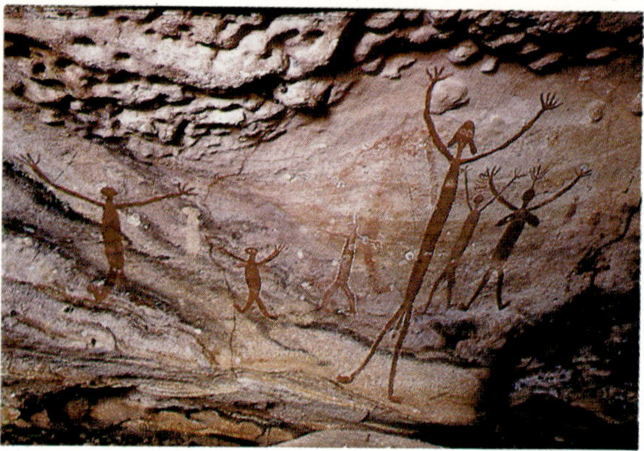

Figure 105. Human figures of Quinkan shelter, Quinkan reserve, Queensland, Australia. Compare Human figures in Māndāsor on page 42, from Shāmlā hills on page 45, Mahādeo hills on page 60 (Fig. 64.).

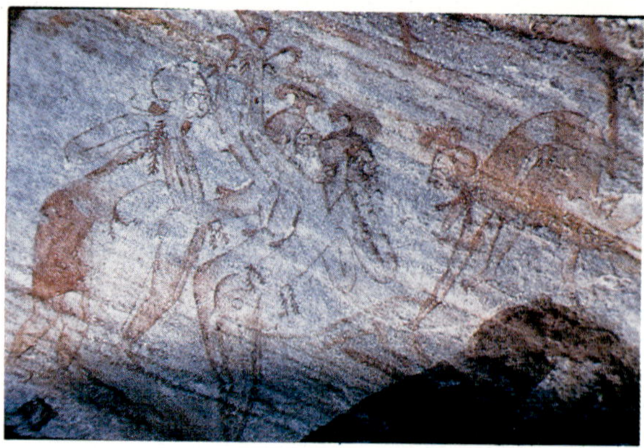

Figure 106. Rock painting of Final Bovidian tradition, men with markings on faces, Tahilahi, Tassili, Algeria. Compare human figures from Mahādeo hills on page 60 (Fig. 65.).

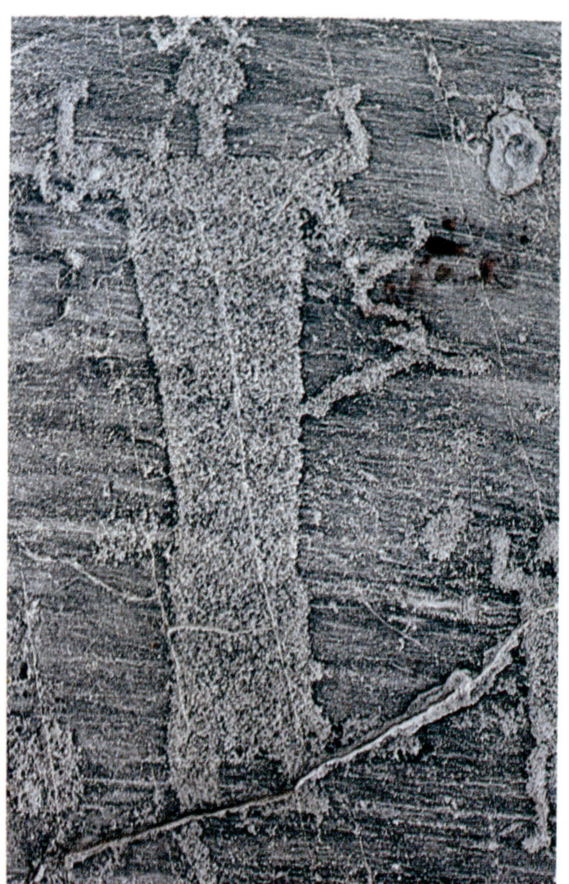

Figure 107. Standing Headgeared human figure, Naquane,Val Camonica, Italy. Compare engraving from Chaturbhujnāth Nālā on

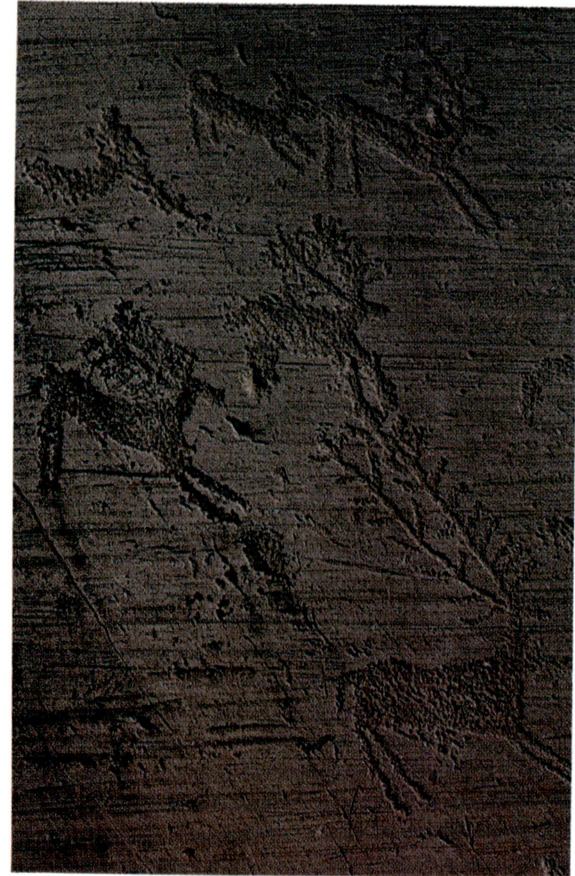

Figure 108. Group of stags, Naquane,Val Camonica, Italy. Compare antelope, Ketāvaram on page 73.

carrying people across the cosmic ocean, reproductive magic of soul birds climbing out of the horns of sun cattle, the Indian and German heaven, *Swarga* and *Walhalla,* epic motifs of the time wheel or lotus bearing image of epic heroes like Krishna, Vedic deities like Agni Daksha, Dhenu Aditih, or Indra Vajra-vāhu, and the theme of release of excremental balls by Rhinos or Bulls have been seen as common to paintings from Bhīmbetkā, Chaturbhujnāth Nālā, Gāndhisāgar, Chibbarnālā, Ādamgarh, Tiklā, Ādhārshilā, Jāorā in central India, and contemporary folk and temple art of central India on the one hand and Swedish (especially the Bahuslan rock engraving), French (release of balls by Rhino at Lascaux), or maritime Alps (Vallée des Merveilles), Monte Bego, Russian and Egyptian paintings (see Lothar Wanke, Tillner, Wakankar, Bhatnagar, Choudhary, Pancholi and others in the volumes of *Jahrbuch Der Ge.Fe.Bi.* 1977/78, 1993/94; Roland Dufrienne, *Bollettino del centro camuno di preistorici* 22: 110-16, Shigenobu Kimura, *ISBN 4-87576-205-4,* 1984, Japan). Depiction of animated humans in green are found in central India in early dynamic style of Australia or in the Levantine style of Eastern Spain, and head trophies are depicted in central India and Peru.

Within Central India itself, comparisons have been made of the Pāchmārhi man, carrying elephant, with the Gilgamesh of Sumerian mobilary art, and of funeral prayer boards with depiction of horses and riders on decorated teak wood memorials used by Korkus, with Pāchmārhi Rock Art. The mythology of the deer in Rock Art of India and Europe has been studied (Camuri, Fossati, Mathpal, *Deer in Rock art of India and Europe,* IGNCA, New Delhi 1993) without any attempt to relate or compare the role of deer in different ecologies.

Comparisons have been made, in an analogical fashion, of the style of Indian and other rock art. The complex network of intermeshed lines in the Edakkal rock engravings of Kerala may be paralleled in the art of the north American Indian at Texas, and stylistic categories like symbolic, generalised, classic, complex, figurative may be established for the Australian as well as Indian rock art (Emmanuel Anati in UNESCO world report on rock art *BCSP* 21, 1984: 13-55; S.K. Pandey, *Rock Art in India)* Figural types with half circular head dress, flaring lower garments, drooping arms, elongated bodies of lightning men of Arnhem land of Australia, may bear some comparison with the figural style of the headhunters of Mahādev hills in Pāchmārhi.

Many stylistic features like the elongation of the upper trunk, diminution of head, accentuation of different body parts, superimposition of squares and triangles in human figures, human bodies interlaced in linear arrays, the X-ray style showing the innards of animals,

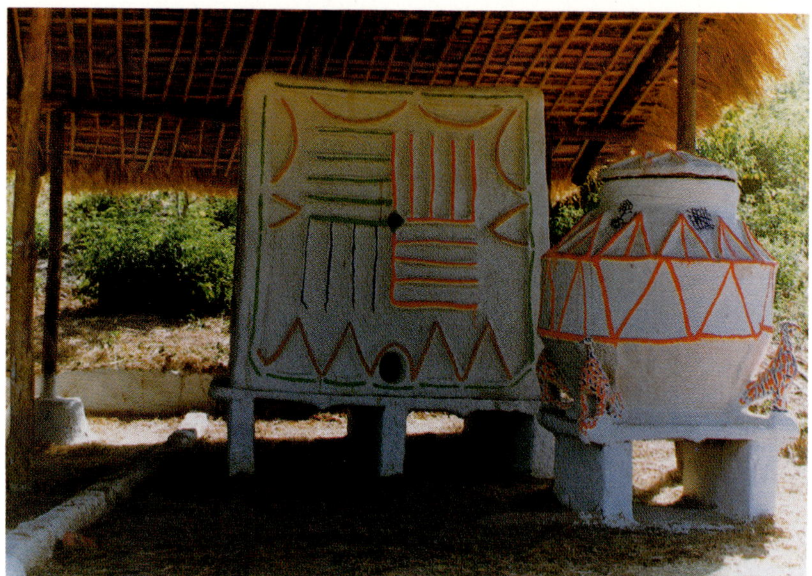

Figure 109. An Earthen grain storage bin with geometric patterns, relief and painting from Chhattisgarh region of Madhya Pradesh in IGRMS premises, Shāmlā hills, Bhopal, Madhya Pradesh, Central India.

the perspective tordue of horns and antlers, combination of the front and profile conventions, are found not only in prehistoric Indian and other rock art in the world, but also in the tribal style in India, illustrated by the magic writing or drawing of the hill-Korwās of Rāigarh or Sargujā, the x-ray style of rendering birds by Pradhān Gonds of Mālwā, the sweeping lines and circles and squares, preferred respectively by Nāgesiyās and Oraons on the one hand, Binjwārs on the other, in Rāigarh, the straight raised lines of Jhārā and Garhwā metal craft of Rāigarh and Bastār, the schematic forms of horses in Pithorā Bhīl and Rāthwā painting of Jhābuā and Gujarat, the stickmen figures of animals, men and deities in wood and bronze made by Gonds of Bastār.

No nominal, substantial or artefactual basis for any common ritualistic symbolism or exegesis can be derived from such comparisons. The ceremonial renewal through retouch, of dreaming or rain making, by the body gyrations of the specially intiated rock art maker, by intercession with his spiritual ancestors, using rock art as process rather than as product, in Manitoba, Canada, West Kimberley or Arnhemland in Australia, the dance of the Bushman medicinemen of south African rock art, for capturing the Eland, the rain animal, can hardly be used to read similar dancing figures in Indian rock art as crystallised metaphors of rain or fertility inducing rituals. The current myths can offer tools for analysis and elements for thought, not readymade answers. The distance between author and subject will have to be kept in case of Rock Art, which is to be seen as a strip cartoon about the past rather than as a picture book painted for us (Michael Lorblanchet, Introduction, *Rock Art in the Old World,* 1992: XXIX).

The apparent similarity of motifs and figures in different parts of the world, cannot suggest either mutual borrowing or priority of origin at any one source. In the absence of relative dating and evidence on cross cultural migration, this can only suggest parallel development of the human imagination in similar grooves. Hominids with similar cognitive building blocks will develop similar graphic marking traditions, and there is no reason for cognitive differentiation between human subspecies in the same broad period as more primitive or advanced than one another. In order to link history of occupation episodes with chronology and level of development, nano-stratigraphic analysis of the painted wall crusts needs to be combined with intra-site spatial analysis, which has hardly been undertaken feasibly. (Campbell, *AURA Occasional Publication* 8, 1993: 57-63). Even if the art of fishermen, hunter gatherers or pastoral populations, distant from one another, betrays similar stylistic traits, this may well reveal different mental horizons or existential relationships among man, nature and the super-natural.

To read contemporary ethnographic rituals into ancient art may not be quite appropriate in spite of some common traits. Though parallels exist between ancient rock art and contemporary patterns of art on different media including rock, made by contemporary folk, tribal and analogous groups classified as modern primitives, these contemporary groups may be quite unlike their Palaeolothic and Neolithic ancestors. While the continuity of motifs from the art of the prehistoric to that of contemporary communities may suggest an identical, cognitive reaction to the world, no common corpus of magical motivation or creation mythology can be suggested on the basis of such evidence without a complete command over the available material around the globe in terms of dating, and sequential, contextual analysis. Even assuming a spatial and temporal invariance of natural laws, it will always be speculative to compare similar graphic or figural patterns in the existing ethnographic record with the archaeological record of rock art, because similar patterns may well be the results of different behavioural processes in the past and the present. The original core of meaning can change in different generations with changing needs, resulting in the reuse of the same tradition for different purposes. In the absence of a constant and testable correlation between the changing behavioural processes and the material conditions, the process which has resulted in a contemporary ethnographic condition should not be used to identify the process used in the prehistoric material condition. (David W Cameron, *RAR* 10.1, 1993: 3-10). Assertion of bio-neurological universals in the study of Rock Art should not also blind us to differences in the application of tool, pigment, use of hand, line, volume, frame, ground or space. Indeed, the spiral, and other geometric squares, hexagons, zigzags or cross hatch motifs at Childant, Kathotiyā suggest that the entoptic designs are not confined only to the Palaeolithic period, but have spread to other periods.

A

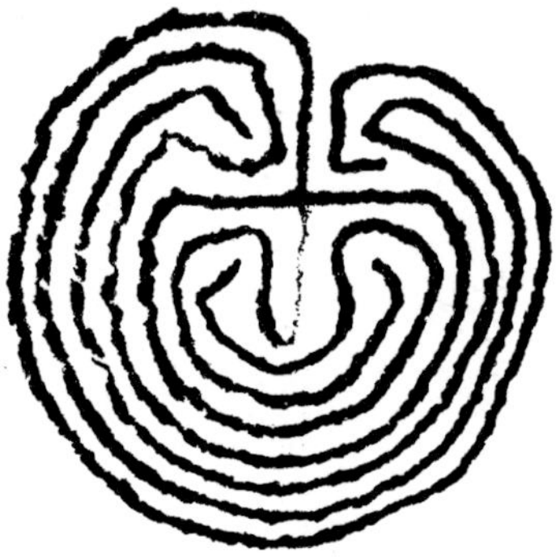

A1

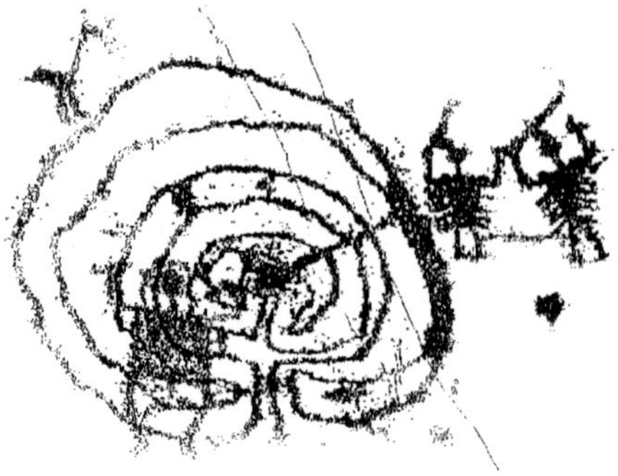

B

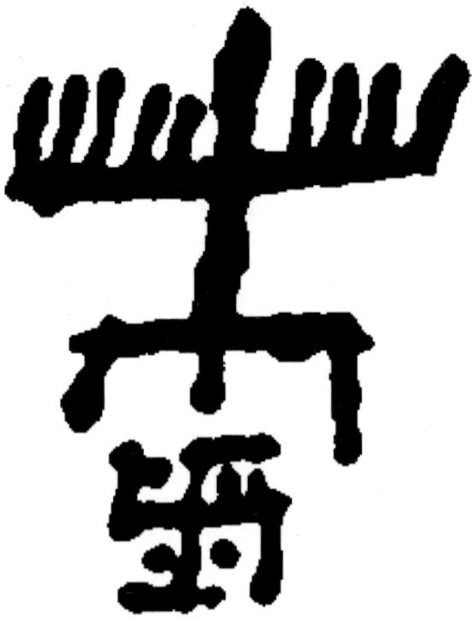

B1

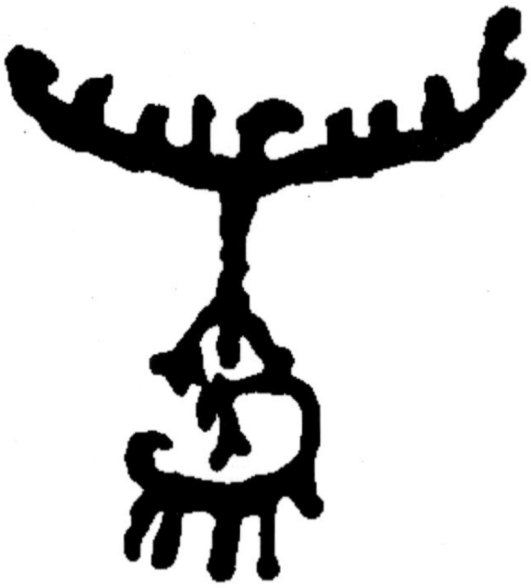

C

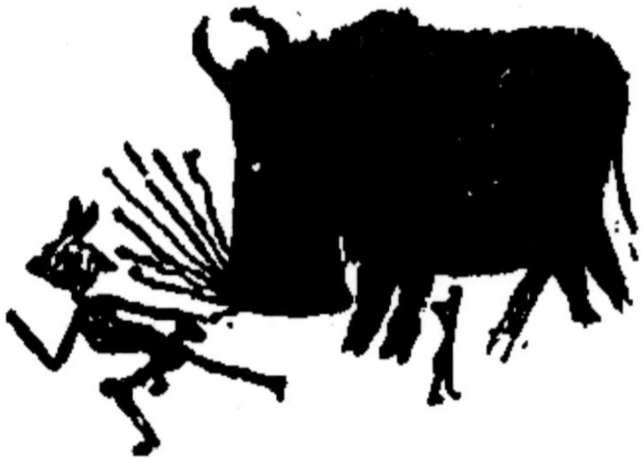

C1

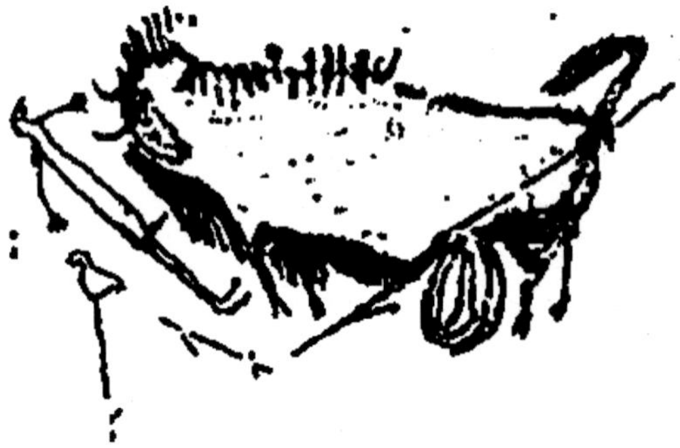

D

D1

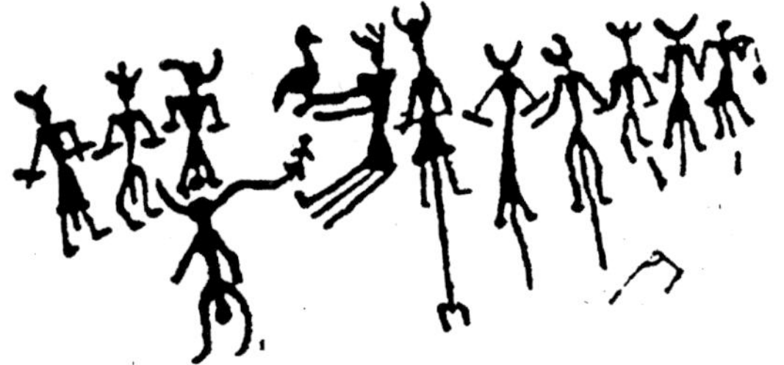

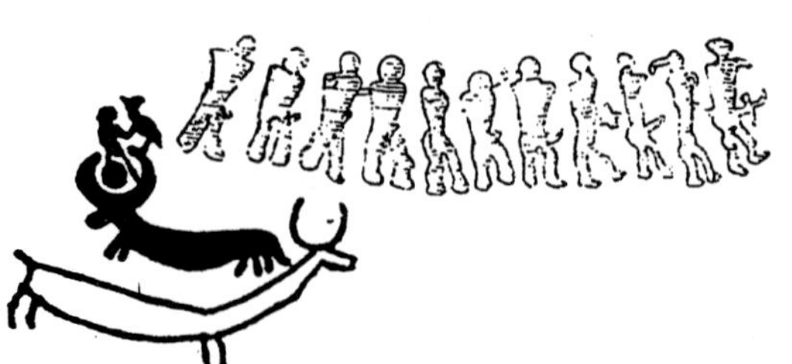

Illustrative comparisons of rock art styles.

(**A:** Pengavān, Rāisen, Madhya Pradesh, Central India, **A1:** Valcamonica, Italy-**Labyrinth**);

(**B:** Ādharshilā, Diken, Māndāsor, Madhya Pradesh, Central India, **B1:** Chilas, Pakistan-**Flying figures**);

(**C:** Pengavān, Rāisen, Madhya Pradesh, Central India, **C1:** Lascaux, France-**Animal Chasing**);

(**D:** Chaturbujnāth Nālā, Chambal valley, Māndāsor, Madhya Pradesh, Central India, **D1:** Aspeberget, Sweden- **'Hornbirth'**)

See Lothar Wanke, Tillner, Wakankar, Bhatnagar, Choudhary, Pancholi and others in the volumes of *Jahrbuch Der Ge.Fe.Bi.* 1977/78, 1993/94.

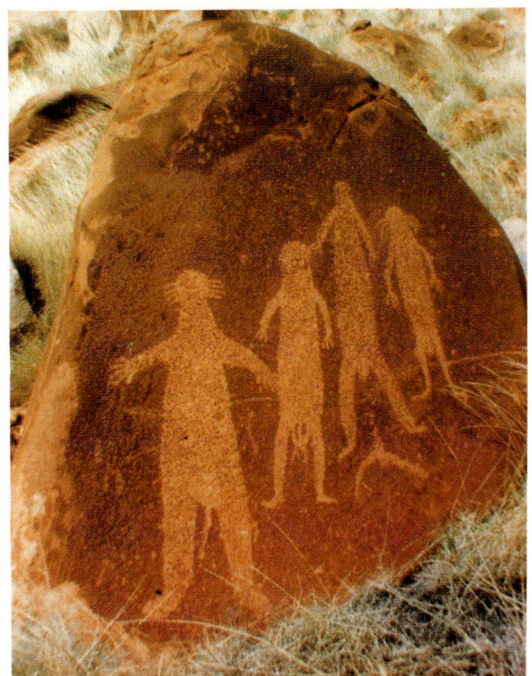

Figure 182-a (refer page no.176 & 177 also). Patinated granite with petroglyphs, Spear hill complex, Pilbara, Western Australia. Compare human figures from Ālmorā on page 37.

hard wired excitation. Finally, the space and information age has suggested a computational model of the brain derived from information processing theory, and interpreters have transplanted this model to rock art to see it as a semantic and ethnographic data bank. Such perceptions have reflected the ethnocentric views of scholars rather than the truth.

In fact, the archaeological or ethnographic identification of the common elements shared by rock art has been found to be laden with the stylistic, cognitive, epistemic, cultural and political biases of the researchers and has remained an oxymoron. Thus, the view of Indian or global rock art, as being designed to only decorate and please, has reflected the contemporary art for art's sake view. The suggestion of such art being a shamanistic instrument to incite bounty and wellbeing has emerged from utilitarian, ethnographic theories of ongones, mediating by sympathetic magic between different worlds. The structural and sexual bifurcation of the rock art has reflected recent theories of psycho-analytical exploration, anthropological structuralism or topographical determinism. Neurology, cognitive and developmental psychology, have also played a role in explaining rock art by

Problem of understanding

Since it is still a problem to identify a method whereby the causes of change can be identified outside the process of change in the body of rock art, it is necessary to identify that part of the behavioural debris which is not the result of taphonomic processes. Otherwise, rock art study will have to confine itself to the dating and analysis of the changes in the shape of the art, an analysis which is replicable and falsifiable (Bednarik, *RAR* 10.1, 1993: 11- 12). Such study may not escape the onus of sensationalism, if not fetishism. The question of how to study Palaeoart outside of human reactions to it (Bednarik, *AURA Newsletter* 11.2, 1994: 12) has been answered by the questioner himself in another place by suggesting caution in indiscriminate invention of order, in the process of mapping reality, by either creating artificial, apparently scientific but self-confirming and non-refutable taxonomies, or by exploiting ambiguity in the search for symbols (Bednarik, *RAR* 11.1, 1994: 42-3). It can be demonstrated that the San or Aboriginal (or, for that matter, Indian) rock art has used motifs which may simultaneously represent several items. Just as organisms have evolved to some complexity before developing parts capable of fossilisation, so human cultures have also begun by developing cognition and communication systems which have left no record. By extending this analogy it can be seen that the existing body of rock art is not exhausted by what is represented, since there is a lot which is too faded, incomplete or irregular to classify. Hence, one has to be wary of imposing an artificial order on the basis of either ethnographic parallels or bio-neurological models. (Robert Layton, in Ladislav Holy, ed., *Comparative Anthropology*1987: 210-39).

Conclusion

To accept the impossibility of objective human understanding within the flawed subjectivism of the human cognitive realm, is to resign onself to mere dating exercises, which, however useful for identifying a site, or for understanding its temporal and spatial relation with other sites of human civilization, remain hobbled by contamination of data and obsession with surface concerns. While it is agreed that the artefact cannot be used as culturally dignostic in the absence of semiological markers, which are undeniably associated with culturally mediated traces of behaviour, there is scope for a comprehensive interpretation, done metamorphologically, after resolution of ranges of probabilities (Bednarik, *Oxford Journal of Archaeology,* 14.2, 1995: 117 - 22). Just as modern science is not irrational by abondoning rational intuitive, space time, subject object dichotomy, so formal arrangements of rock art can be seen as not only modes of representation but also as expressively significant, as not only phraseologically oriented but also ideologically. Hence, a physical and mental reiteration of the process in rock art, an attempt to understand the product through systematic in depth regional studies, and, to combine this with multi-dimensional appreciation of the various concepts of reality, may help us to read meanings back into forms, left out of them by us because of the loss of recollection.

Though human encephalisation was completed 100,000 years ago in terms of the cortical hardware and neural structures, the ontological constructs and metaphysical models of reality have changed from the early period of rock art to the present (Bednarik, *The Artefact,* 17: 4-5) because, one would assume, the human being has changed his environment faster than he can biologically adapt himself to it. Post-processual archaeology has demonstrated the anthropocentricity and socio-political solipsism of contemporary interpretation of older human activity. All objects are now seen as processes in universal flux; certainties are making way for probabilities; subject-object distinctions are being dissolved with the observer becoming a participator, who is changing reality by his observation. What we observe therefore is not nature itself, but nature exposed to and influenced by our method of questioning.

The analysis of the rock art of the world and in India, has been often hamstrung by the Hegelian approach of the interpreter who has assumed for himself and the dominant tradition he represents, a historical entelechy, and has tried to objectify, master and appropriate the other traditions in his own tradition. A reversal of this approach is needed. The interpreter should not stand over and objectify history but be borne on its movement, being subject and object at the same time, using, what Heidegger called, the hermeneutic circular movement, to move back and forth, from the part to the whole, from his own tradition to the other tradition, his self-understanding being fulfilled by an understanding of the other (J.L. Mehta, *India and the West*, 1985; *Philosophy and Religion*,1990). The use of abstraction to represent and transform aspects of the physical world or of naturalism, to define and concretise the spiritual environment in a process of creative inversion, has been suggested as an explanation of Warlpiri art in Australia (Paul Faulstich in *AURA Occasional Publication* 5: 19-23). It would appear to be an explanation of a similar intellectual movement, between the idea and the image, the self and the other, to effect a true home coming to the roots of one's own tradition. Irrespective of the validity of such an explanation and irrespective of the fact that the socio-cultural significance of rock art sites to the surrounding local populations in India may not be the same as that for the original makers of such art, there is a need to recollect the cognitive and physical process of production of this art, to effectively repossess the cultural landscape from which we stand alienated today.

The procedure recommended for this is not one of physical recovery of the cultural landscape behind Indian rock art, through introduction of retouch of the painting tradition, where none exists, but one of repeating, recapitulating, retracing the beginning once again. 'Pantheistic' traditions continue among folk and tribal communities of India in the vast rural hinterlands living around the rock shelter sites for thousands of years. Their life and art are still one and not divorced from one another. They hew, sculpt and paint in different media, paint their body, costume, house walls, floors and livestock, make art to celebrate all the rites of passage, and people such art with meaning and myth through song and dance, which respond to the rhythm of seasons, nature and life. They see every stone, plant, flower, bird, animal and living creature, every implement and tool of daily use as instinct with life, vibration and purpose, and worship them with equal fervour. They endow every occasion of life, calamity and festival with its God and its demon. They still live in perpetual communion, illustrating, what Heidegger calls, the unified four-fold play of the earth and the heaven, Gods and mortals, in which man dwells on earth as his home, under the heaven, in friendly commerce with God, with his fellow men and with things, building and making untiring, with thoughts, words, and things. They dwell in the four-fold to save and not master the earth or wear it out. They receive the sky as sky and do not turn night into day nor day into a harassed unrest. They wait for intimation of the coming of the divinity, and do not mistake signs of their absence. They initiate their own nature, being capable of death as death. Dwelling in such simple oneness of the four, they dwell poetically (Martin Heidegger, *Poetry, Language and Thought*, 1971: 150-51, 227-29).

For the interpreter of Indian rock art or of its context in the world of rock art, the task therefore is to overcome the alienation from that immediacy of living, in which rock art appears to have been at once man's way of experiencing and responding to the reality. The interpreter has to see the beginnings of rock art as uncanny and mighty and not as feeble and awkward, which hold potentials yet to be spelt out for the future. These potentials can be captured by him stepping back, by beginning the beginning once again, by using all the available evidence. Thereby he will step forward to a post rather than pre-scientific mode of understanding. With the growing understanding of the absence of any partition between observer and observed in the physical sciences, or of the isomorphism of genetic and verbal codes, it should become possible to see the mental and physical sets in a human creative activity simultaneously, and look for the beginning of Indian rock art and its global context. In the bargain, it may be possible to rethink what has been thought; to get a glimpse of what has remained unthought, in embryo; to acknowledge the past or other traditions in their otherness; and to turn homeward to the present, to our own respective traditions. The dialogue can restore to each tradition what it once was and can become. It will leave the beginning of the tradition undepleted, and enrich its future. ❑

• THE REST OF ASIA •

THE REST OF ASIA

The rock arts found in the remaining parts of Asia are of a geographical distribution that is probably very similar to the uneven intensity of research work in these two different factors. Limitations in the international dissemination of knowledge about the massive corpus of rock art found in China has been severely hampered until very recently. No scientific report about this national heritage had appeared in any language other than Chinese until 1984, the year the first article about it appeared in Australia. And yet there are some 10,000 rock art sites known in China! Moreover, China boasts the earliest published recordings of rock art in the world, produced over 1500 years ago!

In various other parts of Asia, this state of a paucity of inforamtion still persists, and there is considerable scope for researchers to improve our knowledge. For instance, rock art is known to exist in most if not all Southeast Asian countries, but reliable knowledge about it is often very scarce indeed. There are a few scientific reports available about these regions, some even providing an inkling of perhaps major assemblages, e.g. in Thailand, Indonesia, Korea and Japan. The occurrence of rock art has even been reported from such small regions as Macao and Hong Kong. But the extensive publications we can draw upon in India and China are not available in other regions of Asia, and our knowledge of them remains extremely circumscribed. Specialists in rock art studies are usually lacking in these countries. For instance. only one rock art researcher is internationally known in

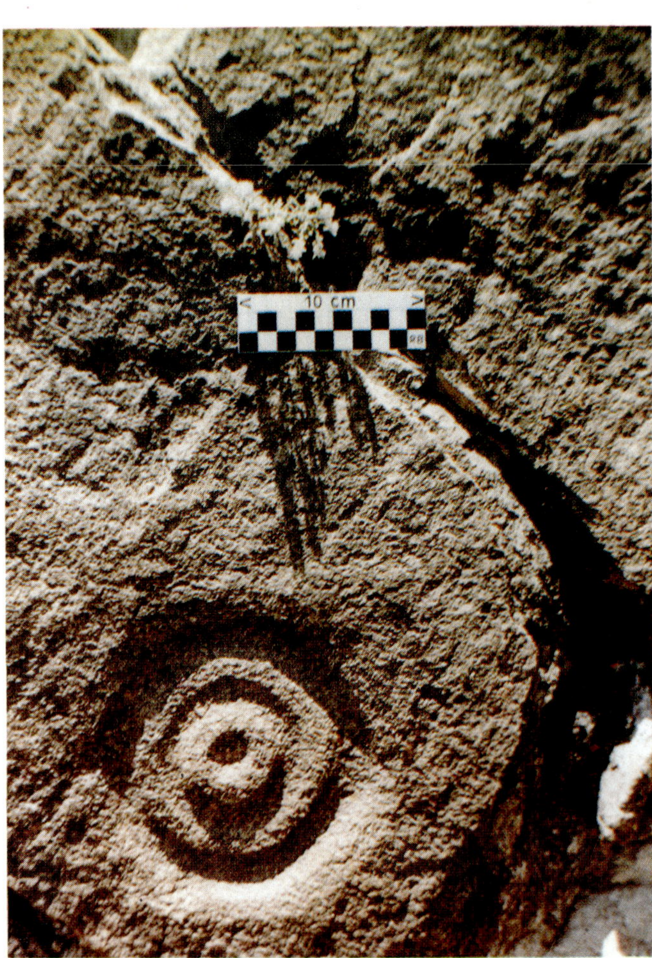

Figure 110. Concentric circle petroglyph in rhyolite, Helankou, Helanshan, Ningxia Hui Province, China.

Figure 111. Petroglyph at Suyukou. Helanshan, Ningxia Hui Province, China.

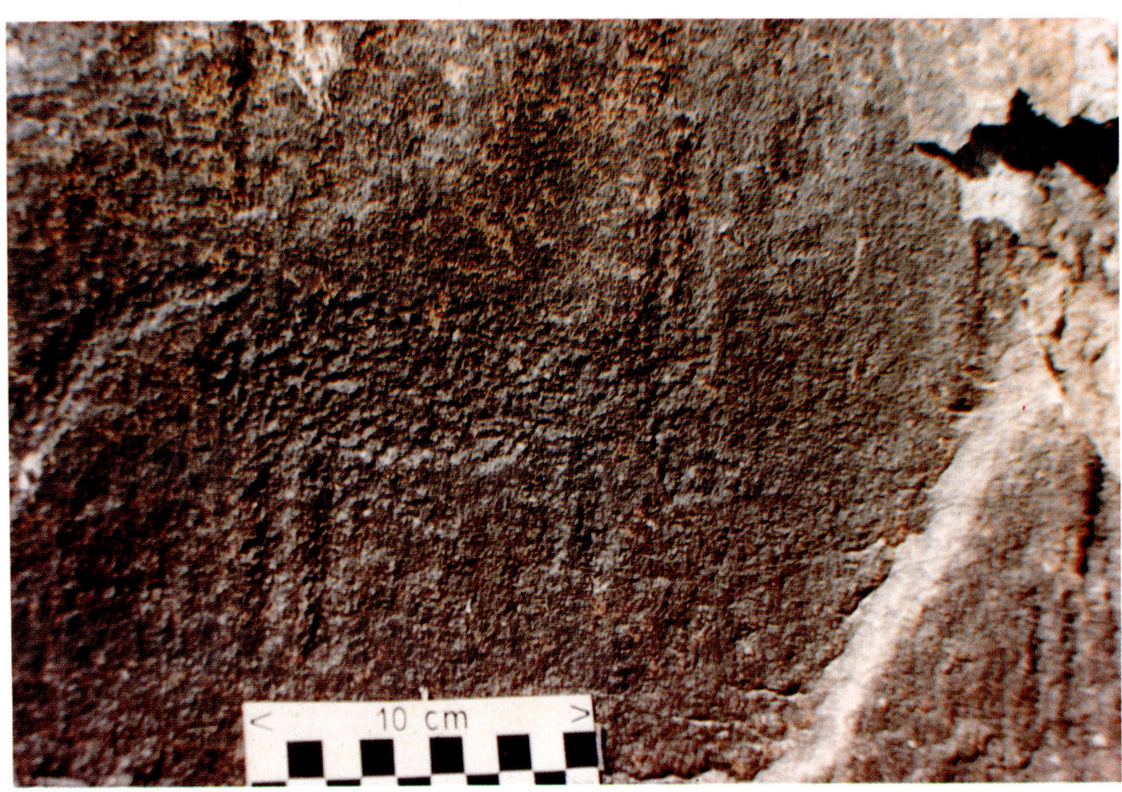

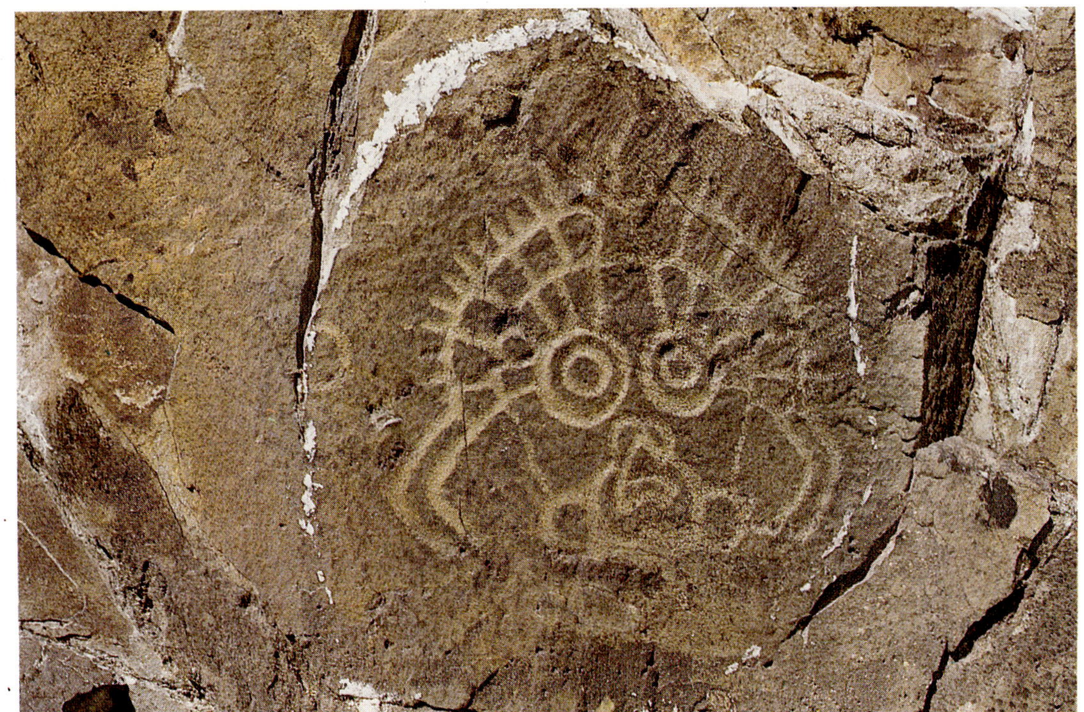

Figure 112. 'Mask'petroglyph, Helankou, Helanshan, Ningxia Hui Province, China.

Japan, Masaru Ogawa, and yet he specialises in Spanish rock art rather than Japanese.

The state of knowledge is significantly better in China, Siberia and parts of south-western Asia (Saudi Arabia, Israel, Turkey). China now boasts several hundred students of rock art, ably led by the doyen of Chinese rock art studies, Chen Zhaofu. Current knowledge indicates an uneven distribution of rock art across the country, with a clear predominance of rock paintings in the south, while petroglyphs are generally much more prominent in northern and western China. The vast petroglyph concentrations in the northern provinces, particularly Inner Mongolia, have been studied thoroughly by several authors, and most especially by Gai Shanlin. They occur in mountainous regions as well as on steppes, and consist mostly of impact (or percussion) petroglyphs hammered into deeply patinated rock.

Much the same pertains to the dense concentrations of petroglyph sites in Ningxia Hui Province, to the west, with the most spectacular sites found in the Helan Mountains (Figures 110 and 111). Among their gorges occur large sites with long sequences of rock art, in which many different traditions are represented. As in most of these art systems, animal figures often predominate, but as one proceeds further northwards and especially westwards, there is a growing proportion of figures that resemble ornate human faces. They are generally described as 'masks', which is indeed what they may well represent (Figure 112). These same mask motifs continue into Mongolia and southern Siberia, as far as the upper Yenisey valley, where they are particularly prominent.

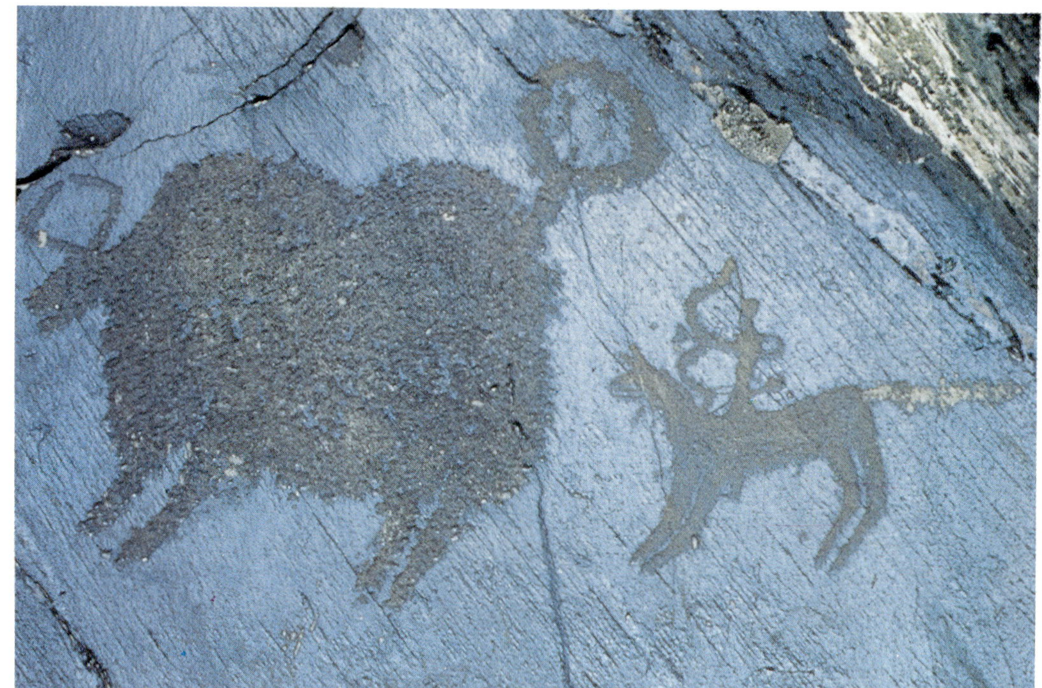

Figure 113. Apparent hunting scene from the Shebuqi site, Gangcha County, Qinghai Province, China.

As we continue to travel around China, we reach the vast plateaus of Qinghai and Tibet. Again, several petroglyph traditions have been distinguished: early animal figures (Figures 113 and 114), followed by more recent pastoral depictions and the appearance of written characters. Of particular interest is the fashion in which the religious competition between Bonism, the ancient shamanistic beliefs of Tibet, and the invading Buddhism can be observed in the sequence of rock art (as studied especially by Tang Huisheng). This struggle eventually resulted in Lamaism, the recent form of Tibetan Buddhism, which is a combination of both these religious currents.

The traces of another religious struggle can also be found in western Chinese rock art: the Buddhist shrines, frequently in rock-hewn caverns, became themselves the targets of widespread iconoclast destruction, when Islam

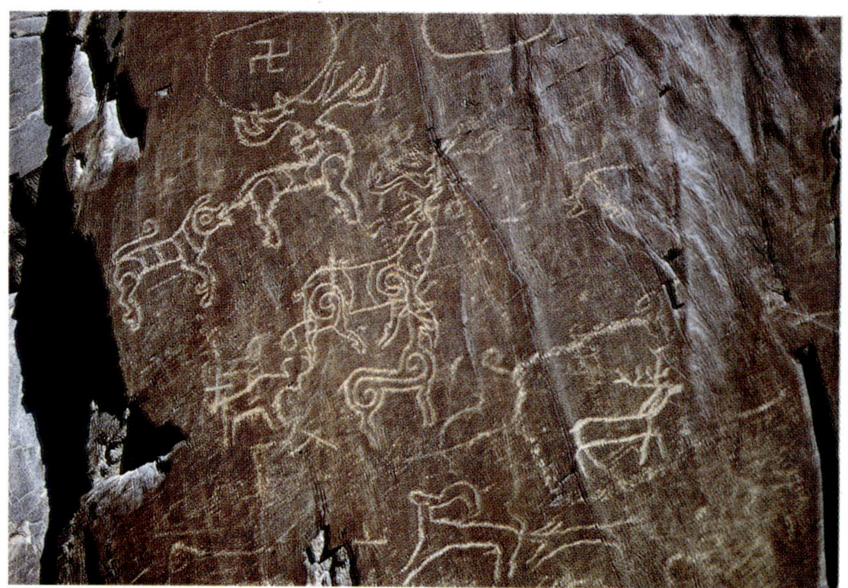

Figure 114. Several petroglyphs of animal figures from the Renmudong site, Rity County, Tibet. The apparent stag and feline figures are depicted in a style resembling Scythian art, which is found widely in central.

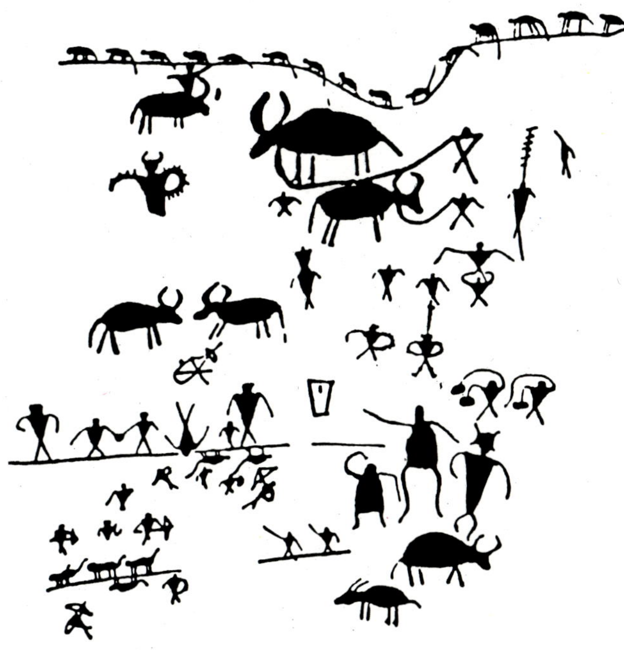

Figure 115. Red rock paintings on the limestone cliff of Site 1, Cangyuan, Yunnan Province, China.

expanded along the Silk Road and enforced its opposition to iconography. Countless Buddhist paintings and inscriptions were destroyed in the process. Indeed, western China is perhaps one of the world's prime locations to study the interaction of major religions in world rock art.

The great rock painting murals of southern China are among the most spectacular sites of rock art in the world. The many painting panels found on the limestone cliffs of Cangyuan, Yunnan Province, have been studied in detail, especially by Wang Ningsheng (Figure 115). Others, including Li Fushun, have examined the impressive Huashan site in Guangxi Province, where hundreds of large red paintings cover a huge vertical cliff up to a height of some forty metres (Figure 116). Some of this art, overlooking a river, has been dated to around 2300 years, using modern methods of direct dating.

Figure 116. Massive panel of red rock paintings on large cliff at Huashan, overlooking the Ming river, Ningming County, Guangxi Zhuang Province, China.

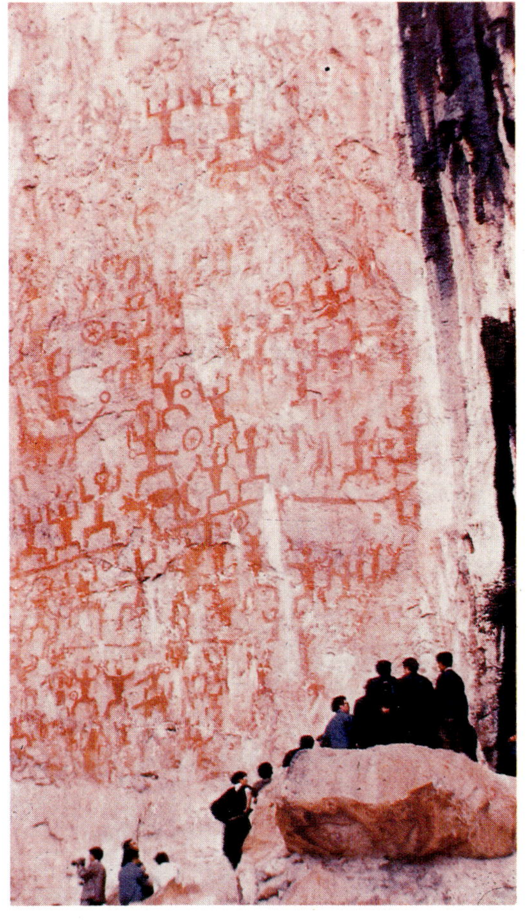

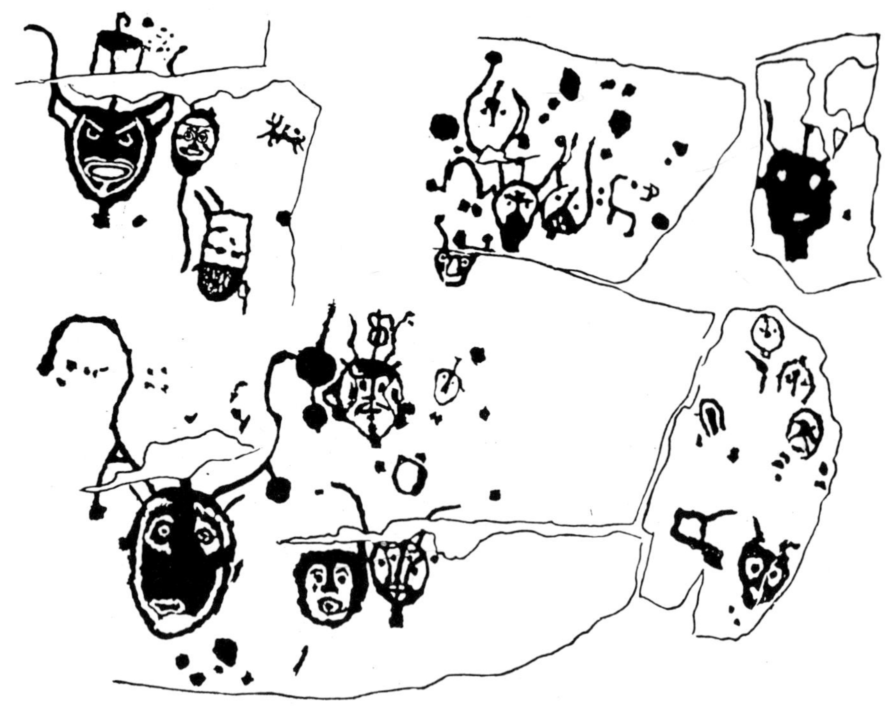

Figure 117. Petroglyphs supposedly depicting masks. upper Yenisey River, Siberia.

In Siberia, too, rock art has been studied in considerable detail. Among the best known concentrations are those on the upper Yenisey and on the upper Lena River. The former concentration, of petroglyphs, appears to be a natural continuation of the art traditions in central Asia, with a rich variety of 'masks' being the outstanding component (Figure 117). This region was studied most thoroughly by Marianna Devlet, a dedicated scholar from the Russian Academy of Sciences, while the great Russian researcher A. P. Okladnikov is perhaps best known for his work on the Lena rock art. This latter region is particularly noteworthy, for its great stylistic variety as well as for the frequent co-occurrence of both paintings and petroglyphs. Some of the Lena sites, such as Vorobiovo (Figure 118) and Kartuchai, comprise only petroglyphs, and often these are percussion (impact) petroglyphs. The vast majority of Lena valley petroglyphs, however, are incisions or engravings, they were created by abrasion rather than by impact. This is particularly the case at the main site, Shishkino, which is about one kilometer long, on a series of cliffs overlooking the Lena (Figure 119). A noteworthy component are a few large rock paintings which Okladnikov suspected to be of the Ice Age, together with one more painting at the Tal'ma site, on a remote tributary of the Lena. However, these attributions to the Ice Age have been rejected recently. Most of the Lena rock art is probably of Historic age, as suggested by the types of motifs and the fine line work

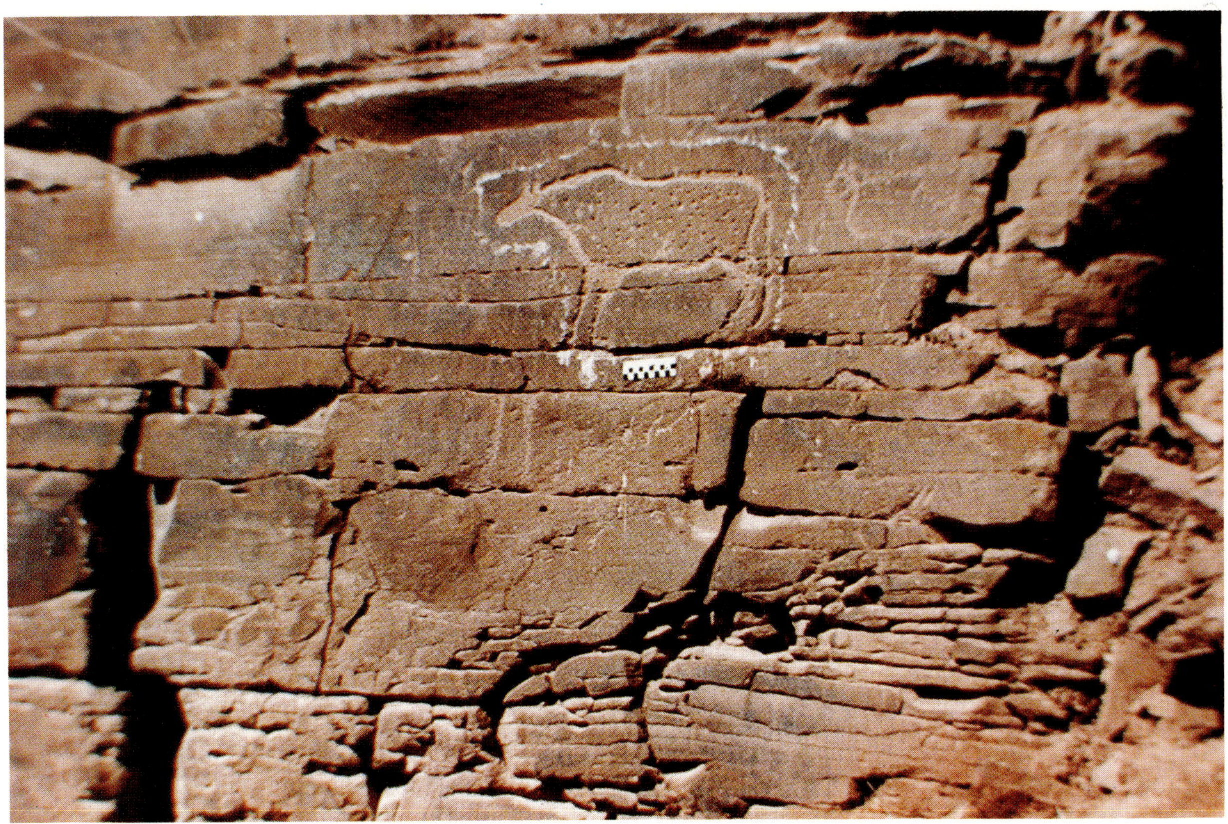

Figure 118. Petroglyph depicting a bovid, Vorobiovo site, Lena valley, central Siberia.
The white traces are latex residues, showing the effects of incompetent recording work.

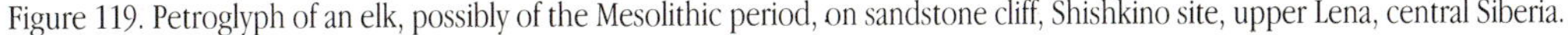

Figure 119. Petroglyph of an elk, possibly of the Mesolithic period, on sandstone cliff, Shishkino site, upper Lena, central Siberia.

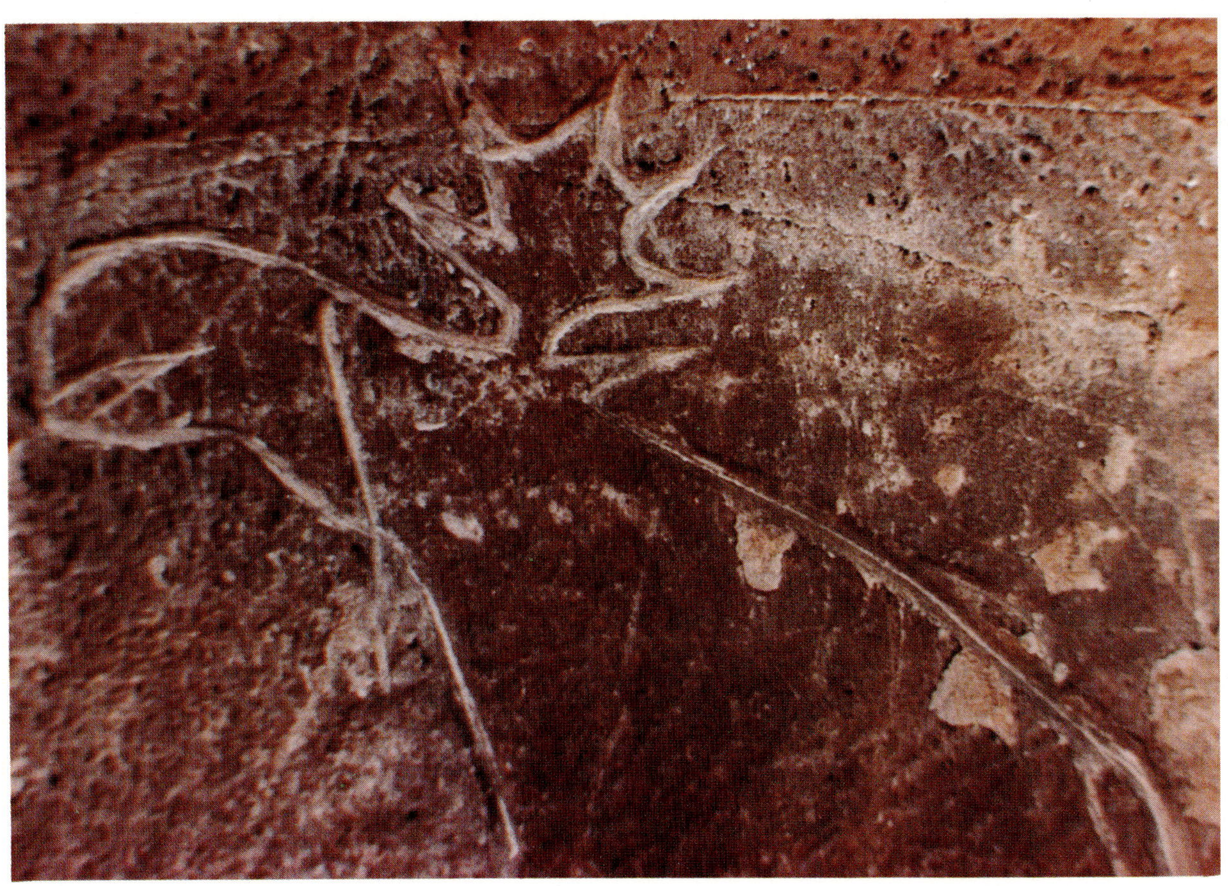

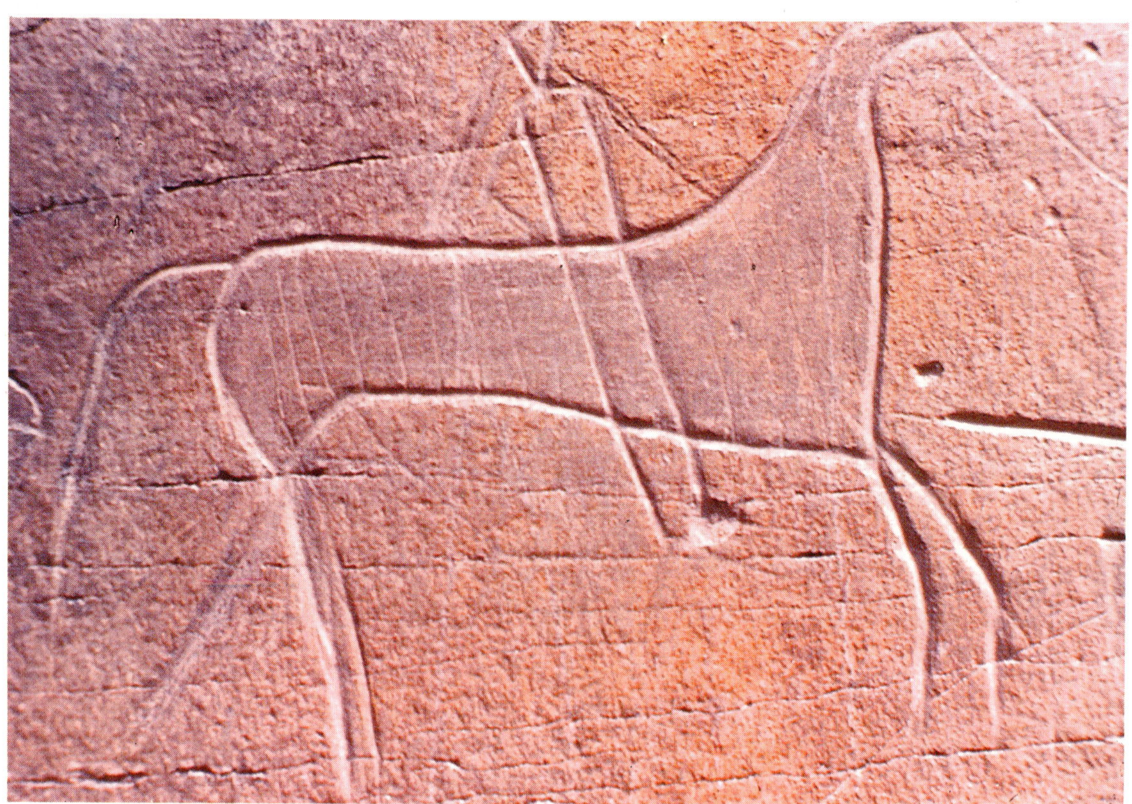

Figure 120. Engraving of horse and rider. on the sandstone cliffs of Shishkino site, upper Lena, central Siberia.

in the petroglyphs. Among these motifs, those of horses and riders are commonly found (Figure 120).

Elsewhere in Siberia and in the central regions of Asia, rock art also occurs widely, but it is in most cases less well known. Examples are the Altay region and parts of Kazakhstan, on the upper Irtysh and Ob Rivers, several regions along the Amur River, and the Kuril Islands between Kamchatka and Japan. We should not omit to mention here the rich portable art finds of the Siberian Early Stone Age (the Upper Palaeolithic). Even though they are not rock art, they do relate to our general subject (Figure 121). Found at some twenty sites so far, these finds bear witness to a rich tradition of art production spanning perhaps the last 35,000 years. In fact the finds include the oldest currently known full sculpture in the world, an animal head carved on a rhinoceros bone from the site Tolbaga (Figure 122). Best known among the Siberian sites of portable Ice Age art are Buret' and Mal'ta, on the Angara River and one of its tributaries respectively. They are famous for the many human figurines of mammoth ivory they yielded, and for the beads, pendants and other ornaments fashioned from the same material. Other sites of portable Ice Age art are located around Lake Baykal, also elsewhere on the Angara, and on the Yenisey and Ob Rivers. There is even one site in far northern Siberia, on the Arctic Sea: Berelekh, the northernmost known Ice Age settlement site in the world. It produced a juvenile mammoth tusk

Figure 121. Three small Paleolithic figurines from Siberia. The two on the left are of ivory and from Mal'ta, the one on the right is of steatite and from Buret', Angara River, about 15,000 years old.

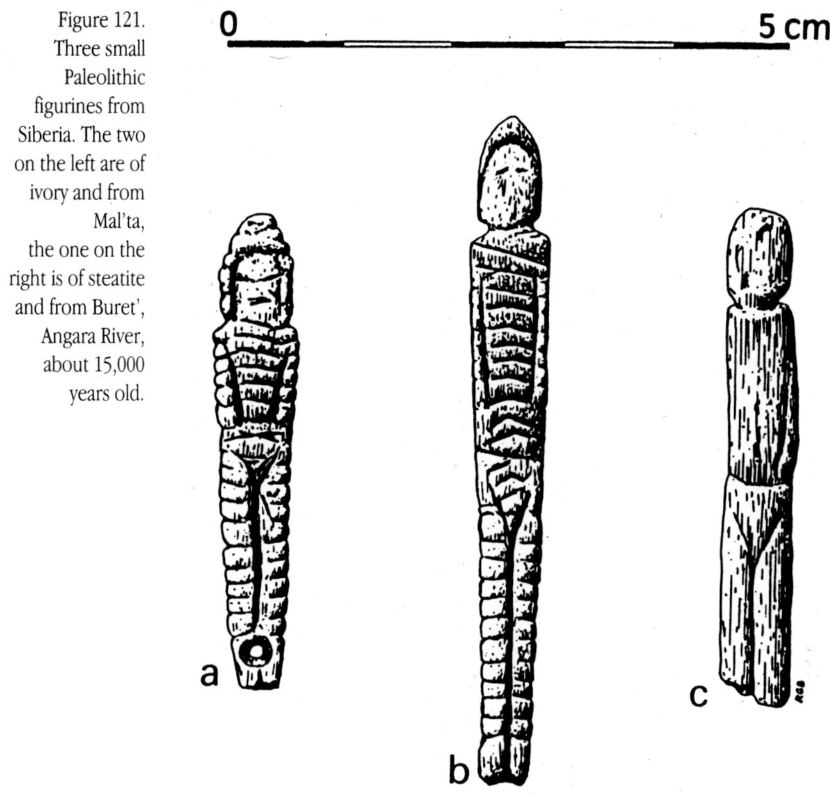

Figure 122. Sculpture of animal head on a vertebra of an extinct rhinoceros, Tolbaga, southern Siberia, perhaps 35,000 years old.

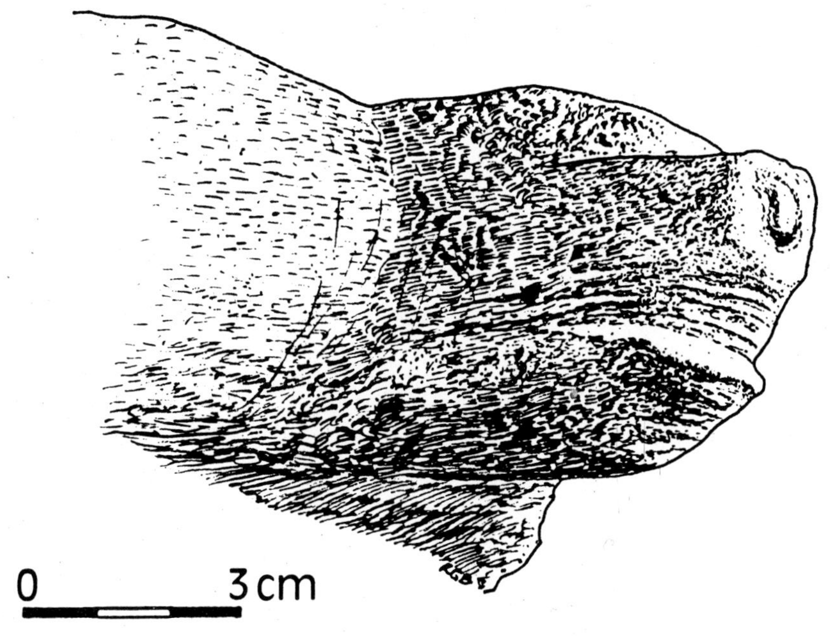

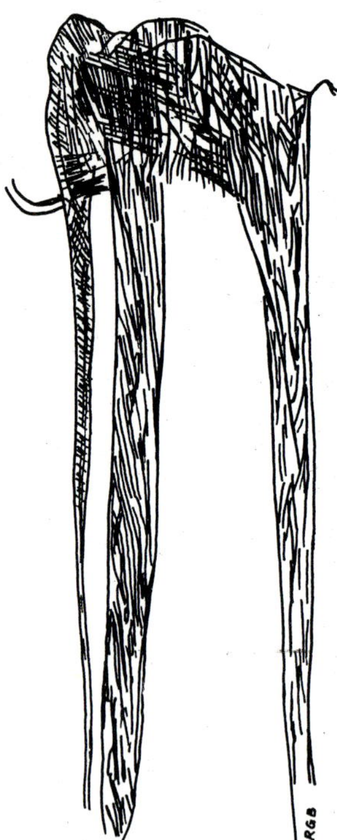

Figure 123. Engraving of a mammoth, on a mammoth tusk from Berelekh, northern Siberia.

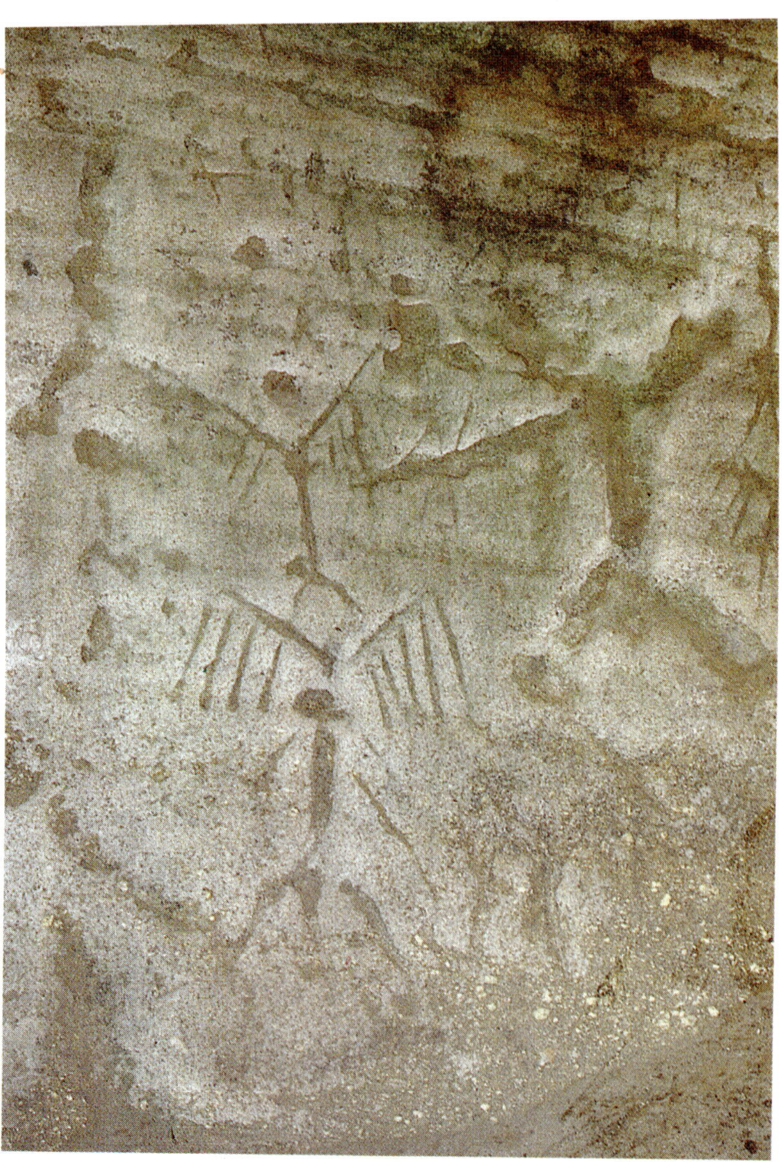

Figure 124. Petroglyphs of human figures in Fugoppe Cave, Yoichi-cho, Hokkaido, northern Japan.

bearing the engraving of a mammoth (Figure 123).

Rock art occurs in Japan, but surprisingly little reliable information about it is available. It occurs often on boulders and stelae found across the country, as simple markings that may resemble written characters and are erroneously interpreted as the writing of foreign seafaring peoples. However, there are exceptions, such as the remarkable petroglyphs in Fugoppe Cave in northern Japan (Figure 124).

In completing our journey around Asia we come to the Middle East and adjacent regions. Here, rock art is again found in all countries, usually in the form of petroglyphs on patinated rock surfaces. Such surfaces survived best in arid regions, which is perhaps why the best preserved concentrations are found in the Negev Desert of Israel and in Saudi Arabia (Figures 125 and 126). Both these occurrences were studied and published by Emmanuel Anati, an Italian rock art specialist. Together with the general region's rock art, Arabic and other inscriptions can often be found. They may assist the researcher in the approximate dating of the art (which is sometimes possible also in India and China, as we have seen). Detailed pictographic and epigraphic studies, concerned with the origins of writing, have been conducted by Majeed Khan in northern Saudi Arabia. Petroglyphs occur also in Oman, Yemen, Turkey, Iraq - in fact throughout the region. It is noteworthy that at one site in Israel, Mount Carmel, engravings in an ancient occupation cave have been suggested to be of the Ice Age. This is quite possibly correct, because Israeli archaeologists have produced a number of other very early evidences of art. These include several engraved or sculpted portable items, of limestone and even of chert, and we have already mentioned that some of the world's oldest possible evidence of art is from Israel. The region's geographical key position may be reflected in the occurrence of such early evidence, as may be the particularly strong research efforts of Israeli archaeologists.

In summary, rock art occurs widely in Asia, but study efforts have been very uneven regionally. The next continent we will examine has received far more attention in this area of study, and this has predictably resulted in much better knowledge about its rock art. ❐

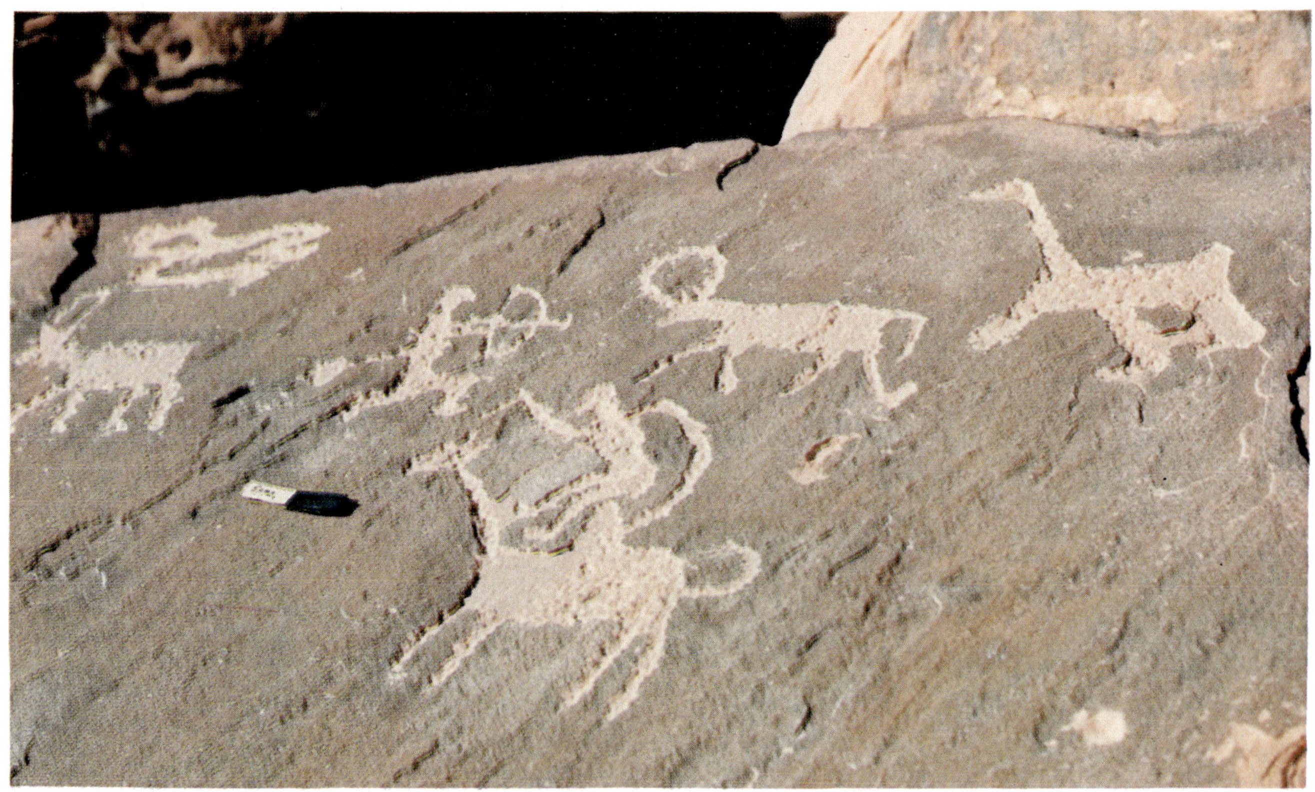

Figure 125. Apparent hunting scene of petroglyphs on patinated rock in the al-Jouf area, northern Saudi Arabia. This panel is typical of the rich rock art in this region.

Figure 126. Camel depictions such as these are found in the recent rock art of Arabia. Note the bullet hole in one of them. The older human figure is thought to be 2000-2500 years old. Pocalid Tabun, northern Saudi Arabia.

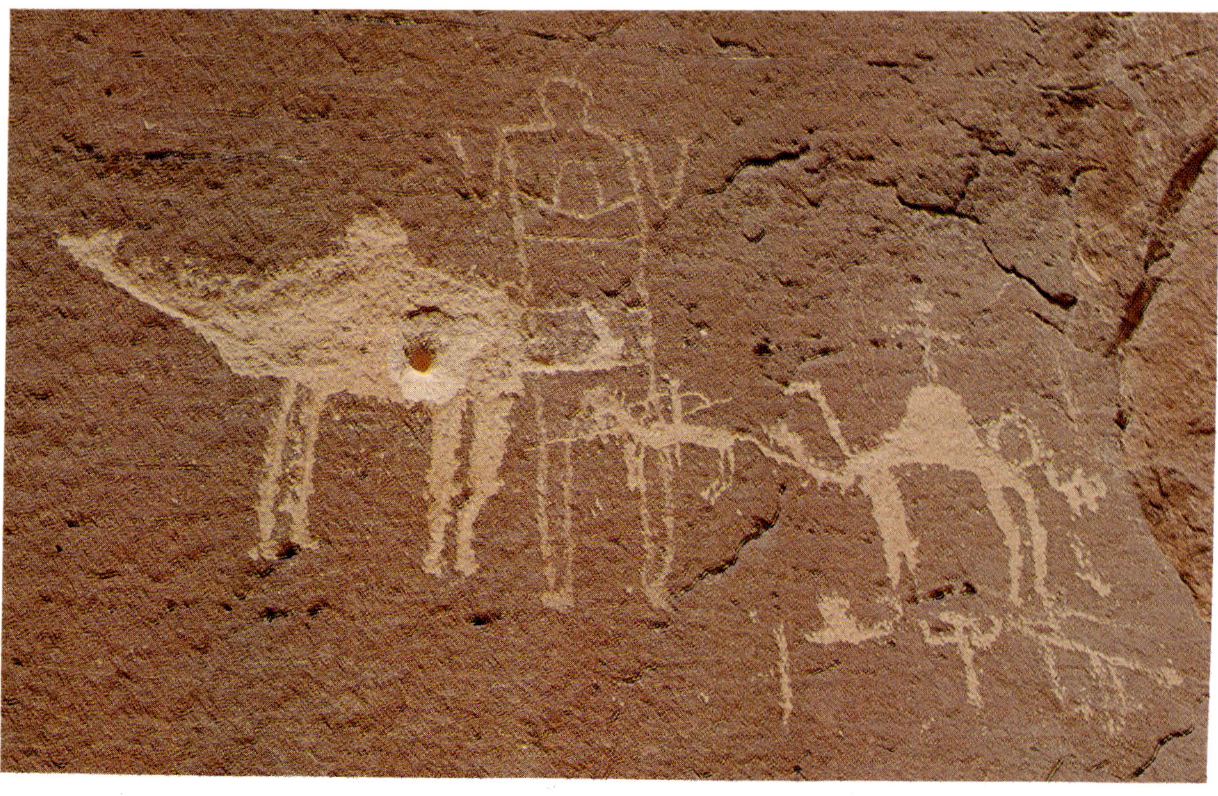

• EUROPE'S ROCK ART HERITAGE •

EUROPE'S ROCK ART HERITAGE

Europe, the western extension of the Eurasian land mass, is the natural way of continuing our world journey. In continuing also our description of Siberia it is appropriate to consider the European Russian rock art next. Here, suitable landforms, such as rockshelters, are not very common. The only well-known rock art region is that of Karelia, which geographically belongs to Scandinavia. Studied by several researchers, the region has been most thoroughly described by Juri Savvateyev. The sweeping granite pavements of this sub-arctic region, scraped clean by the advancing and retreating glaciers of the last Ice Age, have provided an excellent rock 'canvas' for the artists of the Late Stone Age (Neolithic), the Bronze Age and the Iron Age. The sites occur typically near water, on major rivers, lake shores, promontories and even on islands. The largest site complex is located where the River Vyg joins the White Sea, and it is dominated by Zalavruga Novaja. A large granite pavement, still showing the heavy wear traces of the Scandinavian glacier that last retreated 10,000 years ago, bears many hundreds of impact petroglyphs. They depict numerous scenes from the lives of ancient societies, including hunting scenes, a very large composition of several deer (Figure 127), boats with many oarsmen, even pictures of skiers (Figure 128). In some of these compositions, deliberate use has been made of the pavement's relief, which has been used skilfully to indicate topographical features such as hills and valleys. We know this because of the way

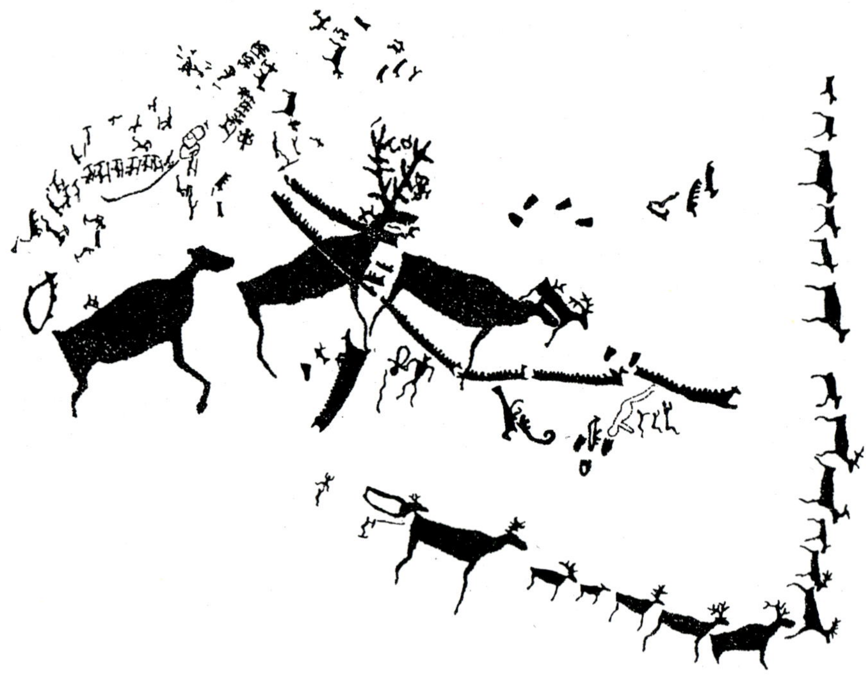

Figure 127. Petroglyphs of numerous deer or reindeer and other objects on granite pavement of Zalavruga Novaja, northern Karelia, Russia. Possibly of the Neolithic or later.

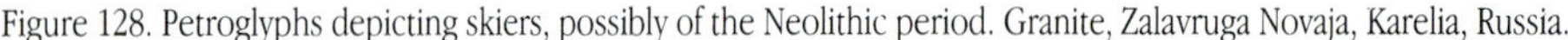

Figure 128. Petroglyphs depicting skiers, possibly of the Neolithic period. Granite, Zalavruga Novaja, Karelia, Russia.

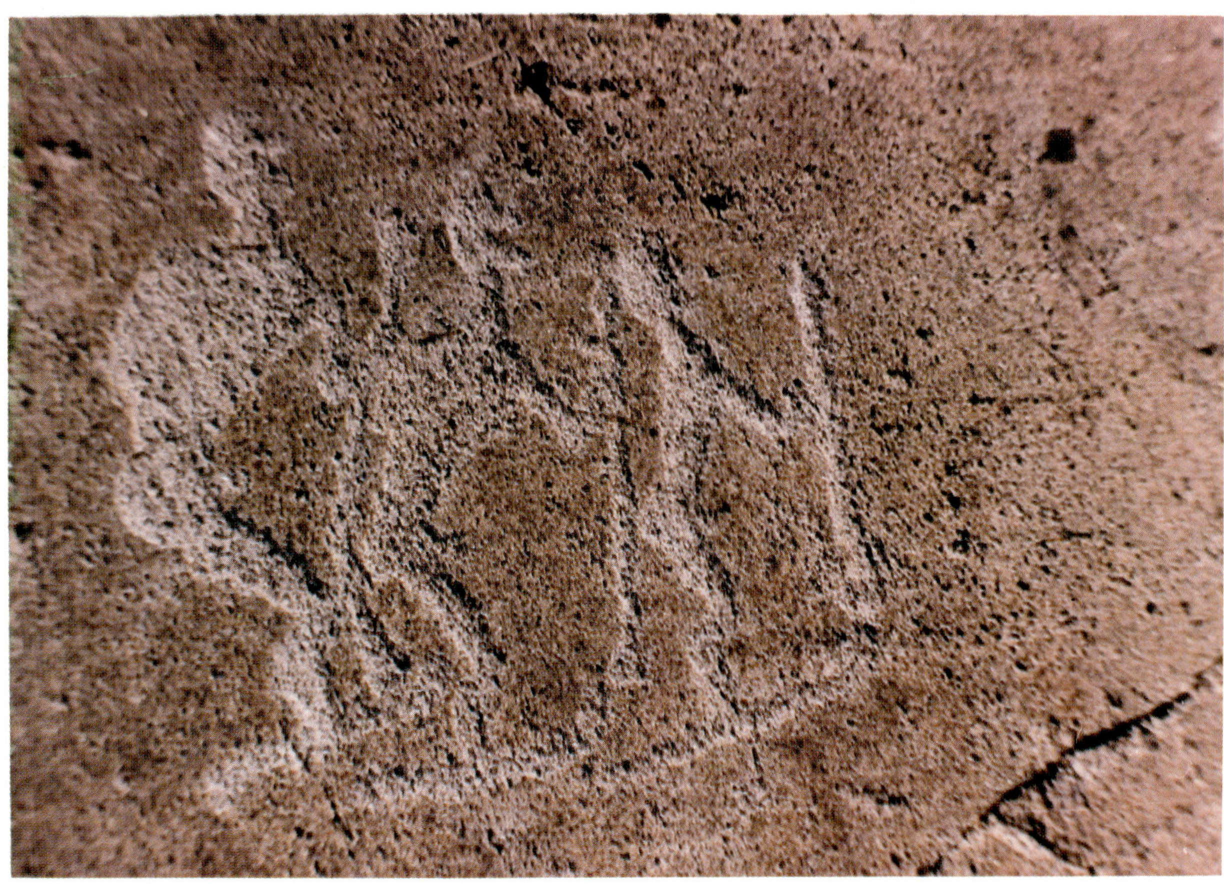

the ski tracks are depicted on these contour maps: they are continuous and sweeping downhill, but interrupted and accompanied by the marks left by the ski poles where the skier had to walk uphill. Arsen Faradzhev has shown that a variety of natural rock features have been skilfully incorporated in individual depictions.

Such economical methods of depiction are but one of many examples of the genial solutions rock artists explored in their work. They also show us that, far from always following rigorous cultural rules and patterns, the artists often enjoyed considerable freedom of expression, and their inventiveness sometimes led them to unique graphic and technical solutions. Such exploration of possibilities is found in rock art traditions the world over, including the innovative use of rock features, the play of light and shadow, and many other artistic devices. It begins right from the earliest art forms we know of, in the Older Stone Age, and it continues right to the present day in art.

The second major petroglyph concentration of Karelia is on the east shore of Lake Onega, where a series of twenty-two sites comprises a rich repertoire of motifs. Pictures of swans occur often, also unexplained depictions of apparent objects which Russian researchers have suggested depict animal traps. Aquatic animal species are common in this area's rock art, as well as pictures of elks and reindeer. The most famous figure at Lake Onega is that of the 'demon' at Besov Nos, which was the first rock art motif dated by the microerosion dating method (Figure 129). It is about 4000 years old. About 500 years ago, Christian monks from a nearby monastery placed a cross petroglyph over this human figure, apparently as a religious measure of 'neutralising' the 'pagan art'. Finally, there are a few sites on Kola Peninsula and elsewhere in Russian Lapland, and they even include rock paintings. They are the northernmost sites of rock art known in the world, being inside the Arctic Circle. Only portable art has been found further north, in Siberia and on islands north of Canada.

Elsewhere in Russia, rock art is not very common. The only other major concentration is in the mountains of the Caucasus and nearby regions, where many thousands of petroglyphs have been discovered in recent years. They are said to be from different phases of the last ten millennia, with the Neolithic component being prominent. However, these traditions remain poorly explored and undated. There are some very small occurrences of rock art also in the Ukraine.

Petroglyph traditions continue further to the west, across the Scandinavian countries. Throughout this

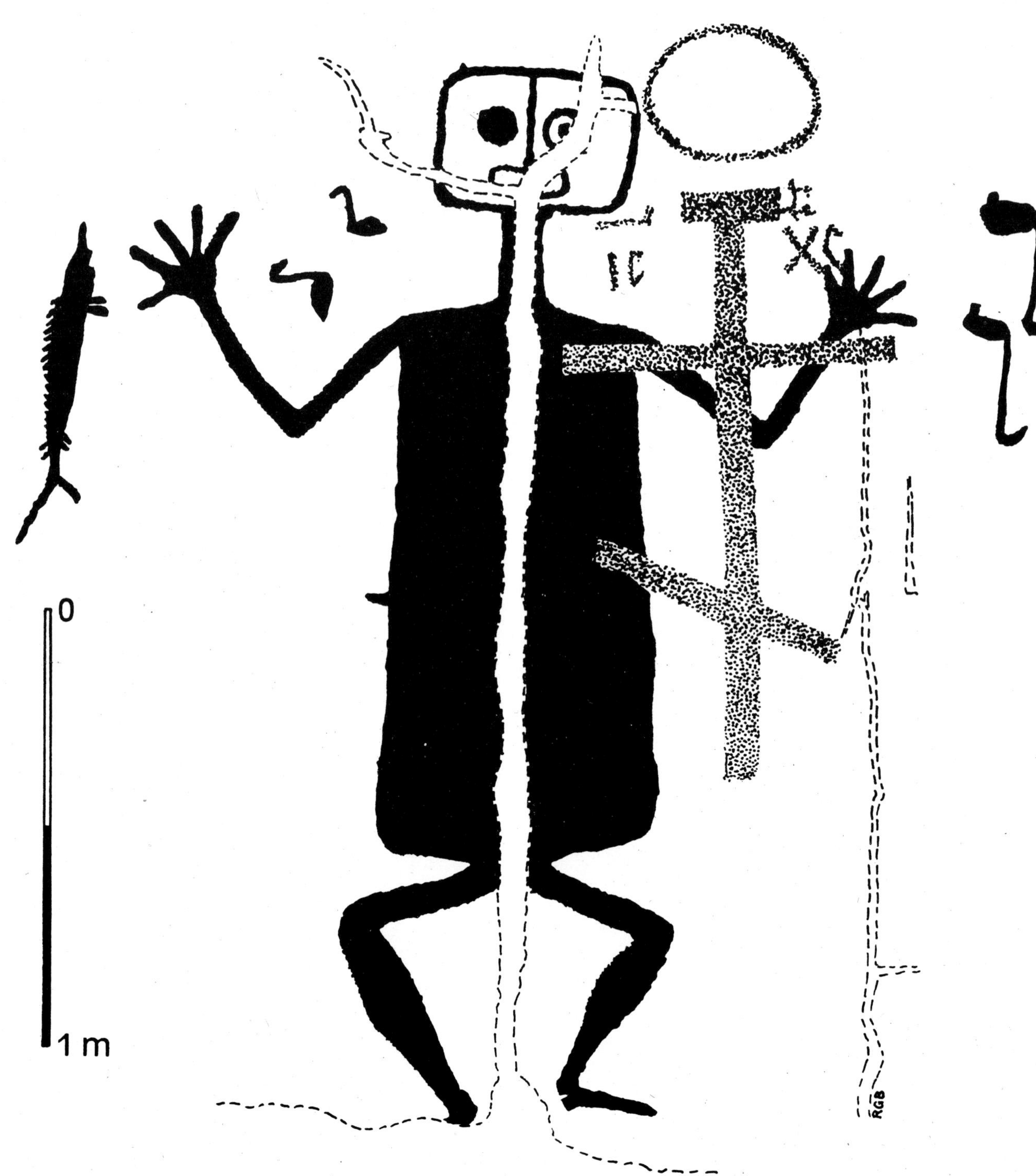

Figure 129. Petroglyph of the so-called demon at Besov Nos, at c. 4000 years old, of the Neolithic, eastern shore of Lake Onega, Karelia, Russia.

region, the rock art must be more recent than the last glacial period, the last Ice Age. The glaciers scoured the landscape so extensively that no Ice Age settlement evidence or rock art have ever been found in the region - if indeed such settlements ever existed there. Hence Scandinavian rock art is generally assumed to be of the post-glacial period, which includes the Late Stone Age (Mesolithic and Neolithic) and the metal ages (Bronze and Iron Ages). However, the ages that have been assigned to individual motifs, sites or rock art traditions are not secure, and are largely based on speculation.

In Finland we find many rock painting sites among the countless lakes of that country, but in Sweden, Norway and Denmark, the rock art consists almost entirely of petroglyphs (Figure 130). Their study and recording has been keenly pursued by the Scandinavians for a long time. Indeed, one of the oldest published records of rock art is from Sweden, from the seventeenth century.

Scandinavian petroglyphs are dominated by boat figures, comprising from 25-60%, not counting cupules (cup-shaped marks). Circles and circles with internal crosses are also common, with depictions of humans and animals being the least common group. Some of the major concentrations are very well known, such as Alta in Norway. The old tradition of studying Scandinavian rock art is being continued by many contemporary scholars, among them Mats Malmer, Ulf Bertilsson and Jarl Nordbladh in Sweden; Knut Helmskog, Kalle Sognnes and Gro Mandt in Norway; and Gerhard Milstreu in Denmark. The state of rock art recording, accordingly, is excellent, and perhaps among the best in the world. Rock art dating, however, is less secure, and largely related to archaeological speculation, and the interpretation of apparent figurative content. Many of the chronological pronouncements of Scandinavian rock art students are no doubt correct, but their validity needs to be demonstrated by scientific dating where possible. Surprisingly, there is also a problem with the conservation of this art in Scandinavia, in that students have been careless in their enthusiasm. Many past recording projects may have affected the scientific research potential of the art, through the application of various enhancing substances.

The British Isles are also rich in petroglyphic rock arts, which are surprisingly little known internationally. Except where they relate to megalithic structures and similar archaeological features, they have attracted comparatively little sustained research effort. The British rock art is entirely non-figurative, i.e. no depicted objects can be

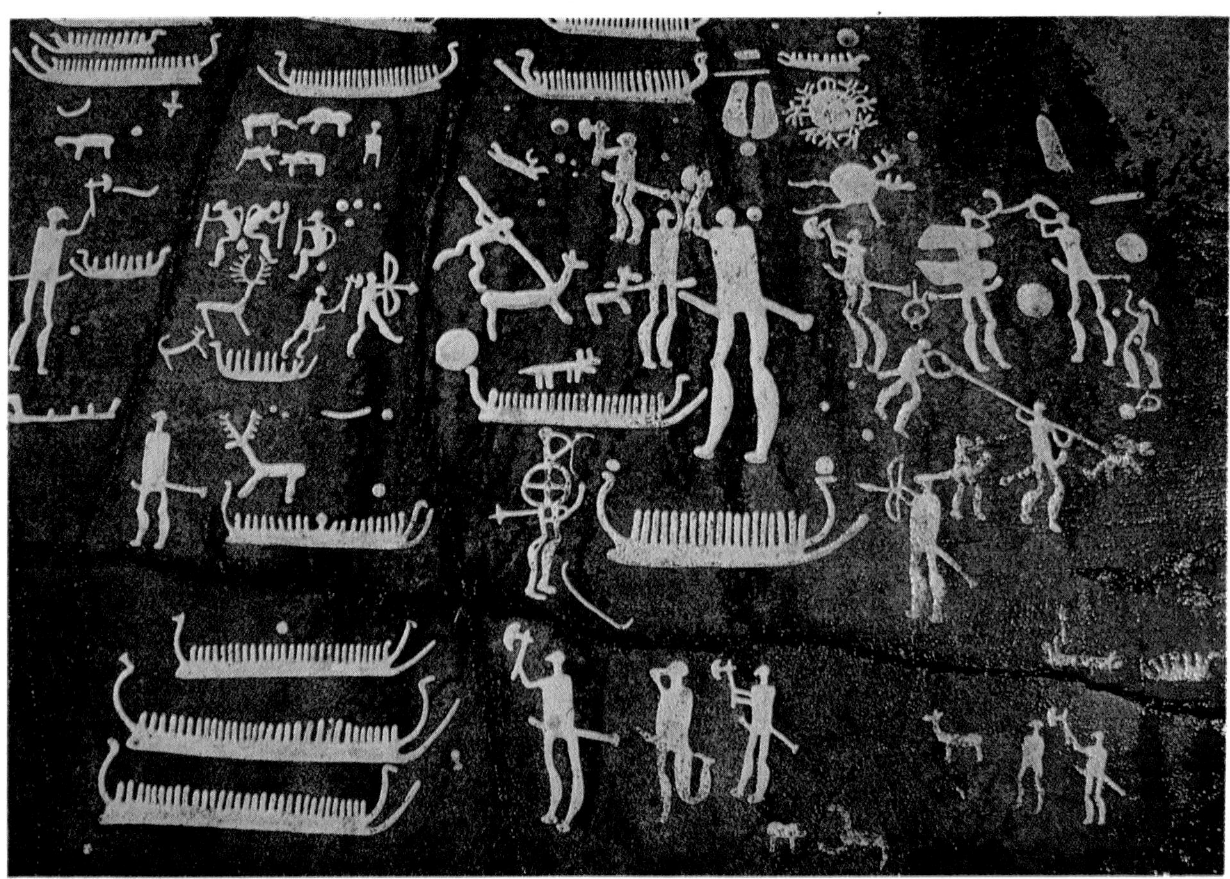

Figure 130. Petroglyphs on pavement at Fossum, Bohuslän, Sweden. These figures, like so many others in the Scandinavian countries, have unfortunately been painted, which means that they have become undatable because of the contamination this vandalism involves.

recognized in it by us. They consist frequently of cupules, spirals, concentric circles and complex geometric mazes. Traditionally it has been thought that they are essentially of recent pre-Historic periods, and necessarily associated with the stone structures on which they are sometimes found. However, real dating evidence is not so readily available, and two Canadian researchers have recently pointed out that there is no proof that some of these traditions may not be considerably older, and may in fact be of hunter- gatherer societies. One of the valid points made in this context is that some of the rocks incorporated in monumental structures were in fact already decorated with petroglyphs at the time they were used in monument construction. Throughout the world we have evidence that rock art was used and re-used by subsequent cultures, often without any knowledge of the people who originally created the art. The art was simply recognised as a non-natural feature in the natural landscape, and thus attributed to some powerful spirit beings, such as the creators of the world. It is therefore quite possible that rocks of special significance, because they were decorated, were intentionally incorporated in the construction of megalithic structures. This rock art occurs particularly in northern England, Scotland and parts of Ireland.

A very similar rock art tradition can be found on the Iberian Peninsula, notably in Portugal. But besides the typical British motif repertoire it includes an additional component, figurative pictures. There is a considerable variety of other rock art to be found in Portugal, including a few sites of presumed Upper Palaeolithic art (of the Older Stone Age, and thus over 10,000 years old). Among them are Mazouco and the recently discovered site Canada do Inferno, in the Côa valley. Interestingly, these are open sites, which contrasts with the belief that the Palaeolithic art of western Europe is endemic to caves. The Côa petroglyphs, however, have recently been dated to a much more recent age, of only a few thousand years.

The rest of the Iberian Peninsula, occupied by Spain, offers a rich selection of rock art traditions, from the Upper Palaeolithic to the recent Historical periods. Again, there are open air Palaeolithic rock art sites, but their dating remains to be confirmed scientifically. Particularly well known are the cave sites of the Upper Palaeolithic, mainly in the north of the country, in Cantabria. The most famous of all is Altamira, discovered well over a century ago, but rejected for decades by the archaeologists of the time. The density of such cave art sites found in the Cantabrian mountains is matched only in the Pyrenean mountains and in the French Dordogne. In all there are about 120 Palaeolithic rock art sites in Spain.

The second famous Spanish rock art tradition is the Levantine shelter art, in the country's eastern provinces. It consists entirely of rock paintings, usually in red, which are distinguished by their dynamic style (Figure 131). In contrast to Palaeolithic rock art, which features almost no human figures (it consists largely of animal pictures and various geometric signs or other non-figurative arrangements), Levantine art offers many lively scenes involving humans, engaged in various activities, including hunting and honey gathering.

The age of this art body was originally assumed to be over 10,000 years (i.e. Palaeolithic), then it was for many decades attributed to the subsequent Mesolithic period. Recently, however, Spanish researchers have again revised the chronological position of this art, placing it into the even more recent Neolithic age (the latest Stone Age). This is a good example of the subjectivity of so much rock art dating of past years. Time and again, researchers have found that rock art attribution to 'hunting peoples' on the basis of apparent pictorial content turned out to be wrong, whereas true hunting and gathering societies produced not a single depiction of hunting, and even depicted animals only rarely in their rock art (e.g. Bradshaw art in Kimberley, Australia). Spain has boasted many eminent rock art scholars over the past century, but among those still active today, Antonio Beltran has perhaps been the most productive.

In France, the Upper Palaeolithic rock art of the limestone caves occurs in 150 sites. The best known among them are perhaps Lascaux, Font-de-Gaume, Rouffignac (Figures 132 and 133), Les Combarelles (all in the Dordogne), Pech Merle (Figure 134), Cougnac (Figure 135) (both in Lot), Les Trois Frères, Niaux and Montespan (all in the Pyrenees). Just a few years ago, in 1991, a particularly spectacular site was discovered on the Mediterranean coast, near Marseilles: Cosquer Cave, perhaps the crown jewel among the French sites. It was soon rejected publicly as a fraud by eminent French prehistorians, without any examination, precisely as had happened a century earlier with Altamira. The archaeological establishment does not seem to learn from its historical mistakes. Discovered by the diver Henri Cosquer, its long entrance tunnel is now totally beneath the sea, with the entrance itself over forty metres below sea level. Entry remains extremely dangerous, and in two separate tragic accidents, several divers have already died trying to find their way through the entrance tunnel.

Experienced French Navy divers remain terrified of the site and its dangers. At the time of the Ice Age, the entrance was well above sea level, but with the rise of the oceans due to the melting of the polar ice caps, the entrance tunnel became flooded, and the art inside the deepest chamber was preserved in pristine condition. The rock art has been studied by France's most eminent rock art scholar, Jean Clottes, without ever setting foot in it: divers took a video camera and radio equipment into the art gallery, while Dr. Clottes directed them from a boat nearby to examine every detail on a video monitor. Very few people have ever been in Cosquer Cave so far, so it remains the perhaps best preserved example we have of European Ice Age cave art.

Other cave sites in France are accessible to the public, but some have had to be closed, or numbers of visitors have had to be severely restricted for the protection of the fragile art. Lascaux, discovered in 1940, has been closed to the public for many years, and only five people per day are allowed to enter now, under strictly controlled conditions. Visitors introduce microscopic organic particles and bacteria into the highly

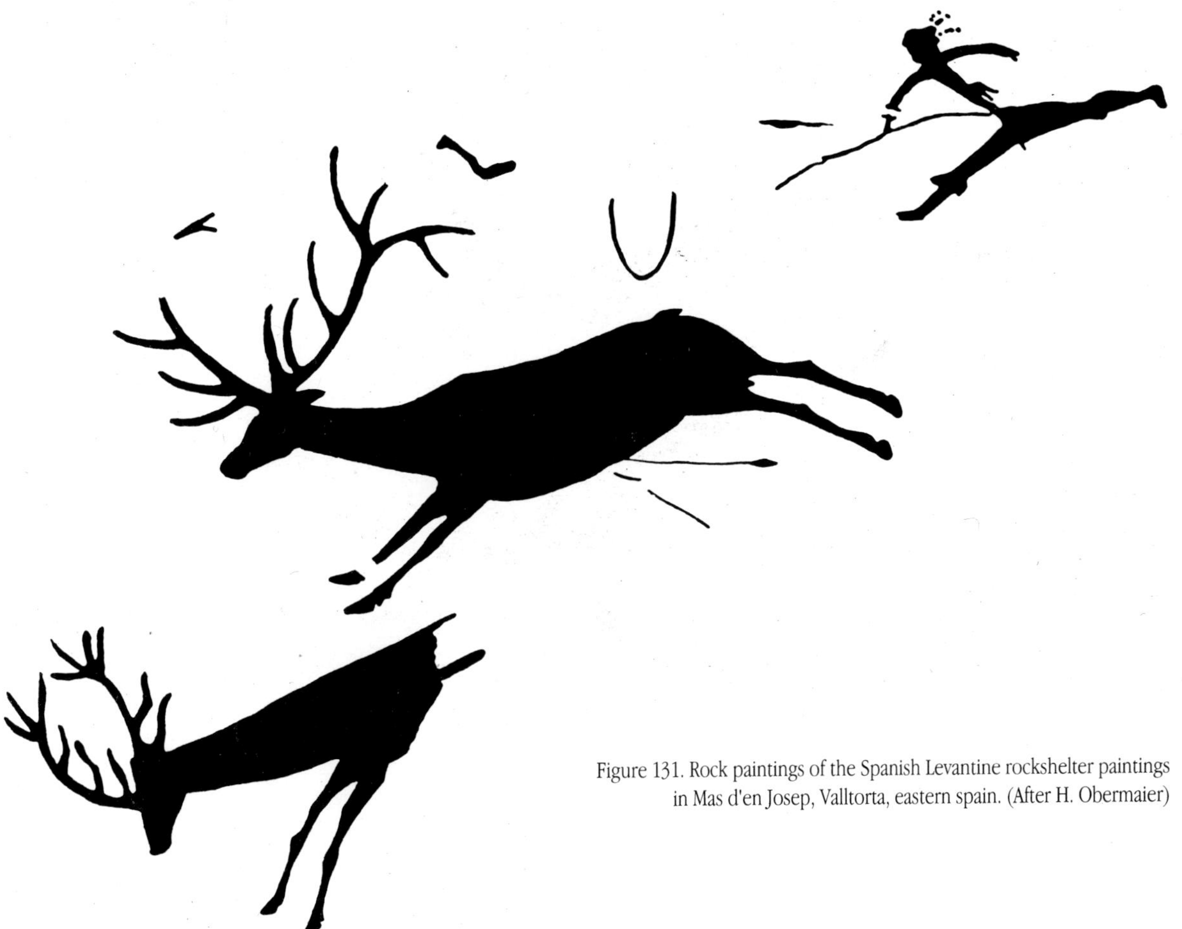

Figure 131. Rock paintings of the Spanish Levantine rockshelter paintings in Mas d'en Josep, Valltorta, eastern spain. (After H. Obermaier)

fragile cave environment, they alter temperature, relative air humidity and carbon dioxide content of the cave atmosphere. All of this is detrimental to the delicate rock art. The entire art of Lascaux has been replicated at the cost of some eight million dollars, in a facsimile of the cave painstakingly constructed in a nearby quarry. That site is called Lascaux II, it is a faithful reproduction of the original, and it attracts hundreds of thousands of tourists annually.

The work of the Upper Palaeolithic artists, like that of so many rock art traditions around the world, is characterised by an elegant, sophisticated economy of depiction, and by the same artistic maturity as found in most other rock arts. Both paintings and engravings occur, and in a number of sites one finds also extensive panels of finger markings on soft, or formerly soft, surfaces. Numerous scholars have dedicated their life work to the study of this art corpus, but the most famous were perhaps Henri Breuil and André Leroi-Gourhan. While their models may now be superseded, at least partially, their pioneer work remains crucially important to the discipline.

Upper Palaeolithic rock art is not the only form of rock art found in France, but its significance has completely overshadowed the study of all other rock art regions and periods in that country.

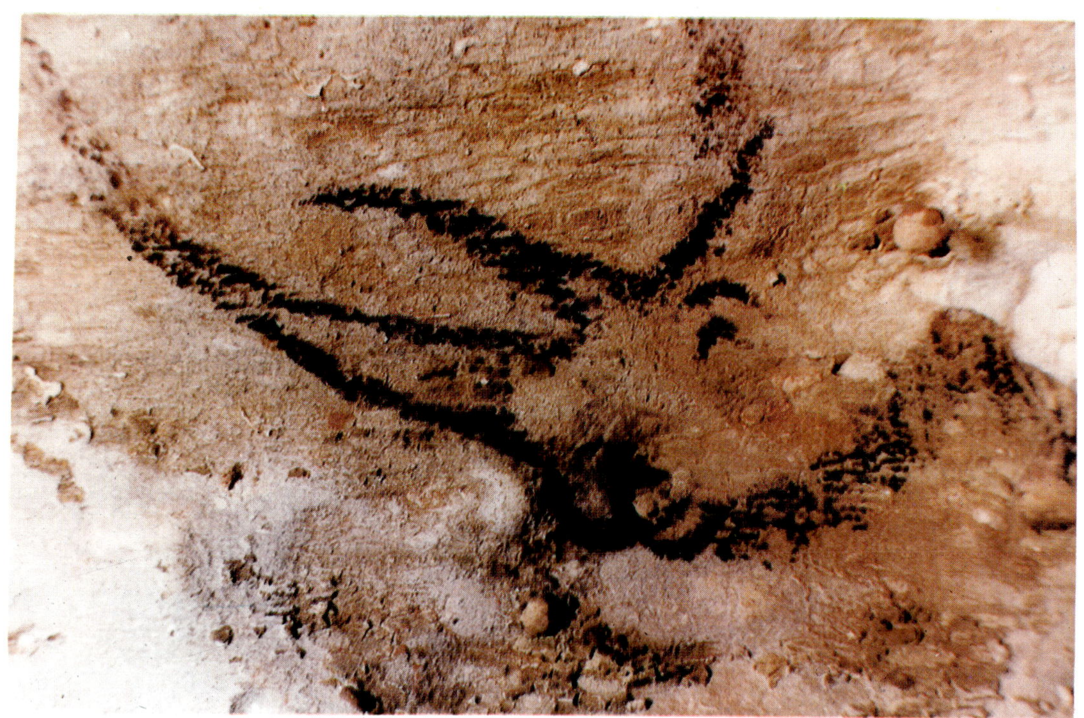

Figure 132. Painting of a woolly rhinoceros, Upper Palaeolithic, Rouffignac Cave, Dordogne, France.

One such example is a large corpus of rock art found in the rockshelters of a sandstone massif just south of Paris, Fontainebleau, where nearly a thousand sites are now documented. This art consists entirely of petroglyphs, and is frequently found as geometric, non-figurative deep incisions and engravings (Figure 136). Some of this art includes written characters and inscriptions, and is obviously of Historical age, while other components appear to be much older. Even a very small Palaeolithic component may be present.

A second regional petroglyph tradition found in France occurs in the western Alps, at considerable elevations. This is actually part of a major petroglyph body typical of the Alpine valleys and mountains, where it may be found at 2000 to 3000 metres above sea level. This rock art region extends from eastern France across the north of Italy, and to some extent into the Austrian Alps. The perhaps best known sites are Mont Bego, Merveilles and Fontainebleau in France, but other concentrations are also notable, for instance in Val di Aosta, Valtellina, and most particularly the famous rock art corpus of Val Camonica (all in Italy). Val Camonica, a beautiful Alpine valley near Milan, has been estimated to contain up to 300,000 petroglyphs. The true number may be somewhat lower, but there can be no doubt that this is one of Europe's most outstanding rock art assemblages (Figure 137-a, b, c). It has been studied most thoroughly by Emmanuel Anati, who has established an international rock art study centre in the valley, at Capo di Ponte. Another eminent rock art scholar working with his team in the southern Alps is Dario Seglie, who hails from the historical city Pinerolo, near Turin.

The Alpine petroglyphs often occur on rock exposures that have been scoured by the glaciers of the last Ice

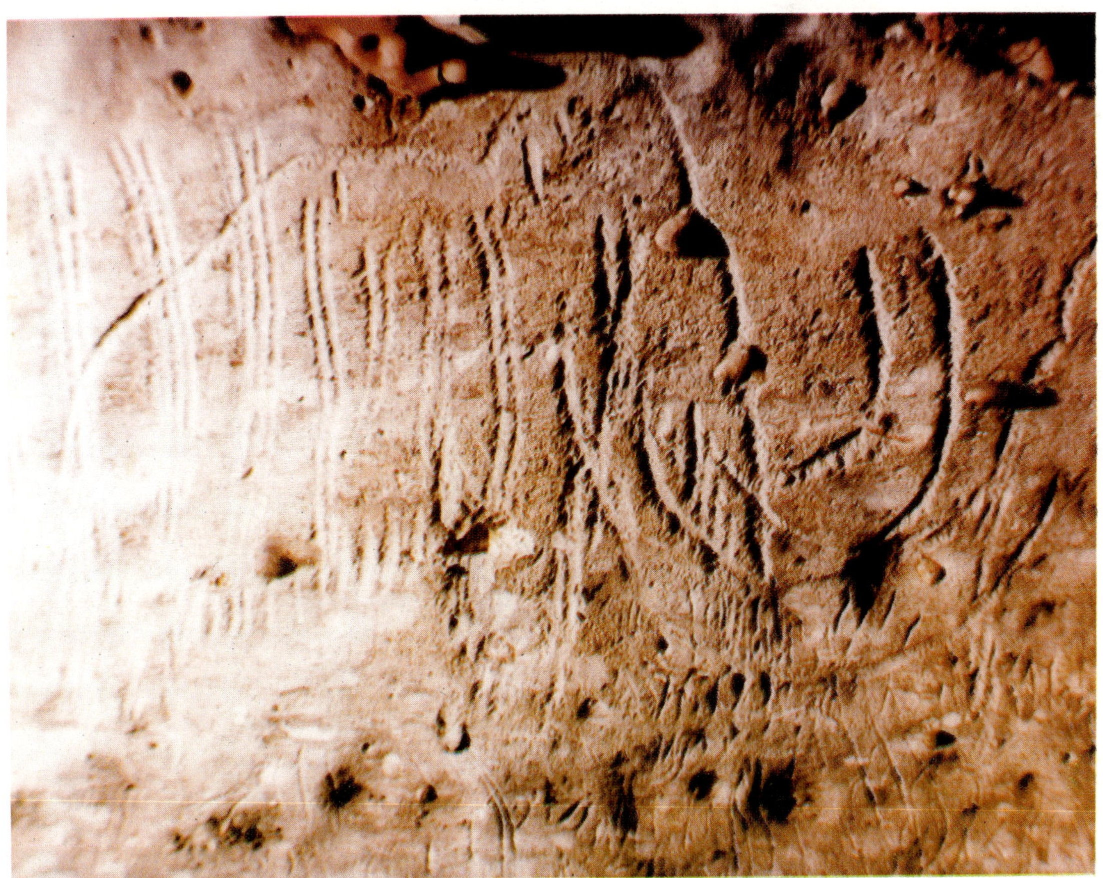

Figure 133. Engraving of a mammoth and finger markings as well as cave bear scratches, Upper Palaeolithic, Rouffignac Cave, Dordogne, France.

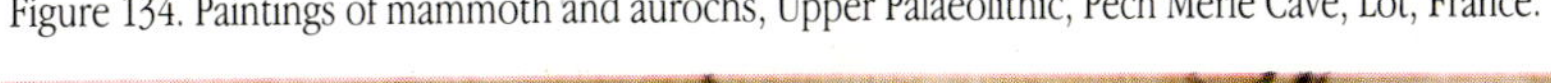

Figure 134. Paintings of mammoth and aurochs, Upper Palaeolithic, Pech Merle Cave, Lot, France.

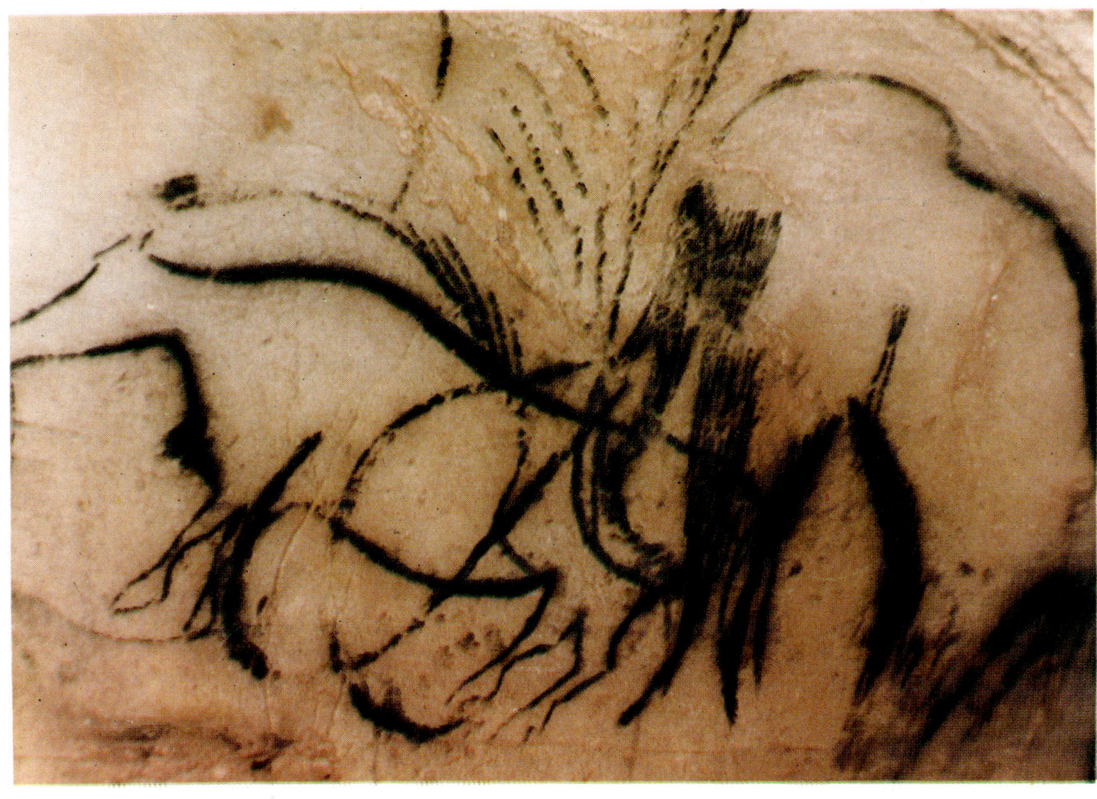

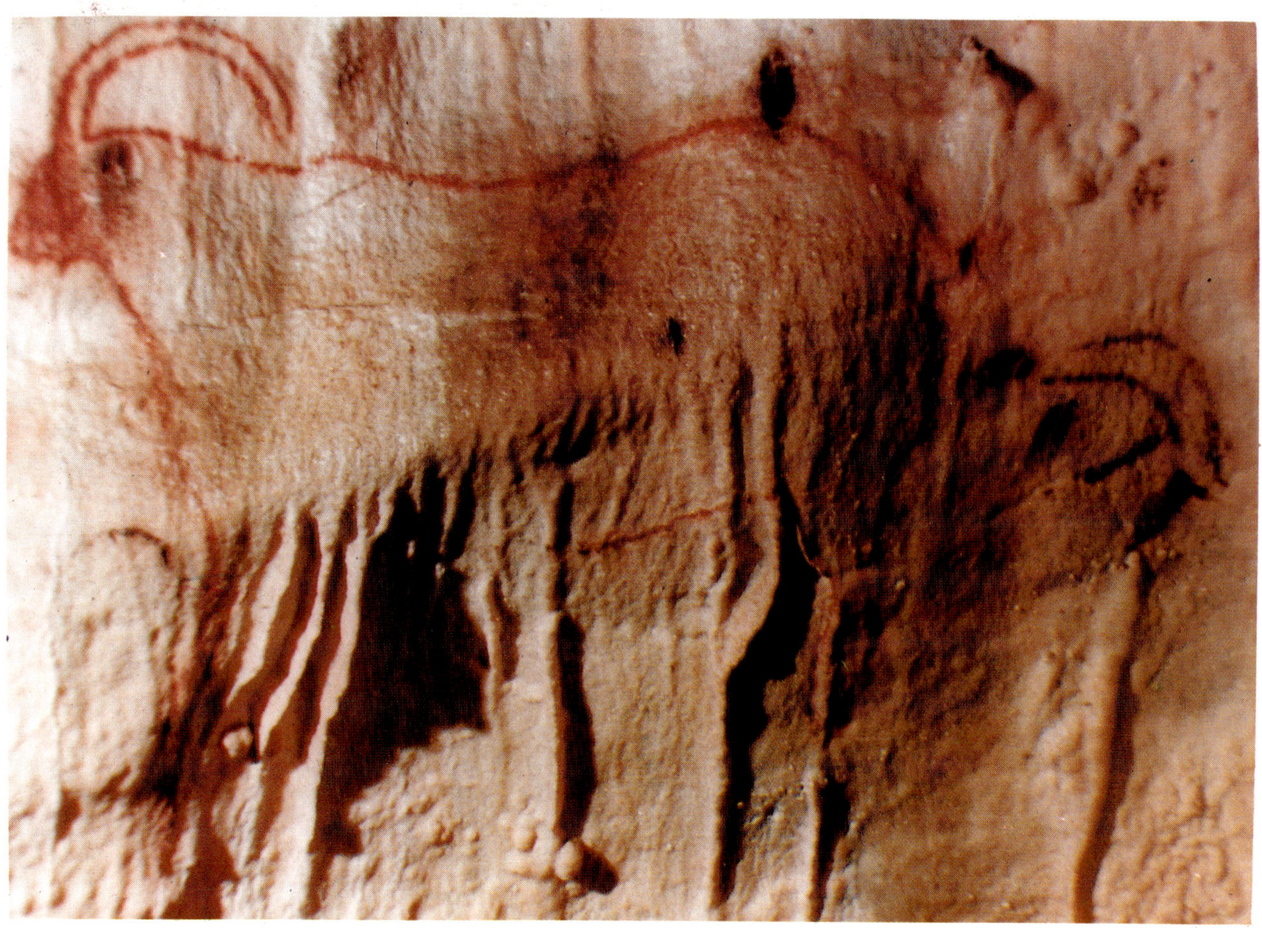

Figure 135. Painting of megaloceros, Upper Palaeolithic, Cougnac, Lot, France.

Age, as we have seen is also the case in Scandinavia and Karelia. These smooth, striated surfaces provided the blackboards of artists from many traditions. The art seems to begin with Epi-Palaeolithic figures, not very much younger than 10,000 years. It documents the later rise of agriculture, the emergence of warriors and armed conflict in the metal ages, and ultimately the appearance of writing.

While the Alpine petroglyph tradition extends into Austria, it seems to consist only of the more recent phases there. The major concentration in this country is that of the Totes Gebirge, in the province of Upper Austria. Dating is again by apparent subject content and by the interpretation of inscriptions and symbols. Small rock art corpora are found in various parts of the Balkans, for instance in the former Yugoslavia, in Macedonia, Bulgaria, Rumania, Albania and Greece. There are even a very few isolated examples of probably Upper Palaeolithic art (in Yugoslavia, Bulgaria and even in the Ural Mountains of Russia). Not much is known about these traditions, however. Hence even in Europe, where some rock art corpora are no doubt better explored than any others in the world, there remain significant lacunae in our knowledge. ❐

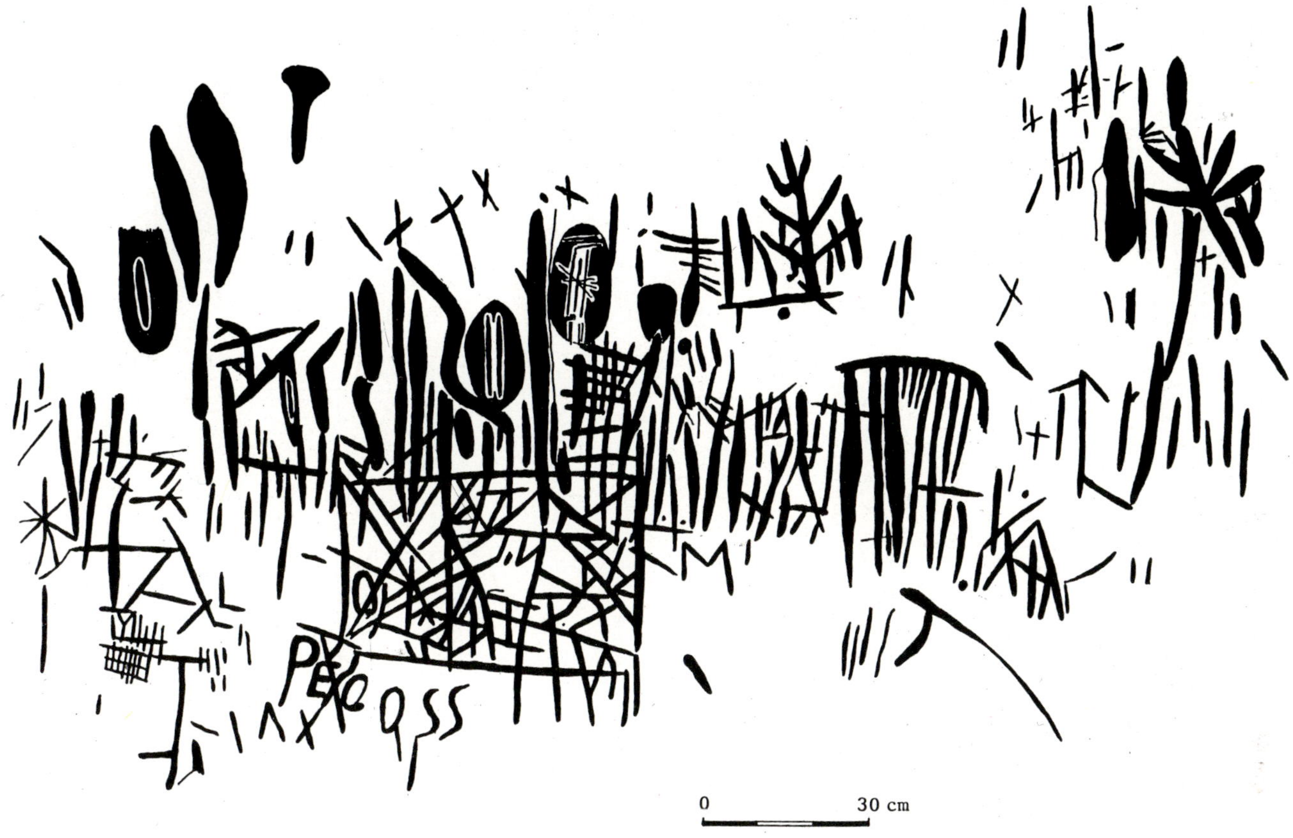

Figure 136. Geometric engravings in the sandstone shelter Caveme du Chamois, Fontainebleau Massif, south of Paris, France.

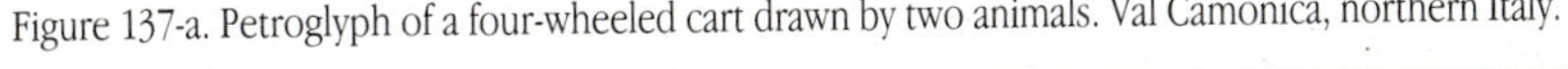
Figure 137-a. Petroglyph of a four-wheeled cart drawn by two animals. Val Camonica, northern Italy.

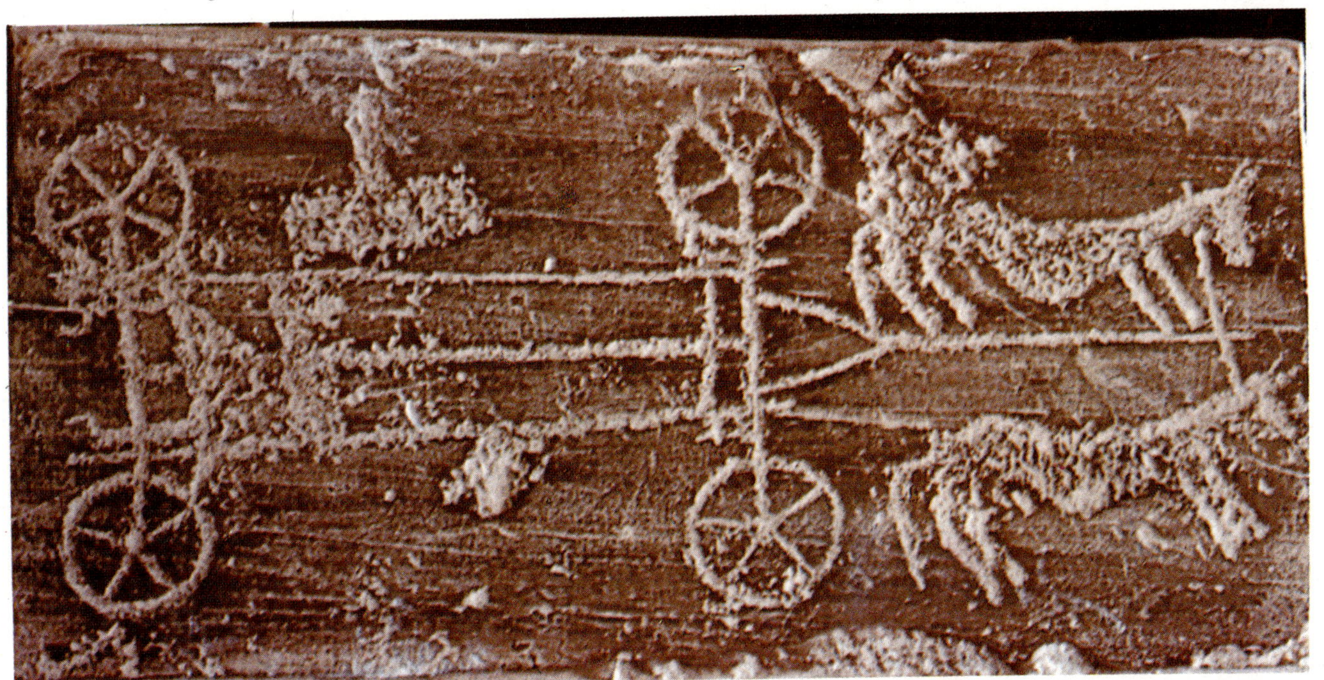

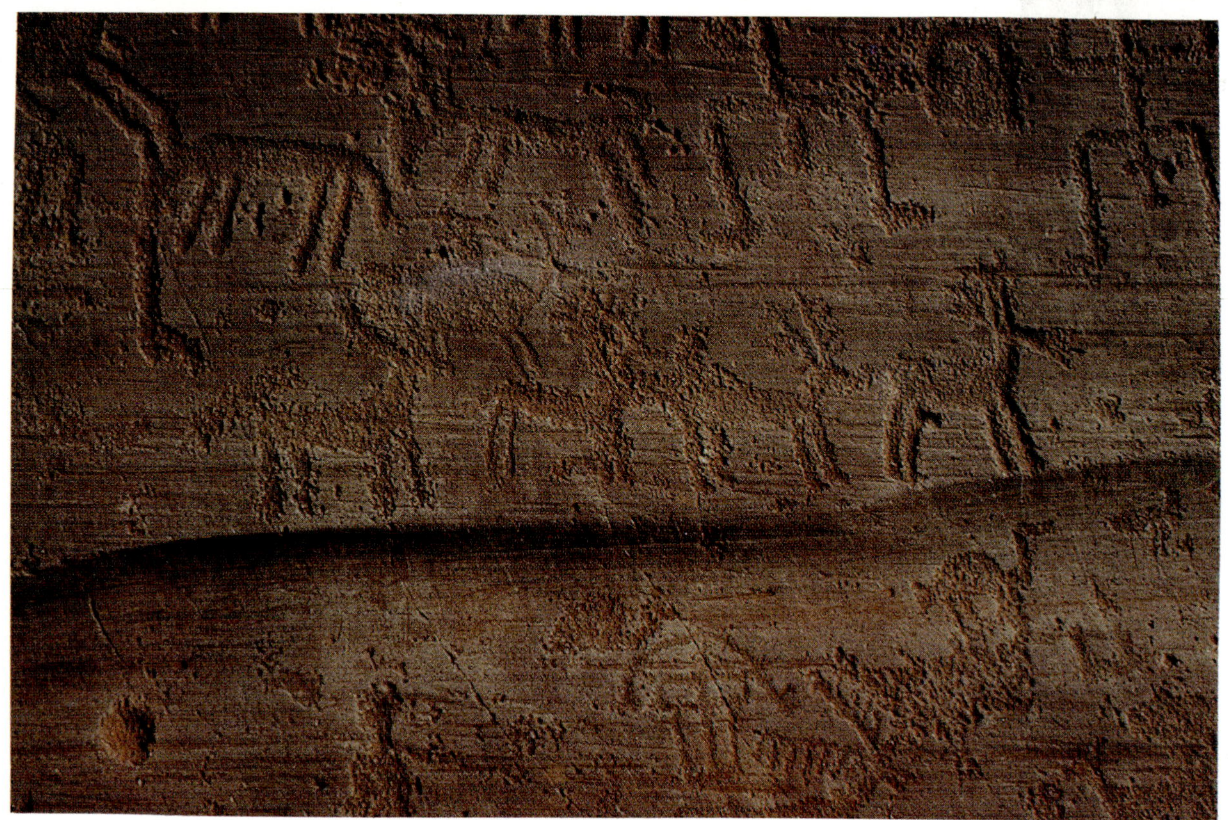

Figure 137-b. Group of stags, Naquane, Val Camonica, Italy

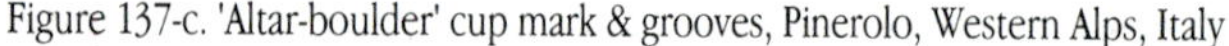

Figure 137-c. 'Altar-boulder' cup mark & grooves, Pinerolo, Western Alps, Italy

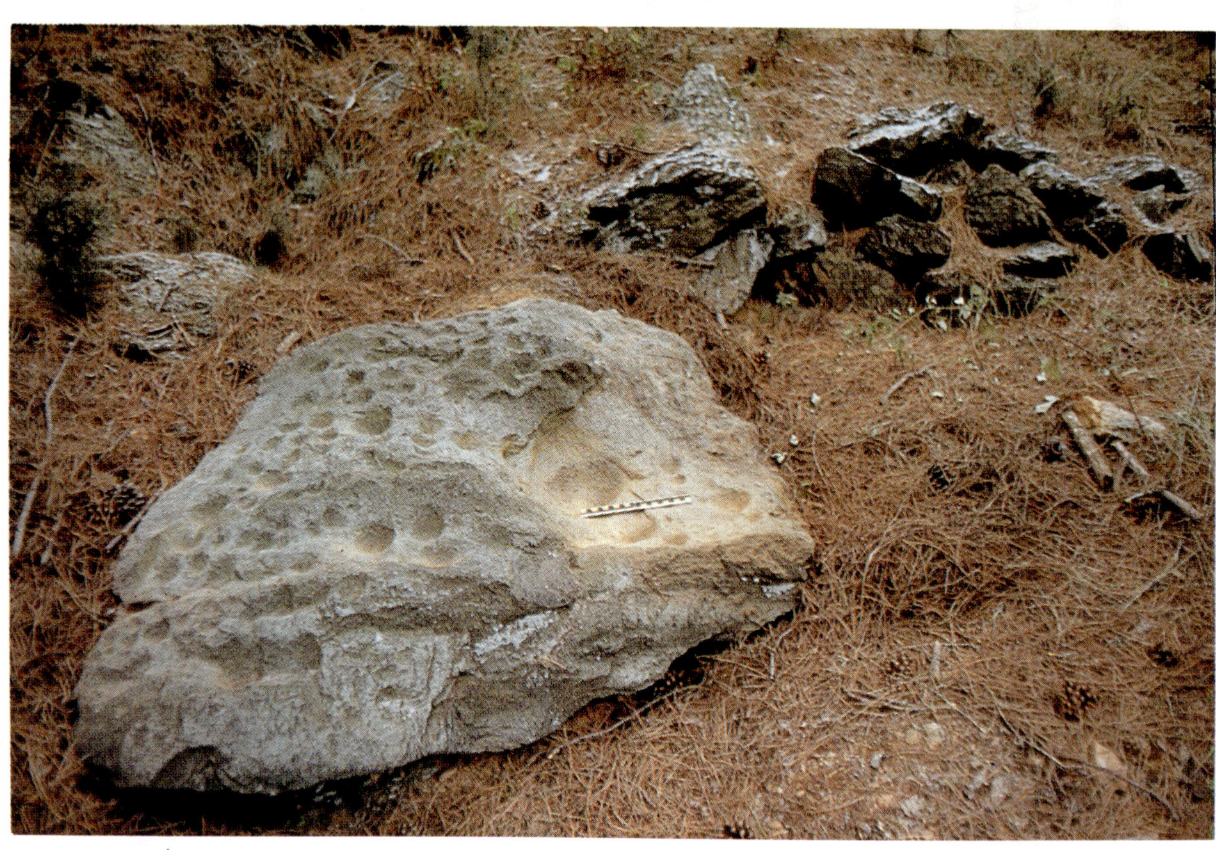

• THE EARLY ART OF AFRICA •

THE EARLY ART OF AFRICA

In considering the earliest arts of Africa we will travel through the continent from north to south. The best-explored regions, apart from southern Africa, are those of the largest desert on earth, the Sahara. Traditionally, European researchers have taken a great interest in this large corpus of rock art, particularly those from Italy, France and Germany. More recently, however, local researchers have made important contributions also, particularly in Algeria and Morocco.

First reports about Saharan rock art appeared in 1830, and in 1850, Heinrich Barth reported petroglyphs of the 'Bubaline school' in the Oued Mathendous, Libya. The famous rock paintings of the Tassili were first reported about 1910, and an initial attempt to summarise Saharan rock art appeared eleven years later. With the work of L. Frobenius and H. Obermaier in 1925, systematic studies commenced, and with them the thorny problem of identifying specific traditions and assigning approximate ages to them. Italian researchers such as P. Graziosi focused on Libyan art bodies, while the French worked mostly in Algeria. Some prominent scholars upheld an Ice Age antiquity for the older component, and diffusionist ideas were favoured for decades. In the 1950s, Henri Lhote emerged as the major scholar in the area, and since his work in the subsequent decades, several recent specialists have

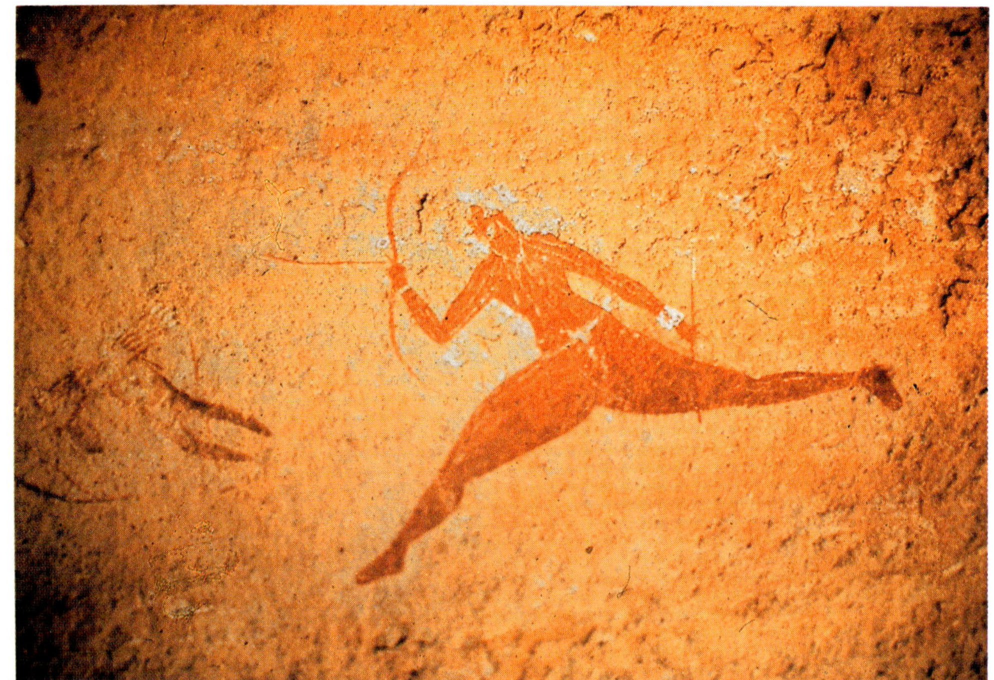

Figure 138. Rock painting interpreted as that of a running archer, Early Bovidian tradition, Sefar, Tassili-n- Ajjer, Algeria.

provided important improvements. Among them are F. Mori, who provided supplementary dating evidence in the Abacus mountains; François Soleilhavoup, producing very detailed technical recordings of petroglyphs on which he includes geomorphological details; Alfred Muzzolini, who clarified important chronological points; Jean-Loïc Le Quellec, contributing new approaches to questions of interpretation; and Karl-Heinz Striedter, who worked in the southern Sahara, in Niger and Mali.

Both petroglyphs and rock paintings are amply represented across northern Africa, from Morocco to the shores of the Red Sea, from the Atlas mountains to Lake Chad. Even on the Canary Islands, off the African west coast, rock art is quite common, and is found as both petroglyphs and paintings. The major, or best known, corpora are those of the Atlas region, the Ahaggar (Algeria), the Fezzan (Libya), the Aïr (Niger), Tibesti and Ennedi (Chad). The rock art does continue further east, through Egypt and Sudan. The Tassili murals, in southern Algeria, are perhaps the most famous Saharan rock art (Figure 138). Characterised by sophisticated and often highly ornate styles, these arts provide a wealth of graphic details about the societies that produced them.

The chronological attributions of Saharan rock arts have followed a pattern that is rather similar to that which we have noted in the Spanish Levantine rock art. After an initial belief that Ice Age art occurs in each region, this was modified to the succeeding Mesolithic period. But more recently that pronouncement was also rejected and a Neolithic age was demonstrated for the older component. In the case of the Sahara, the latter re-assignment was based on the observation that the tradition generally agreed to be

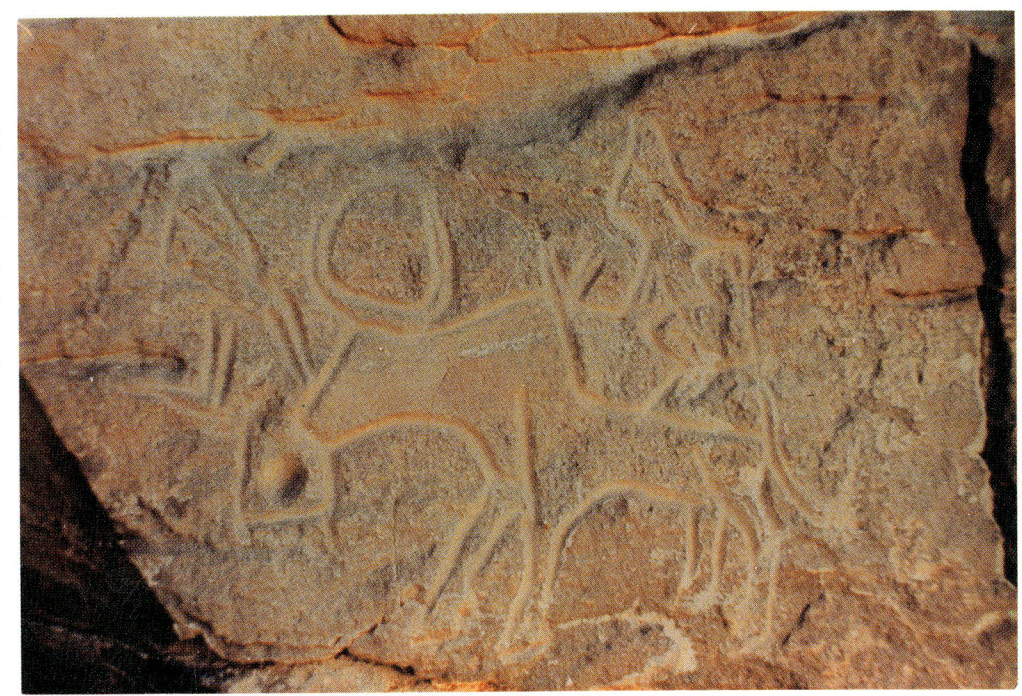

Figure 139. Petroglyphs of man seated on ox, woman walking. Naturalistic Bubaline tradition, Mathendous, Libya.

the oldest, called Naturalistic Bubaline school (Figure 139), includes clear depictions of sheep. This species was introduced in domesticated form only in the Neolithic period, 4000 to 6000 years ago. Therefore we have no unambiguous evidence that any rock art older than this time exists in the Sahara. Nevertheless, controversy concerning several details of the Saharan rock art chronology still lingers on, and there is no general agreement concerning the true ages, or even the true relative sequence. Not a single motif has been dated by direct dating, and until the results of such work become available it is appropriate to consider all these chronological models as tentative and speculative.

Another problem with much of the Saharan rock art is that it became immensely popular with cultural tourists in the 1970s and 1980s, without adequate protection of remote sites. This trend now endangers much of the most spectacular rock art of Africa, which should be a warning to rock art authors: if there are no means of effective protection, rock art must not be popularised, and publications should not provide Information on site locations. This applies not just to the popular literature, it applies to specialist literature as well. The only people who need to know the locations of sites are those whose responsibility it is to manage them.

There can be no doubt that a great many Saharan animal depictions refer to climatic and environmental conditions at the time the art was created that were significantly different from those found today. Pictures of buffaloes, elephants, giraffes and hippos, among many other species, bear witness to the many regional extinctions caused by the gradual desertification of most of northern Africa. The early Bubaline school is found in various regions, from

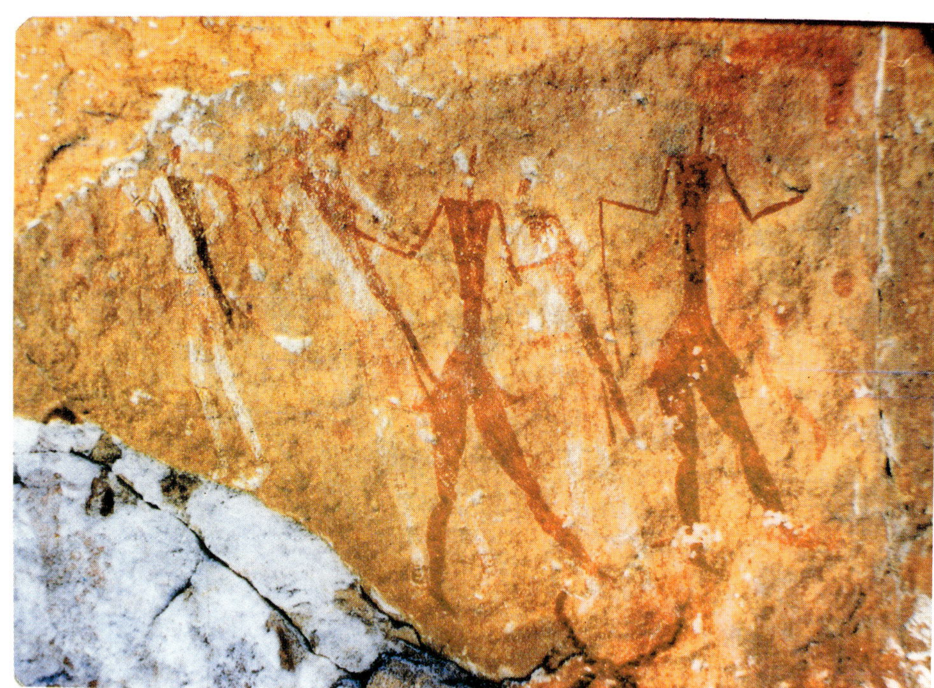

Figure 140-a. Three figures of the Early Horse Period and two classical Caballine figures, Imesseridjen, Tassili-n-Ajjer, Algeria.

the Atlas ranges to some of the Libyan art corpora. The contemporary to somewhat younger Round Head school is distinguished by its faceless human figures, and found especially in parts of the Tassili. The figures are thought to depict mythical beings, even though their interpretation as spacemen may be more popular. The Early Bovidian school (Figure 138) may also begin quite early, with cattle depictions being a prominent component. It continues to perhaps 3000 years ago, to be succeeded by the Horse Period (Figure 140-a,b), and by the appearance of written inscriptions. Finally, there is a Camel Period also, which might be suggestive of increasingly arid conditions, and which commences from about 2000 years ago. In some places, rock art has continued to be produced in recent time. In part of the Atlas, human footprint petroglyphs mark a continuing custom of eternalising the feet of bride and bridegroom at the time of their wedding.

With the discovery of the granite massif of Jebel Uweinat in 1923, the Saharan rock art body was seen to be connected to the much earlier known rock art of the Nile Valley and adjacent desert regions. It was in fact on the upper Nile, in Sudan, that Belzoni, an Italian archaeologist, first contemplated the possibility of scientific dating of rock art. He observed the different states of repatination on the petroglyphs there in the early nineteenth century. In 1820 he proposed that these patination differences might help in determining the ages of the various figures. Rock art is also found to the east of the Nile, for instance in the Nubian Desert. There, numerous depictions of pharaonic boats have been described. Of course a great deal of pharaonic monumental art work exists in Egypt, but it is not considered

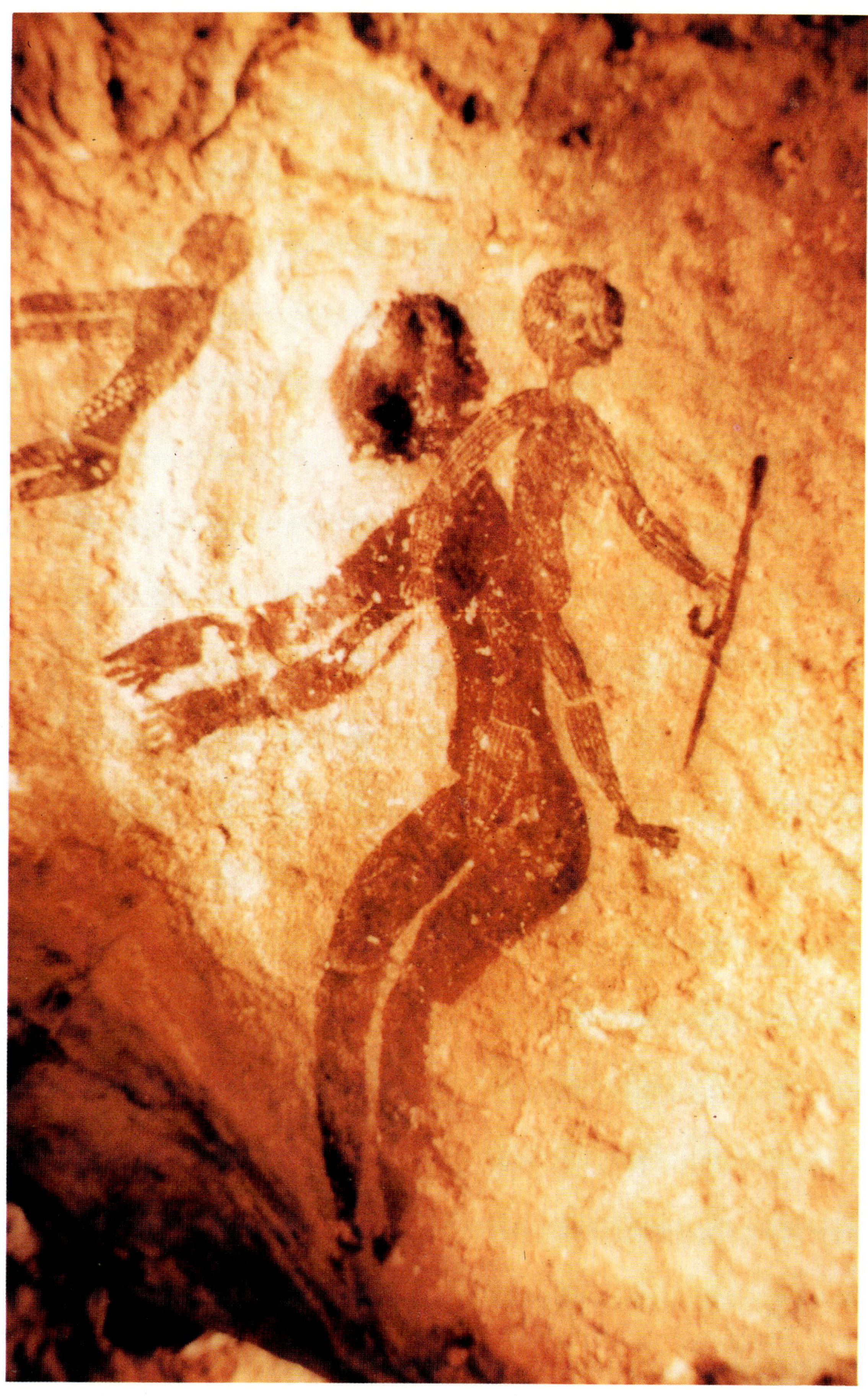

Figure 140-b. Rock paintings, Final Round Head tradition, 4000-5000 years old, Tan-Zoumaîtak, Tassili, Algeria.

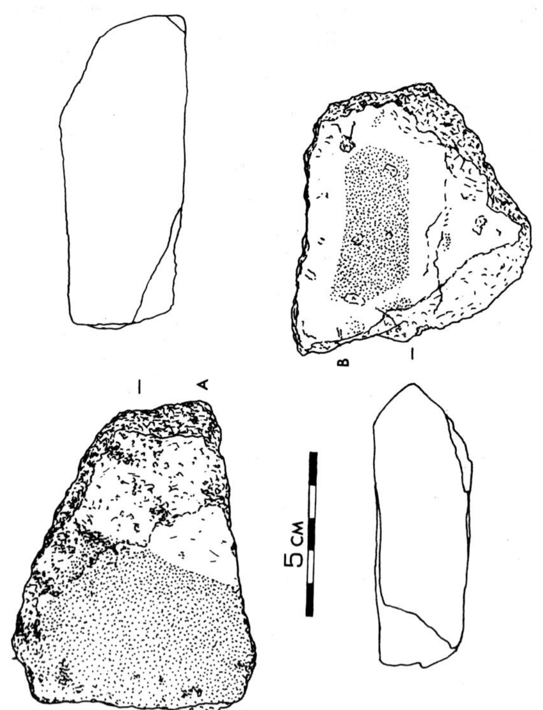

Figure 141. Two stone slabs with ochre patches, of the Middle Stone Age, Pomongwe Cave, Matopos, Zimbabwe. (After Nicholas Walker.)

under the general rubric of rock art.

As one proceeds south through Africa, there is hardly a country that lacks rock art altogether. Densities of sites and sizes of corpora may differ, and most particularly, reliable information is often not available. For instance there are reports from Ethiopia, Zaire and Gabon (petroglyphs only), but little sustained research work has been reported internationally. Our knowledge is considerably better in Kenya, especially from the work of Osaga Odak. He has provided detailed descriptions of Kenyan cupule petroglyphs, together with their ethnological interpretation. They were used in a kind of board game. In neighbouring Tanzania, Fidelius Masao is active, and Emmanuel Anati has provided an outline of Tanzanian rock art. But it should be emphasised that, contrary to popular misconception, Anati has not offered any early dating evidence for this art. He merely noted the very early presence of excavated ochre in Kisese 2, and he reminded us that in Namibia, a few thousand kilometres to the south-west, portable painted art of the Ice Age has been found. None of this is particularly relevant to the antiquity of rock art in Tanzania, however. Evidence of ochre or haematite use in southern Africa extends to earlier times than anywhere else in the world, and the use of such pigments does not necessarily indicate that it was employed in rock art production.

In Zimbabwe, a country about whose rock art we are comparatively well informed, portable stones bearing traces of red pigment have been found in extremely early archaeological contexts, in Bambata and Pomongwe Caves (Figure 141). The Charama levels of Bambata Cave yielded ochre fragments supposedly 125,000 years old. However, this is still exceeded in age by similar finds further south. In Lions' Cavern, South Africa, large-scale ochre mining traces have been observed along with large numbers of stone tools, and a radiocarbon date of 43,000 years confirms that this evidence is of the period called the Middle Stone Age in sub-Saharan Africa. But in the huge Wonderwork Cave, excavated by Peter Beaumont, haematite is found right down to the lowest living floors of the Acheulian. This is the very same, extremely old stone tool industry from which we have encountered very archaic evidence elsewhere. At this site, the lower strata remain undated, but have been suggested to be up to 800,000 or 900,000 years old. If it should prove correct that the use of ochre does extend to such extremely remote periods, then some of our ideas of early cognitive evolution of humans may be in need of further radical revision.

The rock art of Zimbabwe is found as both petroglyphs and paintings, and a rough chronology has been proposed for it (Figure 142). The largest concentration is located in the Matopos region, in the country's south. Less is known about the rock art of neighbouring Mozambique, but such art does occur there, and also continues to the south, through Botswana, Namibia, ultimately culminating in one of the greatest and most spectacular concentrations of the world, in South Africa.

The most prominent, and by far the best known rock art of southern Africa, is the art attributed to the Bushman or San people (Figure 143). Several very major concentrations of this art occur, in the Drakensberg Range, Ndedema Gorge, in Lesotho, on the Brandberg in Namibia, to name just the best-known concentrations. This art consists of paintings, it is among the most detailed rock art forms in the world, and it is often considered to be one of the most aesthetic traditions.

Its sheer numbers alone are impressive enough, but the detail found in it, the skilful use of colour to depict surface features, and the supreme control of painting techniques makes this one of the most highly valued rock arts in the entire world. Paintings include depictions of numerous animal species, of which those of the eland antelope have attracted much interest. There are also countless depictions of human figures, some of which have animal heads (depicting the use of masks or mythical beings?). A notable motif are the 'alites' or 'flying bucks', which seem to fly or float in the air (Figure 144).

Through its artistic sophistication this art has attracted the attention of many scholars, but the greatest contribution to its documentation is unquestionably that of Harald Pager, who was the greatest rock art recorder of this century. Other notable researchers of this

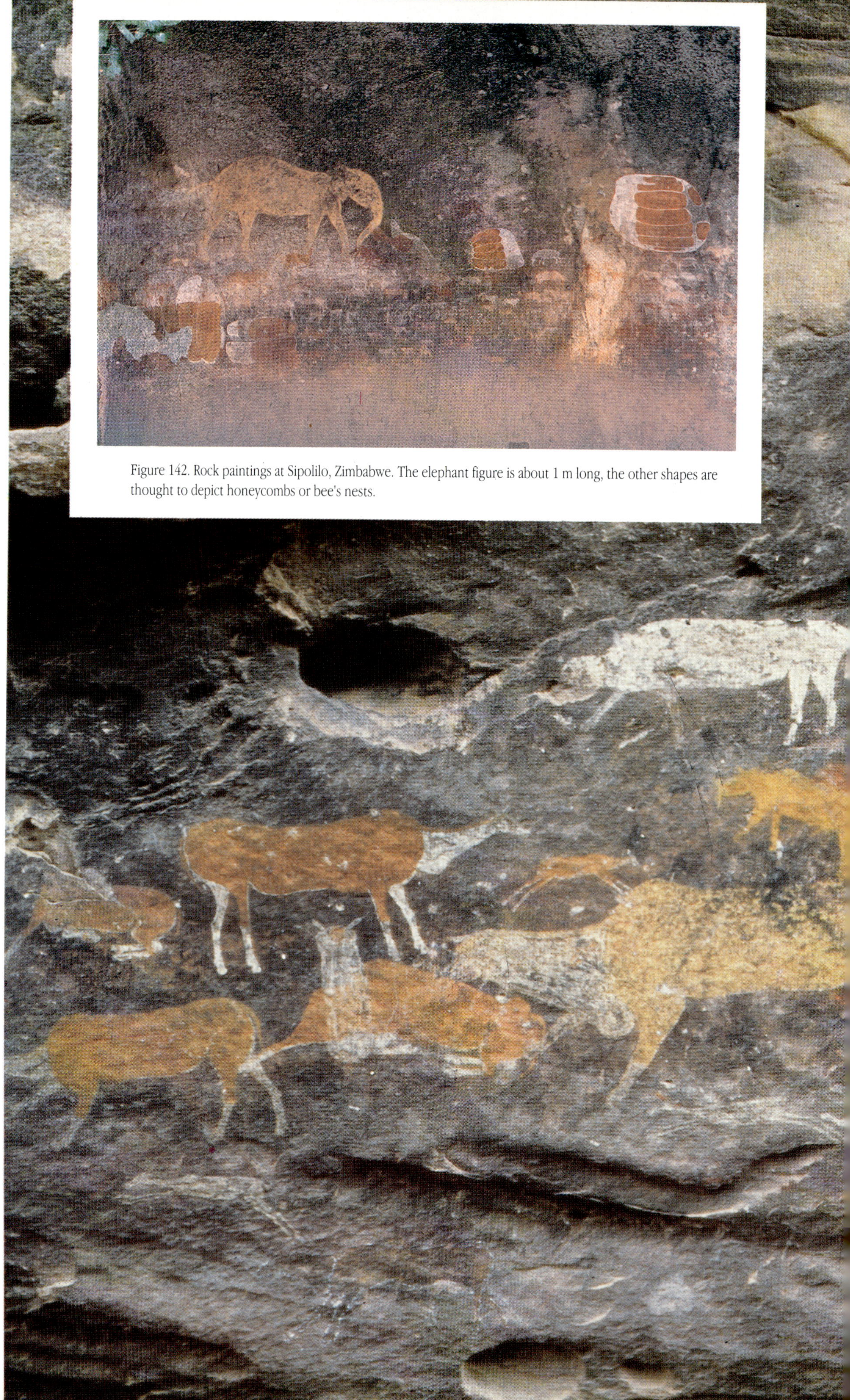

Figure 142. Rock paintings at Sipolilo, Zimbabwe. The elephant figure is about 1 m long, the other shapes are thought to depict honeycombs or bee's nests.

Figure 143. Group of painted eland antelopes, but the top centre animal has cattle horns. Cattle were introduced approximately 1500 years ago. Farm Post Catherine, Indwe District, Eastern Cape Province, South Africa.

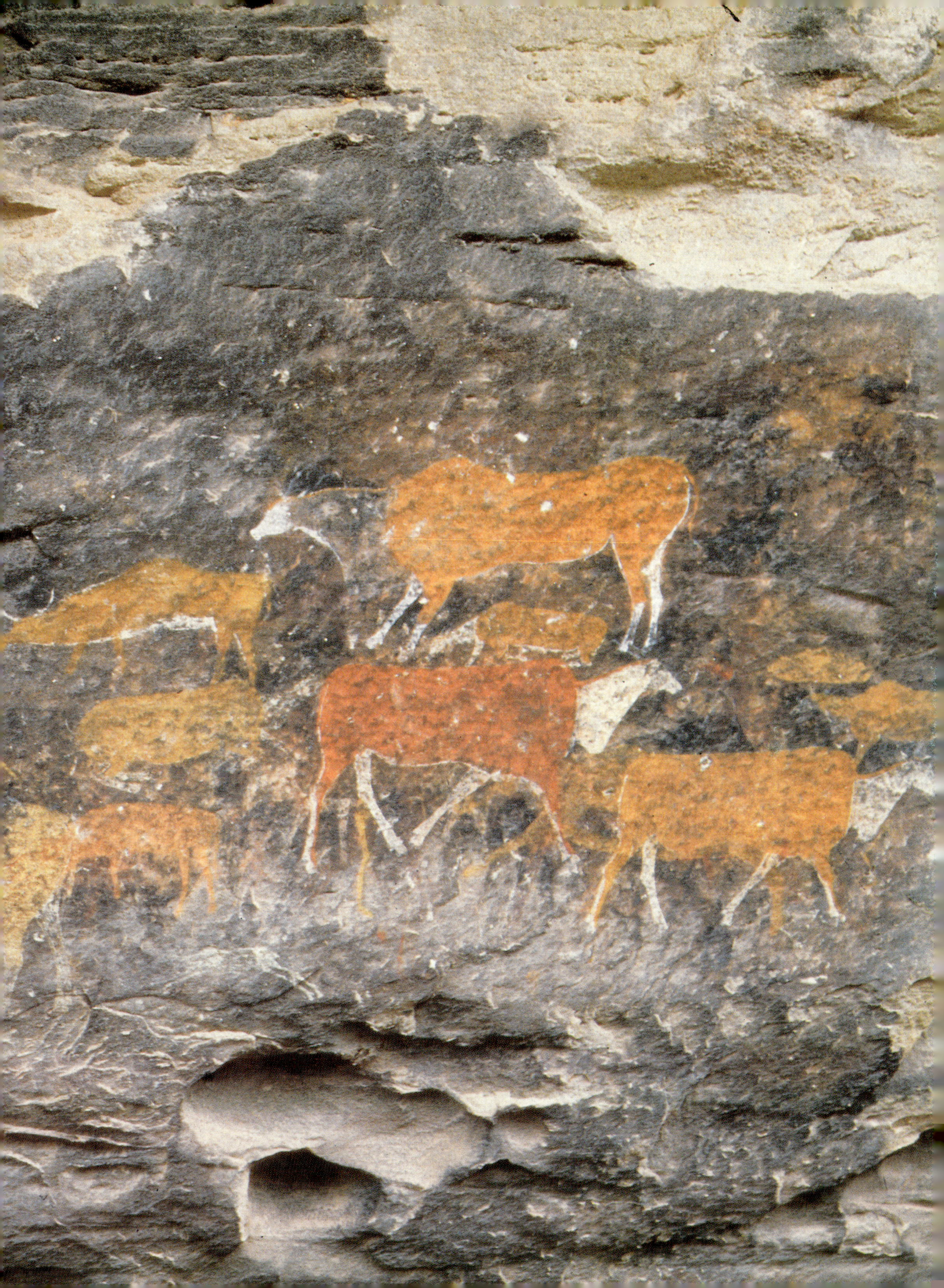

region are Alex Willcox, Patricia Vinnicombe, David Lewis-Williams and Bert Woodhouse. Over-enthusiastic interpretation of this vast art corpus has led to a great deal of interpretative speculation (as we have seen happen in other parts of the world). Much of this concerns issues of trance imagery and the involvement of shamanism in rock art production. However, as in most other areas of subjective rock art interpretation, these kinds of speculations have not resulted in any falsifiable propositions or scientific knowledge. Essentially, the claim of the supporters of these ideas is that all Bushman rock paintings depict trance experiences, and that they are all the work of shamans. It is then argued that there are specific features in the art which demonstrate that it is such shamanistic art, and since these same features can be found in many other rock arts the world over, the same interpretation is extrapolated to world rock art. For instance, the Stone Age cave art of European caves is argued to be shamanistic, as are many other arts in other continents.

There is little doubt that some of the Bushman rock paintings do refer to trance experiences, but various objections have been raised against the shamanistic model as a general explanation. Firstly, the claimed ethnographic evidence from southern Africa almost evaporates when it is closely examined: there is very little, if any, in favour of trance imagery having been depicted, or indicating that the art production was the privilege of a specific class of people, such as medicine men. Moreover, the trance dances of the Bushmen were certainly not limited to shamans, many of the tribe's adults joined in; they were communal affairs. Such knowledge was certainly not restricted to medicine men or some such special class, and it may not even be justified to equate the role of the medicine man or rain maker (Figure 145) with the Eurasian/American shaman, even though there are certain parallels. Finally, and perhaps most importantly, it is false to extrapolate to the rock art of the rest of the world, whatever explanation may be adopted in southern Africa. In some regions we possess considerable ethnological knowledge about the motivations of rock artists. Australia is foremost in this respect, and there is not even any evidence of shamanism in that country. Rock art production and renewal was perhaps the responsibility of senior people, the custodians of the sites, the elders of the group. But there was certainly no trance involved, nor does most of the art in Australia refer to anything like trance depictions. We know of various forms of sympathetic magic, such as love magic or

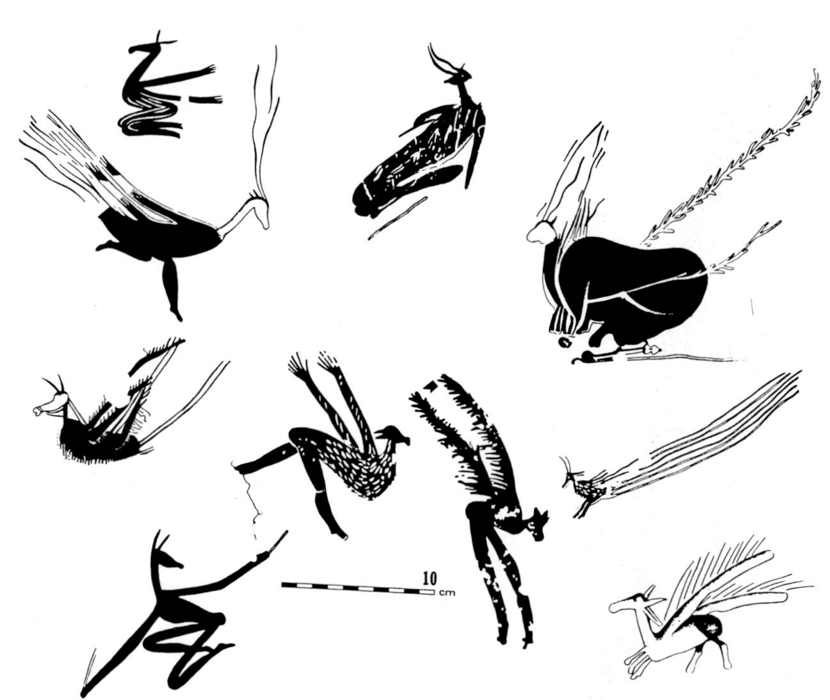

Figure 144. Some examples of alites or flying bucks from different rockshelters of the Natal Drakensberg, South Africa. (After Harald Pager.)

hunting magic, we know of many totemic meanings, of sorcery art, and of rock arts being records of some form or other. But most importantly, Australian rock art is connected with the stories of Creation - it depicts, records and demonstrates the eternal truths of the deeds of the Dreamtime heroes, as do many topographical features in the landscape, and it explains human existence and the rules governing it. It is the visual manifestation of The Law. To misinterpret such powerful imagery, which externalises the values and beliefs of a society, by attributing it to trance visions or explaining it in some other simplistic fashion that academics of an alien society can comprehend would not do justice to any of these cognitively and culturally sophisticated societies; it would debase them.

In the same sense, the oversimplification involved in the application of the trance/shaman hypothesis to Bushman art, while probably including some truths, does not do justice to Bushman culture in its totality. Some of the Bushman art clearly relates to the contact period (Figure 146) while other depictions are of specific communal activities (Figure 147). The mature sophistication of this art, its obvious complexity and even the iconographic content all negate a simplistic and superficial, wholesale explanation. A variety of alternative interpretations have been proposed, but the surprisingly poor ethnographic record we have renders evaluation difficult. It is limited to only a very few reliable sources, and they are very brief on the subject of rock art. The interpretations of researchers all suffer from their reliance on the interpreters' intuition. In fact there is not even any substantial evidence as to which arts can realistically be attributed to the Bushmen (Figure 148). It is often so identified

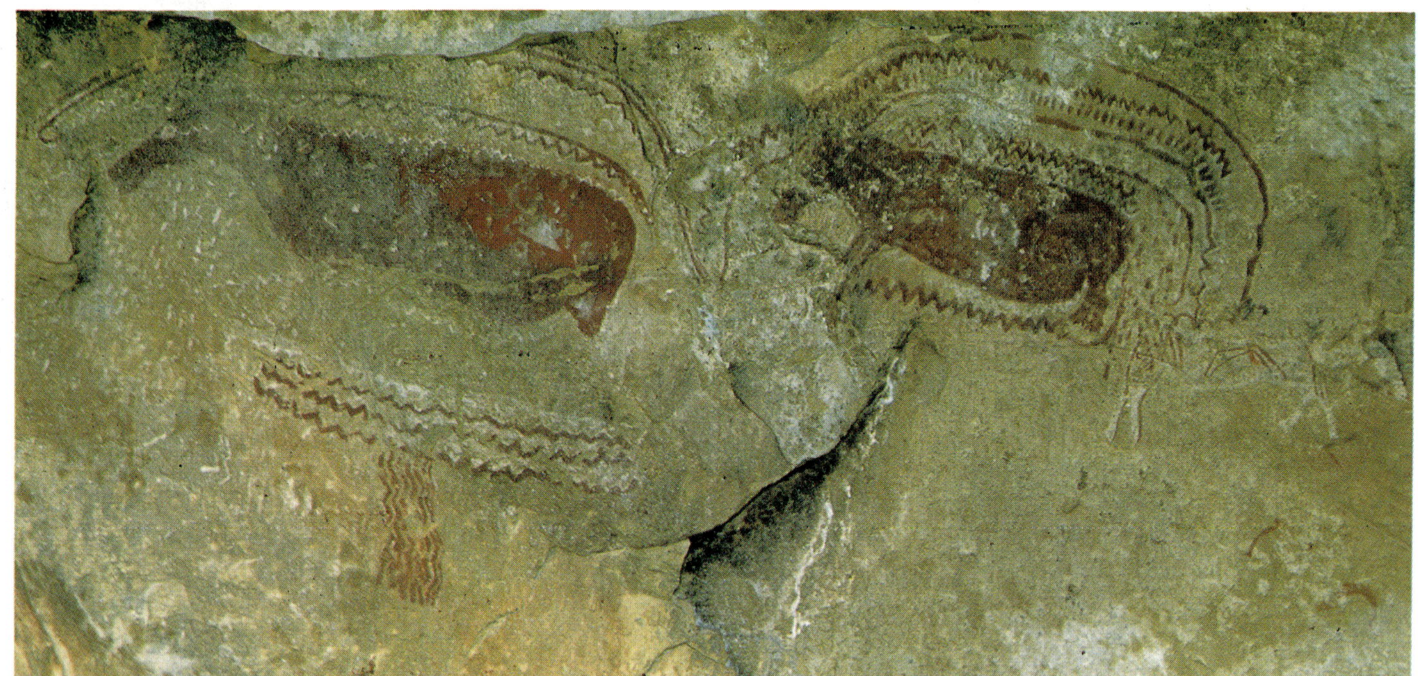

Figure 145. Rain animals, which illustrate the Bushman concept of animals in the cumulo-nimbus clouds that send thunder, lightning, rain and hail. La Rochelle, Bethlem District, Orange Free State, South Africa.

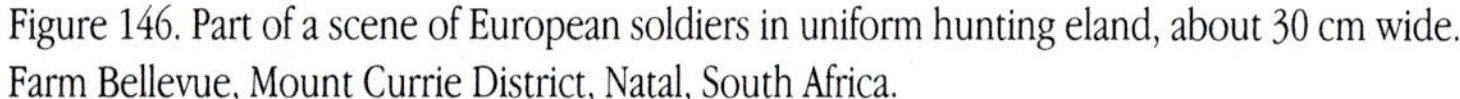

Figure 146. Part of a scene of European soldiers in uniform hunting eland, about 30 cm wide.
Farm Bellevue, Mount Currie District, Natal, South Africa.

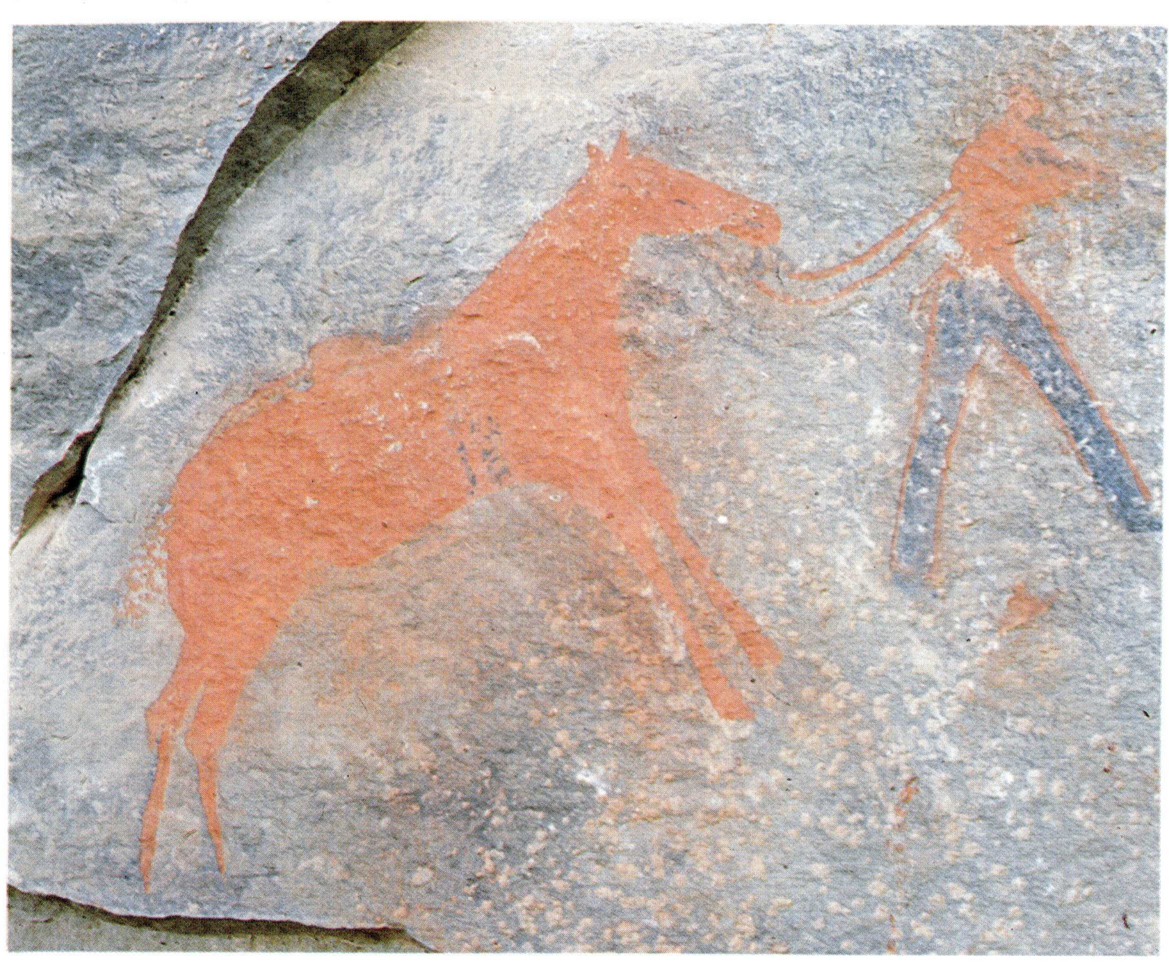

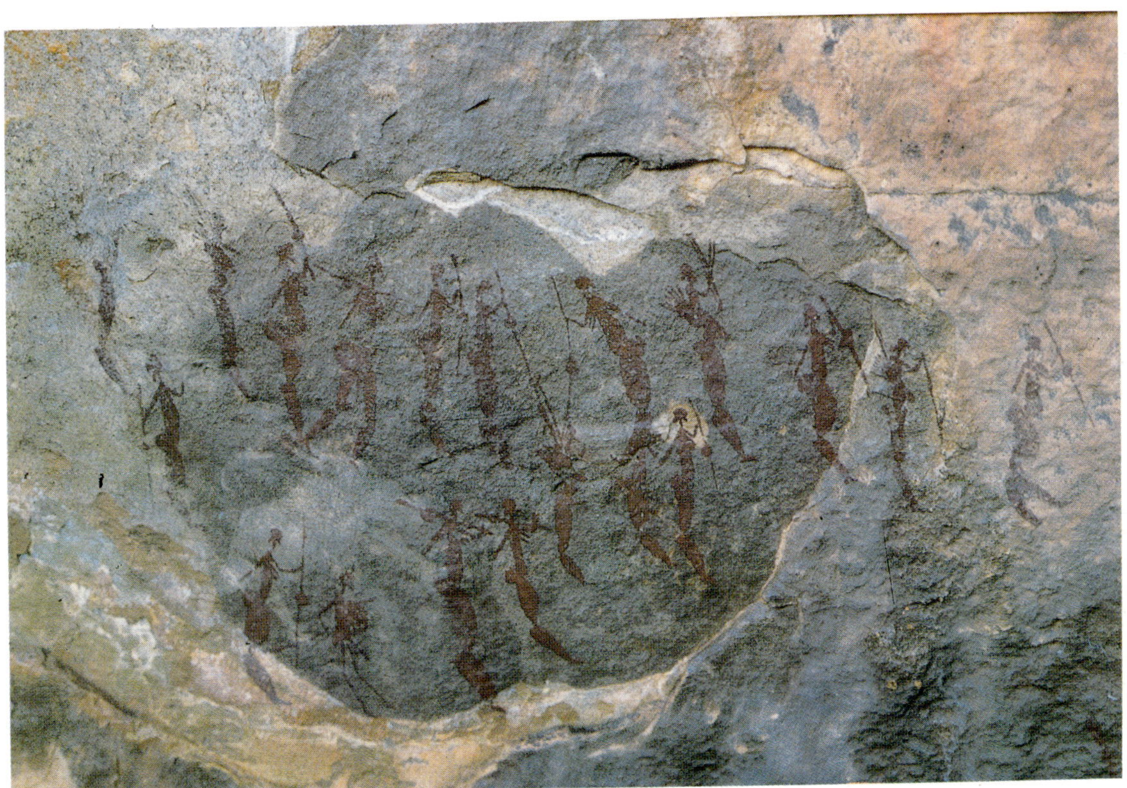

Figure 147. Apparent scene depicting women gathering roots with the use of weighted digging sticks. The figures average about 20 cm. Farm Tripolitania, Ladybrand, Orange Free State, South Africa.

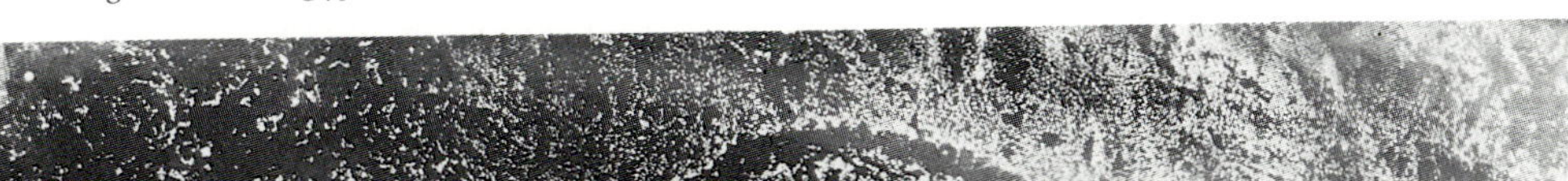

Figure 148. Petroglyph of a charging rhinoceros, approximately 50 cm long. Orford s Farm, Klerksdorp, South Africa.

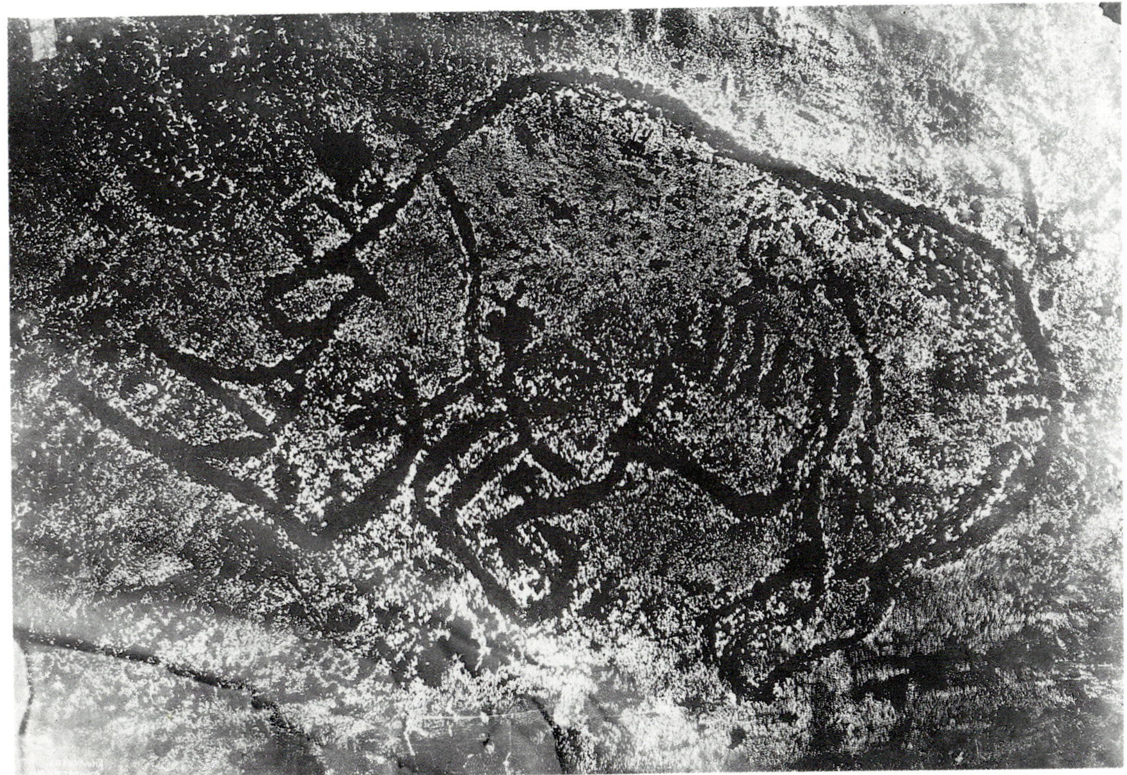

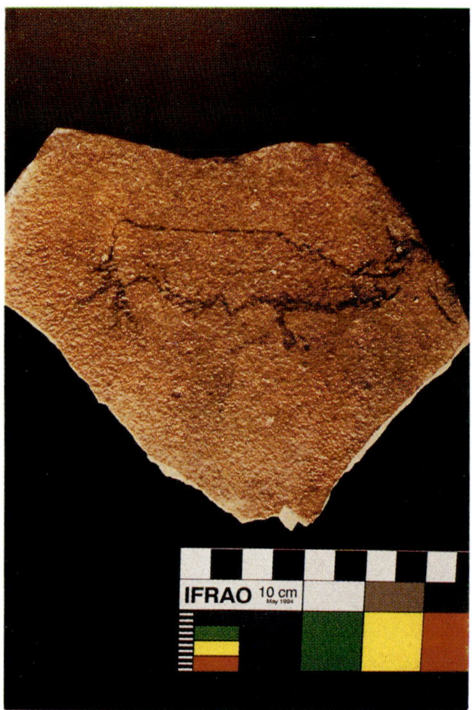

Figure 149. One of the stone tablets from Apollo 11 Cave, Namibia, Middle Stone Age, thought to be 26,000 to 28,000 years old.

merely on the basis of perceived style. Also, reliable dating is restricted to only a few instances, all of which refer to comparatively recent art.

The lack of knowledge about much earlier rock art in southern Africa is perplexing. There are rock arts that differ significantly from that attributed to the Bushmen. In particular, there is a large series of petroglyph sites in the Western Cape region, consisting of non-figurative motifs. But nothing is known about its age. And yet, one of the most fascinating features of southern African palaeoart is the occurrence, in Namibia, of some of the oldest known figurative paintings in the world. At the Apollo 11 Cave, W. E. Wendt excavated several stone plaques with paint traces in an occupation layer of the Middle Stone Age, thought to date from about 26,000 to 28,000 years ago. About five of these stone tablets bear animal figures (Figure 149). They are among the oldest recognisable pictures of objects that have so far been found and dated, anywhere in the world.

They add another facet to the extremely ancient cultural traditions of Africa, about which we have no more than very few, tantalising clues so far. It is clear that some art forms have existed in southern Africa for hundreds of thousands of years, as is the case also in Asia. We know this from very early portable articles, and from the even earlier evidence of ochre mining and use. But like in Asia, the evidence is few and far between, it provides no more than some minute glimpses. We can only hope that future research will provide better knowledge, because our present information is certainly most inadequate to speculate about the subject of art beginnings. ❐

• THE ROCK ART OF THE AMERICAS •

THE ROCK ART OF THE AMERICAS

It is generally assumed by archaeologists, and with good reason, that the Americas were initially occupied by humans from the north, via Bering Strait. There is, however, considerable disagreement concerning the timing of this initial immigration from Asia. This is because evidence of human settlement has been found in South America which dates to 40,000 or 50,000 years ago, while there is a distinct lack of acceptable settlement evidence in North America that is older than 13,000 years. Clearly this creates a dilemma for North American scholars: how did the initial settlers manage to tiptoe through the continent of North America without leaving traces that have so far been found?

Several answers are possible to this conundrum, but the one most likely to be correct is that the initial thrust of human occupation was by a coastal people, possessing a coastal economy and some seafaring ability. They limited their expansion mostly to the western coastal zone, proceeding south and reaching South America before achieving high enough population densities to become archaeologically 'visible' across North America's interior. With the rising sea level at the end of the Ice Age (the sea had been 100 - 150 metres lower than today) the coastal settlement traces became inundated, so they are no longer available for study. This seems to be the most logical explanation, but that does not necessarily mean that it must be correct. Interestingly enough, the earliest safely dated American rock art is also found in South America rather than in

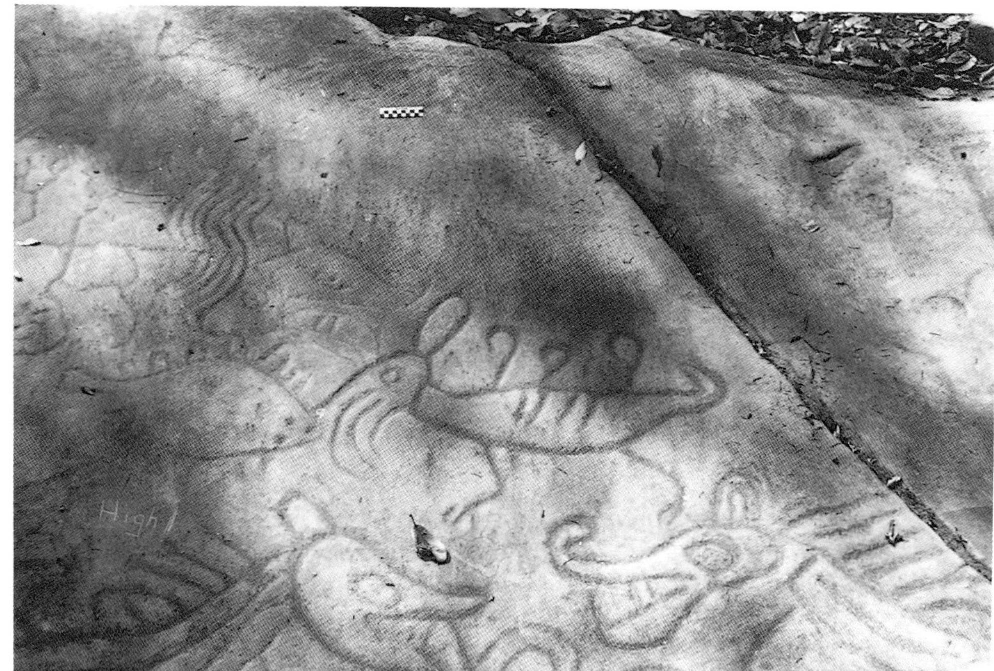

Figure 150. Engraved pavement in Nanaimo Petroglyph Park, near Nanaimo, Vancouver Island, Canada, showing several sea monsters.

North America - where one would expect to find it.

But we shall travel through the American continents from north to south, following the direction most probably taken by the early immigrants. At whatever time they arrived, their first landfall was probably in Alaska. Rock art, in the form of petroglyphs, occurs even on the Aleutian Islands, which form a line of rocky outcrops between Alaska and the Kamchatka Peninsula of Siberia. These sites are poorly known, however, partly because of their poor accessibility. Petroglyphs then occur in Alaska, and down the west coast of Canada. The number of known sites is not very great, being only in the order of a few dozen, and motif numbers are also low at most localities. However, they include spectacular examples, for instance mythological, fantastic animal figures, resembling dragons and sea monsters (Figure 150), or complex and stylised human faces with an uncanny resemblance to the 'masks' of Asian rock art regions. They and the dragon-like figures, which resemble Chinese depictions, have been cited as possible indications of cultural influence from China. However, as we have mentioned above, such diffusionist explanations are usually very tenuous. The real connection may be more related to cognitive universals in the human species, as we will see below.

Most of these sites occur close to the coast, a few on rivers and lakes, for instance on Vancouver Island. There, sites such as Sproat Lake and Nanaimo provide classical examples of the rich graphic traditions expressed in Northwest Coast petroglyphs (Figure 151). Of particular interest is the occurrence of rock art right at sea level, and apparently even below it. A large

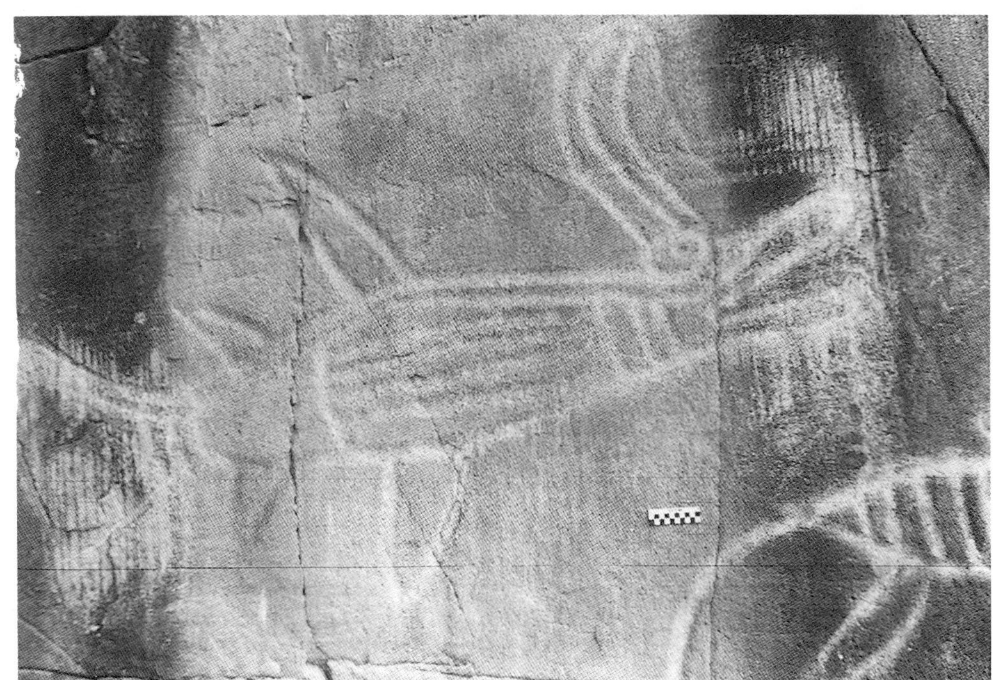

Figure 151. Abraded design of a sea monster on vertical cliff of very hard quartzite rising immediately from Sproat Lake, Vancouver Island, Canada.

boulder in Oyster Bay on Vancouver Island was located in the sea before loggers dragged it to the shore, only to discover a complex mythical creature depicted wrapped around it (Figure 152). A huge granite boulder on the beach near Victor (Washington State, U.S.A.) is entirely covered by a maze of petroglyphs. These were found to extend below the water level after an attempt to move it with a tug boat failed early this century. We cannot be sure whether these features relate to a geologically recent adjustment in plate tectonics, or whether the petroglyphs genuinely relate to a lower sea level. In the latter case they could date from the late Ice Age. It is relevant to note that a boulder with an incised human face was found on Vancouver Island in the 1920s, some three metres below the roots of a cedar tree that was itself over a thousand years old. While not providing conclusive dating, this does suggest that human faces or masks in this region may be at least a few millennia old.

Generally speaking, almost no rock art in North America has been soundly dated. One of the few exceptions is Mud Portage in Manitoba, Canada, where Jack Steinbring obtained a rough dating of between 5000 and 9000 years on the basis of archaeological deductions. Numerous dating claims have appeared in the United States, but most of them are questionable. For instance, in recent years much use has been made of a direct method called cation-ratio dating. The dates may seem credible, but the method is not, and it has been rejected now by most researchers in the field. It involves far too many variables and its results have been found to be not repeatable in Australian work. Much the same applies to several other American rock art dating attempts, the notable

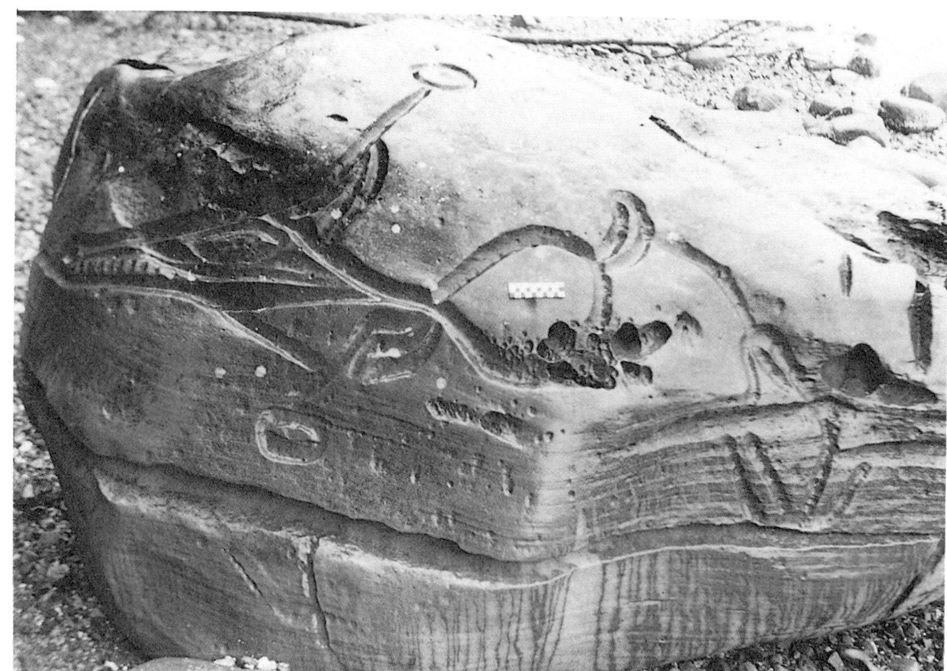

Figure 152. Depiction of a monster wrapped around a boulder in Oyster Bay, Vancouver Island, Canada.

exception being work done in Texas under the direction of Marvin Rowe, in which rock paints are dated directly. In a general sense, however, there appears to be wide agreement that the earliest rock art tradition one tends to find in North America is one consisting of cup marks (cupules) and grooves (linear, usually abraded lines). Such petroglyphs are found especially along the continent's west coast, all the way up to Alaska. This is of considerable interest because these kinds of rock art have been consistently found to be the oldest in other continents also, notably in Asia, Australia, Europe and South America. This is therefore a global pattern - one of several universal patterns one finds in rock art.

In Canada, rock art occurs not only as petroglyphs but also as rock paintings, especially inland. Sites are not numerous across this vast land but they occur in many regions, including British Columbia, Alberta, Saskatchewan, Manitoba, Ontario, along the Atlantic seaboard, around the Great Lakes system, and even in the far north. Indeed, the northernmost rock art in the Americas is found at Bering Strait and in central Alaska, while in eastern Canada, three petroglyph sites occur on the northern Ungava Peninsula. Portable art, however, is found much further to the north, on the Queen Elizabeth Islands and Baffin Island. A well-known site in Canada is the Petroglyphs Provincial Park near Woodview, Ontario (Figure 153), where petroglyphs have unfortunately been filled with paint before they were covered with a protective building of steel and glass in 1984. An unusual form of rock art was produced by the Micmac Indians in Nova Scotia, scratched into a soft and fine-grained slate. The production of rock art was continued on their sites by French and English settlers in recent centuries.

In the United States, rock art is

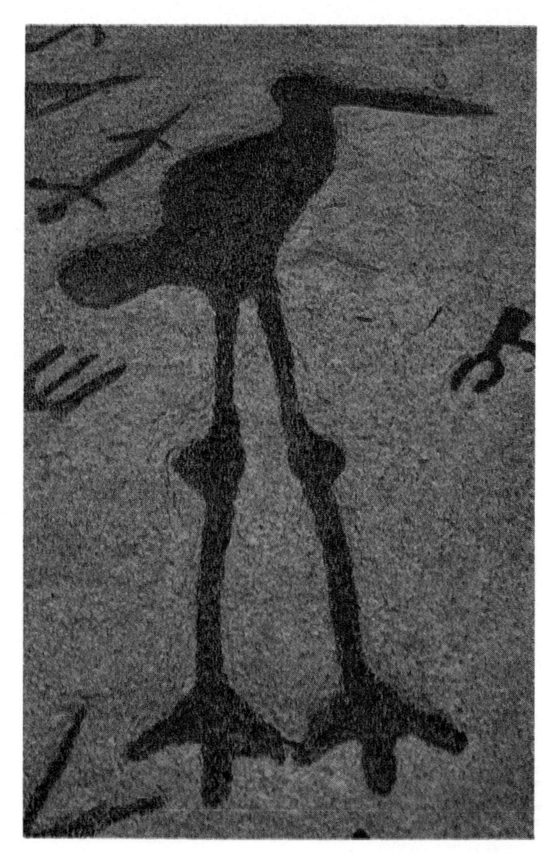

Figure 153. Petroglyphs on marble (metamorphosed limestone) pavement, filled in with black paint, a vandalistic practice. Petroglyphs Provincial Park, Ontario, Canada.

considerably more common, but the main concentrations are those of the south-western States: California, Arizona, New Mexico, Nevada and Utah. Outside this massive concentration, rock art does occur in most parts of U.S.A. but it is considerably less common. Research efforts, too, have been uneven, with more work done in some states than in others. An unusual discovery was made in Tennessee, when petroglyphs were found in a series of deep caves, particularly Mud Glyph Cave. Rock art in actual caves (as distinct from rockshelters) remains limited to specific world regions, and it is common only in four others: the Caribbean, Yucatán, southern Australia and south-western Europe. Another interesting rock art site is The Dalles, on the Columbia River (Washington), where some petroglyphs were saved during the construction of a massive dam project, but many others are now submerged beneath the water.

The major divisions of rock art regions in the United States are those of the Columbia-Fraser drainage system (which is shared with Canada), California, the Great Basin, the Great Plains, the Temperate Woodlands of the east, and the Southwest, which extends also into Mexico. The recent pioneers in the study of these vast corpora are Klaus Wellmann, Campbell Grant, Georgia Lee and Polly Schaafsma, but a large number of further researchers have also made significant contributions. A very important work in the early understanding of American art was that by Garrick Mallery at the end of the nineteenth century.

The rock art of the Great Plains

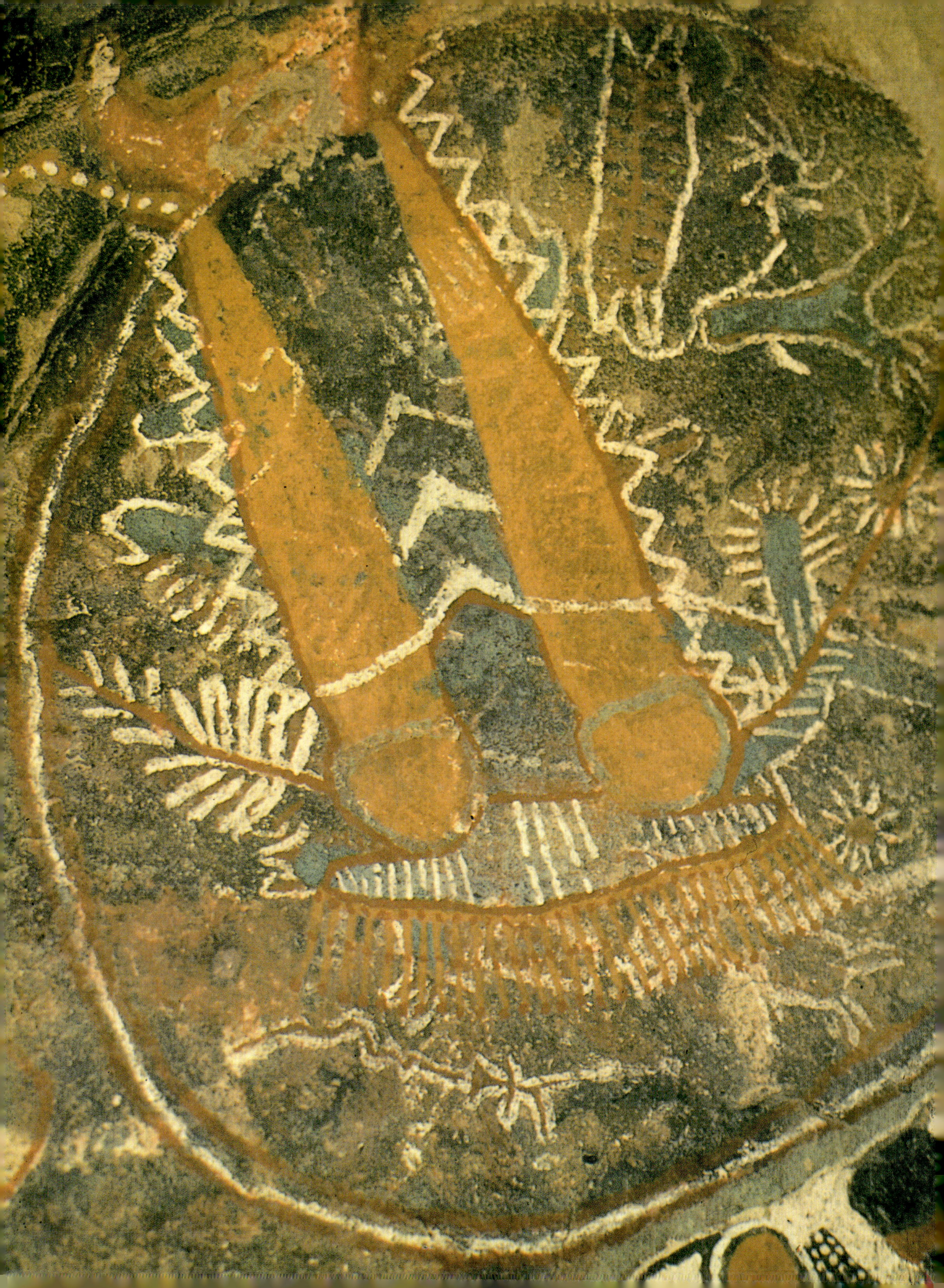

Figure 154. Chumash rock paintings at San Emigdio, California, U.S.A. The motifs in this rock art have been attributed to the use of narcotics. (facing page)

extends from southern Canada to Texas. Typical components are the shield figures, which are human figures largely concealed by circular shields with individual designs, the V-necked figures, and the locally restricted Dinwoody figures which occur only in one part of Wyoming. The rock art of the eastern states is thought to belong to the Woodland Culture or the subsequent Mississippian. Among its features are the 'thunder-bird' and the heart line of some figures. Like many sequences of rock art, the eastern woodlands art begins with cupules and linear grooves.

Although both rock paintings and petroglyphs are well represented in the United States, the latter seem to predominate in most traditions. A notable exception is the particularly striking painting tradition of the Chumash in California (Figure 154), in the coastal ranges and on the Carrizo Plain which has been researched by Georgia Lee and William Hyder. Its colourful geometric imagery is unmistakable (Figure 155). Other distinctive and well-known traditions are the petroglyphs of the Coso Range, with their bighorn sheep and other figures pounded into the area's patinated boulders; the delicately pecked petroglyphs of the Fremont Style; and the large and brooding, mummy-like human figures of the painted Barrier Canyon Style (Figure 156). Nearer the coast, for instance around San Diego and San Francisco, one finds cupule-covered boulders and 'rock gongs' (lithophones, i.e. rocks that were pounded in order to produce loud, ringing sounds). Such features, conversely, are also known from other parts of the world, for instance in Kenya, and even from a few of the caves used by Upper Palaeolithic people in south-western Europe where stalactites served as lithophones. Again, we find that this is a universal feature found in many unconnected cultures of the world.

It is not possible to list here all the inferred styles and traditions of Southwestern rock art, nor the tentative chronological schemes that have been enunciated for them. The major traditions, however, are the Hohokam, Mogollon, Anasazi, Navaho, Fremont, Barrier Canyon and Pecos River styles. There is a good deal of preliminary dating available, and sound dating methods have been introduced. The first credible results were obtained in the Lower Pecos, Texas, where specific motifs are now known to be approximately 3800 years old. More information of this kind is expected to become available soon. Relative dating is sometimes possible from pottery decoration, especially for the Hohokam and Mogollon traditions.

A few of the distinctive features in these major rock art traditions are

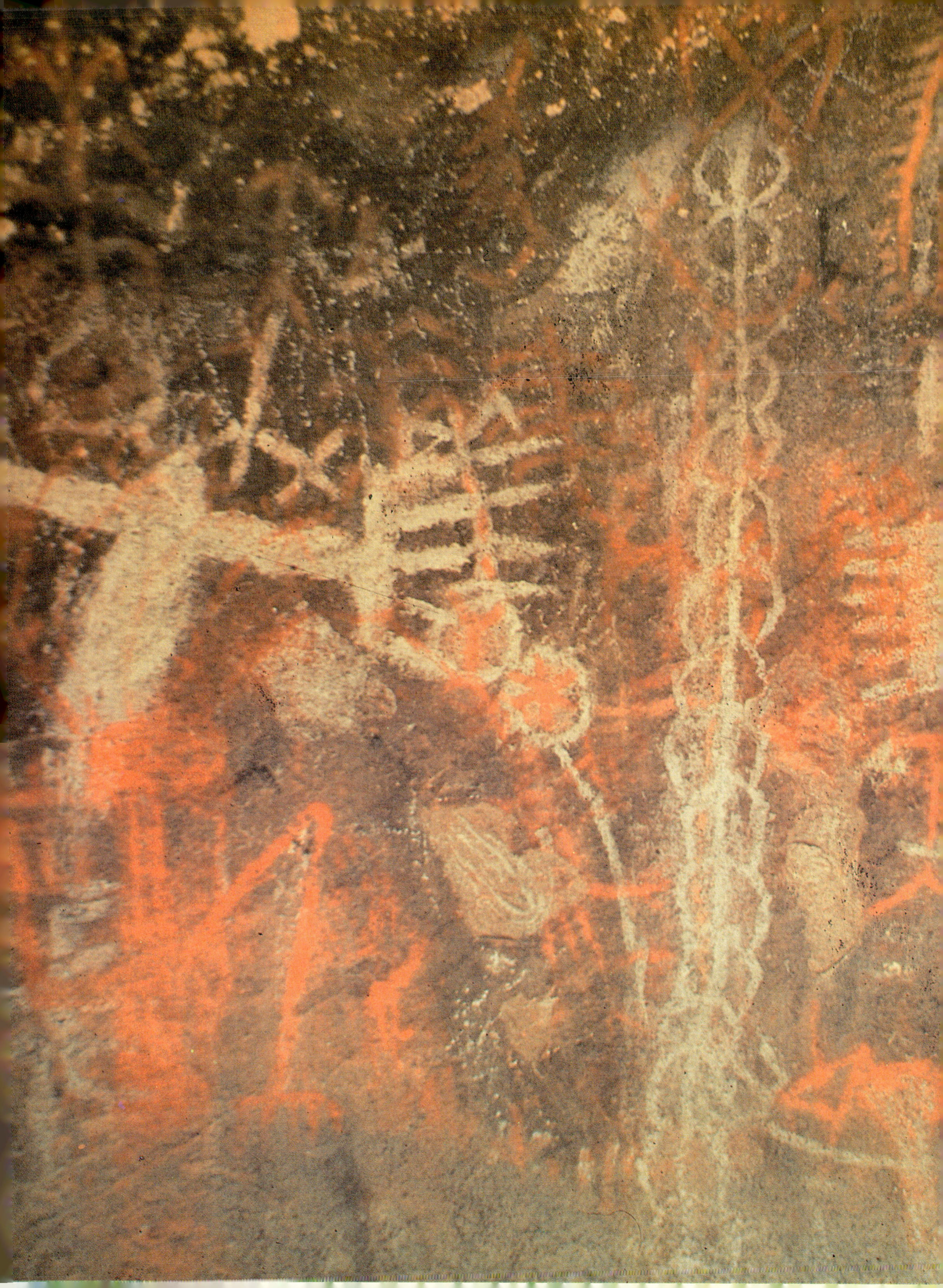

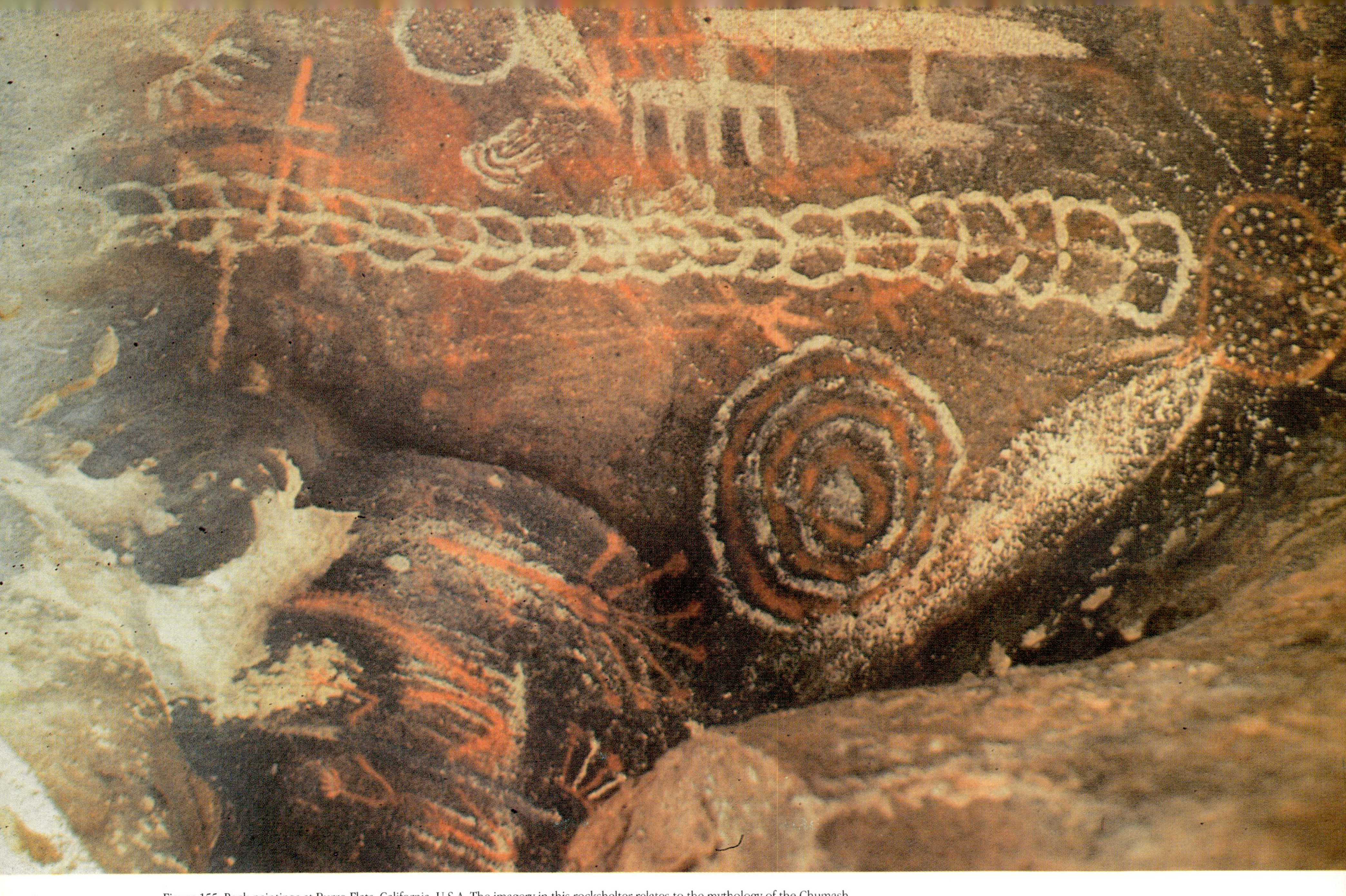

Figure 155. Pock paintings at Burro Flats, California, U.S.A. The imagery in this rockshelter relates to the mythology of the Chumash.

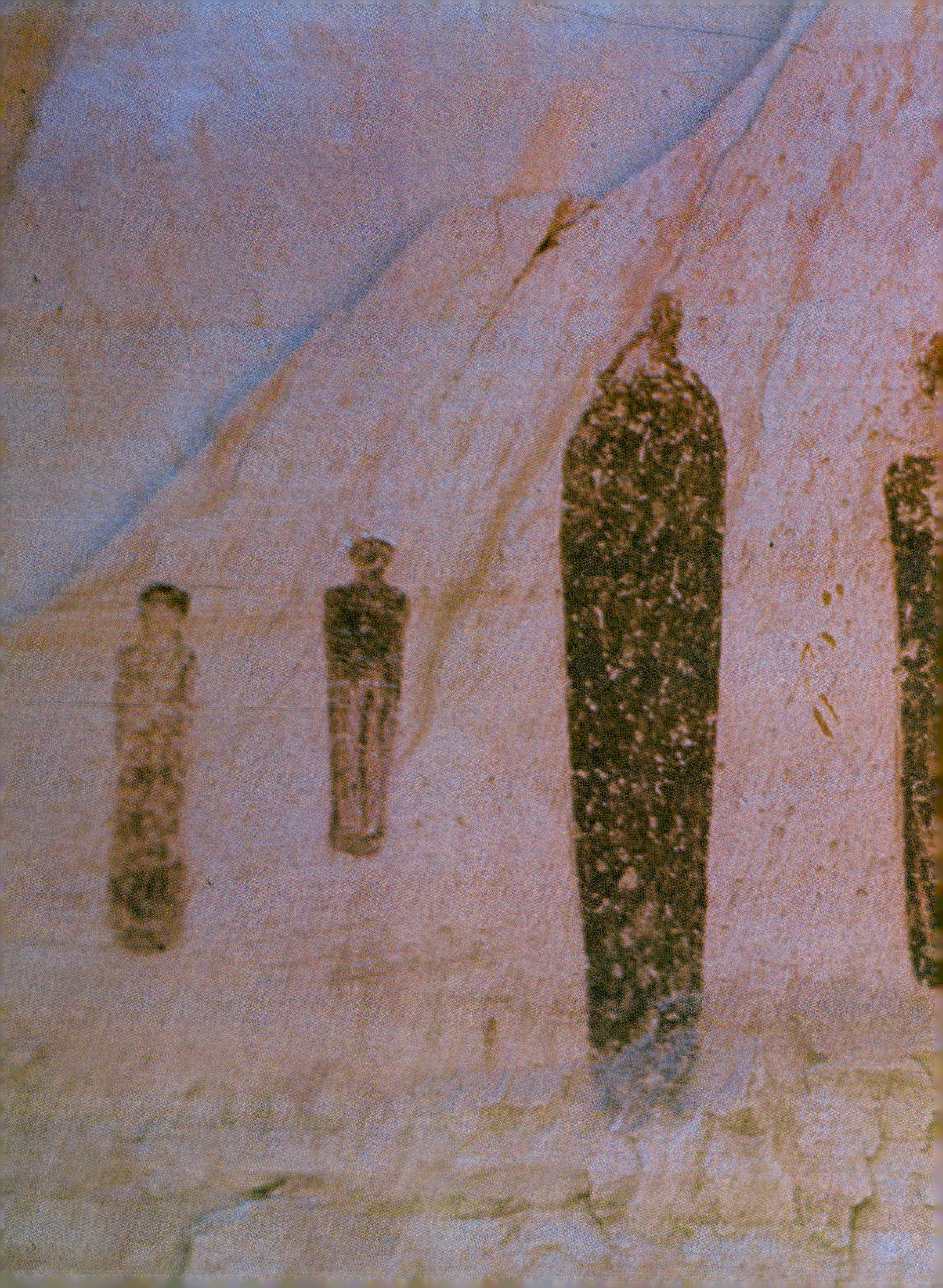

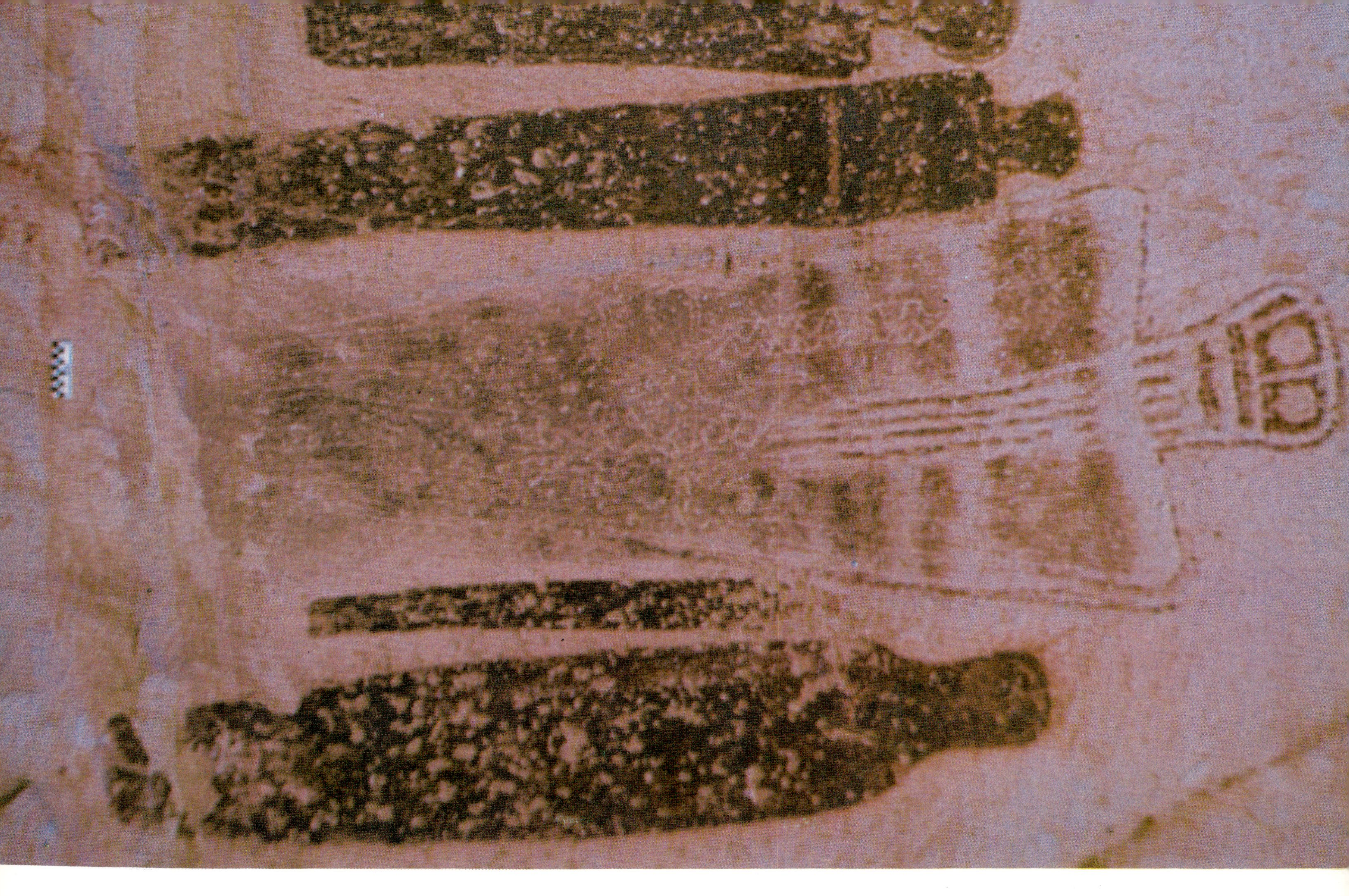

Figure 156. Section of the main gallery at the Barrier Canyon site, Horseshoe Canyon, Utah, U.S.A. The painted figures are 2-3 m high.

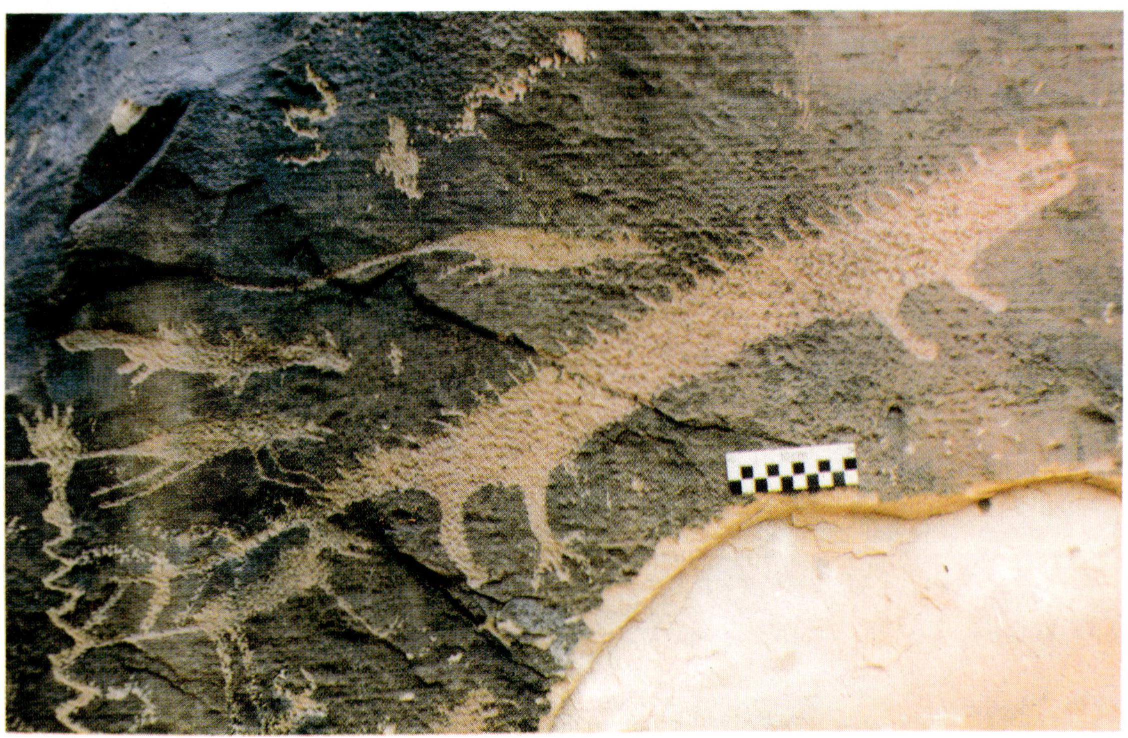

Figure 157. Petroglyph of a fantastic animal, Rochester Creek Site, Utah, U.S.A.

Kokopelli, a hunchbacked and often phallic flute player of the Anasazi tradition; and the broad-shouldered humans with horns, helmets and ear pendants of the Fremont Culture. Some of the outstanding and best known individual sites are perhaps Petroglyph Canyon (the major Coso rock art site), the Barrier Canyon type site (paintings only, unsuccessful dating attempt), Newspaper Rock, Rochester Creek (scene of another unsuccessful dating attempt; Figure 157), Butler Wash (spectacular recent petroglyphs), Cottonwood Canyon (numerous sites) and Parowan Gap (a complex sequence of styles and traditions, with some very old petroglyphs present; Figure 158).

This rich rock art tradition continues unabated across the Mexican border, culminating in spectacular painting sites found in various parts of Baja California, the Californian Peninsula. In this rugged and mountainous region, dissected by deep arroyos or gorges, one finds large, often polychrome paintings of human figures as well as animals. However, there are also many petroglyphs, usually older than the paintings, which include the apparent vulva designs at San Javier and the drilled designs in the soft tuff of Agua Honda. Rather more accessible are the major Mexican site complexes of the Sonora desert and elsewhere in northern Mexico. Two famous examples are those of Cerro Blanco, close to the town of Caborca, and La Pintada, south of Hermosillo. Cerro Blanco consists of a prominent group of hills, some kilometres across, with many concentrations of petroglyphs. Among the boulder slopes and on bedrock

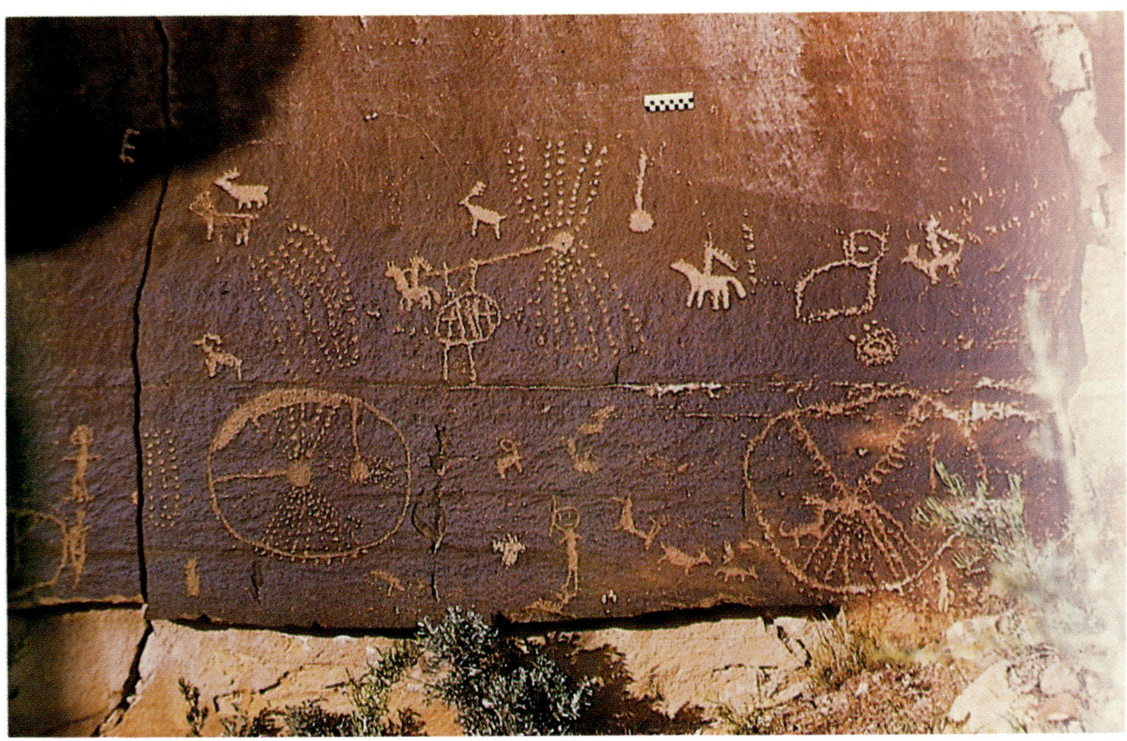

Figure 158. Petroglyphs of the Fremont Style, at Parowan Gap, Utah, U.S.A.

surfaces, all of which are patinated to a dark-brown colour, one finds thousands of motifs: geometric patterns, some resembling the decoration on pottery sherds, as well as countless animal figures and some larger human depictions. La Pintada is a complex of several painting sites arranged around a narrow and steep canyon, vaguely resembling painting traditions further north (Figure 159). But included are many specific elements: the ubiquitous 'flying condor' symbol which occurs widely in the Americas, other brightly coloured symbols, and some extremely small paintings. These miniatures of animal and human figures are sometimes just a couple of centimetres high, and yet they show considerable anatomical detail, or the use of two different colours.

Elsewhere in northern Mexico, notably in Chihuahua and Nuevo Leon, one observes frequent arrangements of dot patterns, occurring in distinctly structured groups (Figure 160). They have prompted some scholars, for instance William Breen Murray, to suggest that their use was in some way mathematically inspired. Further south in Mexico, rock art continues, but is mostly known in the form of the inscriptions of the Aztec, Mayan and Oltec empires, which are not considered as part of prehistoric rock arts. However, a particularly notable rock art tradition has been studied on the peninsula of Yucatán, in southern Mexico. Matthias Strecker and others have reported rock art from a series of deep caves in this region. The art includes painted hieroglyphic inscriptions as well as pictures. It has been suggested to have

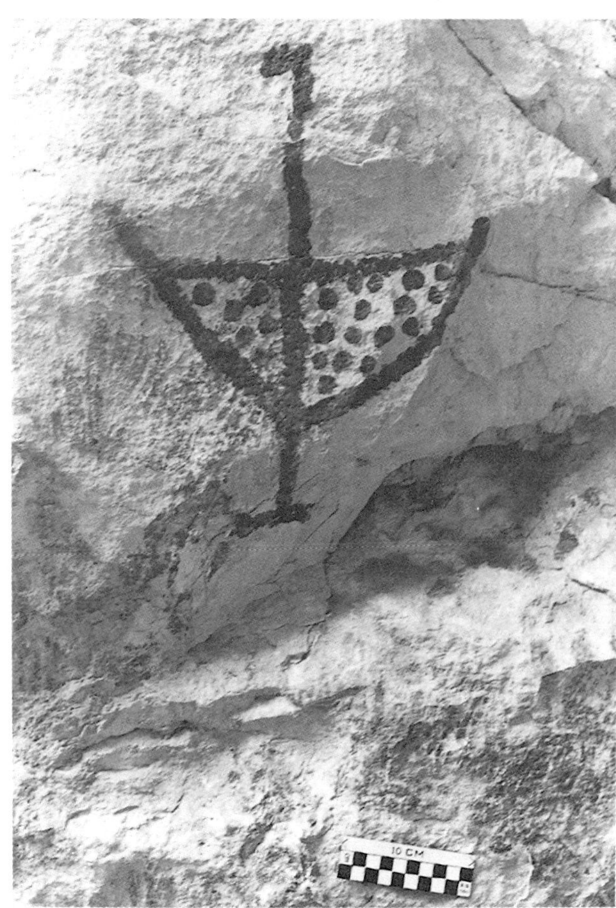

Figure 159. Stylised image of a bird with outstretched wings, La Pintada, Sonora, Mexico.

been connected with rituals that may have taken place in these subterranean locations. Cave art, i.e. rock art traditions frequently found in true caves, is limited to a few world regions, as we have seen above. A notable feature in Yucatán is the use of a blue pigment, Maya Blue, which has resisted all scientific attempts to determine its manufacturing process.

Rock art then continues through the Mesoamerican countries, where it seems to occur in all of them. Again, published information is limited, but it is available from Guatemala, Belize, Honduras and Costa Rica, and rock art is known to occur in Nicaragua and Panama. The rock art of the Greater and Lesser Antilles, however, is somewhat better known. Again, there is a notable component of true cave art found, especially on Cuba, Hispaniola and Puerto Rico. On the first two islands, a series of limestone cave sites have been published, mostly in Spanish. The larger concentration occurs in the Dominican Republic, where deep caves with both rock paintings and petroglyphs occur in a few concentrations. Best known are perhaps such sites as the Bourbon caves, including Cueva del Puente, north-west of Santo Domingo (Figure 161). This spectacular cave site consists of a deep chasm, above which are precariously located numerous black paintings, of small human figures, fierce-looking faces, animals and various geometric or non-figurative designs. Petroglyphs, usually of humans, are sometimes carved into

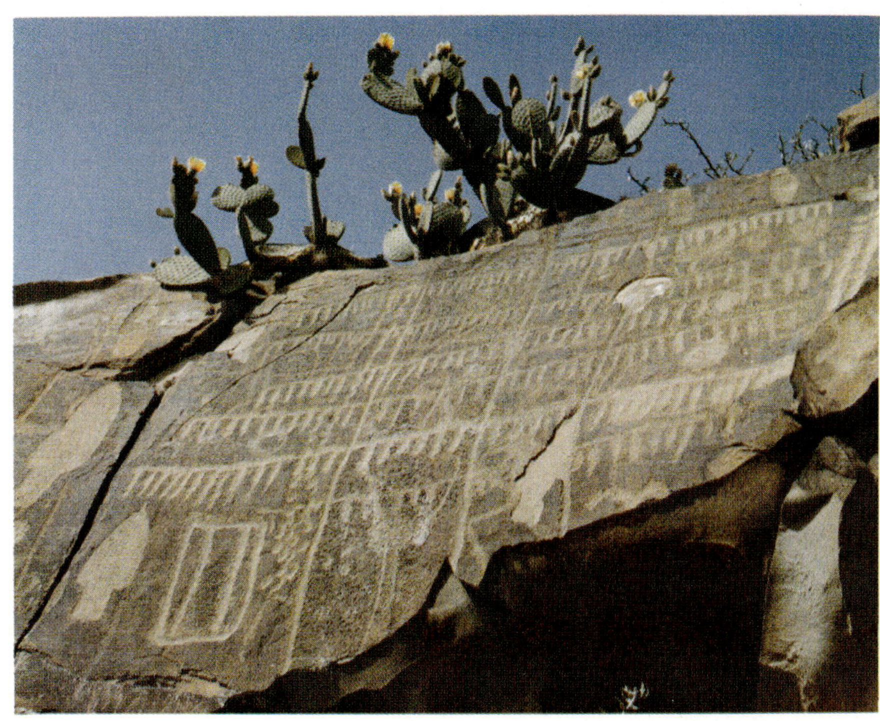

Figure 160. Presumed tally petroglyphs, Presa de La Mula, Nuevo León, Mexico.

stalagmites. This combination of black charcoal paintings and carved petroglyphs is repeated in many caves. The perhaps most spectacular concentration of Caribbean rock art sites is found in a national park in the north of Hispaniola Island, on a remote coast that has in the past been a favoured haunting place of explorers, mariners and buccaneers. Their inscriptions, too, can be found in the caves, often with historically significant comments and the dates of the visit noted. They are inscribed with such materials as tar paint, and they usually record the visits of landing parties from anchored ships, seeking drinking water and food provisions to replenish their stores.

The stunning setting of these sites and their rock art both provide these places with a powerful atmosphere. There is apparent evidence of past cannibalism to be found, in the form of burnt skeletal remains of humans. Such bones can be found even on the surface of some cave deposits, strewn among the rubble. At sites such as Cueva del Ferrocarril (Figure 162), the rock art comprises many hundreds of motifs. The many hidden coves and sheltered rock niches along the mountainous coast add to the region's atmosphere of mystery, and the settings of some of the sites are spectacular. For instance the entrance of Cueva Arena, lapped by the sea, is guarded on each side by large, menacing human figures (Figure 163). They are carved into ancient stalagmites. Inside, in a hall with rock art and Historical inscriptions, is a large pool of crystal-clear freshwater, a welcome resource for the mariners of past centuries.

Besides the spectacular cave art, rock art can also be found in the open on both Hispaniola and Cuba, for example on basalt boulders. On Puerto Rico,

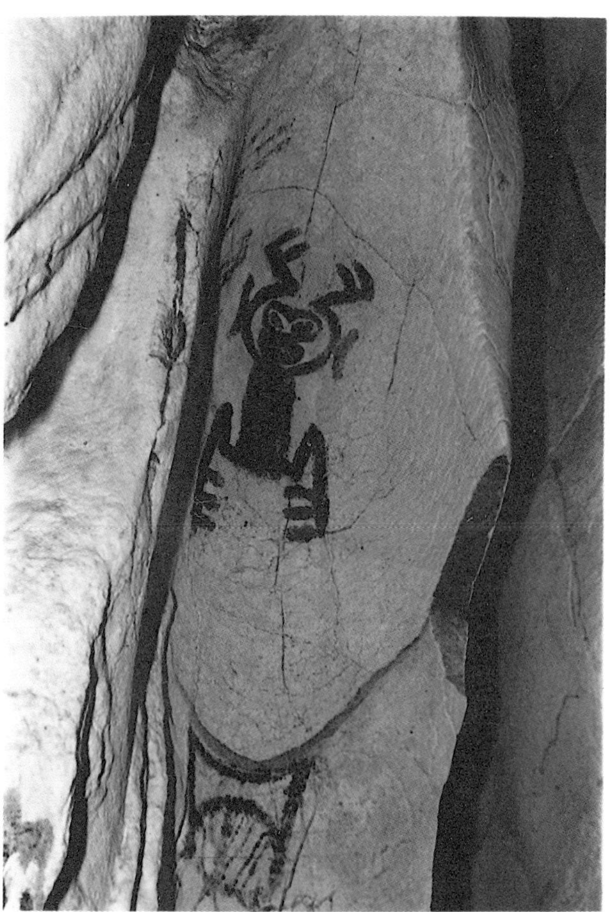

Figure 161. Black painting in a small alcove in Cueva del Puente, Borbón, Dominican Republic.

American speleologists have developed one site of cave art for tourist access, but the remaining cave sites are not open to the public. Rock art also occurs on some of the islands of the Lesser Antilles where it has been studied for the past thirty years by the Dutch scholar C. N. Dubelaar. In addition, several local researchers have contributed to the exploration of Caribbean rock art, among them Antonio Núñez Jiménez and Fernando Morban Laucer.

We thus arrive in South America, from whence the Caribbean is thought to have been settled initially. In this continent, rock art occurs again in all countries, from Venezuela and Colombia in the north to Terra del Fuego in the far south. As we have seen in other continents, the rock art is again highly diverse, consisting of many traditions and divided into many regional schools. Perhaps the best studied regional corpora are those of specific parts of Brazil, Peru, Bolivia, Chile and Argentina. The outstanding scholars in the study of this massive body include Niède Guidon, Anne-Marie Pessis and André Prous in Brazil, María Mercedes Podestá, Carlos Gradin, María Onetto and Juan Schobinger in Argentina, Mario Consens in Uruguay, Eloy Linares Málaga in Peru, and Roy Querejazu and Matthias Strecker in Bolivia. Together, these and many other researchers have pieced together a remarkable tapestry of ancient and not so

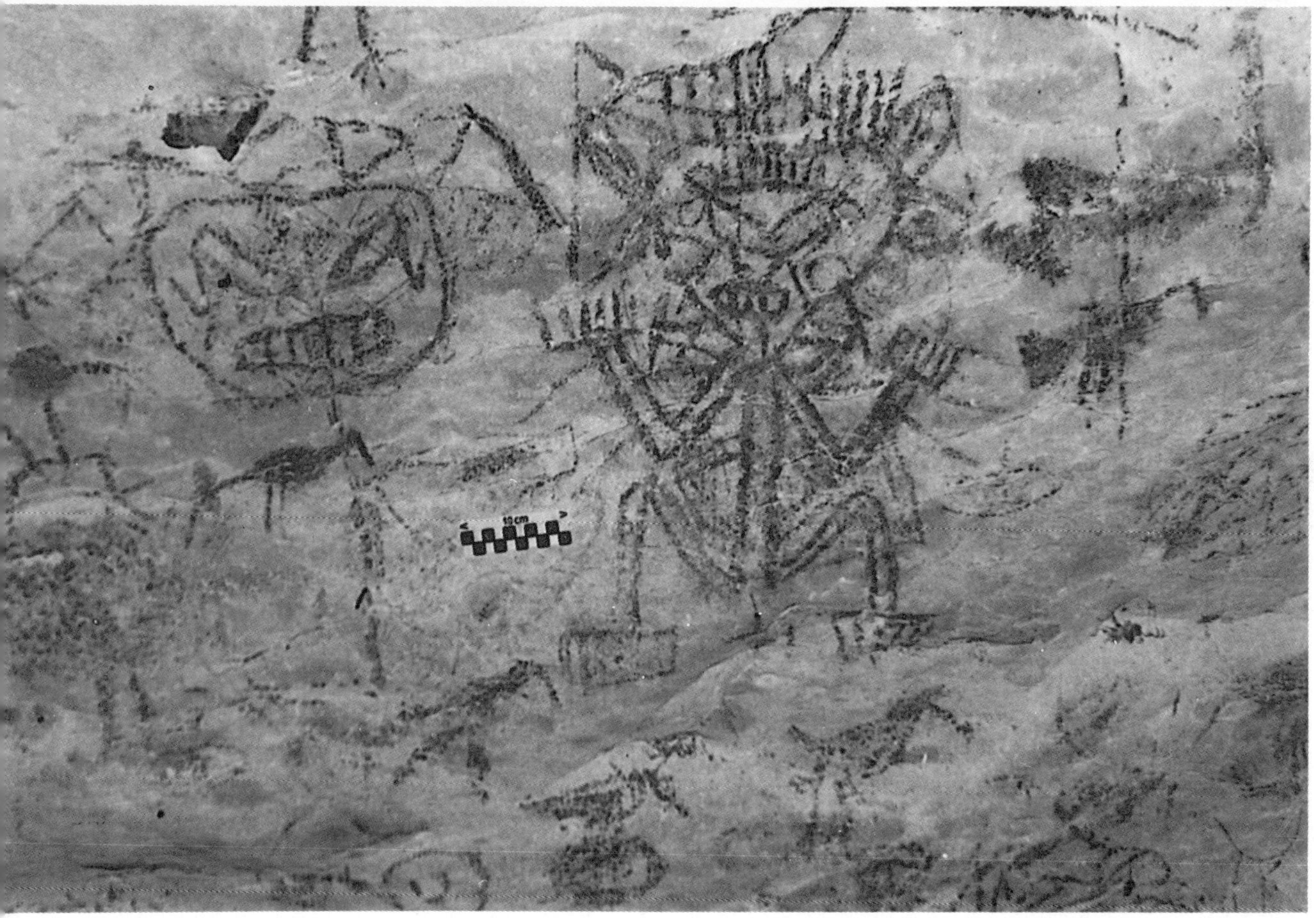

Figure 162. Rock paintings in the large cave of Cueva del Ferrocarril, Samaná, Dominican Republic.

Figure 163. Bas relief of a fierce human face carved onto a stalagmite at the entrance of Cueva Arena, Samaná, Dominican Republic.

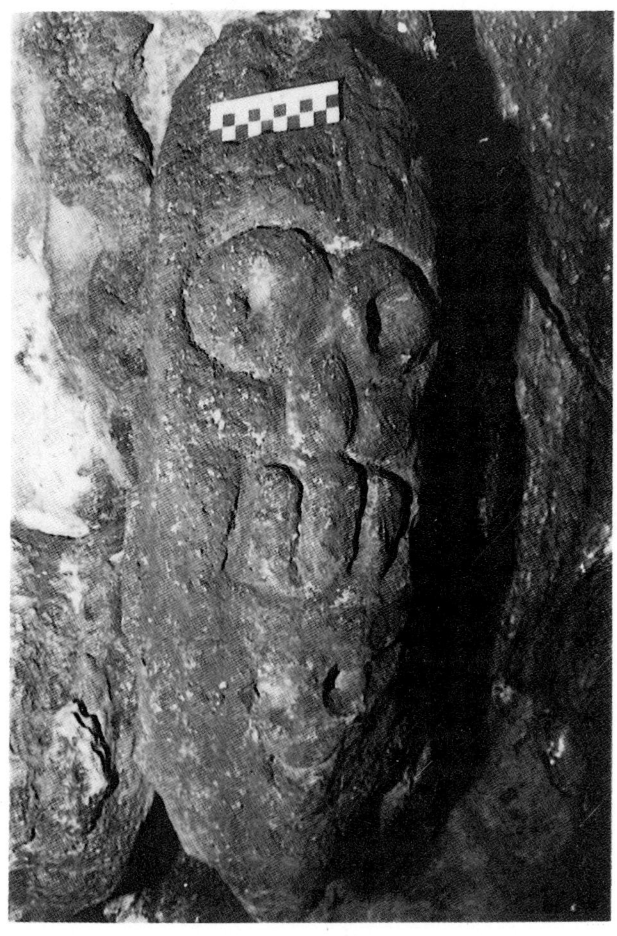

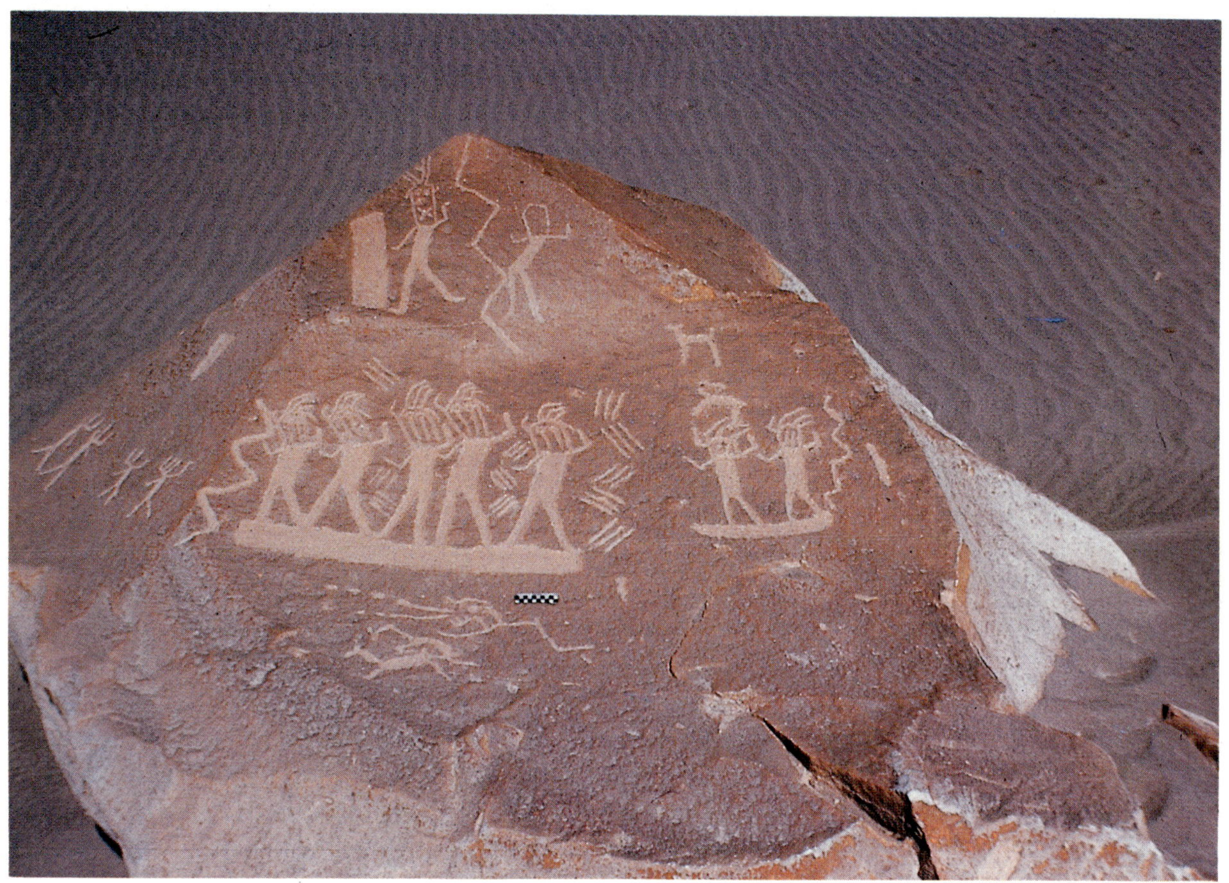

Figure 164. Tufa block bearing petroglyphs, Toro Muerto site complex, Aplao, Arequipa, Peru.

ancient artistic traditions. Some research work is also being conducted in most of the remaining countries of South America, in Colombia, Venezuela, Guyana and Surinam. In the latter countries, Dutchman Dubelaar has again been particularly active.

The rock art of Peru, summarised in four volumes by the above-mentioned Cuban Núñez Jiménez (former Cuban Minister of Culture), is among the best known and most spectacular of South America. Above all, the huge site of Toro Muerto in the country's south requires special mention. Measuring some four kilometres across, this massive assemblage of petroglyphs has been carved on thousands of large, angular blocks of volcanic tufa strewn over the desert site (Figure 164). The flat surfaces of this comparatively soft rock have provided excellent panels for countless artists, who carved many tens of thousands of motifs into them. There are spectacular geometric patterns, often composed of zigzags, dots and parallel sets of lines. The figurative component seems dominated by highly distinctive human figures. They are invariably depicted in animated poses, as if dancing, with limbs shown in various contorted positions. Their heads resemble masks, with zigzag lines emanating from the large eyes, and there are lines emanating from the top of the head (Figure 165). They are depicted singly or in groups,

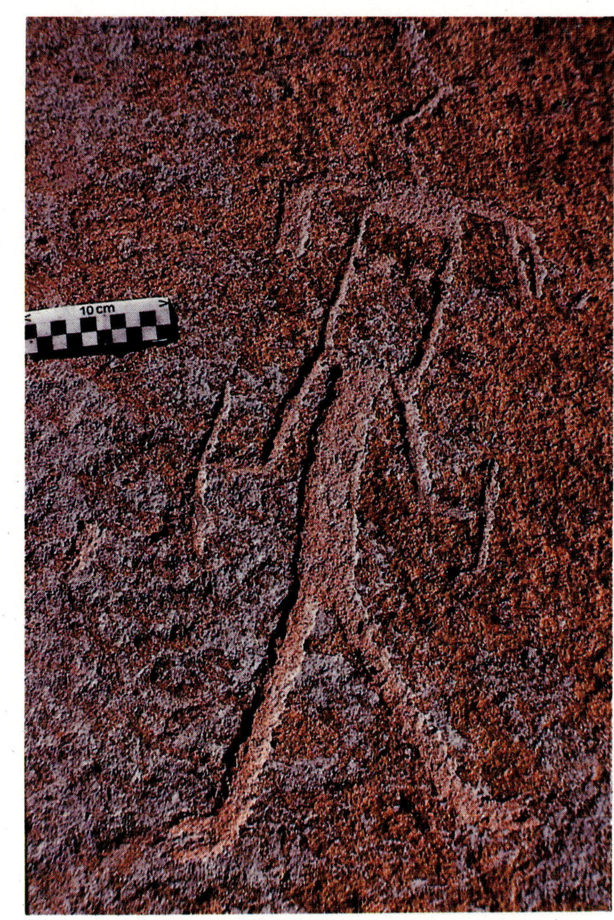

Figure 165. Apparently dancing human figure, possibly influenced by drugs or trance, Toro Muerto site complex, Aplao, Arequipa, Peru.

often surrounded by zigzags and other geometric forms. The component of animal figures is just as distinctive: it includes especially birds of prey, snakes and spotted cats, presumably jaguars (Figure 166). They occur in combinations, and there are even instances where transformations from one species into another appear to be depicted (Figure 167). Some figures feature most exotic and sophisticated stylistic conventions and graphic solutions, very reminiscent of the work of modern abstract artists (Figure 168). One can find many compositions resembling the style of Picasso and others, not only at Toro Muerto but also at many other Peruvian sites. The distinctive motif repertoire of sites such as this one has prompted speculation that the imagery of this powerful art may be related to drug-induced visions of the artists. It seems that they may have recorded the strange imagery artists experienced during ritual use of hallucinogens, especially such substances as *ayahuasca* and *yaye*. We know that these harmaline and ibogane-based narcotics produce visions of phosphenes (specific geometric patterns), large cats, eagles and serpents, and the universal image of the dragon or *Lindwurm* is a collage of the distinguishing features of these three animals. Such mythical beings are found in many parts of the world, and they occur often in rock arts (the dragon of eastern Asia, the 'sea wolf' of the Canadian west coast, or the Rainbow Serpent of Australia are just some examples), even where intentional use of narcotics is not known. It must be remembered, however, that many societies ingested such drugs unintentionally, including the people of the European Middle Ages (in the form

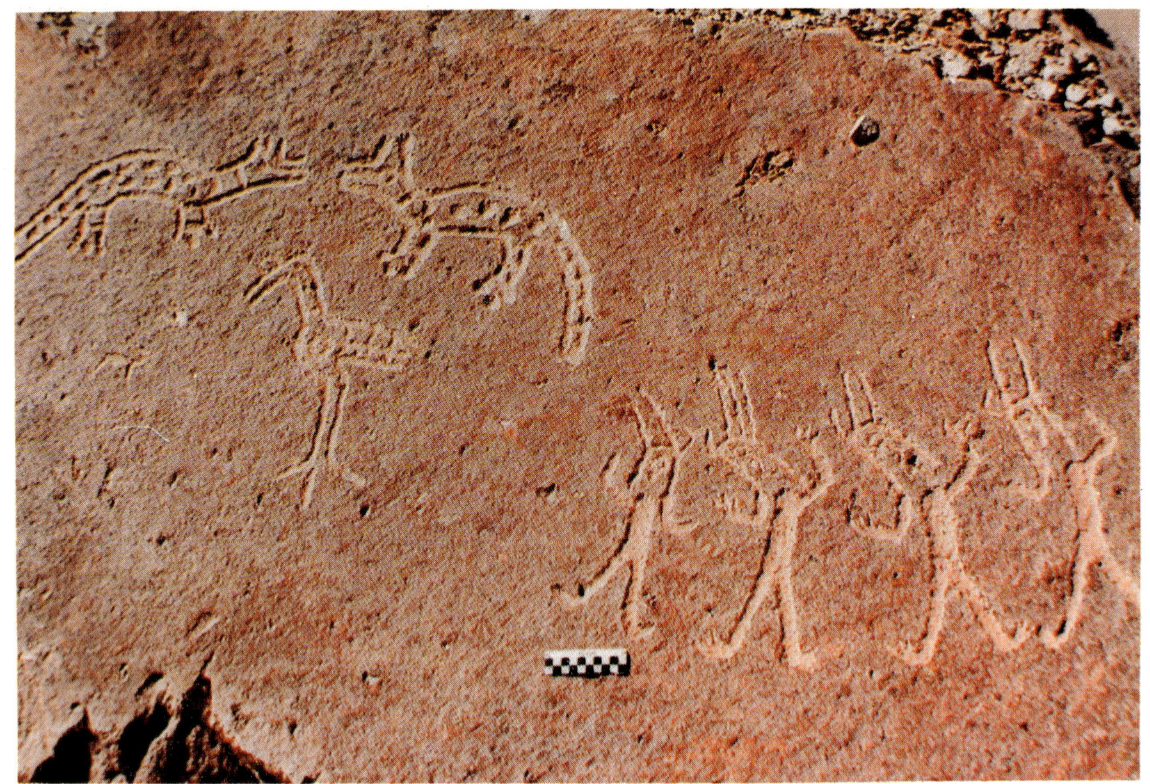

Figure 166. Two apparent jaguars, a bird and four dancers, of the Collawa period. Toro Muerto site complex, Aplao, Arequipa, Peru.

Figure 167. Apparent depiction of narcotics-induced imagery involving serpent, cat and bird of prey. Petroglyphs of Toro Muerto, Aplao, Arequipa, Peru.

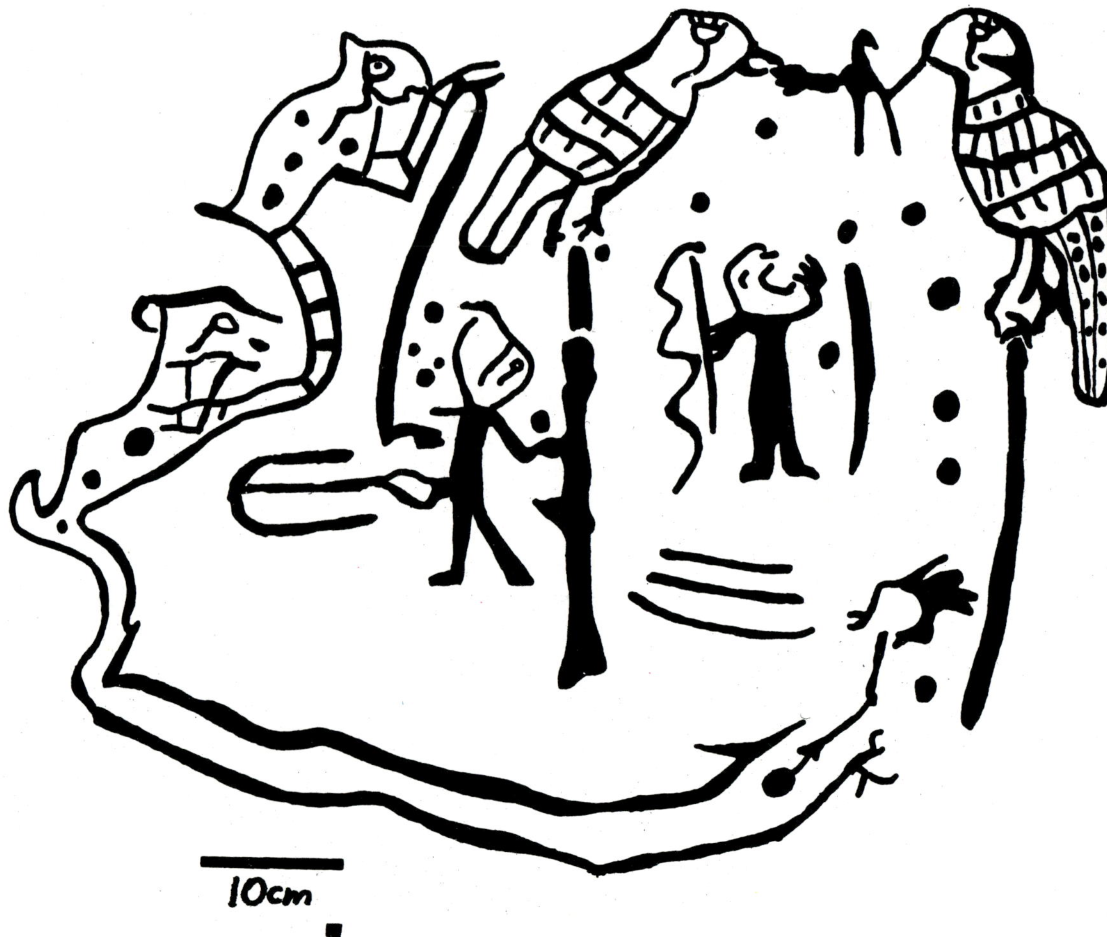

Figure 168. A selection of petroglyph motifs from Alto de la Guitarra, Trujillo, Peru. (After A. Núñez Jiménez.)

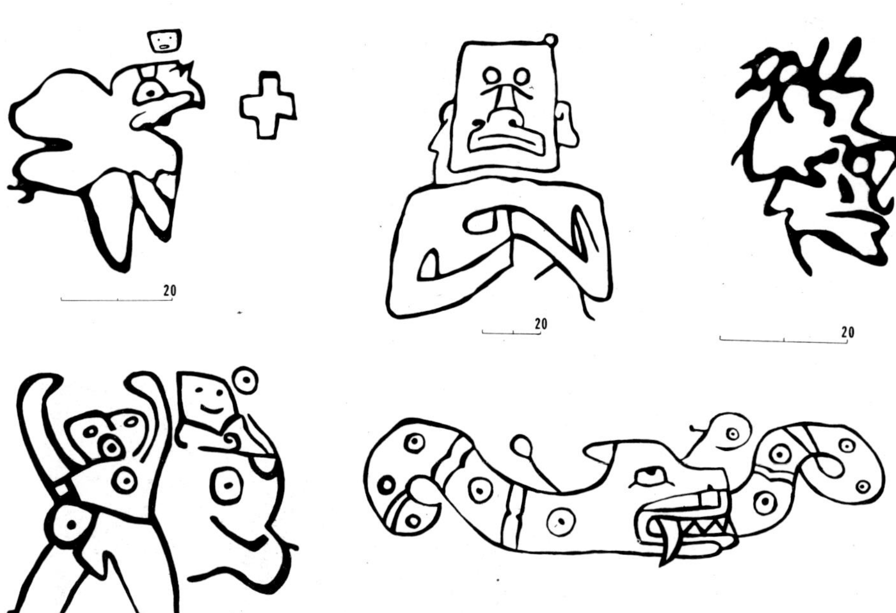

of ergot, a fungus infecting grain foods). Similar visions may have even been induced by other means, such as trance.

The most frequent examples of such imagery - which provides us with yet another case of universals found in global rock art - occur in South America, and here they are perhaps most prominent in Peru. This is not surprising, the peoples of the Andean region have been traditionally the world's experts in the cultural and ritual use of narcotics. Peruvian rock art sites are dominated by petroglyphs, but paintings also occur in that country. In the valley of the Río Siguas, huge petroglyphs are often found twenty or thirty metres high up on vertical, unscalable cliffs (Figure 169). Like the giant geoglyphs (stone arrangements, commonly measuring hundreds of metres) of the same area (Figure 170), they are barely visible to the visitor, rather they seem to be intended to be seen from positions above the land surface - perhaps by deities. At some sites, Historical inscriptions by the Spanish invaders of past centuries can be found, sometimes together with rock art. Speculative dating of the petroglyphs places most of them into the pre-Incan period, with a large number of images being attributed to the Collawa culture. A macabre component are apparent depictions of humans holding what seem to be human head trophies (Figure 171). We have seen that such imagery also occurs in India, at Pachmarhi. Portable art also occurs, in several forms, one of which is of 'naturalistic' style and seems to date from perhaps 7000 years ago. A very specific form of portable art is called 'sandwich'. It consist of flat, circular river pebbles, the size of a hand, which are found in pairs. They bear ochre patterns on one side, and sandwiched between them is a thin sheet of precious metal,

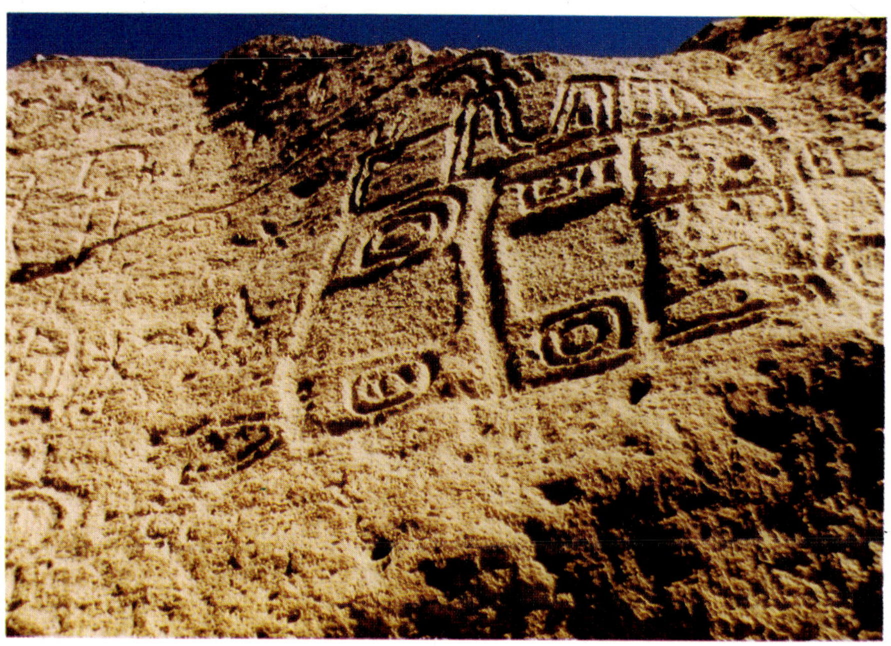

Figure 169. Large petroglyph high up on vertical tufa cliff in the Siguas valley, Arequipa, Peru.

gold or silver. They occur typically in children's graves. Some of these portable art forms have been used to provide tentative age estimates for rock art, but as in most parts of the world, solid dating evidence remains elusive.

In neighbouring Bolivia, very little was known about rock art in the mid-1980s. The establishment of a very active research association has resulted in significant improvements, and that country's rock art is now among the best explored national bodies in South America. The number of known sites is still small, a few hundred, but they include some fascinating examples. Paintings are more common than petroglyphs in Bolivia. Recently it has been established that some of the rock art sites there are still places of worship to the indigenous peoples, notably the Aymara. Traditional communities still provide offerings to the deities at such sites. They sacrifice animals, and they bury such items as bottles of drink in the floor of rock art shelters. The rock art traditions themselves also continue with modern motifs, suggesting the involvement of sympathetic magic (wish fulfilment, which is well documented from Australian rock art too).

Another fascinating discovery in Bolivian rock art concerns the evidence of religious iconoclasm - the intentional destruction of art. We have considered this subject in Asia and in Europe, and it is also found in the Americas. In North America, we know of many sites desecrated in recent times, by rifle bullets and other means. In Bolivia, at the site Peña Escrita, numerous Christian crosses were found engraved over the rock paintings (Figure 172). They had been added several centuries ago, sometimes superimposed directly over human figures, as if to exorcise them. R. G.

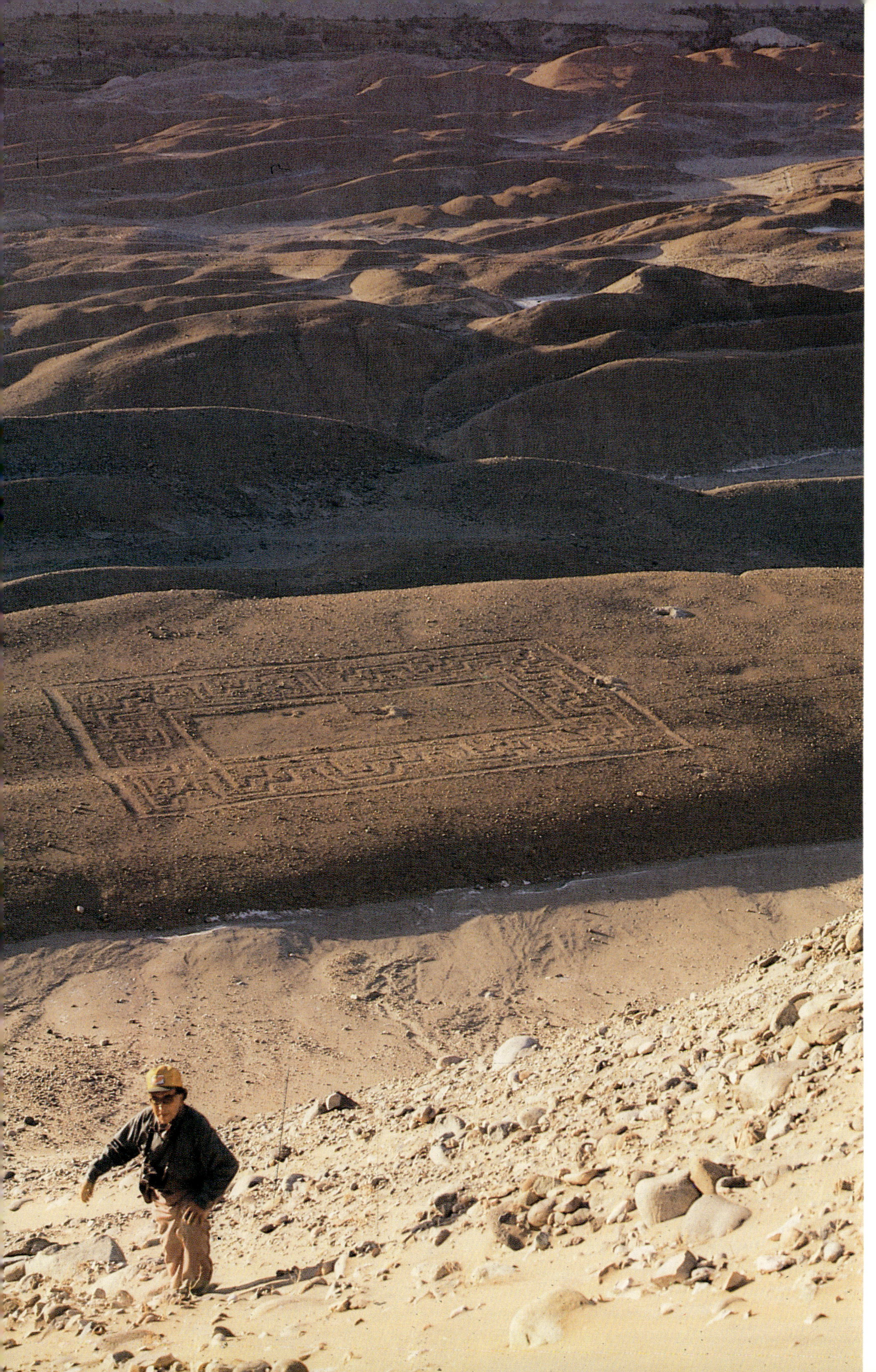

Figure 170. Negative geoglyph measuring several hundred metres, Professor E. Linares Málaga in the foreground. Pampa Siguas, Siguas valley, Arequipa, Peru.

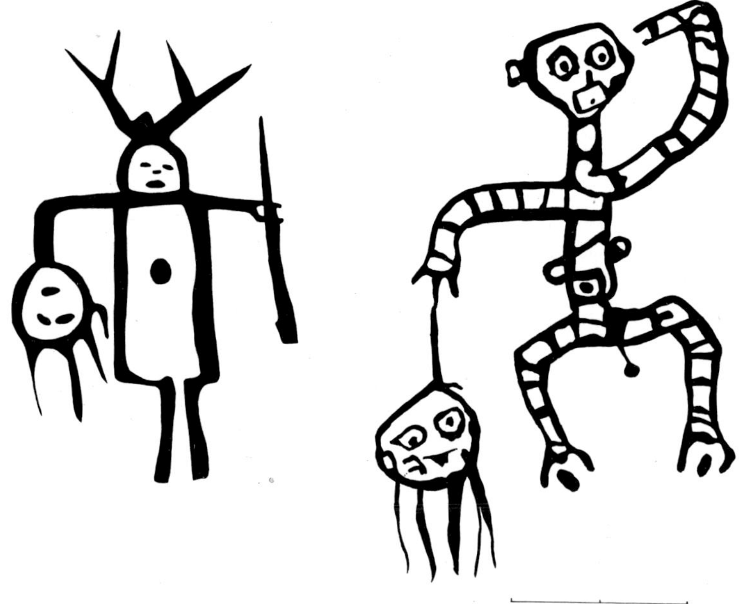

Figure 171. Two petroglyphs, apparently of humans holding severed human heads, from rock 34 at Huancor (left) and Toro Muerto (right), Peru.

Bednarik suggested that this was the work of the missionaries accompanying the Spanish conquistadors. Historical research soon showed that an edict by the colonial government in Lima had indeed decreed the destruction of indigenous sites of 'idolatry' in 1567, thus confirming the validity of the findings of rock art researchers.

Brazil, a huge country, offers several rock art regions, but the perhaps most important is in the country's semi-arid north-east. In parts of Pernambuco and Piauí, a rich concentration of painting sites has been explored by several researchers over the past twenty years. In particular, the area of Serra da Capivara in southern Piauí has attained world significance, through the discovery of the earliest current evidence of a human presence in the Americas. At the site Pedra Furada (Figure 173), near Sao Raimundo Nonato, and at other localities, Ice Age living floors have been discovered, some of them at rock art sites. At Pedra Furada, a rock fragment bearing some paint traces was found at a level dating from 17,000 years ago, but it has been argued that this does not represent reliable dating of the art. Indeed, the rock art at most of these sites is exfoliating rapidly, and is not very ancient. Some 300 rock art sites are now known in a small area, much of which has recently been declared a national park, and they include a few very ancient petroglyph galleries as well, such as Caicaras. The petroglyphs are entirely non-figurative and usually deeply patinated. Their motif range is very similar to the oldest petroglyph traditions in most other continents. The much more recent paintings are of several styles, some simple, others very complex and ornate. A key site in this region is the large rockshelter of Perna 1, because it contains the currently oldest reliably dated rock art in the Americas. A panel of perhaps a hundred small animal and human figures, in a very faded red pigment, was found at the back wall of the shelter, concealed by the entire upper part of the floor sediment (Figure 174). It is most unusual to find rock paintings below ground level; extremely dry soil conditions are necessary for this to be possible. The paintings extend right down to a massive occupation layer of almost solidly packed charcoal, which we know is about 10,000 years old. We also know that the site was denuded of any sediment when it was flooded 13,000 years ago, so it is obvious that the paintings must be between these two ages, and probably close to the first.

Other important rock art regions exist in Brazil, for instance in regions near Belo Horizonte and Sao Paulo, both in the country's south, and in the western state Mato Grosso. They are less spectacular and less well known. Numerous boulders with petroglyphs have also been reported on various upper tributaries of the Amazon, but until recently it had been assumed that the lower Amazon basin was entirely devoid of rock art. However, even here, rock art was finally discovered, and in considerable quantity. In a series of caves in the dense jungle near the town of Monte Alegré, on the lower Amazon, an expedition found numerous paintings in 1987. This suggests that there may be a great deal more still to be discovered in the less explored regions of Brazil.

In Chile and Argentina, rock art studies is a field with a long history, dating back to the work of such pioneers as Oswald Menghin. The main concentrations of rock art are found in the foothills and lower ranges of the Andes, and they extend down on both sides of this massive divide. Argentine rock art is perhaps best known for its spectacular sites of hand stencils in Patagonia, notably at Cueva de las Manos (Figure 175). In this form of rock painting, which is yet another universal form we find in rock art, an object (most frequently a human hand) is held against the rock, and the artist then sprays the area around it with paint from his (or her) mouth. This is a very fast and effective way of creating an image, taking only seconds, and it is found most highly developed in Australia. However, there are various other forms of rock art found in Argentina, the main art regions being the north-west, the Sierras Centrales, Cuyo, Neuquen and Patagonia. One painted site in the latter region, Cueva Grande del Arroyo Feo, has yielded occupation evidence that is up to 9300 years old. Despite the better-known paintings, petroglyphs are well represented in the traditions of the southern Andes.

In Chile, particularly in the northern parts of that country, the geoglyph traditions we have already

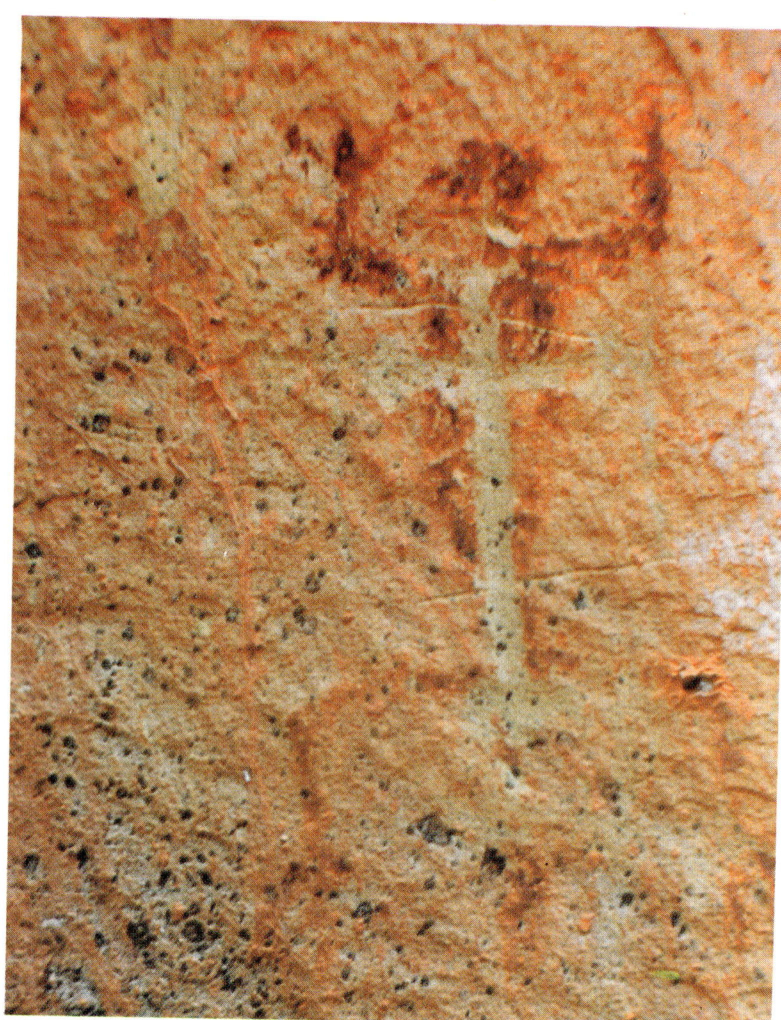

Figure 172. Painting of human, with superimposed religious vandalism in the form of a Spanish cross petroglyph, Peña Escrita, Cochabamba, Bolivia.

Figure 173. A selection of rockpainting motifs in Pedra Furada rockshelter, Piauí, Brazil.

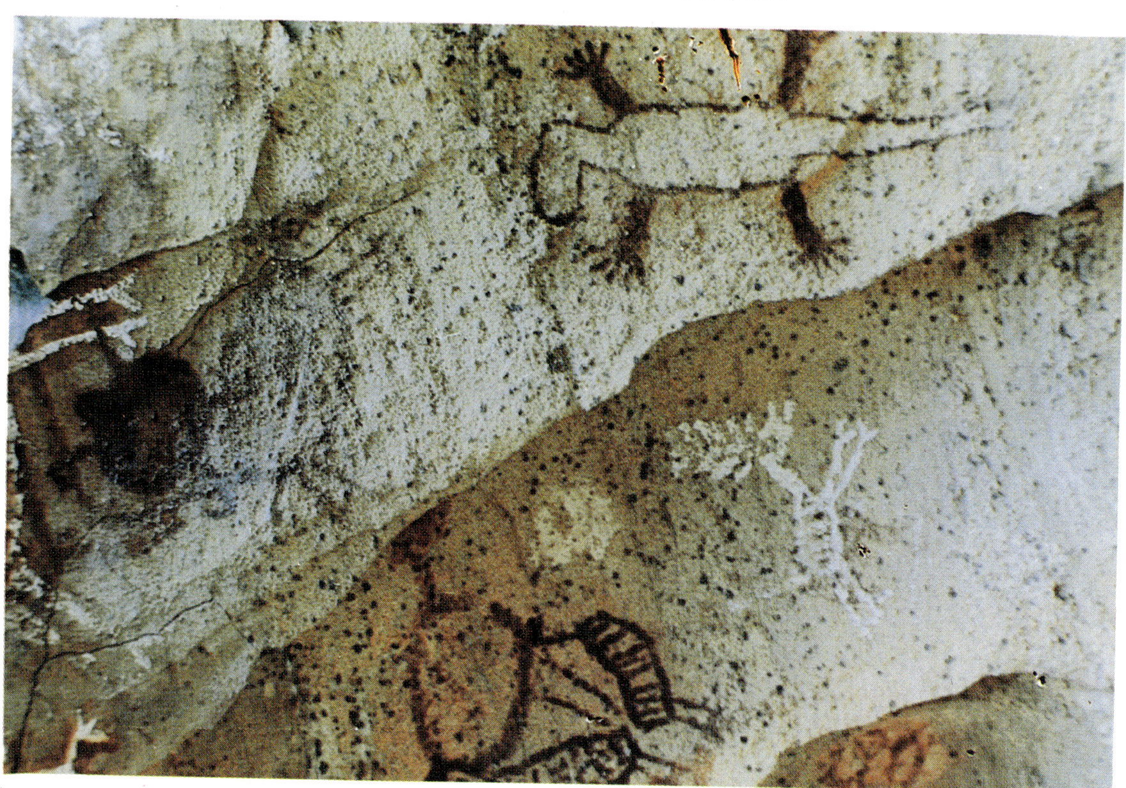

Figure 174. Excavated living floor in Perna 1, Piauí, Brazil. The numerous paintings on the wall were found below the sediment which extended almost to the top of the photograph.

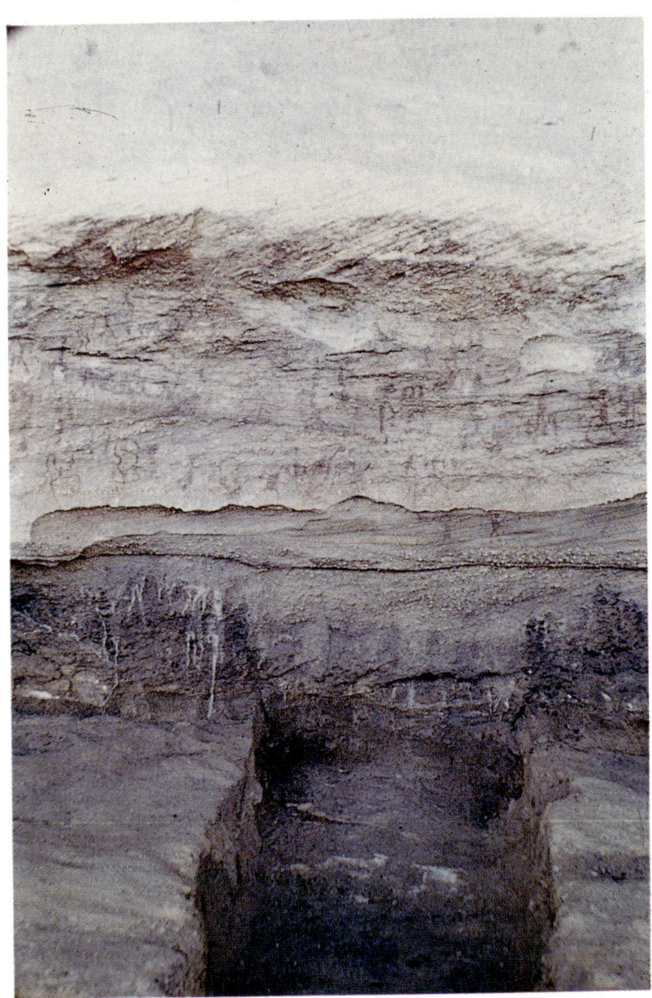

Figure 175. Hand stencil and apparent guanaco hunting scene, Cueva de las Manos, Santa Cruz Province, Patagonia, Argentina.

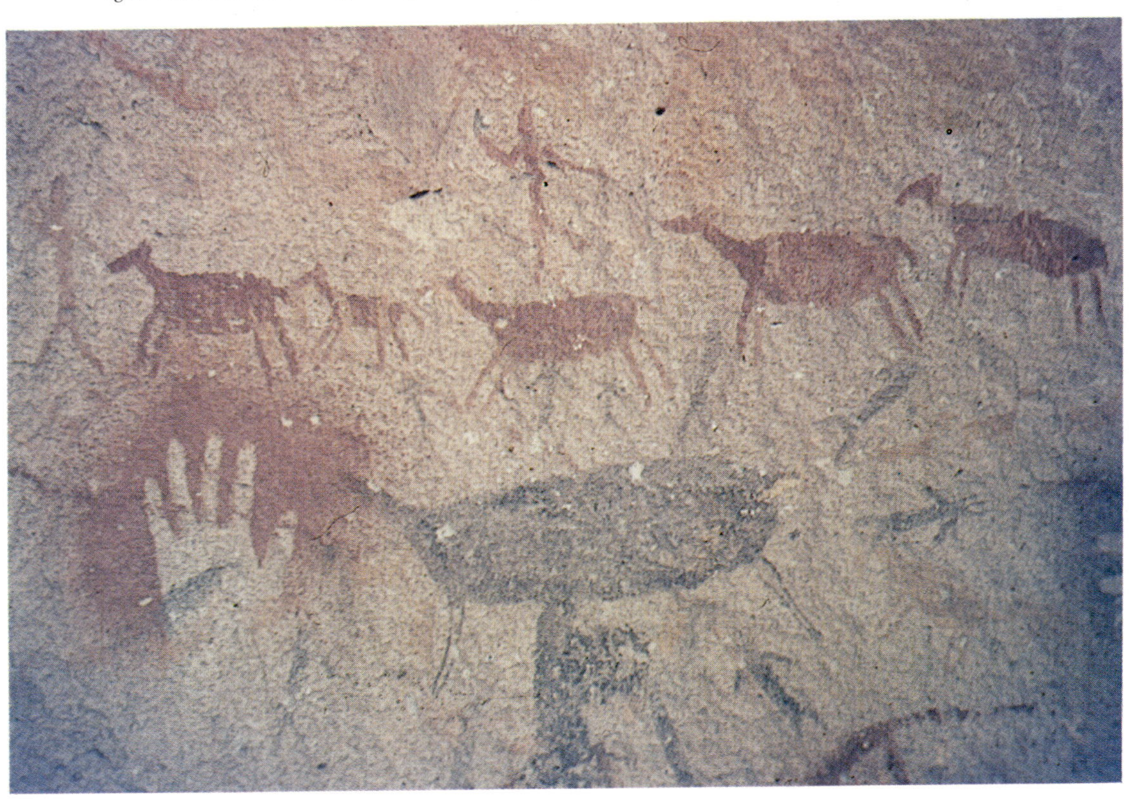

noted in southern Peru continue, and many thousands of these art works have now been recorded. One researcher lists over 8000 such sites. The 'Nazca lines' in Peru are well known, but the greater number of these features occurs in Chile. Strictly speaking, geoglyphs are not considered to be rock art as such, but they are of obvious interest to us still, just as portable art is relevant. Such features, also called stone arrangements, are found in many other world regions, not only in the Andes: for instance in the Southwest of U.S.A., in Australia and in Britain. We distinguish positive and negative forms of geoglyphs: the former were produced by placing large numbers of rocks and boulders in specific patterns, the latter by removing stones from a darkly patinated cobble pavement, thus exposing the lighter coloured stones beneath (see Figure 170).

With the exception of the examples specifically mentioned, little rock art has been dated securely in South America. In Bolivia some basic phases have been distinguished preliminarily. Similarly, in Brazil and Argentina there are plausible models of rock art chronology. On the whole, however, direct dating is desirable before any of these tentative frameworks can be accepted as truly valid. ❐

• AN OVERVIEW OF AUSTRALIAN ROCK ART •

AN OVERVIEW OF AUSTRALIAN ROCK ART

In contrast to the Americas, where the question of initial human settlement remains the subject of a major scientific controversy, the model of the first occupation of the island continent is much more straightforward. Australia is sometimes seen as the 'new continent', in a somewhat Eurocentric perspective. In reality it is a very ancient land: some of its landforms are among the earliest surviving land surfaces on the face of the earth. Genera and classes of animals and plants extinct elsewhere have managed to survive here, and Australia is the home of the oldest surviving culture in the world. This latter characteristic is strongly reflected in the rock art of the continent, all of which is claimed by the Aboriginal people as their own cultural heritage. The Aborigines are descended directly from the heroes of the Dreamtime, who were animals before they became human. Interestingly enough, this belief coincides with the findings of science, that humans have evolved from other animals. But Europeans, who thought that Darwin's findings represented a major breakthrough in human knowledge, regarded the beliefs of Aborigines as pure myths which needed to be replaced with their own, 'true' teachings. Arrogant science has still not learnt that much of its 'new knowledge' has been with us for a long time. Such is the course of science. The Aborigines, unencumbered by fantastical religious beliefs, had always known the truth about evolution. Indeed, many 'facts' already recorded in their oral traditions have had

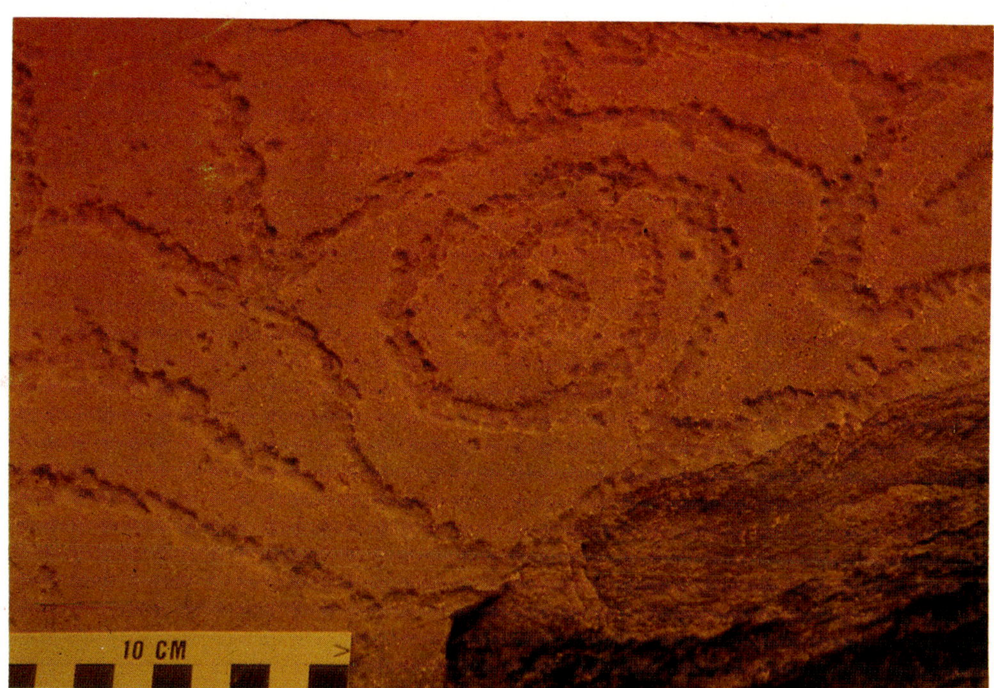

Figure 176. Detail of complex petroglyph maze of the archaic linear tradition, Panaramitee North, South Australia.

to be re-discovered by scientists: that certain islands were once connected to the Australian mainland, that there was a vast lake once where the Gulf of Carpentaria is today, and that volcanoes in two regions of the continent erupted thousands of years ago.

We believe today that humans first arrived in Australia perhaps 60,000 years ago. Even at the lowest sea level in the Ice Age, they still had to cross several stretches of open ocean, sometimes without seeing the land on the other side from the shore of departure. After reaching the then much larger continent of Australia (it included New Guinea and the continental shelf), they proceeded further to New Ireland, and finally from there to Buka Island, crossing 180 kilometres of sea. These accomplished and competent seafarers navigated the ocean almost habitually and probably on many occasions. Sometimes they established new populations in the process. They possessed language, planned their expeditions well, and had seaworthy watercraft. This picture differs significantly from the Eurocentric model, according to which the peoples of this period (called the Middle Palaeolithic) were primitive, lacked speech and other forms of symbolism, and lacked also the capacity of forward planning. That model is, as we have seen above, totally false; it is itself a mythology of poorly informed and excessively conservative scholars, and yet it still dominates university curricula of archaeology around the world!

The earliest rock art in Australia was probably produced soon after the arrival of humans. The ability of symbolic thought and action itself implies a capacity to produce art, in whatever form. In the Olary region of South Australia, minimum dating of well over

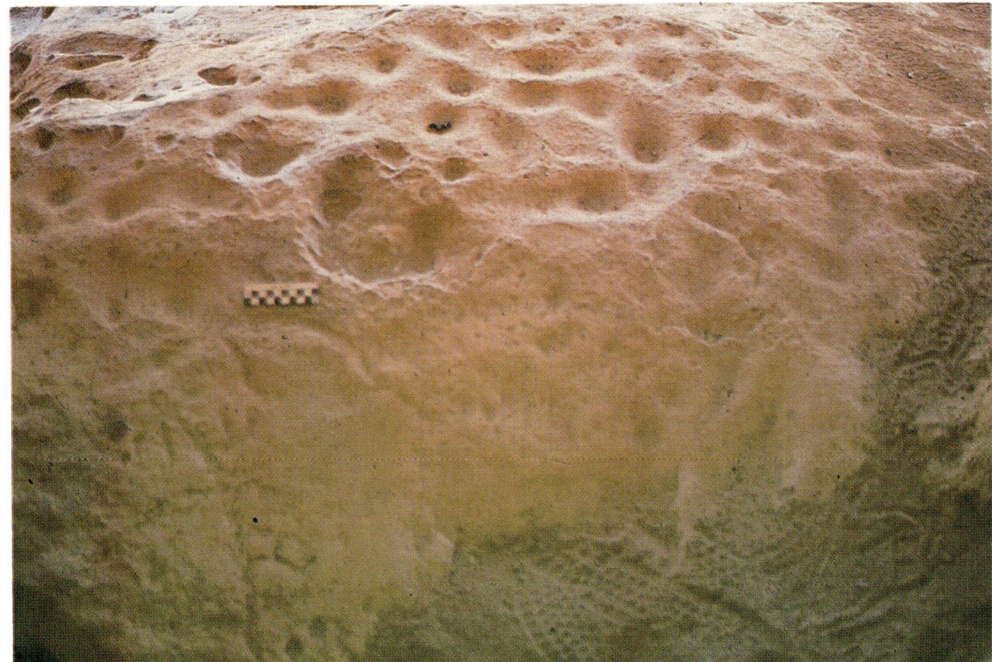

Figure 177. Ice Age cupules or cup marks on the sandstone of Sandy Creek site, Cape York Peninsula, Queensland, Australia.

40,000 years has been obtained directly from several petroglyphs on heavily patinated rock pavements, at the sites Panaramitee North and Wharton Hill, and somewhat younger dates are available from other sites (Figure 176). Elsewhere in Australia, cup marks have been suggested to be particularly ancient, and may prove to be the earliest surviving art form in that continent (Figure 177). This agrees completely with the pattern already established in Europe, Asia and America.

The Archaic Linear Petroglyph Traditions of Australia, which are clearly of the Ice Age, present us with the most complete repertoire of the ancient non-figurative petroglyph traditions which we can find also in other continents. Because so many examples have managed to survive in the favourable environment of Australia, this ancient art is found at literally thousands of sites (Figure 178). Initially, it consists of cupules (cup marks) or dots, parallel lines, arcs and multiple arcs, circles, concentric circles, wave lines or zigzags, spirals, and of what are called CLMs (convergent lines motifs, of a few, usually three, lines bunched together at one end so they look like the track of a bird). Much later, tracks of humans and animals are added, and finally depictions of objects (animal and human figures). These traditions are distributed over much of the continent and they are also found in Tasmania. That island was separated from the mainland by the rising sea level around 10,000 years ago and in recent human history, the Tasmanians were the population longest isolated from any other people. They produced both petroglyphs and cave paintings (hand stencils), but only a few sites have survived. They also used ochre for body painting and their mining operations were described by scholars of

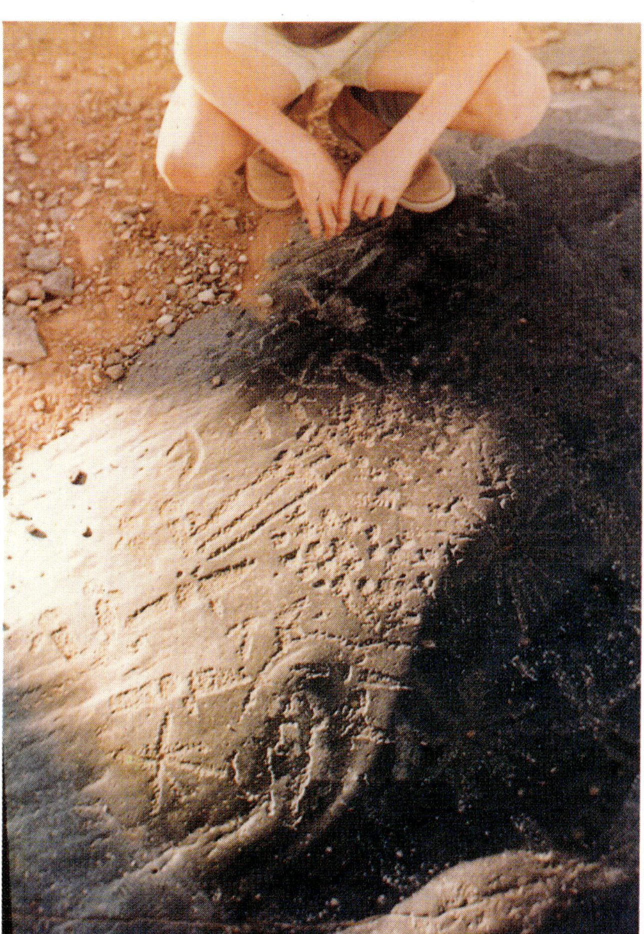

Figure 178. Archaic linear petroglyphs, non-figurative, very early and patinated. Sturts Meadows, New South Wales, Australia.

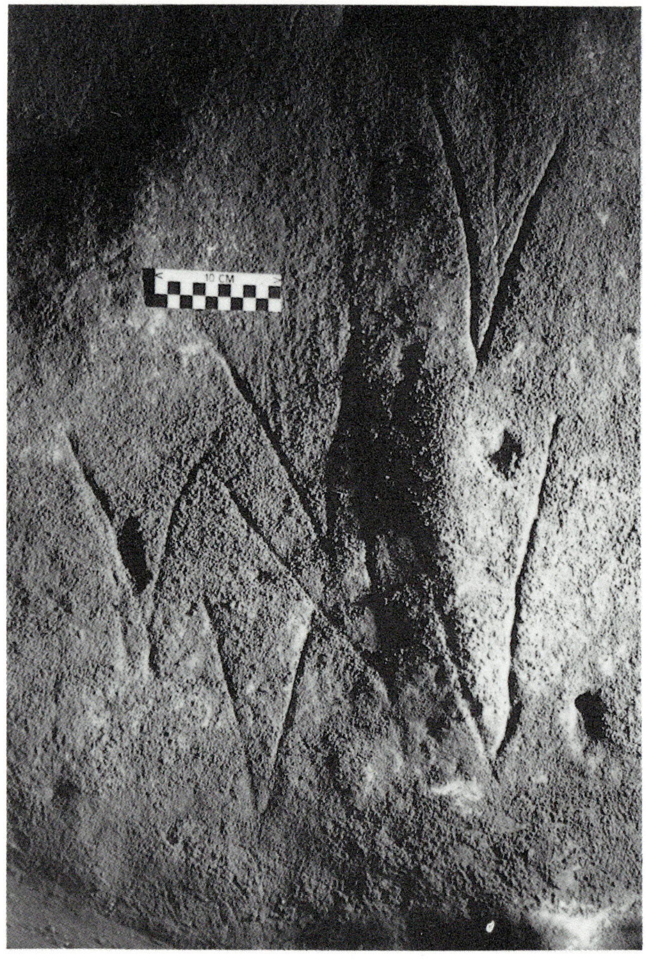

Figure 179. Ancient cave petroglyphs in the permanent darkness of Mooraa Cave, South Australia.

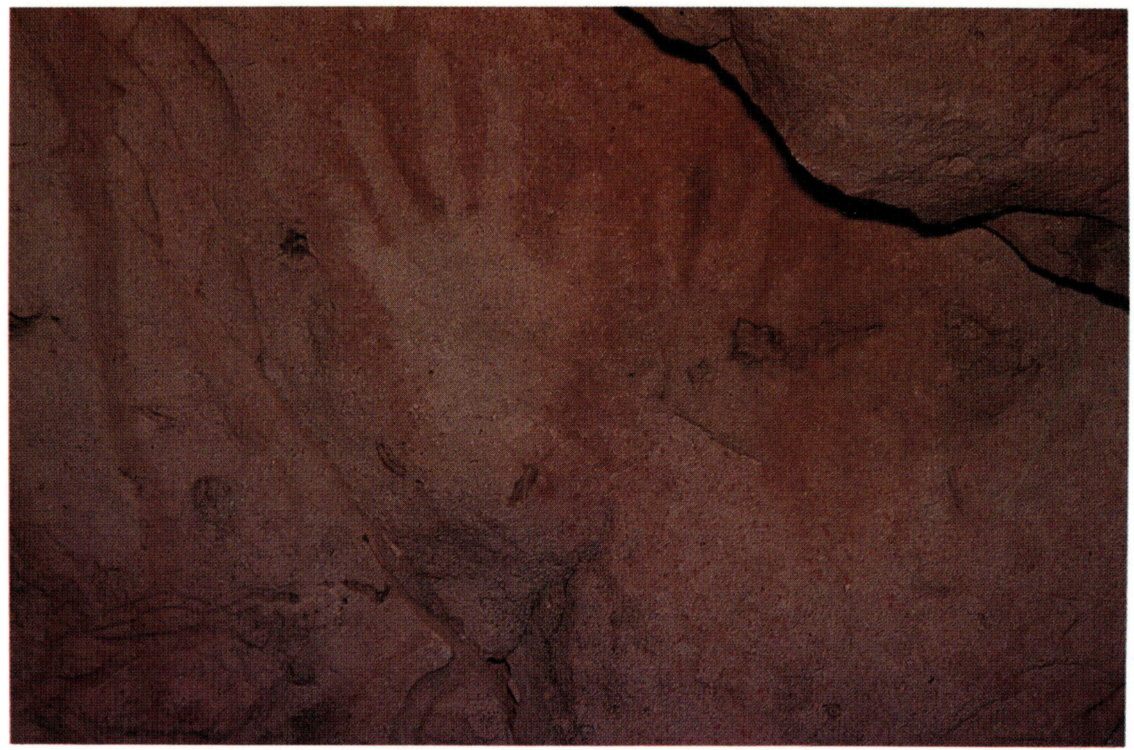

Figure 180. Hand stencils in limestone cave on the Nullarbor Plain. Murrawichina Cave, South Australia.

the last century.

Ochre mining evidence is also widespread on the Australian mainland, the largest site being Wilgie Mia in Western Australia, where thousands of tonnes of the mineral has been quarried. Elsewhere, Ice Age Aborigines mined flint in underground limestone caves. And they produced rock art in such caves, across the southern regions of Australia (Figure 179). Over 100 sites of cave art are presently known, and more are expected to be found. Petroglyphs occur in most of them, as finger markings on formerly soft surfaces, or as deep carvings or shallow engravings. A number of traditions of this cave art are distinguished but all of them are entirely non-figurative. Some resemble the Archaic Linear Tradition found at open sites and certainly extend well into the Ice Age. The greatest concentrations of Australian cave petroglyphs are those of Koonalda Cave, Karlie-ngoingpool Cave and Paroong Cave. In a few caves in south-western Australia, hand stencils can also be found (Figure 180).

Major concentrations of open site rock art occur in the Flinders Ranges of South Australia, as archaic petroglyphs and more recent paintings, and a similar pattern continues from there to the east. Large sites are found around Broken Hill, including Sturts Meadows and the Mootwingee site complex. Central New South Wales offers major painting sites such as Mount Grenfell, and rock art site concentration increases towards the east coast. In the region around Sydney, some 3000 sites have been recorded, of shelter paintings and sandstone pavement petroglyphs. To the south of this zone, rock art incidence decreases notably, with only one concentration worth

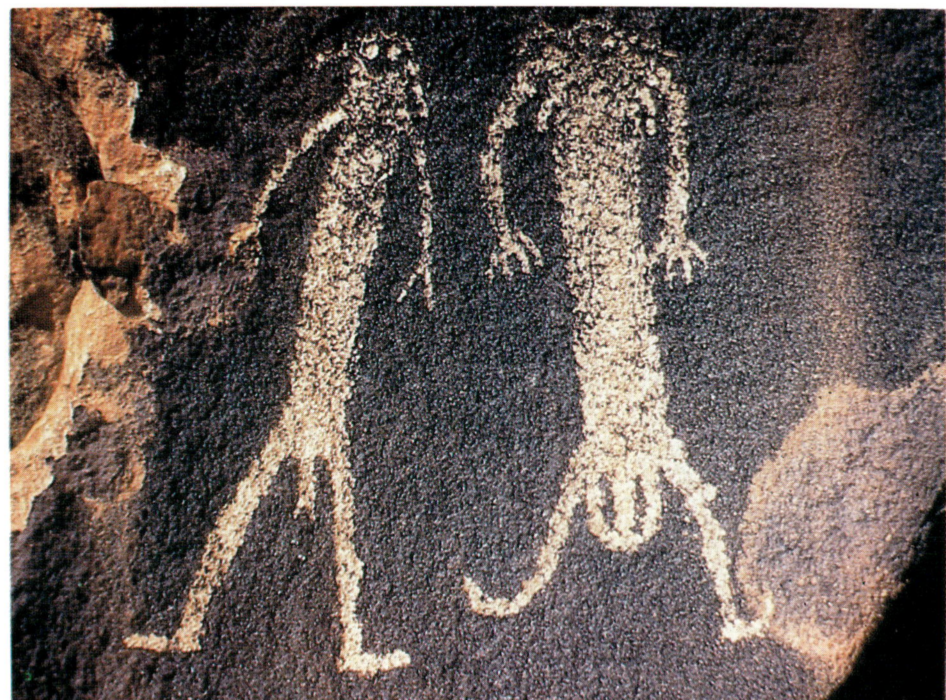

Figure 181. Petroglyphs of male and female humans, Watering Cove, Burrup Peninsula, Pilbara, Western Australia.

mentioning in Victoria, that of the Grampians mountains.

However, as one proceeds further north in Australia, rock art site density increases steadily, until it culminates in the most spectacular galleries found in the world, those of the far northern regions of the continent. The five largest and most spectacular regional concentrations of rock art are all in northern Australia. They are, from west to east, the Pilbara, the Kimberley, the Victoria River district (VRD), Arnhem Land and Cape York Peninsula. Large numbers of sites occur also elsewhere in the north, particularly in the Alice Springs region and in various parts of Queensland, such as at Mount Isa and in the central highlands of that state. In sheer quantity of art, in its visual impact and superb state of preservation, the great rock art zones of Australia's north are unequalled in the world.

The Pilbara is a semi-arid zone of rugged mountains, gorges, vast boulder piles and coastal promontories. It contains great numbers of petroglyph sites, which in the 1960s were found to amount to the largest petroglyph concentration on earth. At one site complex alone, the Burrup Peninsula (Dampier), the number of petroglyphs runs into hundreds of thousands (Figure 181). Other famous site complexes are the over thirty hill sites at Spear Hill (Figure 182-a,b; see page no. 89 also), Woodstock, and the Port Hedland pavements. The vast majority of petroglyphs are found on plutonic rocks that are always deeply patinated. Numerous, still poorly explored traditions are present, and there is no doubt that they begin in the Ice Age. The range of motifs is so vast that it is not possible to provide even a superficial

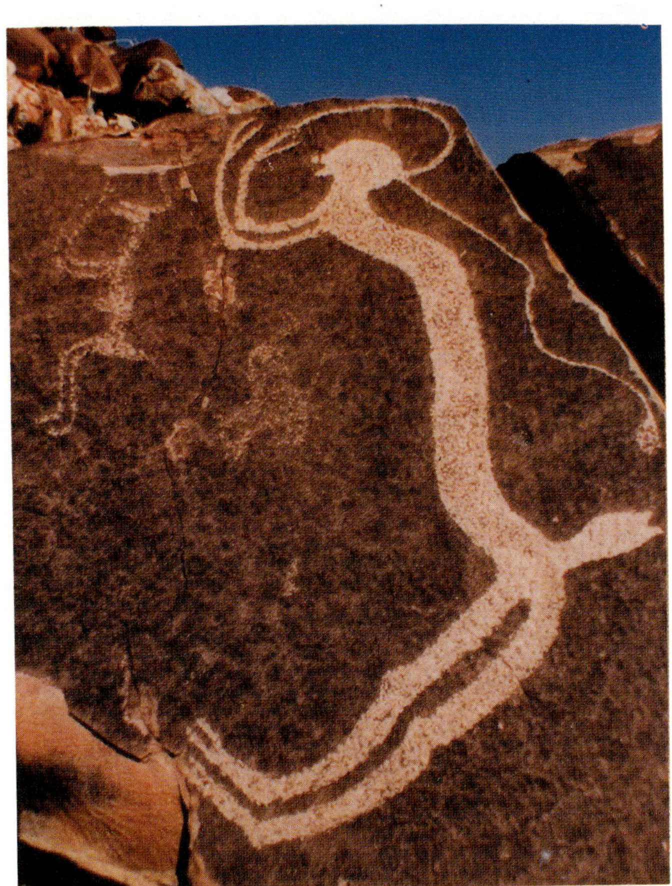

Figure 182-b. Anthropomorphous petroglyph, Woodstock figure, Spear Hill Site 30, Pilbara, Western Australia.

account here. None of this art is dated at present.

Proceeding to the Kimberley region, we find one of the most inaccessible parts of the continent, dissected by rugged ranges and steep canyons, with very few roads. This region forms a fairly continuous corpus with the adjacent VRD, although there exist numerous discrete styles and artistic traditions across this wide expanse of land. The art of both regions remains very poorly explored, and it may well represent the world's largest single rock art body (Figure 183). Systematic survey began less than ten years ago. One researcher, David Welch, has found some 1000 sites in the Kimberley and considers to have 'barely scratched the surface'; he thinks it is possible that there are 100,000 sites in that region alone. Another scholar, Grahame Walsh, has found many more sites, and in one of them a painting that is 43 metres long, the largest rock art motif known in the world (it is partially eroded and was originally over 50 metres, probably depicting a human figure). Figures of monumental sizes are found at various sites, and the many painting traditions can be divided into two main groups: the early Bradshaw figures and the later Wandjina styles. Bradshaws are usually red elaborate paintings of humans, with great care taken to depict details of decoration: headdresses (elongate caps or large wings), tassels, hand-held objects and objects attached to limbs are all shown with great care for

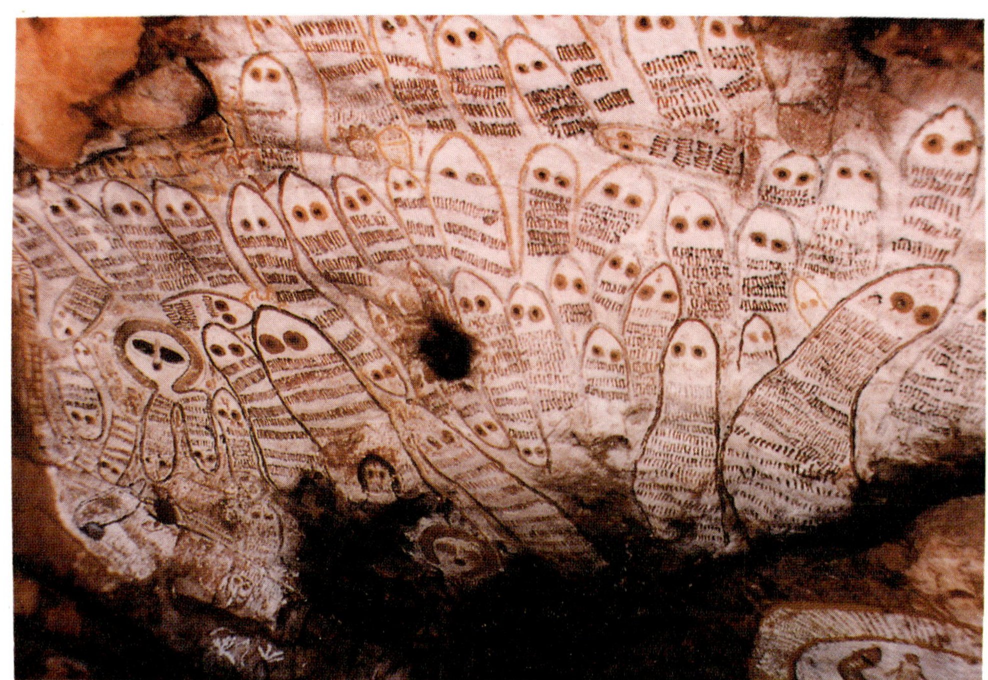

Figure 183. Rainbow Serpent, the world creator, on the lower right, with many baby Rainbow Serpents. Gibb River, Kimberley, Western Australia.

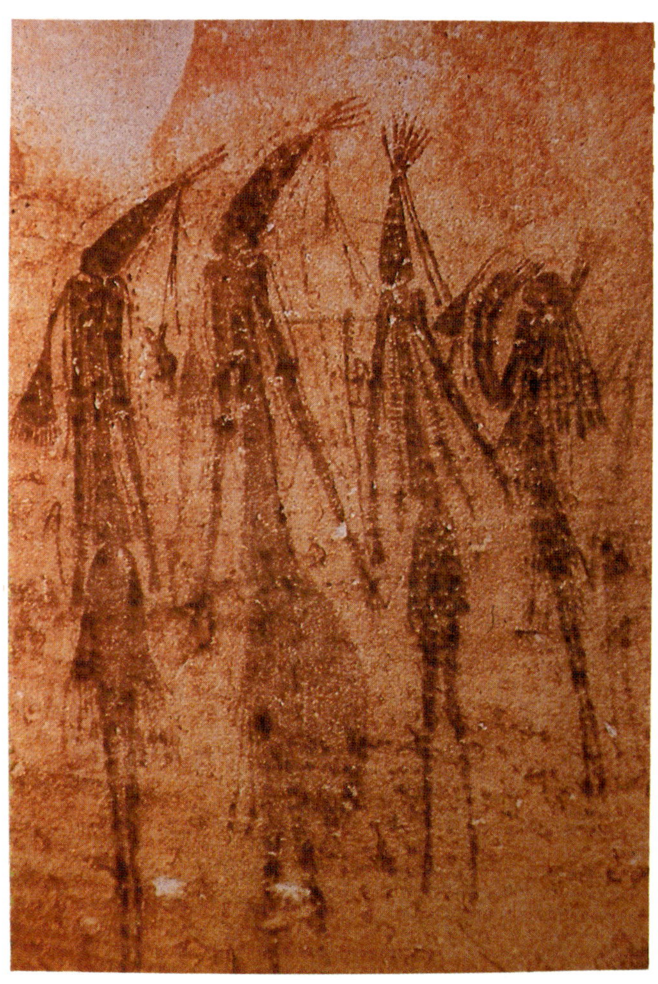

Figure 184. Group of Bradshaw figures, a very early painting tradition of the Kimberley, Western Australia.

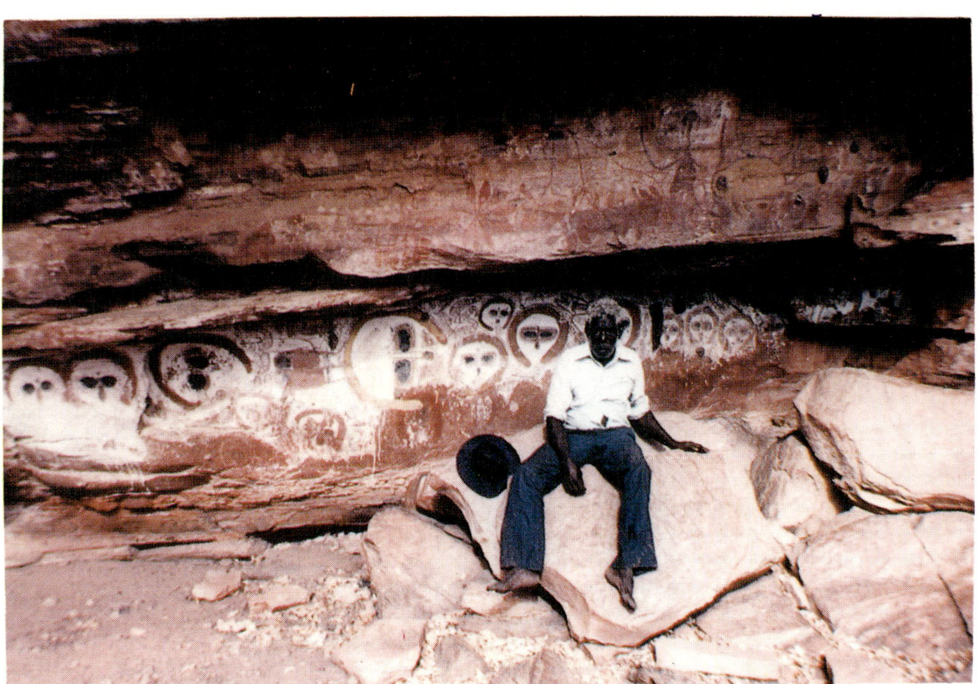

Figure 185. Wandjina rock painting site with its senior Aboriginal site custodian, Kimberley, Western Australia.

detail (Figure 184). The sex is never indicated in these figures, nor are there any depictions of hunt or other activities. These art styles provide the most detailed human figures we have of such great antiquity, anywhere in the world. The figures are often depicted with extraordinary grace, movement and pride, showing us once again that the earlier art traditions are often the ones that appear the most sophisticated to us.

The Wandjinas are the more recent human figures, usually polychrome on white-painted rock panels, with a halo-like feature and lacking mouths. This is of a much more rigid style than the older traditions, and it continues to be maintained by present Aboriginal society (Figure 185). The Wandjinas are the Dreamtime heroes who lived in a period called *Yoriyoro,* the Ice Age. After creating the world they painted themselves onto the rocks as they disappeared into them, instructing the Aboriginal people to maintain their images forever. It remains the responsibility of the most senior elders of the Kimberley tribes to renew or retouch the images whenever they fade (Figure 186). It should be mentioned that all painting traditions of Kimberley are preceded by petroglyphs, including the ubiquitous earliest cupules, assumed to extend to the earliest settlement of the area.

In the neighbouring VRD, which also remains poorly explored, we find a great diversity of yet again different styles (Figure 187). Ancient petroglyphs are found, and here they often occur together with the paintings (Figure 188). The latter dominate clearly, however (Figure 189). Specific features are the Rainbow Serpent, one of the greatest mythical beings in Aboriginal religion, and the Lightning Brothers, relating to a

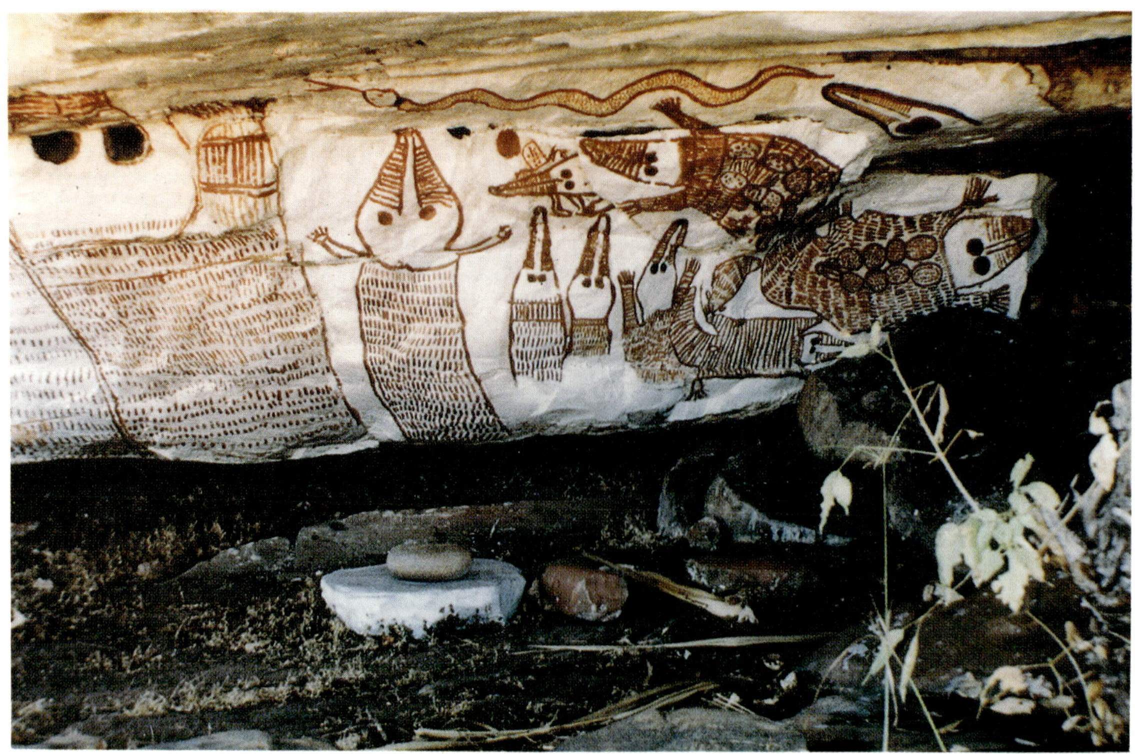

Figure 186. Recently repainted rock art site, with white and red ochre mortars still on floor. Mount Elizabeth, Kimberley, Western Australia.

Figure 187. Painted squatting female spirit being, strings between hands. Western Baines, Victoria River district, Northern Territory, Australia.

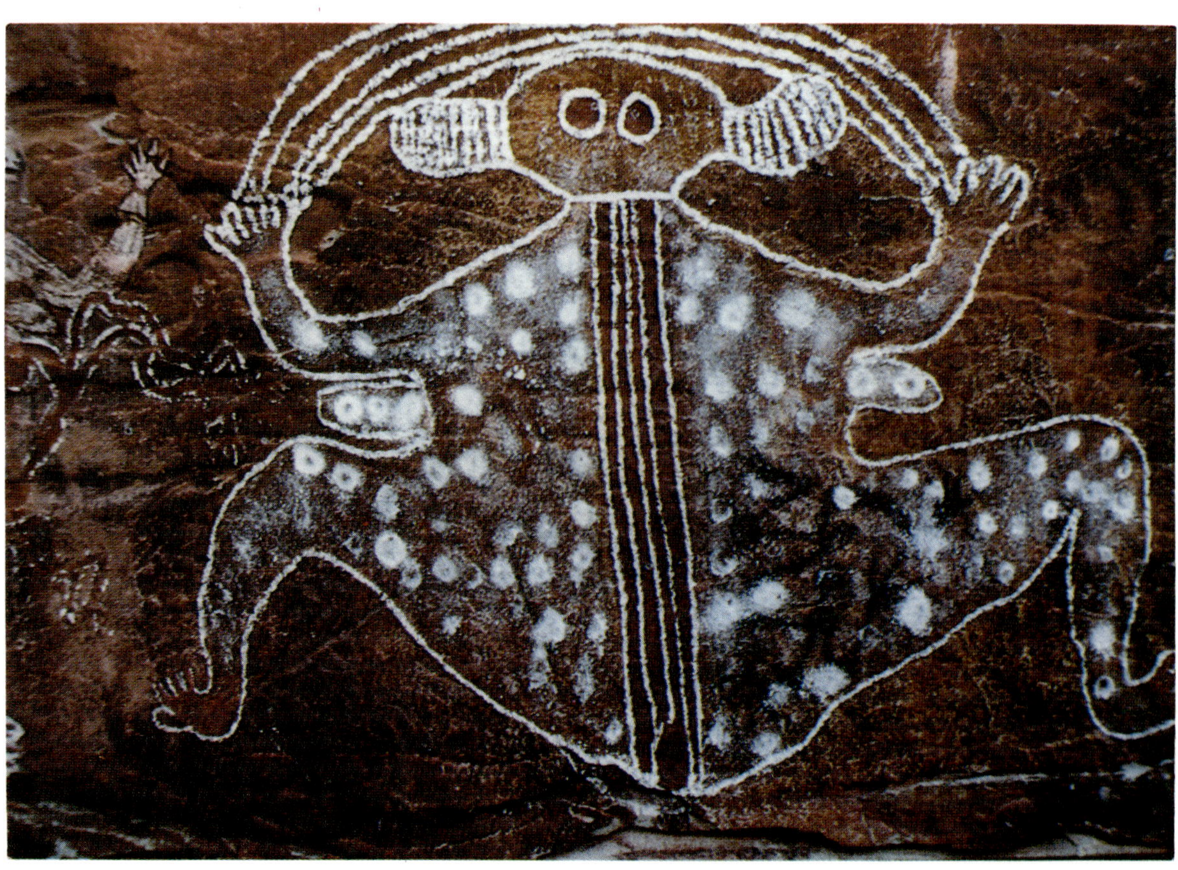

Figure 188. Combination of petroglyphs (cupules and incisions) with paintings, Jalijbang, Victoria River district, Northern Territory, Australia.

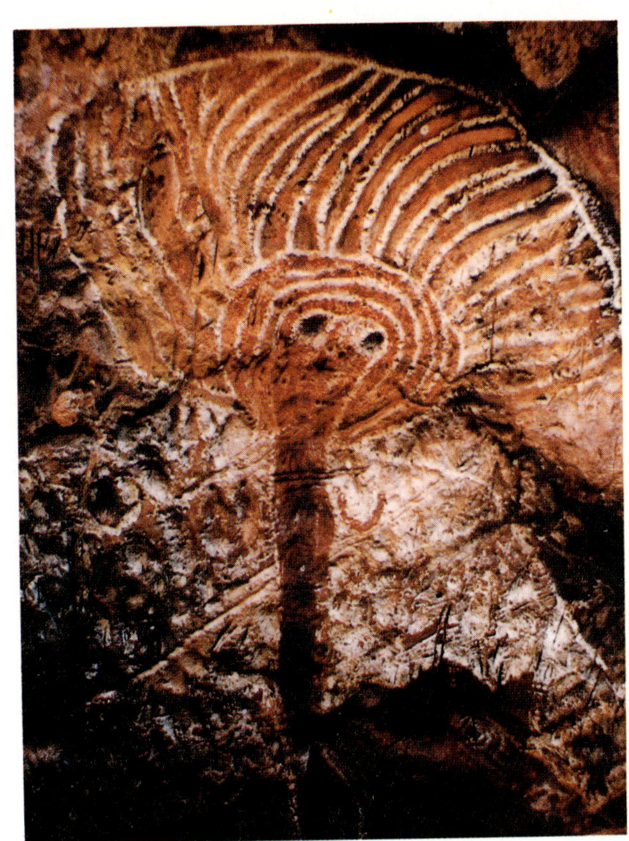

story told in various regions of the Northern Territory. Howard McNickle has begun the first comprehensive survey of the VRD, and Josephine Flood with her team works in the region of the Wardaman people.

One of the world's most famous rock art areas is that of Arnhem Land, best known through the long work of George Chaloupka. Part of this region, which comprises the finest X-ray art we know of, is now a national park and a World Heritage property, and all of Arnhem Land belongs to its traditional Aboriginal owners (as do many other areas of Australia, which often include cultural properties such as rock art sites). Some 10,000 sites have been documented in Arnhem Land, and we shall not even attempt to summarise their styles and traditions. At many sites, layer upon layer of paint has been found, and up to forty such superimposed strata have been counted. Rock art scientist Alan Watchman has even detected such stratigraphies of paintings at other sites where no art at all was visible on the surface. These paint layers are often separated by mineral deposits, some of which are datable. In addition to studying the rock art of Arnhem Land for many years, Chaloupka has also gathered an immense amount of ethnological information through his strong friendships with senior Aboriginal custodians. Today, the Aboriginal society of Arnhem Land manages and preserves its own cultural heritage. Rock art remains a powerful cultural focus of that society, and in some cases has continued

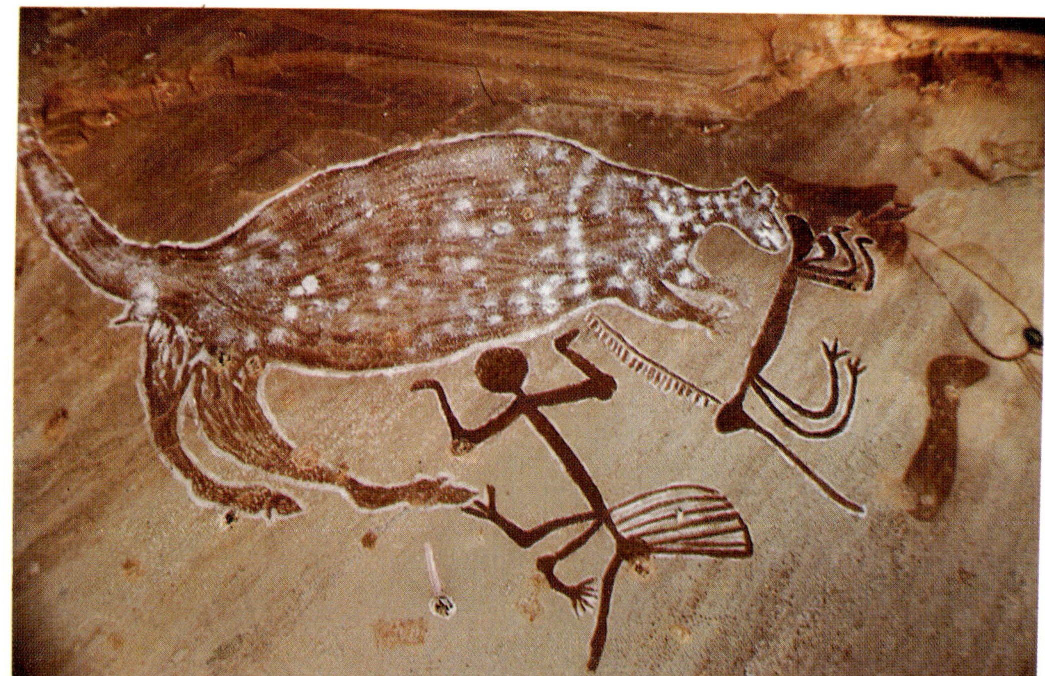

Figure 189. Bichrome rock paintings of kangaroo (2.4 m long) and humans on flat shelter ceiling, Victoria River district, Northern Territory, Australia.

to be produced in recent years (for instance at Nourlangie Rock). A similar trend of cultural assertion can be found almost universally throughout the country.

Some comment is required on the X-ray art (Figure 190). This is again a universal feature in rock art, found in many parts of the world, including India. In this convention of depiction, internal parts of human and animal bodies are depicted as if they were visible - sometimes even internal aspects of inanimate objects. They may indicate the digestive tract, skeletal details, a fetus, or any internal organ. Elaborate X-ray depiction can include considerable anatomical information in this fashion. There is no direct cultural connection between all of the world's art traditions that have used this convention; it has been re-invented independently. But it reaches a sophistication in Arnhem Land that is not approached anywhere else.

Continuing further to the east we reach Cape York Peninsula. Once again we find many styles of rock art, of both paintings and petroglyphs, and in most cases the latter are the older art form. At the sites Early Man Shelter and Sandy Creek 1, petroglyphs have been found under sediment. In the first site they seem to be older than 14,000 years; in the latter, erosion prevents us from seeing how far the cup marks extended down the excavated wall, but we know that occupation began much earlier than 32,000 years at this site. In fact it has yielded the oldest known ground stone axe in the world.

Rock painting traditions of the region are very diverse, but by far the best known is the Quinkan art. Quinkans are spirit beings (sometimes mischievous) of human form, they may be male or female, and they are always

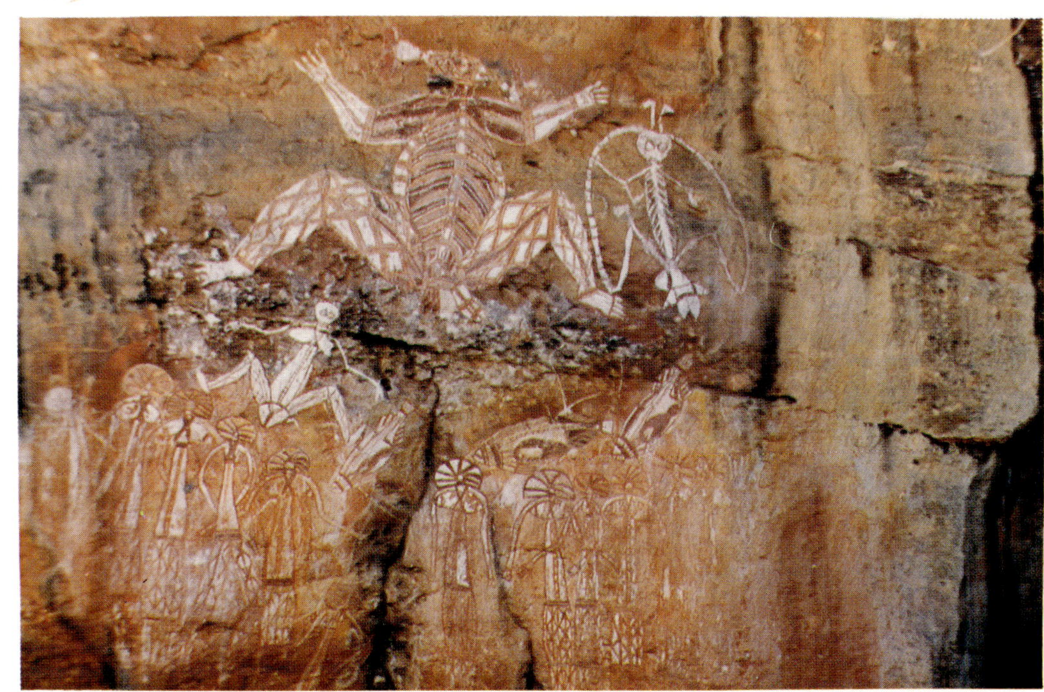

Figure 190. X-ray style paintings executed in 1964 by Nayombolmi, in Anbangbang Shelter, Nourlangie Rock, Arnhem Land, Northern Territory.

painted (Figure 191). The pioneer scholar studying this art body is Percy Trezise, a former pilot who surveyed much of the region from the air before exploring it on foot. Many hundreds of sites are known, thousands may yet be found in the rugged sandstone escarpments. Currently, rock art specialists such as Mike Morwood, Noelene Cole and Bruno David explore the sites and their archaeological settings. The large rock painting concentrations near Laura, at Jowalbinna and in the Quinkan Reserve, are well protected, and the latter is now managed by Ang-Gnarra, the Laura Aboriginal community (Figure 192).

Among the remaining rock art regions in Queensland, two more deserve mention here. One is the 'shield art' in the Townsville region, which is thought to depict intricate shield designs in its paintings (Figure 193). The other comprises the Carnarvon Range stencil sites. Stencils, as we have seen earlier, arc found in many rock arts, the world over, and they often appear in the earliest phases. This art form reaches its greatest sophistication in the central Queensland highlands (Figure 194). Here, it was not just hands that were stencilled, but numerous other objects: many forms of weapons and utensils, ornaments, feet of animals and large birds, arms and feet of humans, and even the whole human body. Naturally, this unique art form provides the researcher with a great deal of reliable information, such as exact shapes and sizes of material culture objects, body sizes, even the approximate ages of the people involved. Hand stencils (sometimes called negatives) are often 'mutilated', i.e. some fingers seem to be missing or shortened. This convention has also been found in other parts of the world, notably in the cave art

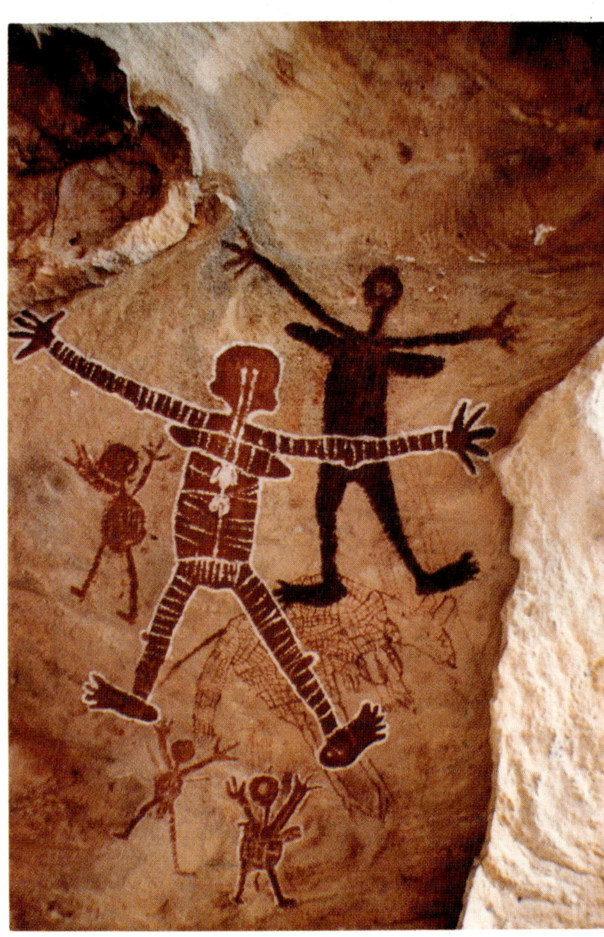

Figure 191. Two female Quinkans (malevolent spirit beings), Quinkan Galleries, Cape York Peninsula, Queensland, Australia.

Figure 192. Section of large painting panel in Ibis Shelter, Quinkan Reserve, Laura, Queensland, Australia.

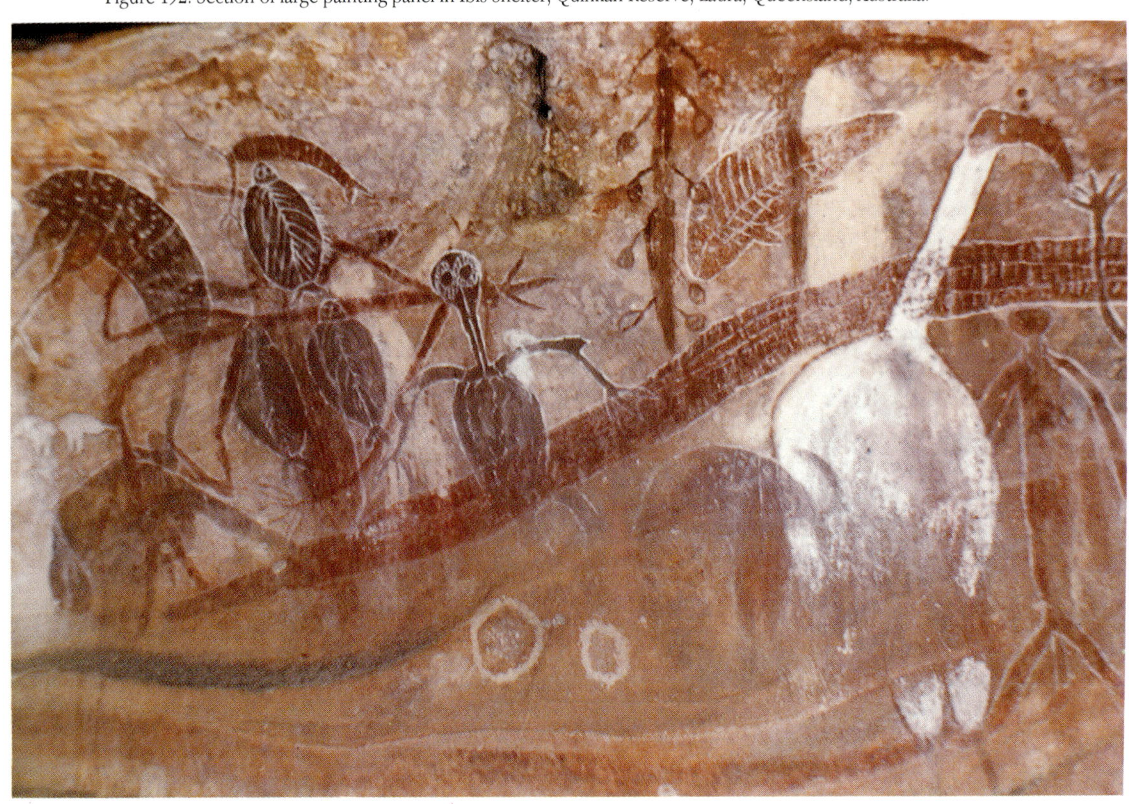

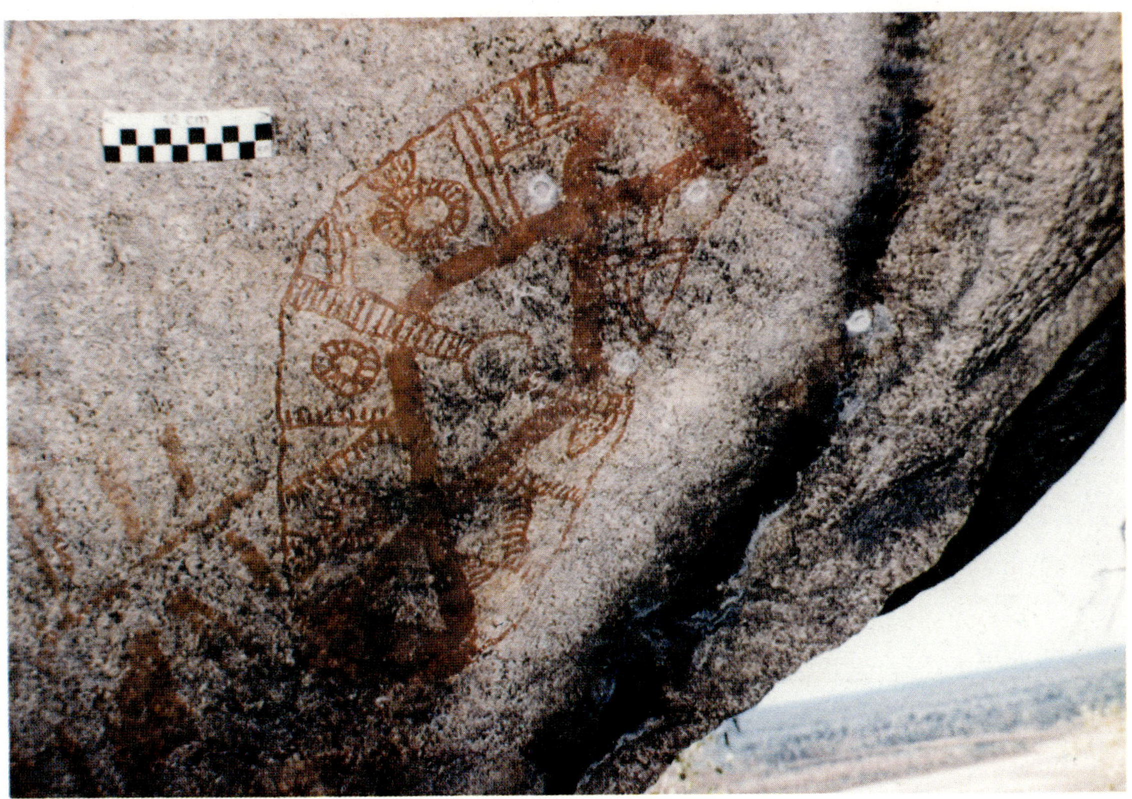

Figure 193. Painted shield designs, in small granite shelter near Townsville, Queensland coast, Australia.

Figure 194. Stencil art of objects including hands, arms, boomerangs, emu feet, shell pendants. Carnarvon Gorge, central Queensland, Australia.

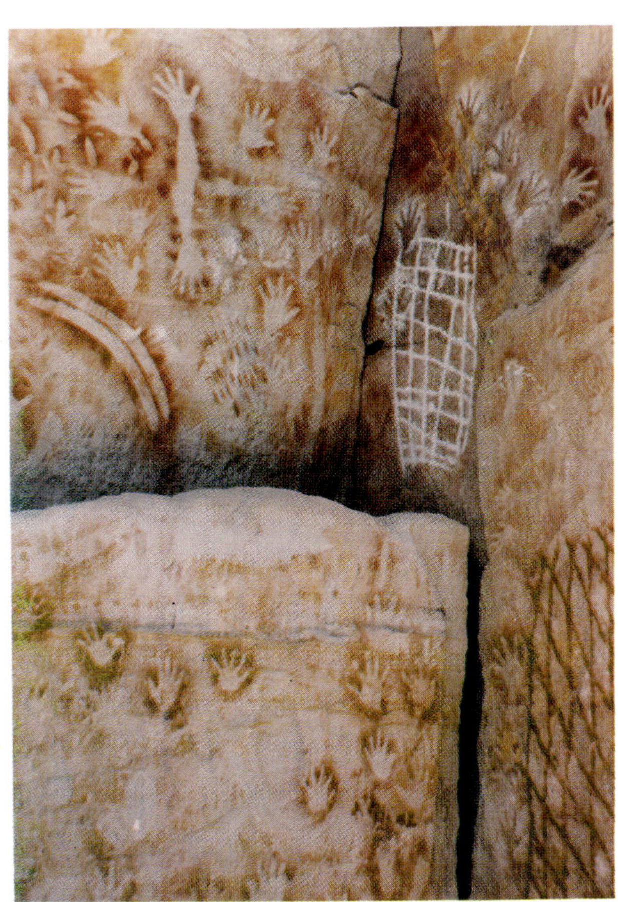

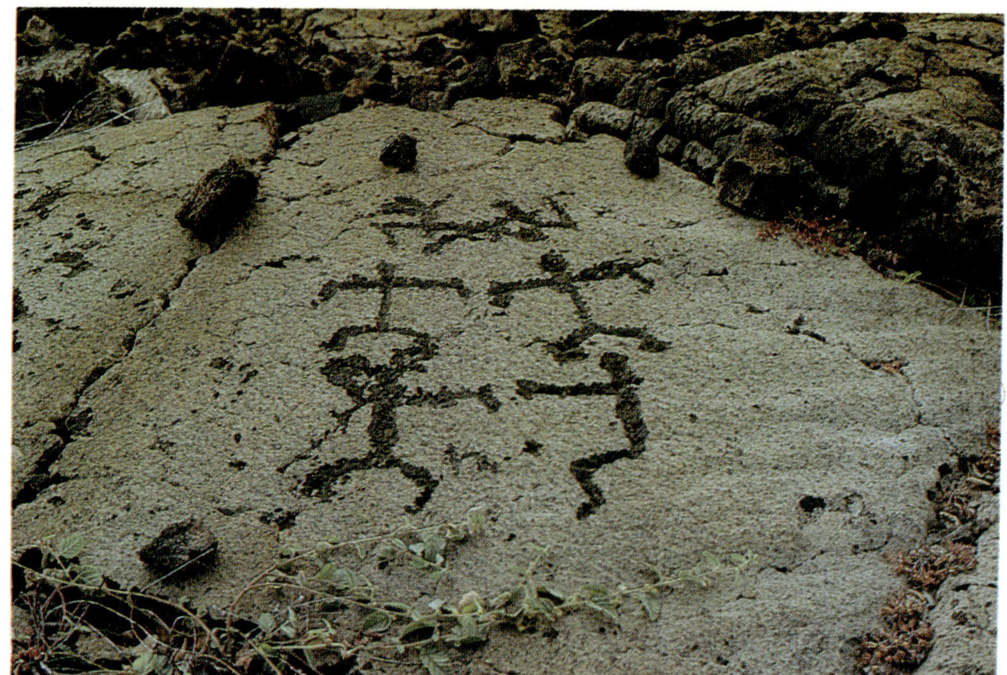

Figure 195. Archaic linear human figure petroglyphs, Kamilo Bay, Hawai'i Island, Hawai'i.

of the European Ice Age. There, it has led to numerous futile speculations, ranging from intentional body mutilation to leprosy and to vitamin deficiency! The Australian evidence, however, points in a very different and more sensible direction. The fingers on these hands were not missing, they were merely folded back when creating the stencils. The significance of this practice is apparently that the finger positions so recorded are related to the sign language the Aborigines sometimes used (for instance while hunting, or when communicating with a person one was not allowed to speak to, such as a mother-in-law). The 'mutilated' hand stencils may thus be the names of the people visiting the site - a kind of signature. They are simply a sophisticated form of communication.

On leaving Australia we should briefly note that rock art is also found on many Pacific islands. In New Zealand it occurs mostly on the northern island, for instance at Rotorua. On New Guinea, rock art has been reported, but remains inadequately explored. The occurrence of finger markings in two deep limestone caves, identical to that found in Australia and south-western Europe, is noteworthy. Rock art, in the form of petroglyphs, occurs on islands of Melanesia.

Further afield in the enormous expanse of the Pacific, numerous petroglyph sites are found on the basalts and lava flows of the islands of Hawai'i where they are being studied by J. Mikilani Ho. Two basic traditions are distinguished by the way humans are depicted: the archaic and older linear style (Figure 195), and the more recent figures with triangular torso which were in use up to the 20th century (Figure 196).

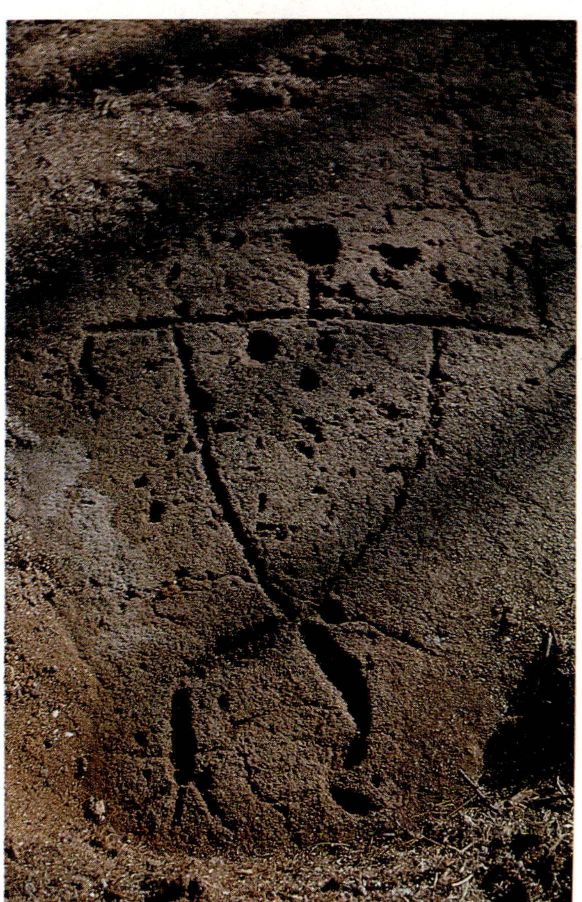

Figure 196. Petroglyph of recent triangle-bodied human figure, Kaluamanini, Hawai'i Island, Hawai'i.

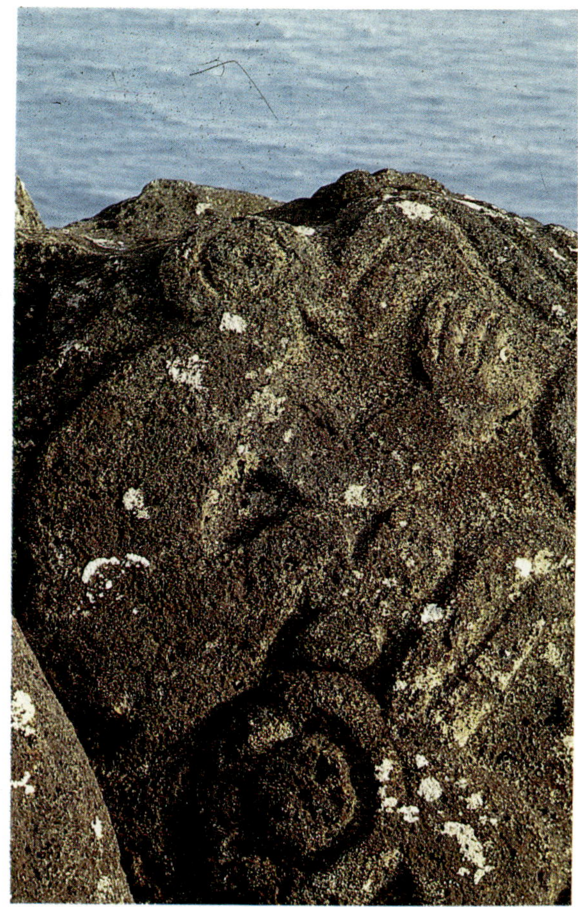

Figure 197. Bas relief of a typical birdman, Orongo, Easter Island.

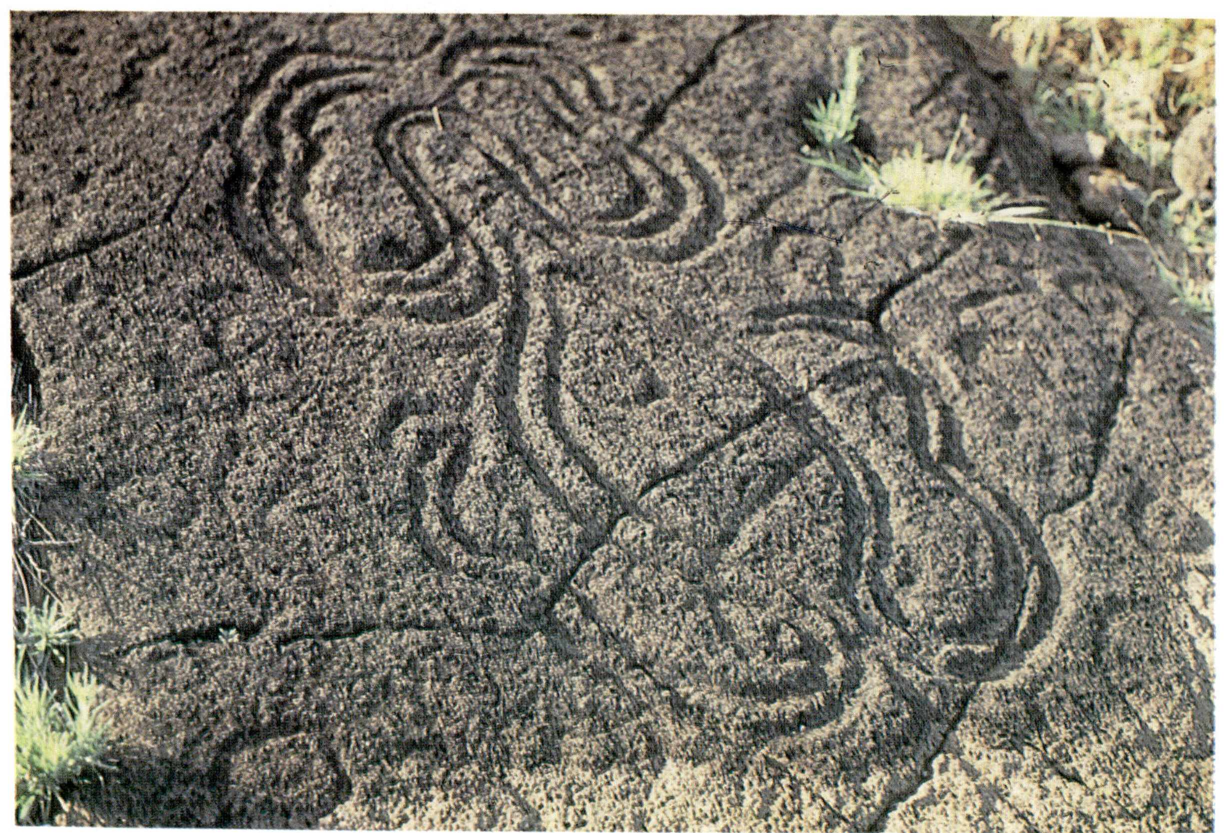

Figure 198. Petroglyph of a stylised octopus, a sacred and mythological creature in Polynesia. La Perouse Bay area,, Easter Island.

Finally, the elaborate rock carvings and bas reliefs on Easter Island must receive mention here, as well as that island's rock paintings. They relate to Easter Island's famous tradition of creating monumental structures and statues, and this rock art has been suggested to pertain to specific rituals. In particular, many images refer to the birdman cult or contest, which is believed to have developed around A.D. 1550, according to Georgia Lee who has conducted the most thorough study of Easter Island rock art (Figure 197). Paintings in small caves are also connected with this ritual, while more conventional petroglyphs on pavements depict animals such as chickens and marine species (Figure 198). ❒

• ROCK ART AND ITS SIGNIFICANCE TO US: A RATIONALE •

ROCK ART AND ITS SIGNIFICANCE TO US: A RATIONALE

India can boast one of the oldest civilisations on earth, and also one of the oldest continuing traditions of scholarship. It is our initial contention that India can continue this ancient tradition, revitalising the intellectual development of humanity, as she has done before, on so many occasions through history. How can we hope to justify such a bold and ambitious proposal?

What we propose here is that the ancient arts of humans, preserved mostly in rock art and so abundant in India, are not just monuments to human artistic achievement - which is how they have been largely viewed so far. Their main role is not to be objects of our admiration, or perhaps of scientific curiosity or contemplation. Similarly, the concept of this corpus being some important heritage of humanity, some valuable cultural patrimony, may be very useful when one tries to gain support for its conservation or protection. But it is not the true reason why we should take a profound interest in this topic. Indeed, none of these points come even near the true significance of ancient art to us - as individuals or as a species. We would suggest here that there should be a considerably more important rationale contemplated and we would like to explore that potential.

Prehistoric rock arts are, foremost of all, records of the mode of perception and cognition of the people who produced them. Human societies of the distant past have experienced the physical world in which they lived by interpreting the sensory information that made it possible for them to relate to this world. Precisely the same applies to modern humans. Each and every one of these countless societies believed very strongly that its perception of the world was valid, that its model of reality was a true reflection of how the world is, and that it was the only valid model. The truth, however, is that none of these models of reality can be seriously considered to bear a close resemblance to objective reality (if indeed there is such a thing). All of them, including our own model, are conceptual artefacts. They are certainly in tune with some aspects of objective reality, but our confidence in our own model is entirely unwarranted. The world does not consist of three-dimensional space, through which time passes as a linear entity that extends indefinitely in two directions. It is not possible to state location and acceleration of an object simultaneously, and all our quantitative statements about the world are only approximations. After all, the dimensions of an object depend on its relative movement, its gravity on its position relative to the centre of gravity it is gravitationally captive to (and which is never stationary, hence gravity must be relative). But most importantly, human sensory faculties have nothing to do with determining how the world is. That was never their role, they were never 'designed' to achieve this. They evolved naturally, and their purpose was merely to maintain the hominids in tune with their biotic environment. For instance, colour vision (the faculty of detecting the wave lengths of reflected light by electrochemical reactions in the retina and transmitting these data neurally to the occipital centre of vision) is only with us because it served certain survival strategies, e.g. the detection of food. It is not a finite or ultimate method of detecting physical surface properties of the world, and with their technological abilities of today, humans can see that there are many properties out there which they cannot detect without technological means (e.g. instruments). It is fairly self-evident that the model of reality developed with the extremely limited means of their cognition, moderated by an endless succession of cultural, ideological and religious paradigms, cannot possibly be expected to have equipped the human species with reliable means of determining the way the world really is.

Our complete confidence in the validity of our own conceptual construct of the world is entirely shared by every society holding an alternative view, however much these models may differ from one another. We can be certain that the cognitive, ontological models of all past societies and civilisations were believed with equal fervour and conviction. None of these many models are in any way inferior or superior, in their true validity. They all contained some truths, and they were all subjective conceptual constructs. What can be superior or inferior, however, is our reaction to these many models and cultures. A superior reaction to them is to recognise that our own model is as ethnocentric and as anthropocentric as that of any other society, in all of human history. There is nothing to prove that our own concept of reality is superior to that which Neanderthals held, nothing at all. In comparing the two models one might find that our's amounts merely to an aggravation of anthropocentricity, a process in which art has played the key role. It is art which permitted the conscious externalisation of human awareness of reality, and its communication to other humans. Art, therefore, is crucial as the foundation of human culture in a much more fundamental fashion than is usually perceived. It is this realization that provides us with a realistic baseline for considering the arts of other societies, and their true significance to modern society.

This position is rather more judicious than the rash naivety of empirical archaeology or anthropology, which is based on totally false assumptions about the cognitive relativity of the 'investigator's' own position. If we accept the fundamental proposition that we lack any means of determining the objective merits of any cognitive construct of reality, including our own, it means that we need to abandon any form of ethnocentricity in how we view rock art as a generic class of evidence. This is what we suggest should be the first precondition of any serious consideration of that topic.

The obvious corollary is that what modern scholars (using their cognitive means) think of, say, Upper Palaeolithic art is no more and no less relevant than what Upper Palaeolithic ethno-scientists would think of modern art (using their cognitive means). Ancient arts need to be seen in this context of scholarly humility, and not in the brash fashion of the empiricist archaeologist, who 'is objective' - or so he or she claims. It is in fact utterly un-scientific for any scholar to claim access to real objectivity. Mere humans may strive towards that noble goal, but there is nothing to encourage any confidence that they will succeed with this pursuit in the short term.

This position confirms the one we have tried to take in this volume: science has no access to the original meanings of ancient arts. But more importantly, it demands considerable restraint in imposing our own construct of reality on the only significant records we have of the modes of perception and cognition of past peoples. Such a form of 'cognitive colonialism' would be a serious flaw in logic and in scholarship. The real significance of these records is that they hold the only key humans have to unlock knowledge about the alternative world models they document. If it is true that these have as much (or, more appropriately, as little) legitimacy as our own, than their value in testing our own construct of reality is immense. It would seem to us that, apart from procedures of pure logic (as one finds in the early philosophies of the Greek and Indian civilisations, for example), this may well be the most promising way of exploring not only how that construct was arrived at, but also how it compares with various of the many alternative ones humans have managed to devise in the past. It is then clear that this kind of enquiry, if conducted in a logically and epistemologically rigorous fashion, would lead to a form of understanding of humans about themselves which has eluded them so far. We are certainly not suggesting that such an enquiry would be easy; it seems almost self-evident that it would be the most ambitious undertaking in the history of science.

Therein lies the real significance of the ancient arts. It is thought that about 98 per cent of the surviving remains of these arts occur in the form of rock arts (the remainder is made up by portable objects of art and other apparently non-utilitarian finds). Our model of the world, like those of all societies before us, is the foundation of all our understanding, our perception of reality and the modes of thought possible for our species. To understand the species of *Homo sapiens* it is essential to understand these origins of our own human-ness.

The point can be well illustrated by exploring the term *human ecology*. Ecology may be the interaction of species with their environment, but the term is frequently misunderstood as merely referring to the place of a species, in our case the human species, within its physical, natural environment. This understanding is based on a very restricted comprehension, which is itself the product of the limited human conception. By far the most important aspect of human ecology is cognitive or intellectual ecology: the way we as a species relate to the real world we exist in. It is extremely important to understand this point, the distinction between physical ecology and cognitive/ intellectual ecology. The former is the sense in which the word ecology is inevitably used in everyday language: how we relate to our environment physically and how we survive in it. We have developed a good understanding of this and we have become very well aware of the effect this understanding has on the continued survival of our species. The more important ecology - the one which concerns the relationship between our limited, anthropocentric model of reality and inaccessible, real reality - has remained unexplored.

Another perspective is also useful in our deliberations. Just as the term ecology is used in a simplified fashion, the term science is usually understood in an intellectually corrupt, banal sense. Science is sometimes given a status that borders on that of religion: a system of knowledge that offers ultimate truths about the world. This is precisely what science is not, and should never pretend (or be perceived) to be. True science possesses no access to truth, and the scientist cannot 'prove' facts, as is popularly believed. The ultimate purpose of science is no different from that of philosophy: to help resolving human confusions (as Ludwig Wittgenstein would say). Science certainly does make an effort to escape the gravitational pull of anthropocentricity, but it rarely succeeds in this. Being very much based on empiricism it, too, is anthropocentric. To go one step further: it often does not even live up to the rigorous demands of empiricism. The concept of empiricism is itself often abused in science. Instead of restricting itself to the definition of empiricism (the realisation that empirical knowledge is the only form available to us about the physical world), it often corrupts that truism and pretends that empirical knowledge tells us how the world is. This is absurd and totally unscientific and yet the point is poorly understood even by many scientists.

In true science we can never attain ultimate truths. We present propositions that are falsifiable (or refutable), which means that they must be formulated in such a fashion that they can be shown to be apparently incorrect (or be susceptible to such formulation). For instance, the proposition that a certain picture in rock art is of a certain age is falsifiable: a method may be applied or some other evidence may become available that shows that the picture cannot be of the age proposed. However, the proposition that the picture represents a crocodile is not falsifiable, it is a subjective pronouncement of the observer, using his or her cortical structures of discriminating iconicity. The discrimination of iconicity is heavily conditioned by cultural and cognitive perception, graphic conventions and other factors, so it can differ significantly among different societies. It is therefore complete nonsense to say that an alien observer, from a totally different culture, can objectively identify objects in an ancient, prehistoric art. Perhaps he or she could actually do this, but since there are usually no ways of testing such subjective identifications they are of no value to rock art science. They are of value only to the psychologist studying the cognitive perception of the rock art researcher (because here, of course, they are testable, and thus susceptible to scientific examination) .

These considerations explain why, in this catalogue, we have deliberately abstained from interpreting the rock art. We are well aware that the many rock arts of the world must have possessed meaning for the people who produced them. We are well aware of modern people's compulsion to fathom these long-lost meanings. But we are equally aware that the subjective pronouncements we are capable of cannot be tested, and may be very different from the meanings originally attributed to the art. We do not, as we have indicated above (in the chapter explaining the purpose of this volume), begrudge the artist, the dreamer, the rock art connoisseur the joy of interpreting the rock art in any way they may like to do this. But we do not claim the privilege of knowing the meanings of the art, and to state our own interpretations would be an infringement of the right of others to interpret to their hearts' desire - as well as a likely misinterpretation of the artists' true intents. We do not know enough about rock art to understand its meanings, and we are also painfully aware of science's limitations. Interpretation of the art lies outside of science's capabilities, and will presumably always remain there. This is and always will be the realm of the artist and the poet, who will retain a complete monopoly in this subjective pursuit. Thus we emphasise that we are not, as might be perceived, hostile to subjective interpretation of rock art. The truth is that as scientists we believe that we have no right to intrude in this world of the dreamer.

To summarise these observations, we could rationalize that the significance of early rock art is twofold. Firstly, this body of evidence, together with portable palaeoart, provides the only major evidence documenting past human models of reality. This evidence may provide us with a balanced perception of our own society's construct of reality, and the understanding of its profound relativity should help us better to understand other cultures, as well as the origins of the human mind and the many constructs of reality it has created. Such understanding can only lead to much greater rigour in our epistemology, our understanding of the nature of human knowledge, and to a more rigorous science. This significance of early arts is such that, by comparison, all other human endeavours (in any field) pale into comparative insignificance. This is not an excessive statement, it is a true reflection of the state of the matter. We are considering the most profound questions humans have been capable of asking, for as long as philosophy has been pursued.

A second, rather different significance of rock arts is its role for those who capture the human concept of reality by intuition rather than by reason: the artists, the creators of new realities. They can readily relate to the arts of other societies, including very early societies, by reacting to these arts in terms of their own cultural and artistic conditioning. We know that such reaction has been practised throughout the history of art. Artists of cultures subsequent to the one that produced rock art observed this art, and reacted to it in their own ways. We know that this has been happening since the Ice Age, and this practice continues today. In fact it is a part of this human reaction which seems to compel us to seek meaning in ancient arts. This significance is acknowledged here, and it is the second form of significance of rock arts. ❐

NOTE BY R. G. BEDNARIK: The bulk of the text in this volume was written over five consecutive days in late November 1994 at the National Museum of Man in Bhopal, immediately before the opening of the exhibition the book is a record of. It is noted that the text was written entirely from memory, without the benefit of any literature references. No references are therefore provided here.

• ROCK ART REGIONS OF THE WORLD & INDIAN ROCK ART REGIONS •

• DIRECT DATING RESULTS FROM ROCK ART •

ROCK ART REGIONS OF THE WORLD & INDIAN ROCK ART SITES

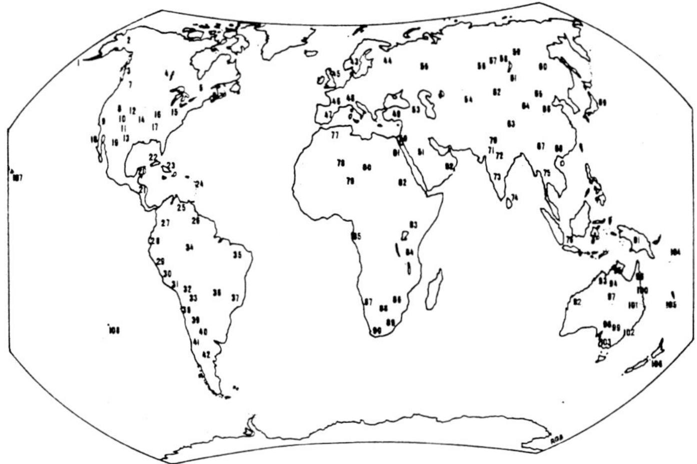

LEGEND FOR ROCK ART WORLD MAP

The regions of major or famous rock art concentrations *(please note : numerous smaller or less known regions are not listed here):*
1. Aleutian Islands; 2. Alaska; 3. Northwest Coast; 4. Canadian Shield; 5 Eastern Canada; 6 Micmac rock art; 7. Columbia-Fraser Plateau; 8. Great Basin; 9. California; 10. Fremont; 11. Barrier Canyon; 12. Dinwoody; 13. Pecos River; 14. Great Plains; 15. Ohio Valley; 16. Missouri; 17. Mississippian; 18. Baha California; 19. Sonora; 20. Yucatan; 21. Mesoamerica; 22. Cuba; 23. Hispaniola; 24. Lesser Antilles; 25. Venezuela; 26. Guyana-Surinam; 27. Colombia; 28. Ecuador; 29. Peruvian north coast; 30. Lima region; 31. Arequipa; 32. Altiplano; 33. Lower Bolivia; 34. Amazon basin; 35. Nordeste traditions; 36. Mato Grosso; 37. Minas Gerais; 38. Chile; 39. Northwest Argentina; 40. Sierra Centrales; 41. Southern Andes; 42. Patagonia; 43. Scandinavia; 44. Karelia; 45. British Isles; 46. Franco-Cantabrian cave art; 47. Levantine shelter art; 48. Alpine petroglyph traditions; 49. Anatolia; 50. Negev Desert; 51. Arabia; 52. Oman; 53. Caucasus region; 54. Central Asian traditions; 55. Urals; 56. Upper Yenisey petroglyphs; 57. Angara river basin; 58. Upper Lena basin; 59. Middle Lena-Olekma basin; 60. Amur region; 61. Lake Baikal-Mongolia; 62. Altay region; 63. Tibet-Qinghai Plateau; 64. Helanshan; 65. Inner Mongolia; 66. Shanxi; 67. Yunnan paintings; 68. Guangxi paintings; 69. Japanese petroglyphs; 70. Southern Himalayas; 71. Chambal valley; 72. Bhopal region; 73. Southern India; 74. Sri Lanka; 75. Thailand; 76. Indonesia; 77. Atlas Mountains; 78. Ahaggar; 79. Southern Sahara; 80. Tibesti; 81. Egypt; 82. Sudan; 83. Kenya; 84. Tanzania; 85. Gabon; 86. Zimbabwe-northern Transvaal; 87. Brandberg-Namibia; 88. Kalahari-Orange region; 89. Drakensberg-Lesotho; 90. Southwestern Cape-Karroo; 91. New Guinea; 92. Pilbara; 93. Kimbereley; 94. Victoria River district; 95. Arnhem Land; 96. Cape York peninsula; 97. Alice Springs region; 98. Flinders Ranges;99. Olary-western News South Wales;100. Queensland coast; 101. Central Queensland Highlands;102. Sydney sandstone region;103. Mt Gambier-Grampians; 104. Western Melanesia; 105. New Caledonia petroglyphs; 106. New Zealand; 107. Hawai'i; 108. Easter Island.

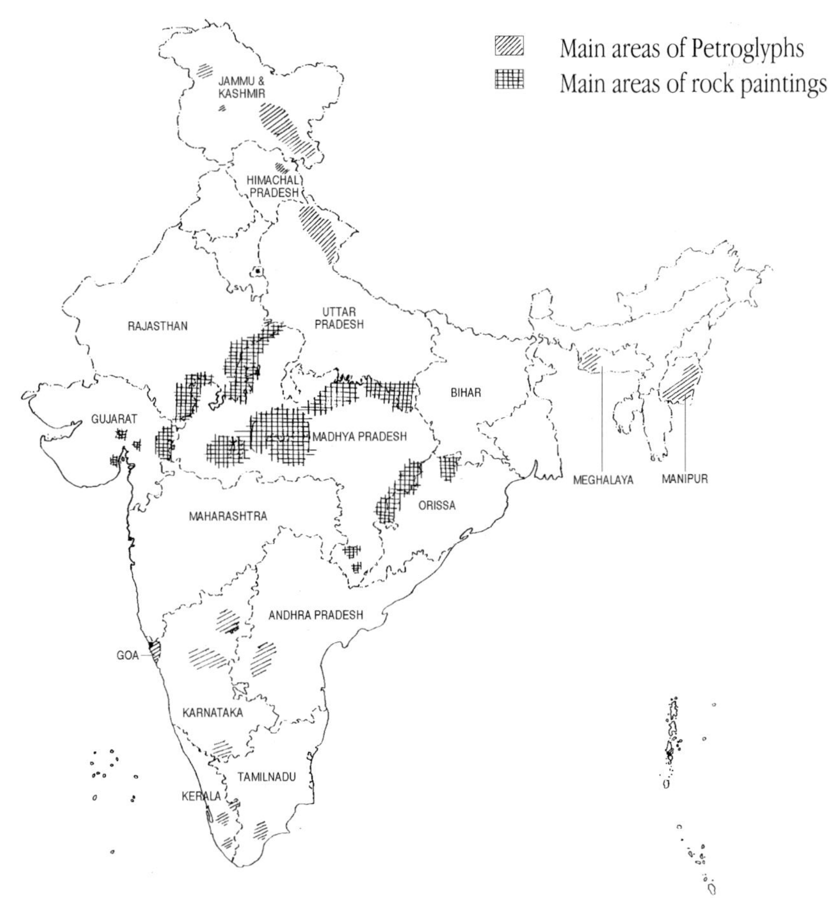

DIRECT DATING RESULTS FROM ROCK ART

Direct dating of rock art was introduced as an alternative to archaeological or stylistic dating, the only methods used until 1980. In recognising the subjective or inductive nature of the traditional approaches, scientists began developing a new methodology in the 1970s and 1980s. Here is a list of the direct dating results so far published. It does not include cation-ration results because these are not considered reliable.

Each entry includes the **year** when the date was either obtained or published, the name of the site or region, the **method** used, the **number** of dates secured, approximate **results,** and the name and country of the **researcher(s)** who produced the results:

1980 Malangine Cave, South Australia - Radiocarbon dating of reprecipitated carbonate over petroglyphs - Two Minimum age of c. 5550 BP - R.G. Bednarik, Australia.

1987 Boontjieskloof, South Africa - AMS radiocarbon dating of charcoal pigment - One - 500 BP - N.J. van der Merwe, J. Sealy, R. Yates, South Africa.

1987 Huashan, China - Radiocarbon dating of reprecipitated carbonate under and over painting - Two for one motif - 2370 BP max. and 2115 BP min. - Qin Shengmin, China.

1990 Kakadu National Park, Australia - Radiocarbon dating of oxalate associated with paintings - Two - Up to c. 8880 BP - A. Watchman, Australia.

1990 Cougnac Cave, France - AMS dating of charcoal pigment - One - 14 300 BP - M. Lorblanchet, France.

1990 Gnatalia Creek, Australia - AMS dating of charcoal pigment - Two - 6000 BP and 29 800 BP from one motif - J. McDonald, K. Officer, T. Jull, D. Donahue, H.Head, B.Ford, Australia.

1990 Waterfall Cave, Australia - AMS dating of charcoal pigment - One - 600 BP - J. McDonald, K. Officer, T. Jull, D. Donahue, H.Head, B.Ford, Australia.

1990 Judds Cavern, Tasmania - AMS dating of blood residue in pigment - Two - 10000 BP - T.H. Loy, R.Jones, D.E.Nelson, B.Meehan, J.Vogel, J.Southon, R.Cosgrove, Australia - Canada.

1990 Laurie Creek, Australia - AMS dating of blood residue in pigment - One - C. 20000 BP - T.H. Loy, R. Jones, D.E.Nelson, B.Meehan, J.Vogel, J.Southon, R.Cosgrove, Australia - Canada. (This result is now doubtful).

1990 Seminole Canyon, Texas - AMS dating of organic carbon in pigment - One - 3900 BP - J. Russ, M. Hyman, H.J. Shafer, M.W. Rowe, USA.

1990 Cangyuan, China - Radiocarbon dating of reprecipitated carbonate under and over painting - Several for one motif - 3100 BP max. and 2960 BP min. - Woo Sheh Ming, China.

1990 Lake Onega, Russia - Microerosion dating of petroglyph - One - E4000 BP - R.G. Bednarik, Australia.

1992 Cosquer Cave, France - AMS dating of charcoal pigment - Seven - Ranging from c. 18000 BP to 27900 BP - J. Clottes, J. Courtin, H. Valladas, France.

1992 Niaux, France - AMS dating of charcoal pigment - Three - Ranging from c. 12900 BP to 13850 BP - H. Valladas, H. Cachier, M. Arnold, F.Bernaldo de Quiros, J.Clottes, P. Uzquiano, France-Spain.

1992 Castillo, Spain - AMS dating of charcoal pigment - Two - C. 13000 BP - H.Valladas, H.Cachier, M.Arnold, F.Bernaldo de Quiros, J. Clottes, P.Uzquiano, France-Spain.

1992 Laura South, Australia - AMS dating of oxalate containing paint residue - One - 24600 BP - A. Watchman.

1993 Olary Province, Australia - AMS dating from organics on petroglyphs - Numerous - Ranging from c. 1500 BP to 43140 BP - M. Nobbs, R.Dorn, Australia-USA.

1993 Cougnac, France - AMS dating of charcoal pigment - Five - Ranging from c. 138000 BP to 25100 BP - M. Lorblanchet, France.

1994 Auditorium Cave, India - Microerosion dating of petroglyphs - One - Beyond range of method - R.G. Bednarik, Australia.

1995 Le Portel, france - AMS dating of charcoal pigment - ??? - M.Rowe, USA.

1995 Grotte Chauvet, France - AMS dating of charcoal pigment and torch soot - Nine - Ranging from c. 26100 to 32400 BP - J. Clottes, J.M.Chauvet, E.Brunel-Deschamps, C.Hillaire, J.P.Daugas, M.Arnold, H.Cachier, J.Evin, P.Fortin, C.Oberlin, N.Tisnerat, H.Valladas, France.

1995 Coa site complex, Portugal - AMS dating from organics on petroglyphs and adjacent surfaces - Several dates - Primary dates ranging from c. 2000 to 7000 BP, corrected to 100 BP to 1700 BP - A. Watchman, Canada.

1995 Coa site complex, Portugal - AMS dating from organics on petroglyphs - Ten - Primary dates from c. 2000 to 5100 BP - R.Dorn, USA.

1995 Coa site complex, Portugal - Microerosion dating of petroglyphs - Numerous - Oldest figure E6500 BP, youngest a few centuries - R.G. Bednarik, Australia.

1995 Grosio, Italy - Microerosion dating of petroglyph - One - E4900 BP - R.G. Bednarik, Australia.

• A GLOSSARY OF KEY WORDS •

A GLOSSARY OF KEYWORDS

INDIA

AREAS, SITES AND FEATURES

NORTHERN INDIA comprises five states, Jammu & Kashmir, Himachal Pradesh, Punjab, Haryana and Delhi; Gangā-Yamunā plains of Uttar Pradesh.

CENTRAL INDIA comprises distinct plateaus, hills, and basins and occupies practically the whole of Madhya Pradesh and Orissa, and parts of the adjoining states of Bihar, Maharashtra and Andhra Pradesh. This area is the richest in rock art and hundreds of sites are found with painted rock-shelters on the sandstone hillocks of Vindhyan, Satpura and Kaimur ranges.

SOUTHERN INDIA lies south of 16°20' N parallel of latitude and extends to the Southern most tip of the country. From west to east, the maximum longitudinal extent of the mainland is 73°24' to 81°54'E, extending all through from coast to coast. The area covers the whole of Kerala, Tamilnadu, Karnataka, Goa, the southern portion of Andhra Pradesh and parts of two districts of Maharashtra: Ratnagiri and Kolhapur. The rock art sites in this area are mainly found in limestone caves and granite boulders.

THE INDIAN HIMALAYAS stretch from Kashmir to Assam and can be divided into the Punjab, Kumāon, Gārhwāl and Assam Himalayas, or, into the Siwaliks, Lesser and Greater Himalayas. In this region, both petroglyphs and petrographs are found, which show remarkable difference from the rock art of other regions.

KUMĀON HILLS are part of the Himalayas, with phases of forest clearence, demonstrated as resulting from human agricultural and other activities, in areas like Naukuchiyatal.

KASHMIR VALLEY has evidence of Megalithic culture and Menhirs, Neolithic culture represented by sites like Burzāhom, spread between Anantnāg and Pāmpur, with pots decorated by oblique, horizontal or vertical grooves and incised lines and infested with pit dwellings, circular, oval, rectangular, or square, cut into the natural loess. Engraved steles from the Neolithic phase, show hunting scenes, double sun, indicating duration of the hunt, and tectiforms suggesting an animal in cage.

KAIMUR RANGE HILLS, situated between Chhatarpur in the west, Robertsganj on the east, Mirzāpur in the north, and Rewā in the south in Madhya Pradesh and Uttar Pradesh, have many factory and rock art sites as well as Mesolithic settlements. The rocky area was suitable for the hunting gathering way of life.

SĀTPURĀ RANGE-The Sātpurās (sātpurā or seven folds), are a hill range in the Vindhyan region, full of parallel ridges rich in caves and rock shelters with Mesolithic deposits and settlements in hills covered with dense, deciduous vegetation, perennial springs, and, till recently, teeming with wild life and plants. Sātpurā range strikes roughly east-west and is separated from the Vindhyan range by Narmadā river. The main peaks of Mahādeo and Pāchmāhri hills are in the Hoshangābād district of Madhya Pradesh. The area around Mahādeo hills and Pāchmāhri hills is covered by rocks of upper Gondwānā group consisting of sand stone, shale and pebble beds.

VINDHYAN RANGE - It is a mountainous tract between the Narmadā and Gangā plains with a restricted estuarine belt of the Narmadā in Gujarat. The Neolithic was generally established as the way of life in propinquity to the truly Chalcolithic and advanced metal using communities, which dominated the area from C.1950 to 1750 BC. Apart from the Sātpurā and Kaimur ranges, the area has riparian tracts, specially the Mālwa plateau, which provided a congenial semi urban settlement topography. The Vindhyan region comprises parts of the states of Rajasthan, Madhya Pradesh and Uttar Pradesh. Physiographically, the area is confined between river Narmadā in South and the fringes of Gangā-Yamunā plains in North; and extends from Māndāsor district in the West to Kātni-Sātnā-Pānnā districts in the East. Consists of the Vindhyan group of rocks comprising sand stone, shale and lime stone. Most of the rock painting sites of India are situated in this range.

ĀRĀVALLI RANGE - Described in plan as two pans joined handle to handle, this land form stretches from Pālānpur in Gujarat through Rajasthan to Delhi. Full of flattopped quartzite ramparts, patinated granitic formations, domes and tors.

BETWĀ SOURCE REGION - A 500 square mile, semicircular flood plain with an average height of about 500 ft. on the foot of the Vindhyan hills in Central India, created by river Betwā and its hill stream tributaries. It is encircled by about 31 sandstone hills explored by Shankar Tiwari, Wakankar and others. Except four, all the hills possess rock shelters and mostly rock paintings. An area with many Chacolithic, early Historic, specially Buddhist sites, the rock shelters being used as dwellings by the Buddhist monks.

NARMADĀ VALLEY - Narmadā basin is formed by the river Narmadā, traversing a distance of 1300 kms from Amarkantak plateau to the sea near Bhāruch in peninsular India. Holds key to quaternary stratigraphy, in which Pleistocene deposits occur in association with Stone age artifacts and animal fossils of different periods. A region rich with finds of the older tool making hominid groups in India. Literally, Narmadā means pleasure giver.

CHAMBAL VALLEY - Formed by river Chambal with numerous Palaeolithic and Microlithic sites and rockshelters. Full of wild glens, gullies and deep ravines.

GAṄGĀ-YAMUNĀ - Two of the principal rivers of north India, forming some of the most fertile alluvial plains with stone-age sites and settlements.

KRISHNĀ-TUNGABHADRĀ VALLEY-Scores of lower Palaeolithic industries have been found in the gravel deposits in the cliff sections of Krishnā river in peninsular India. Animal fossils, ash mounds associated with Neolithic, Megalithic or early Historic humans, and with iron smelting, have been found in the valley. The russet coated painted ware has been found in the valley alongwith Megalithic Urn burials in the lower Deccan with varieties of rectilinear, comblike, dotted and wavy designs.

BUNDELKHAND - The name of the region in Madhya Pradesh bounded by Yamunā river in the north, Vindhyas on the south, Betwā on the East and Tamasā on the West. Before being taken over by the Bundelās in the 14th century, it was known as Jejakabhukti, and was ruled by Chāndelās from the 9th century. It has the world heritage site Khajurāho in Chhātārpur District.

CHHATTISGARH - Literally, 36 forts or houses, Chhattisgarh is the name first used for the districts of eastern Madhya Pradesh in A.D. 1497. It is washed by rivers Mahānadi, Seonāth, Maniyāri, Gopatvanās etc., and is predominantly inhabited by aboriginal tribes.

DAKSHIṆA KOŚALA - An area more or less coterminous with the eastern Madhya Pradesh (known Later as Chattisgarh) and western Orissa. Being hilly, heavily forested, and inhabited mainly by tribal groups, this area has revealed, in recent excavations, the development of an original and innovative style of Indian art from the 5th to the 9th centuries A.D.

CHHOTĀ NĀGPUR PLATEAU -An area full of pāts (high level mesas) in the Uttar Pradesh, Bihar, Madhya Pradesh, Orissa region with Mesolithic factory sites, Neolithic cultures with hand made pottery, bearing cord or basket impressions, Menhirs and Asura sites with extensive use of iron objects. Mirzāpur plateau is full of rock art.

SHĀMLĀ HILL - Situated in the sedimentary lower Vindhyan system, in the city of Bhopāl, capital of Madhya Pradesh. Littered with rockshelters, the hill has yielded Palaeolithic and Mesolithic deposits. About 32 painted rockshelters are situated in the premises of the Indira Gandhi Rāshtriya Mānav Sangrahālāya

(National Museum of Man). The style and the subject matter of these paintings is the same as that of the Betwā source region rock art, including that of Bhīmbetkā.

ĀDAMGARH-In district Hoshangābād, Madhya Pradesh in Vindhyan sandstone hills, 2 kms. south of Narmadā river. Frequented from the Palaeolithic to the Medieval period, the site has yielded undisturbed deposits in painted rock shelters, and has helped in establishing a corelation with the tools associated with the animal fossils in the Narmadā alluvia, and with the material exposed in the cliff sections of the Narmadā between Hoshangābād and Narsinghpur.

BHĪMBETKĀ -In district Rāisen, Madhya Pradesh. A group of 200 caves and rock shelters in the Vindhyan hills, made of naturally weathered soft sand stone. About 1,000 shelters have been fund in the several hills dotted on a 10km. stretch, with Bhimbetkā as a major centre, 500 of them containing prehistoric, transitional and historic paintings. Extensive floor deposits attest habitation of stone age man from the lower Palaeolithic to the late Mesolitic. The cuesta hill of Bhimbetkā is one of the 31 hills, encircling the 1500 ft. high Betwā flood plain, rising to a height of about 1980ft., with rock shelters situated on the dip slope.

BUTTE-A hill with steep sides and flat top.

CUESTA-A hill, with a steep descent on one side, and a gentle slope on the other.

HOG BACK-A rocky ridge created by differential erosion on the edges of tilted strata.

MESA- High and flat tableland with rocky slopes.

TECTIFORM- Sloping down on either side from a central ridge like a roof.

SCUTIFORM- Shield shaped.

PEDIFORM- Foot shaped.

BRECCIA- Angular stone, cemented by finer material.

CRYPTOGAM- Plant without true seeds and flowers: Ferns, fungi, algae and mosses.

PHOSPHENE- Sensation of rings of light produced by pressure on eyeball generated by irritation of retina.

MATERIAL & TIME ZONE

PRE HARAPPAN ceramic assemblage from places like Kālibāngān is characterised by a bichrome ware with black and white decoration on dull surface. The designs include horizontal bands, loops, wavy lines, concentric arches, meanders, dots, cross hatched triangles, tridents and squares, floral and faunal motifs. The pre Harappan culture flourished in the Quetta and Jhob valleys of Baluchistan, in the Punjab and Sindh as also in Gujarat, Rajasthan, and Hariyana. The village communities, using this pottery, flourished from the mid-4th to the end of the 2nd millennium B.C. and represent a semi nomadic to Neolithic phase. The resemblances between pre Harappan ceramic designs and the rock art need not suggest the same people as the artists.

CHALCOLITHIC pottery has been found in different parts of India including Madhya Pradesh, Maharashtra, Rajasthan, Karnataka, Deccan, and is characterised by great variety. The Mālwa ware of Madhya Pradesh, the Jorwe ware on the bank of Paravara, the Sāvāldā ware of Godāvari-Krishnā-Tāpti valleys are some of the well known ceramic cultures and these are characterised by an incredible variety of designs and shapes, occasionally deriving from late Harappan elements, specially in Gujarat. The corpus of designs is expanded in this period to include new linear, geometric, plant and animal motifs. Many of these designs and motifs resemble the rock art motifs, which need not suggest a common origin or inspiration.

MEGALITHS in India are mostly collective burials including a variety of sepulchral and commemorative monuments, built by arranging large stones in circles, squares or series alignments, with hoods, port holes etc. These are found all over India but are concentrated in peninsular India. These are usually associated with a homogeneous group of Black and Red ware and iron tools and weapons. The proximity of the rock art sites to these assemblages has been taken to suggest association of the Megalithic people with rock art.

OSTRICH EGGSHELLS have been found in the plains, hills and river valleys (Chambal, Kālisindh, Darrā etc.) of Rajasthan, Madhya Pradesh, Maharashtra and U.P. in association with scrapers, borers, burins and blades in upper Palaeolithic industry sites. The identification of the bird at sites like Pāchmārhi bazar shelter, Firangi, Kathotiyā in Madhya Pradesh and evidence of anthropic markings on the eggshells has been discussed and questioned. The Ostrich may have disappeared in the Holocene period.

MYTHOLOGY & MEANING

BUDDHISM-The religion founded by Gautama Buddha in the latter half of the 6th century B.C. Buddhism adopted non iconic and iconic motifs from the older Indian art and endowed them with new meaning and fervour.

DHARMA CHAKRA-The gesture of hands, exhibited by Lord Buddha, while preaching his first sermon at Sārnāth. The palms are placed near the breast in the manner of expounding an argument.

SAṀGHA-The Buddhist or the Jaina congregation, a body of religieux, following a corpus of principles and rules of discipline.

STUPA-The Buddhist sanctuary or universe, represented as a square or round tumulus, a truncated, semihemispherical, solid dome, representing the body of Buddha, lying in state at his despiration, or passing away, at the cross roads.

TRIRATNA-The three jewels, knowledge, faith and conduct, which, in Buddhism, are synonymous with Buddha, Dharma and Saṁgha.

JAINISM AND JAINA-Jainism is a religion founded in the 6th century B.C. by Mahavira on the basis of principles taught by earlier Tirthaṅkaras (pathfinders) who became Jinas or conquerors of passions. Hence, his followers were called Jainas. Jainism created a canonical and noncanonical literature, and inspired a large body of Indian art.

VEDIC DEITIES-The Rigveda or the Veda of the verses is the oldest of the Vedas, and its hymns are dedicated to Gods and Goddesses, who are personifications of natural phenomena, such as Sun, Dawn, Fire, Wind, which, in turn, are ultimately seen as manifestations of a single divine being. The pantheistic identification with nature is developed through Vedic literature to culminate in Vedānta philosphy.

AGNI-DAKSHA-Agni is the fire god, the presiding deity of sacrificial rites, while Dakshāyana is a sacrifice. Daksha is one of the Prajāpatis or protectors of men, born of Brahmā the creator, the performer of a great sacrifice.

INDRA VAJRAVĀHU-Indra is the lord of Gods and lord of rain, armed (vāhu, arm) with the thunderbolt (vajra) as his weapon.

DHENU-ADITIH-Dhenu is a gift of articles in imitation of the gift of cows. Mythically, Aditih is the mother of the Gods, daughter of Daksha, wife of Kāshyapa, signifying boundless expanse and freedom, bounty and wellbeing.

GANESHA-Son of Lord Shiva and Pārvati. Has an elephant head with one tusk. Head of Shiva's hosts or gaṇas. Considered to be the bestower of wisdom and remover of obstacles.

LAJJĀ GAURĪ- Is shown as a nude mother goddess sitting with legs apart and raised, exposing her vulva in the frog or Baubo style (the sitting style is Uttānapāda in Sanskrit). She is often shown headless with a lotus in place of her head in terracotta and stone plaques. She is also shown with a torso in the shape of a pot (ghaṭa in Sanskrit), symbolic of the womb. She is the personified fertility goddess.

TRIBAL POPULATION

India abounds in tribal population. An autochthonous ethnic group rooted in its land of origin and claiming a territorial distribution, distinct dialect and religion is known as a tribal group. The tribal groups are still pursuing their traditional way of life and rituals.

BAIGĀS-The Baigās are village priests and medicine men, concentrated in Madhya Pradesh, who consider themselves to be descendants of mother earth. The Binjhwār are one of their subgroups. Baigā women decorate their decor bodies with tattoo marks, while men carve wooden doors, panels, and set up memorial posts for their ancestors in wood and stone.

BHĪLS-The second largest tribe of India, concentrated in southern Rajasthan, western Madhya Pradesh, Gujarat, and northern Maharashtra. The Bhil magician priest paints the sacred Pithorā or the theme of the horse and the riders on the mud walls of their huts in red, yellow and black.

RĀTHWĀS-Rāthwās are a subgroup of Bhīls. Rāthwās are concentrated in Chhotā Udaipur region of Gujarat and in the Jhābuā Disatrict of Madhya Pradesh. They decorate their house walls with Pithorā painting of horses moving in the same direction, unlike in Bhīl Pithorā painting, in which the horses face each other. They also carve the wooden doors and windows of their houses wirh decorative patterns.

BHOṬIĀ- A term derived from Bod, which means Tibet. The Bhoṭiā have been traders, practicing transhumance in the Himalayas.

GONḌS-The largest tribe of India, concentrated in what was known as Gondwānā in Madhya Pradesh and also in hılly Ādılābād distt. of Andhra Pradesh. They trace their origion to the Pāṇḍava 'ıero Bhīmsen, practice ceremonial dances, ancestor worship. They decorate their walls with geometric and natural forms, specially inverted juxtaposed triangles, carve their wooden doors and panels, and tattoo their bodies.

GUNIĀ-The medicinemen or the magic men among the Gond tribals of Chhattisgarh, specially in Bastār.

PRADHĀN GONḌ-A tribe from the ìarger Gond group, situated mostly in Mānḍlā, Madhya Pradesh.

KONḌ-Name of a tribe, probably derived from the Dravidian word Konḍā or hill, living in Orissa, Andhra Pradesh, Madhya Pradesh and Maharashtra. Practice wood carving, tattooing, embroidery and ritual dances.

KORKU-The Korku are a tribe concentrated in Madhya Pradesh and derive their name from the word Karu or man and Ku which makes the name plural.

KORWĀ- The Korwā are a tribe living in the states of Madhya Pradesh, Bihar, Orissa and West Bengal. The name is derived from a tree known as Koderā or the word Dodawās or earth diggers. Used to be, till recently, hunter gatherers.

NĀIK-A tribe known with variations in the name in Maharashtra, Gujarat, Karnataka and Andhra Pradesh. Different groups speak different languages according to their place of residence. In Barodā in Gujarat, they are called Nāikadā, and their women paint walls and draw with ricepowder.

SĀNTHĀL-A major tribe of Bihar and West Bengal, also known as Hor, which simply means a man. Of Dravidian stock. Observe totemism and engage in ceremonial communal hunts, fighting or dances. The Sānthāls carve wooden bridal palanquins, adorn their walls with floral, faunal, human and geometric forms in red and black, while the women tattoo their bodies.

SĀORĀ-A tribe concentrated in Orissa, which derives its name from the Sanskrit word Śavara, a hunter mountaineer. They decorate the wooden doors of their homes with carvings, and paint the red ochre washed clay walls of their huts in white, and their priest draws the Ittal, the ritual fertility diagrams. The women tattoo their bodies.

WĀRLI OR VĀRLI-A tribe inhabiting Maharashtra and Gujarat. They are fond of painting the earth brown walls of their homes in white rice powder with splashes of scintillating Geruā or saffron.

DYNASTIES

GUPTAS - A powerful Hindu dynasty, which ruled northern India from Ca.A.D. 320 till Ca.A.D. 510. The Gupta period witnessed the efflorescence of a highly sophisticated civilisation, classical in terms of the union of ethos and pathos, passion and intelligence. The vocabulary of Indian art was finally shaped; the epics and canonical texts were codified; and the different religions, existing together, yielded their finest flower, in terms of art and culture, during this period.

KATYŪRĪS-A dynasty which is supposed to have ruled Kūrmāchal or Kumāon region of Uttar Pradesh, Himalayas from the 2500 B.C. till 700 A.D. They have left extensive remains of temples and inscriptions in the post Christian period. They founded Kārtikeyapurā, present Baijanāth, near Gomati river.

KṢAHARĀTA-Also called Kshatrapas, a branch of the Shakas, who extended their rule in the western Deccan from the 2nd century A.D. Called Śatrapas in inscriptions, these rulers dedicated several caves with sculpture and art.

KUSHĀṆAS - These were a section of the Yueh Chi nomadic horde, who settled first in Bactria, and then came into northern India, which they ruled from Ca.A.D. 48 to Ca.A.D. 220. The foundation of the Shaka era, dating from A.D. 78, has been attributed to the Kushāṇas.

MAURYAS - The Maurya dynasty ruled northen India from Pātaliputra, now Pātnā, in Bihar, from C. 322 B.C. till 185 B.C. The founder, Chandragupta, drove out the Greeks after Alexander's departure and married the daughter of Saleucos, one of the Greek princes. Ashoka (273 B.C. to 232 B.C.) was the most famous ruler of this dynasty who converted to Buddhism, abjuring a career of violence and conquest, and propagated Buddhism inside and outside India. With this proselytising movement, Buddhist icons and motifs entered all Indian art, including rock art.

VALABHI MAITRAKA-Valabhi(Wala in eastern Kāthiāwār) was the name of the city and kingdom, founded by the Maitrakas, who ruled from early 6th century A.D. till about A.D. 770.

SCRIPTS

BRĀHMĪ - The name applied by Buhler to the script, in which most of the inscriptions of the Mauryan emperor Ashoka were engraved in the 3rd century B.C. Most of the Indian scripts and many south east Asian scripts have developed from Brāhmī.

KHAROSHTHI - Script related to the Aramaic, used from about mid 3rd century B.C. to the 3rd-4th century A.D., mostly in northwestern India, in Ashokan edicts, and in the records of Greek, Scythian, Parthian and Kushāṇa rulers.

SHAṄKHA LIPI - The socalled shell script, a cursive script resembling the shape of a shaṅkha or conchshell, sometimes derived by scholars from Brāhmī, and found to be in use from the 1st century B.C. till about 1000 A.D. The characters of the script are clockwise or anticlockwise in orientation.

EPICS

MAHĀBHĀRATA-The great Indian epic of 100,000 Sanskrit verses, attributed to Vyāsa, which describes the battle of Kauravas and Pāṇḍavas at Kurukshetra near the field of Pānipat in Hariyana. Composed well before the beginning of the Christian era, this epic epitomizes the anxiety and problems of the modern man and contains thousands of stories including the story of Krishna Balarāma, the heroic brothers who were also divinity incarnate. These stories provided the themes of much of the historic art, including rock art. Bhīmsen is the second of the five Pāṇḍava brothers, and was known for his size, strength and appetite.

RĀMĀYAṆA-Considered to be the earliest in Sanskrit poetic literature, Rāmāyaṇa is a great Indian epic, attributed to Vālmiki. It speaks of the battle of Rāma, an incarnation of Lord Vishṇu, one of the holy trinity, with the demon king Rāvaṇa of Laṅkā. The epic speaks of a period of greater certitudes and lesser anxiety than the epic Mahābhārata, and would appear to have been conceived earlier, even if its formal conposition may have been near contemporary to that of Mahābhārata. Along with the Mahābhārata, the Rāmāyaṇa was the other great mine of stories about the exploits of Rāma and his monkey cohorts, which supplied an endless source for Indian Art, including Historic rock art.

AUSTRALIA

Australia is the richest continent in terms of rock art, with some hundreds of thousands of sites. Among the art bodies found are both the oldest we have been able to date so far, and the most recent we know of. The ritual use of rock art is a continuing, living tradition among the Aboriginal people of Australia. Rock art occurs throughout most of the continent, but its frequency increases sharply towards the north.

PILBARA

Petroglyphs are found mostly on dark-brown patinated boulders of plutonic rocks. Some are of great age. This is the largest petroglyph concentration on earth. Along the coast, depictions of marine animals are common, inland one finds unusual human figures, such as the Woodstock figures. Pictures of the Thylacine have also been found.

PATINA - A surface alteration of rock which is distinctly visible and which becomes more intensive with increasing age. It therefore may assist us in dating rock surfaces and petroglyphs. It may be attributable to an accretion, chemical weathering or solution.

PLUTONIC ROCK - A type of rock that derives from molted lava, such as granite, gneiss, rhyolite, basalt, granophyre, gabbro. These are often very ancient rocks, though not necessarily so.

WOODSTOCK FIGURE - A form of petroglyphs depicting a human figure which is found in part of the Pilbara region, north-western Australia. The figure has long, flexible limbs ending in two forked fingers, a large penis and often antennae on the head.

THYLACINE - A dog- like mammal, also called Tasmanian wolf or Tasmanian tiger, with striped body. In recent times it existed only in Tasmania, where it became extinct by about 1940, but millennia ago it also lived on the mainland of Australia. It is sometimes depicted in rock art, where it was first discovered in the Pilbara region in 1968.

KIMBERLEY

A region of north-western Australla featurlng mostly rock paintings, some of which are of enormous sizes. There are two main traditions, the older Bradshaw figures and the younger Wandjina figures. The latter are still being repainted by Aboriginal people as part of a living cultural tradition. Poorly explored rock art region, but a very large number of sites is indicated.

BRADSHAWS - Bradshaw figures are of faded red pigment, and are thought to be very ancient. They are mostly of human figures, which are often very detailed, with extensive decoration, such as headdresses, tassels and various objects worn or hand-held. Occurs at thousands of sites in Kimberley. This is the earliest rock art tradition in the world which features detailed human depictions in great numbers.

WANDJINAS - The Wandjinas lived in Yoriyoro, a time identified with the Ice Age, or the Dreamtime. They were powerful creator beings who instructed the Aboriginal people. Then they walked into the rocks, but in doing so they left their images on the rocks, and instructed the humans to maintain their pictures forever.

LARGEST PAINTINGS - The world's largest paintings are found in the Kimberley region of Australia and in the adjacent Victoria River District. A 43-metre human figure has been found, which is eroded at both ends and was originally over 50 metres long. There is also a 24-metre picture of a snake, and several other extremely large figures. The largest rock art figure outside of Australia is in India, and 10 metres long.

AUSTRALIAN ABORIGINES - The Aboriginal people of Australia are thought to have arrived about 60,000 years ago, from Asia. To reach Australia, they must have crossed several stretches of open sea, sometimes without seeing the other shore at the commencement of the journey. They are the earliest ocean navigators we know of. The Aborigines possess the oldest continuing culture on earth, and one of the most complex and sophisticated belief systems we know about.

VICTORIA RIVER DISTRICT

This region is in the Northern Territory of Australia, and its rock art remains poorly explored. Both petroglyphs and rock paintings are common. Frequent motifs from the Dreamtime stories are the Lightning Brothers and the Rainbow Serpent. There are also many sorcery figures and there is contact a rt .

LIGHTNING BROTHERS - A frequent motif in the rock paintings of the Victoria River District, referring to a creation story of the Aboriginal people. The brothers are always depicted together, side by side, sometimes their thumbs are very long, or a lightning bolt is depicted next to them.

RAINBOW SERPENT - One of the most powerful beings in Aboriginal cosmology. It has a snake-like body, often very thick, and the head of a mammal, with ears or horns. It travelled across the land in the Dreamtime, creating the landscape and many of its features, and now dwells underground.

DREAMTIME - In Aboriginal cosmology, the period at the dawn of time, during which the Dreamtime heroes roamed the earth, often in animal form, creating it and the topographical features of the landscape, as well as some of the rock art. This part of rock art is said not to have been created by humans.

SORCERY ART - A feature of Aboriginal rock art, particularly of northern Australia. This art was created as part of a sorcery ritual, in which the artist wished some calamity to affect an enemy or opponent. Sorcery art can take various forms: a human may be depicted deformed, or in an upside-down position, or attacked by small animals.

CONTACT ART - This is the name given to rock art depicting objects and scenes from the period of first contact between Aborigines and invading Europeans. Such depictions include those of sailing ships, steam boats, rifles, pistols, steel axes and police men in uniforms.

ARNHEM LAND

A very rich rock art region, with 10,000 known sites, often of polychrome paintings. It includes Kakadu National Park. A frequent style is called X-ray art, and there are many layers of paint at the major art sites which may assist in dating. A chronological sequence of this rock art body is based on the depiction of animal species and the environment they relate to. Very recent rock art occurs in addition to ancient.

POLYCHROME - Rock paintings may be monochrome (in a single colour), bichrome (in two different colours) or polychrome (in three or more colours). Polychrome paintings are usually complex depictions, found only in specific world regions. However, in many rock arts, only some of the colours originally used may have su rvived .

KAKADU - Kakadu National Park is a World Heritage property. While there are many thousands of rock art sites in this park, only three of them are accessible to the general public, and they are visited by hundreds of thousands of tourists each year. Kakadu National Park belongs to the Gagadju Association, an Aboriginal community, who leases it to the Commonwealth Government of Australia.

X-RAY ART - In this form of rock art, which is widely found in different parts of the world, some internal features are added to the depiction of surface and form. Most frequently, this art form is applied in the depiction of animals, including humans, in which internal organs or skeletal details may be shown. There are also, however, some pictures of inanimate objects in X-ray style.

ARNHEM LAND CHRONOLOGY - The chronological sequence of Arnhem Land rock art is based on the depiction of saltwater and freshwater species, and the knowledge that the coastal plains were much wider during the lower sea levels of the past, in the late Ice Age. It is assumed that the depiction of freshwater species indicates a greater distance of the sea.

RECENT ROCK ART - In Arnhem Land, as in some other Australian regions, rock art has continued to be produced until very recently, and may even be produced in the present time. A famous example is the X-ray painting panel at Nourlangie Rock, in Angbangbang shelter, which was painted in 1964 by Aboriginal artist Najombolmi.

CAPE YORK PENINSULA

A region of sandstone and granite mountains with several rock art concentrations, the largest of which is located at Laura. Quinkan art is found there, and dating has been possible at Early Man Shelter and Sandy Creek1. Both petroglyphs and rock paintings occur in this region, but the former are usually earlier. This applies generally in rock art.

SANDSTONE - Sandstone is a sedimentary rock composed of former sand grains that have become cemented together. The cement may be silica or carbonate, and it determines the rock's resistance to weathering processes. All sandstones are susceptible to rockshelter formation, and it is in these shelters that rock art occurs most frequently.

QUINKANS - Quinkans are spirit beings of human form. They are sometimes malevolent or mischievous, they can be male or female, and they are always painted. The males can travel fast by bouncing through the landscape on their very large testicles. Quinkans are found only around Laura, especially in the Quinkan Reserve.

EARLY MAN SHELTER - A sandstone shelter near Laura in which petroglyphs were found to be covered by a sequence of archaeological deposits. These provided a series of radiocarbon dates, and the lowest stratum covering petroglyphs is about 14,000 years old. This suggests that the rock art must be older than that age.

SANDY CREEK 1 - A sandstone shelter near Laura with petroglyphs covered by archaeological deposits. Erosion of the rock prevents us from seeing how far the petroglyphs extended down the excavated wall. Occupation of the site began much earlier than 32,000 years ago. The site yielded the earliest ground stone axe so far found in the world.

ARID AUSTRALIA

This includes a very large area of land across the central regions of Australia. Major rock art bodies occur in the southern part of Northern Territory (e.g. at Uluru and Cleland Hills), in the Flinders Ranges and the Olary/Broken Hill region. The latter has produced the world's earliest available direct dates from rock art .

ULURU - Formerly called Ayers Rock by European explorers, this massive rock is now known by its original name. Uluru National Park is owned by the traditional Aboriginal custodians who lease it to the Commonwealth Government of Australia as a national park. Uluru is said to be the largest monolith in the world, and rock art•occurs in some of its peripheral rockshelters.

CLELAND HILLS - Rediscovered in the 1 960s, this remote rock art site features hundreds of petroglyphs, among which some highly stylized human faces are prominent. At the time this was suggested to be a particularly ancient art form, due to its patination, but today we know of much earlier rock art traditions in Australia.

FLINDERS RANGES - A series of rugged mountain ranges featuring a series of rock art sites. They include very early petroglyphs at water holes and in canyons, as well as paintings in rockshelters. Non-figurative art predominates, and styles resemble those of other arid regions of Australia.

OLARY SITES - Mostly of very deeply patinated and archaic petroglyphs on dolomite, and of much more recent paintings in granite shelters. At the sites Panaramitee North and Wharton Hill, the world's oldest direct dates from any rock art have been obtained, which are in the vicinity of 40,000 to 45,000 years before present. These are minimum dates as they refer to the patina covering the art .

BROKEN HILL - Near this town occur several well-studied site complexes of rock art, including Euriowie, Sturts Meadows and Mootwingie. The former include only petroglyphs, showing the development from very early traditions to more recent, the latter combines several painting and spectacular petroglyph sites which have serious conservation problems.

EASTERN AUSTRALIA

Along the eastern coast of Australia, major concentrations of rock art include the Townsville rock art and cupules on granite, Carnarvon stencil art on sandstone, and the Sydney sandstone region. Styles are very diverse, with both petroglyphs and rock paintings well represented.

TOWNSVILLE - In the shelters of this granite region of northern Queensland, painted designs resembling the area's complex decorative patterns found on wooden shields are commonly found. It is thought that they depict specific shield designs relating to individual warriors, as was the practice among European knights of the Middle Ages. In addition, extremely old cupules have also been found in this region.

CUPULES - One of the oldest forms of rock art in the world, known to extend tens, even hundreds, of thousands of years into the past (e.g. in India). Cupules, or cup marks, are circular, dish-shaped depressions produced by hammering with a pointed stone tool. They may occur in small numbers or as very large accumulations, numbering many hundreds, and they may be of very great age or comparatively recent. Their use is unknown.

CARNARVON - Sandstone highlands in central Queensland with the greatest concentration of stencil art known in the world. The most famous sites are in Carnarvon Gorge, a National Park. Together with the dominant stencil art, usually in red paint, occur also many earlier petroglyphs, usually non-figurative.

STENCIL ART - This was produced by holding an object against the rock surface and spraying paint around its margins, producing a silhouette image of it (also called a 'negative'). The object so depicted is most frequently a hand, but in Australia many other objects were also used: weapons and utensils, ornaments, feet of animals and large birds, ams and feet of humans, even the whole human body. Stencils occur in many parts of the world.

SYDNEY - The sandstone region around Sydney contains some 3000 known rock art sites of two types: rock paintings in rockshelters, and petroglyphs of often large sizes on horizontal rock pavements. The latter depict human figures and marine animals, and may mark ceremonial sites called Bora grounds.

SOUTHERN AUSTRALIA

This region extends mostly along the southern coast of Australia, containing a great variety of styles and techniques, but small number of sites. It includes the cave art on the Nullarbor and near Mount Gambier, the lower Murray art and the Grampians rock art, besides several smaller concentrations. The density of sites is significantly lower than in northern Australia, with only a few hundred sites in total.

CAVE ART - Rock art in deep limestone cave occurs in few parts of the world. The second largest known concentration is along the south coast of Australia, with the largest sites being Koonalda, Karlie- ngoinpool, Nung-kol, Prung-kart, Karake and Paroong Caves. The cave art consists of several distinctive traditions, all of which are non- figurative. Australian cave art has been found in over 100 caves.

NULLARBOR - A tree-less limestone plain with 1600 known caves, some of which contain rock art. It occurs in two forms here: as red hand stencils and as very ancient finger lines. Some of these vast underground systems contain also evidence of flint mining which is known to date from the Ice Age, being 20,000 to 30,000 years old.

MOUNT GAMBIER - A limestone area in south-eastern South Australia, dotted with very recent volcanoes. Among the 400 known caves, 35 contain cave art in the form of several petroglyph traditions. These sites have been discovered only during the 1 980s. Their art begins with finger lines on soft surfaces in the Ice Age. Flint mining evidence occurs in six caves.

LOWER MURRAY - Along the lower Murray River, in South Australia, occur a number of rockshelters with mostly engraved rock art. Stylistically this art resembles that of some of the typically non- figurative cave petroglyphs at Mount Gambier to the south, as well as very ancient rock art to the north, such as that in the Olary reg ion .

GRAMPIANS - A sandstone mountain region of western Victoria, now re-named with its Aboriginal name Gariwerd. It contains a minor concentration of painted rock art, numbering less than 100 sites. Many of them are protected by excellent site management measures. Hand stencils and simple painted motifs occur.

TASMANIA

This island to the south of Australia was inhabited by the Tasmanians. They are known to have conducted ochre mining and painted their bodies with this mineral. In the distant past, they painted also in deep caves. The number of rock art sites in Tasmania is minute but it includes a few petroglyph sites of the Karake style.

TASMANIANS - The Tasmanians have been longer isolated from the rest of humanity than any other people known: the island was cut off from the Australian mainland by the rising sea level about 10,000 years ago. The stormy southern seas were not navigable with small watercraft .

OCHRE MINING - Like the Aborigines on the Australian mainland, and many prehistoric peoples in Africa and Europe, the Tasmanians are known to have conducted underground mining of ochre. This red, brown or yellow mineral pigment consists of iron oxides or iron hydroxides, and was the favoured pigment of most early societies.

CAVE ART - Only three sites of cave art are known in Tasmania, and nearly all motifs are hand stencils. In one of the sites, Judd's Cavern, the rock art paint was found to contain traces of human blood which had been mixed with the ochre. It was radiocarbon-dated to about 10,000 years before present.

KARAKE STYLE - This style of deeply carved mazes of circular and circilinear forms was first recognized in Karake Cave on the Australian mainland, opposite Tasmania. The occurrence of the style on both sides of Bass Strait, which separates Tasmania from Australia, suggests that the two occurrences either predate the severance of Tasmania 10,000 years ago, or that the style continued to be used later.

EUROPE

The rock art of Europe is the smallest body of any continent, but it is also the best studied and the most widely published in the world. Nevertheless, there are still considerable differences in the degree of attention given to the various rock art traditions and regions. The Ice Age art of the Upper Palaeolithic period, found mostly in France and Spain, is by far the best studied.

FRANCO-CANTABRIA

The Upper Palaeolithic rock art of the Franco-Cantabrian region is concentrated in south-western France and northern Spain. It occurs mostly in limestone caves, although open sites have also been discovered recently. Considered to be between 10,000 and 30,000 years old, this art consists of painted and engraved motifs, mostly of animals and abstract signs. A tentative chronology has been constructed for it over the past centu ry.

UPPER PALAEOLITHIC - This is the last major period of the era called the Palaeolithic, or the Old Stone Age, the earliest phase of human culture. The people of the Upper Palaeolithic were modern humans, they were technologically very advanced, and lived as hunters and gatherers, mostly in tents. Occasionally they made use of caves and rockshelters, including in producing their rock art. Where they did this the art has often managed to survive.

FRANCO-CANTABRIA - This region of Upper Palaeolithic rock art encompasses especially the regions of the French Dordogne, Lot, the French Pyrenees and Cantabria in northern Spain. Besides rock art, portable art also occurs, but has a much wider distribution than the rock art of the period.

OPEN SITES - Contrary to the popular belief that the rock art of the European Upper Palaeolithic period was created exclusively in caves, it is much more likely that only that part of it that was located in such sheltered places had a good chance of surviving. Recently, several rock art sites of the same period have been found at open sites in the Pyrenees, northern Spain and Portugal, but their dating remains unproven.

ICE AGE ANIMALS - The best-known subject of Upper Palaeolithic rock art are the Ice Age animal pictures of mammoths, woolly rhinos, horses, bison, aur oxens, ibex, bears and other species. However, these number only about 2500 from all sites in Europe, and are greatly exceeded in number by the non-figurative component of this rock art corpus.

SIGNS - The non-figurative motifs of Upper Palaeolithic European rock art are usually called 'signs', although we cannot know whether these were indeed signs, or what their meanings might have been. They are also called 'abstracts', an equally contentious term. Certain recurrent motifs are being distinguished, and we have various speculations concerning their significance.

CHRONOLOGY - The tentative chronological sequence of supposed rock art traditions of the Upper Palaeolithic rock art has been based on stylistic reasoning, and some archaeologically derived dating information. Individual researchers differ concerning various details of this sequence, and recent results of direct dating methods often disagree significantly with the traditional models.

SPANISH LEVANT

This distinctive corpus of rock art occurs among the rockshelters of eastern Spain. Its faded red paintings are of a dynamic style, frequently featuring human figures that are sometimes engaged in activities, such as hunting or honey gathering. The chronological attribution of this art corpus remains controversial. The art has been assigned successively to the Palaeolithic, Mesolithic and Neolithic periods.

DYNAMIC STYLE - Human and animal figures in rock art can be depicted in a 'static' or 'dynamic' style. The latter is found in various parts of the world, frequently in very early traditions: in central India, Australia, southern Africa, and here, in the Levantine region of Spain. Dynamic art styles depict movement in addition to form .

HUNTING SCENES - Many apparent compositions in rock art have been interpreted as hunting scenes. However, it is essential that the interpreter's subjectivity is not imposed on the rock art. The most detailed and dynamic arts are the most likely to permit reliable detection of hunting scenes, such as those of the Levantine art.

HONEY GATHERING - Apparent depictions of honey gathering in rock arts have been reported from several parts of the world, including southern African Bushmen art, India and Australia. In the Levantine art of Spain, such depiction also seems to occur. Honey was an extremely important nutritional supplement for most human societies since the dawn of time.

MESOLITHIC - The archaeologically perceived technological period between the Palaeolithic and the Neolithic. It is characterized by very small stone tools (microliths) and occurs between about 10,000 and 5,000 years ago. Having been assigned Palaeolithic age first, Levantine art was then placed into the Mesolithic, but recently this was also rejected, in favour of assignment to the Neolithic.

NEOLITHIC - The period between the Mesolithic and the introduction of Bronze, often characterized by stone drilling, pottery, domestication and permanent settlements. After recent discoveries and stylistic comparisons with decorations on Neolithic pottery sherds, the Levantine shelter art was re-assigned to the Neolithic period .

ALPINE REGION

Encompassing parts of eastern France, Switzerland, northern Italy and Austria. The Alpine rock art occurs sometimes high on mountains, such as Mount Bego or the Totes Gebirge, or in mountain valleys, such as Val Camonica. Many different cultures have contributed to these traditions, which consist almost entirely of petroglyphs. Technological details often assist in estimating the age of traditions, and with their help, a tentative chronological sequence has been constructed.

MOUNT BEGO - This mountain in the western Alps is famous for its large body of petroglyphs, occurring at an elevation of almost 3000 metres. The concentration has been considered to show that Mount Bego was a 'sacred mountain' to the peoples of the past.

TOTES GEBIRGE - Located in the north-eastern Alps, this group of limestone mountains comprises a great number of sites of petroglyphs. Most of this rock art has been attributed to comparatively recent, historical periods, essentially on the basis of apparent subject content and by the interpretation of symbols and m sc ri ptl o n s .

VAL CAMONICA - At possibly up to 300,000 figures, the rock art of Val Camonica is one of the largest local concentrations of Europe. The petroglyphs are often executed on rock exposures near the base of the valley that have been scoured smooth by the glaciers of the final Ice Age, sometimes on erect stelae. The art seems to document all cultural phases of the post-glacial period, from the Epi-Palaeolithic to the historical period.

TECHNOLOGY - Depictions permitting technological deductions are crucial to determining the chronologies of the Alpine rock art. For instance, pictures of warriors can be placed chronologically from the weapons they hold or the armour they wear, or equipment such as ploughs or wheeled vehicles may be recognized in the art.

CHRONOLOGY - The chronological sequence of the Alpine art is based on technological detail perceived, and on style, superimposition and, for the most recent phases, inscriptions or other historically datable features.

BALKANS

Small rock art corpora are found in many parts of the Balkans, for instance in parts of the former Yugoslavia, Bulgaria, Romania, Albania and Greece. There is, however, no well-known major corpus of rock art in this region, and little is known about the art. Two sites are thought to have Upper Palaeolithic rock art, one in Bulgaria, one in Croatia.

SCANDINAVIA

Northern Europe possesses some major concentrations of rock art. Petroglyphs occur in Denmark, Norway and Sweden, while paintings can be found in Finland. A Russian continuation of this art corpus can be found in Karelia and Russian Lappland. Tentative dating of these corpora attributes them to Mesolithic to Historic times.

NORWAY - Petroglyphs include several concentrations, notably the Alta corpus which has received World Heritage listing. As in some other parts of Scandinavia, there is an unfortunate tendency to emphasize rock art motifs with various substances for physical enhancement and a neglect of conservation and proper scientific study.

SWEDEN - Sweden boasts some of the earliest published recordings of rock art in the world, dating from the early sixteenth century. Petroglyphs include figures of humans, animals, boats, other objects that are not so readily identifiable, and apparently non-figurative objects.

RUSSIAN LAPPLAND - In one of the northernmost rock art regions, on the coast of the White Sea and on Kola Peninsula, occur a few rock art sites. Rock paintings occur in a small cave, and petroglyphs are found on a number of boulders and pavements, usually near rivers .

KARELIA - Two concentrations of petroglyphs on granite pavements occur, one at Zalavruga, the other on the east shore of Lake Onega. The motif repertoire of western Scandinavia is repeated to some extent, but there are also regionally distinctive motifs present. At Zalavruga, scenes occur, at Lake Onega, swans are a common motif.

CHRONOLOGY - The rock art chronology of Scandinavia is largely derived from the subjective identification of individual motifs, supposed past water levels, presumed stylistic traits and nearby archaeological occupation evidence. Scientific dating evidence exists only at one site, Besov Nos in Russia.

WESTERN EUROPE, LATE

The late prehistoric periods of western Europe have left a great number of regional rock art traditions that have been neglected in favour of the Upper Palaeolithic evidence. Major such concentrations occur in Britain, Portugal and France, and they include various traditions from the Mesolithic to the historical periods.

BRITAIN - The petroglyphic traditions of the British Isles have been largely neglected, except in terms of studying them as relating to megalithic structures. This rock art is entirely non-figurative. It consists frequently of cupules, spirals, concentric circles and complex geometric mazes, and occurs in northern England, Scotland and parts of Ireland.

PORTUGAL - The petroglyph traditions of Portugal and adjacent parts of Spain are very similar to those of Britain, except that they also comprise a notable figurative component. As in Britain, dating is only by associative deduction.

FRANCE - In France, too, rock art traditions postdating the Palaeolithic have been neglected. For example, some 800 decorated rockshelters have been found in a sandstone massif just south of Paris. The art seems to related to a considerable range of traditions. Geometric, deeply carved patterns dominate, and there are also some inscriptions present at these sites.

CHRONOLOGY - The difficulty in determining the true age is illustrated by a recent claim that some of the rocks incorporated in megalithic structures were already decorated before they were used in this way. It is therefore possible that the art was merely considered important and thus included in the monument construction. Thus the structure does not tell us the age of the rock art.

NORTH AMERICA

Rock art occurs in most parts of North America, from the Arctic to Mesoamerica and the Caribbean. Nevertheless, there are great variations in the density of art and in the level of its exploration. The main concentration is in the Southwest of the United States and adjacent parts of Mexico.

ARCTIC

The Arctic region, across the north of the continent, is the home of Eskimos, Aleuts and Chugach. Very few rock art sites have been found in this harsh region, the only concentrations known being those of southern Alaska, Cook Inlet and Wakeham Bay. This includes incisions and cupules which are regarded further south as the oldest tradition of the continent.

ESKIMOS - The Eskimos are a hunter-gatherer people of the Arctic. They still produce portable art objects made of bone, ivory, soapstone and other materials. In the past they also created rock art in the bleak islands north of Hudson Bay. These are the northernmost rock art sites known in the world.

ALEUTS - They are the occupants of the Aleutian Islands, which form a large arc from the Kamchatka Peninsula of Siberia to Alaska. Some of these rocky outcrops possess rock art in the form of petroglyphs, but they are poorly studied because of their inaccessibility. In some cases access involves the use of helicopters.

CHUGACH - They occupy the Cook Inlet area where petroglyphs include depictions of marine and land animals, boats, men, birds and apparent bird tracks. This art occurs both as rock paintings in shelters and as petroglyphs at open sites.

ALASKA - Some petroglyphs have been suggested to resemble corn cobs. Deeply incised lines can be tool sharpening grooves or they belong to the cup-and-groove tradition. Cupules also occur in this region, together with as a limited component of figurative depictions.

WAKEHAM BAY - Located in northern Quebec, near the Atlantic coast, this site consists of steatite ledges. The soft rock bears over fifty depictions of Eskimo masks as well as human and animal pictures. It has been suggested that the figures are stylistically similar to stone masks of the Dorset Culture, which might make them between 1000 and 2700 years old.

NORTHWEST COAST

Extending from southern Alaska to the northern end of California, this is a comparatively uniform petroglyph region. Sites of red paintings occur in the region of the Coast Salish. Motifs include masks or faces, sea monsters, realistic marine animals, coppers and cupules. The major concentration of sites is on Vancouver Island.

MASKS - Petroglphs that seem to depict masks or human faces occur widely in both north- eastern Asia and north-western North America. In many of these regions, from southern Siberia to British Columbia, the prominent use of ceremonial masks is well documented ethnographically. Some of this art is thought to be shamanistic.

SEA MONSTERS - Ornate petroglyphs depicting fantastic animals, sometimes described as sea-wolves, can be found along the west coast of Canada. Excellent examples are found on Vancouver Island. These combine the body of a marine creature with the dog-like head of a carnivore.

COPPERS - Coppers is the name used for roughly rectangular copper plates that were about a metre long. Elaborately decorated with mythical figures, their function was to indicate a high social status of the owner. They were in use on the west coast of Canada and their depictions can be frequently found in rock art.

CUPULES - The hemispherical cup marks that were hammered into the rock. In North America they often occur as the main component of the pit-and-groove style, which is regarded as the oldest rock art form of that continent. Cupules are among the earliest rock art of Eurasia and Australia as well.

NORTHERN WOODLAND

The rock art is concentrated on the Canadian Shield, occurring as paintings and petroglyphs. Dating has been attempted at Mud Portage. Well-known assemblages occur at Peterborough and Lake Kejimkoojik. Generally, sites are thinly distributed, with Algonquian and Micmac art best represented.

CANADIAN SHIELD - A vast expanse of pre-Cambrian rock covering much of Canada, and consisting generally of granites. In this huge area, paintings occur mostly along rivers and lakes. The rock art of the Woodland Algonquians, from British Columbia to Quebec Province, is fairly uniform. Petroglyphs occur also.

MUD PORTAGE - A site in Manitoba, central Canada, where an excavation of a large occupation site uncovered a granite pavement bearing a number of petroglyphs. Using the minimum dates from the sediment deposit and some stratigraphical extrapolative reasoning, a minimum age of 5000 years was obtained for the rock art. A maximum age is provided by the fact that the site was flooded prior to 9000 years ago.

PETERBOROUGH - An Algonquian petroglyph site in Ontario, engraved on metamorphosed limestone (marble). There are over 300 motifs on the pavement, part of which has recently been protected by an air-conditioned building erected over the site. There are male and female humans with genitalia, some with headdresses, reptiles, mammals, animal tracks, projectile points, boats and unidentifiable, perhaps non-figurative forms.

ALGONQUIAN - The rock art of the Woodland Algonquians is very homogeneous, from British Columbia to Quebec Province. Painted motifs include human figures with bird wings, 'thunderbirds' and other fantastic animals, men in canoes, contact art (in which European objects are present), animals and non-figurative motifs.

MICMAC - The Micmac Indians of Lake Kejimkoojik in Nova Scotia, in the east of Canada, produced a distinctive rock art that is scratched into the soft, fine-grained slate of the lake shore. This seems to be a fairly recent tradition, and it was continued at the same site by French and English settlers, who added their own petroglyphs to those of the Micmac.

COLUMBIA-FRASER

This region includes a small section of south-western Canada and Washington State of U.S.A., drained by the Columbia and Fraser rivers. Rock art occurs on the Okanagan River, at The Dalles and generally on the region's plateau. It resembles in part the rock art of the Northwest Coast but also shows similarities to the Great Basin rock art to the south.

OKANAGAN RIVER - Located in the southernmost part of British Columbia, Canada, this rock art region contains small numbers of painting sites, mostly of red figures such as humans, bear tracks, 'thunderbirds', animals and a variety of non-figurative designs. Most of this art seems to be comparatively recent.

THE DALLES - Also called Long Narrows, this stretch of rapids on the Columbia River is about two kilometres long. An important salmon fishing point, it is the greatest rock art concentration of the Columbia-Fraser region. Most of the petroglyphs are now submerged under a dam, some were rescued during the dam's construction.

COLUMBIA-FRASER PLATEAU - This corpus of rock paintings is thought to be only a few centuries old. Some of it is known to have been made at the beginning of the twentieth century, and the motifs include various recent types, such as horse pictures. Some paintings are connected with puberty rites which also continued into recent history.

CALIFORNIA

The rock art of California includes a surprising variety of major traditions. Among these are the Chumash paintings in the south, the Rectilinear Abstract Style, the South Coast paintings, the rock art of the Central Sierra and the petroglyphs on the northern coast of California. In the east of California State the Coso Range rock art occurs, but it is part of the Great Basin traditions.

CHUMASH PAINTINGS - This dramatic painted rock art is often geometric and polychrome, but not necessarily so. Among its non-figurative motifs, star, circle and multiple zigzag designs may be prominent. Highly stylized human and animal forms also occur. Numerous different colours may be distinguished. Paintings are sometimes found high on cliffs, in recesses and small caves.

RECTILINEAR ABSTRACT - Found in southern California, this style occurs in sheltered positions under granite boulders. These paintings are usually in red, and non-figurative. They consist of simple geometric figures, such as straight lines, zigzags and chevrons, and hands are occasionally found.

SOUTH COAST PAINTINGS - Found in the Santa Lucia Range and in the Salinas river basin, at a small number of sites. Human stick figures, dot patterns and rectangles are dominant motifs, but white hand prints occur also. Sometimes this style resembles that of the nearby Chumash painting tradition.

CENTRAL SIERRA - A rock art body of both petroglyphs and paintings is found in the Sierra Nevada ranges of central California. It consists largely of geometric forms, with very few figurative elements. Generally, the motifs resemble those of the Great Basin styles further east, but their distinctive animal figures are lacking.

NORTHERN COAST - In the coastal regions of northern California, rock art consists mainly of the pit-and-groove type, featuring cupules and linear incised grooves. At some sites only the cupules occur, often densely covering a boulder. Similar traditions are also found in coastal areas to the south and north, even inland, and the tradition is usually assumed to be the earliest we know of.

GREAT BASIN

Including portions of Oregon, Utah, Nevada and California, this large region of the western U.S.A. features several distinctive rock art traditions. The major ones are of geometric, scratched or figurative petroglyphs, and of the Great Basin painting style. A more local tradition of rock paintings is the Sevier Style in Utah.

GEOMETRIC PETROGLYPHS - Two styles are distinguished, the curvilinear and the rectilinear style. The differentiation may be arbitrary, however. Both are distinguished by an absence of recognizably figurative components. The motifs are often complex arrangements of linear motifs on patinated boulders.

SCRATCHED PETROGLYPHS - In contrast to most petroglyph traditions, which are pecked or hammered, this form is incised or scratched with a sharp stone tool. These engravings are always non-figurative. Their distribution seems to extend beyond the Great Basin and similar sites occur very close to the West Coast, for instance at Agua Dulce near Los Angeles.

FIGURATIVE PETROGLYPHS - The representative or figurative petroglyphs of the Great Basin are dominated by depictions of the bighorn sheep. Some sheep pictures have two heads. The major concentration of this style is found in the Coso Range of eastern California, where direct rock art dating has been attempted in the 1980s.

GREAT BASIN PAINTINGS - Occurring in parts of Nevada and Northern California, this tradition consists largely of non-figurative or geometric designs, but human figures do occur occasionally. In neighbouring Utah, which possesses a high concentration of rock art sites, these paintings are often found together with the motifs of other traditions.

SEVIER STYLE - This localized style consists mainly of petroglyphs but it includes also some rock paintings in red pigment. It occurs in the area of the Sevier River. Motifs include Fremont human figures, with typical triangular bodies and decoration, as well as bighorn sheep and geometric patterns resembling those on ceramics and textiles.

PLAINS

The Great Plains are the vast grasslands in the central region of the U.S.A., from southern Canada to Texas. Typical human designs found in the rock art of these prairies are the shield figures, the V-necked figures and the therianthropic Dinwoody figures. In additions, there are also numerous depictions of animals and artefacts, and locally there is recent missionary - influenced art.

SHIELD FIGURES - These human figures are partially or almost completely concealed behind circular shields. Usually only the head and legs protrude from the shield, or a spear or club is visible. The shields are often decorated with non-figurative designs which vary so greatly that they seem to designate individual warriors. Shield figures are found equally as rock paintings and as petroglyphs in this individualistic art.

V-NECKED FIGURES - Another common anthropomorph style of the Great Plains consists of elongated, rectangular torsos with V-shaped shoulder to neck connection and linear limbs. These petroglyphs may occur together with the shield figures, and they are often found with depictions of horses. The sex is frequently indicated on these human figures.

DINWOODY FIGURES - These intricate and distinctive human figures are named after Dinwoodyy Lake, and they are of local distribution only, occuring in a small mountainous part of Wyoming. They are of rectangular but rounded shape, often with wing-like arms and ornate geometric decoration. Dinwoody figures occur only as petroglyphs and are thought to be much older than the shield and V-necked figures of the plains.

THERIANTHROPES - The Dinwoody figures, with their owl-like appearance, are often thought to be therianthropes. Such figures combine human attributes with those of other animals. Therianthropes occur in numerous rock art traditions throughout the world, and in many combinations. Some may depict humans wearing animal attributes, others may be mythical beings or creation heroes, or depict trance experiences or shamans.

ANIMAL FIGURES - The most common animal depiction in Great Plains rock art are those of horses. Since these were introduced by European colonisers, the rock art must be of recent centuries. Other animals found in the rock art are bison, roe, deer, antelope and bighorn sheep, sometimes birds and turtles. Animal tracks are also common in this art.

ARTEFACT PICTURES - Depictions of weapons range from those of lances, spears, bows and arrows; clubs, to flintlock rifles. The tipi, the characteristic tent of the prairie, is sometimes found in the rock art of the Great Plains.

MISSIONARY ART - In parts of central and western Texas, rock paintings of missions and missionary - inspired motifs are found. They include depictions of mission churches with windows, spires and crosses. Even depictions of the devil with tail and fork have been found here, and can only date from the late 18th or the 19th centuries.

EASTERN TEMPERATE

Covering the area between the Great Lakes and Florida, this includes all of the eastern U.S.A. In this vast region, the earlier Woodland Culture is succeeded by the Mississippian. The three principal rock art regions are in the Ohio, Missouri and Mississippi valleys. Frequent motifs are 'thunder-birds' and 'heart lines'.

WOODLAND CULTURE - This cultural phase of eastern North America dates from approximately 1000 B.C. to A.D. 800. Pottery was used and maize was planted. The period is characterised by the production of burial mounds, sometimes in the form of effigy mounds. The latter are shaped to resemble objects, including animals forms. The culture's principal centres were the Illinois and Ohio valleys. Rock art occurs there also.

MISSISSIPPIAN - Lasting from approximately 800 B.C. to the Historic Period, this consists of a series of related cultural complexes. These agriculturalists planted maize, beans and squash. The rock art of their cultural sequence consists of petroglyphs, which often include imagery of spirit beings such as 'thunder-birds'.

OHIO VALLEY - Among the petroglyphs of this region, human figures with round heads or masks, often decorated with horns or feathers, occur frequently. Other motifs are birds, quadrupeds, snakes, animal tracks and human hands. Animal figures with 'heart lines' are found, and there are numerous non-figurative motif types: circles, spirals, stars, crescents and others.

MISSOURI - This rock art region includes parts of Missouri, southern Illinois and western Kentucky, as well as Tennessee, Georgia, Alabama and North Carolina. Human figures include some with bird heads, others with what appear to be speech blobs in front of their mouths. Human feet or tracks are common, also animal tracks. Non-figurative or geometric petroglyphs occur frequently.

MISSISSIPPI VALLEY - Petroglyphs of human forms are usually sitck men, but they include sometimes mask-like faces, horns or pointed headdresses. At the quartizite site of Jeffers, numerous depictions of artefacts have been found, especially of projectile points and atlatls (spear throwers). The 'thunder-bird' occurs, as do other depictions of animals, quadrupeds as well as fish, snakes and turtles.

THUNDER-BIRD - This motif, which is re-cycled in Western heraldry, is common in many rock art traditions of North America. It is found from Canada to Mexico, and similar motifs also occur in northern regions of South America. It consists of a bird figure depicted with outstretched wings, often resembling an eagle or condor. Its head is typically turned to the side. It causes lightning with its eyes and thunder with its wings, but protects humans.

HEART LINE - Thought to relate to mythological beings, this line connects the head or mouth of beings with a blob in the heart area. In the eastern temperate region, it belongs to the Mississippian culture. It has been used in hunting magic when occurring in animal figures, but it may alternatively, especially in human or therianthropic figures, indicate supernatural status.

CHRONOLOGY - The cupules, sometimes occurring together with linear grooves, as they are found especially in northern Georgia and the adjacent parts of Tennessee, Alabama and North Carolina, are thought to be the earliest form of rock art in the eastern temperate region of North America. This is consistent with the findings in other parts of the continent, including the Great Basin and the west coast.

SOUTHWEST

One of the culturally most differentiated regions of North America, this includes Colorado, New Mexico, Arizona, as well as parts of Utah, Texas, Wyoming, Nevada and California. This partly mountainous, partly arid region comprises the richest rock art occurrence of North America. It includes such major traditions as Hohokam, Mogollon, Anasazi, Navaho, Fremont, Barrier Canyon and Pecos River.

HOHOKAM - This culture of sedentary peoples developed just over 2000 years ago in the arid regions of northern Mexico and adjacent parts of the United States. Rock art features stick men or hour-glass human figures, sometimes with other objects, as well as deer, bighorn sheep, lizards and other animals. The overwhelming part of Hohokam rock art consists of distinctive geometric motifs. These and some figurative elements occur also on pottery.

MOGOLLON - In southern New Mexico and adjacent Texas, the Mogollon tribes coincided with the Hohokam chronologically. The imagery of their rock art occurs widely in their pottery. Rock art is found in the form of both petroglyphs and paintings, and as often spectacular combinations of figurative and geometric motifs. Human figures may be decorated in textile-like patterns.

ANASAZI - Located in the canyon country shared by Utah, Arizona, Colorado and New Mexico, the Anasazi sequence includes the Basketmaker and Pueblo culltures. Petroglyphs and paintings of stylistic diversity belong to it, including distinctive elements such as Kokopelli, a hunchbacked and often phallic flute player, and a feathered or horned serpent. Besides human forms, numerous animal species are depicted.

NAVAHO - In 1969, Pueblo - Indians from the Rio Grande sought escape from Spanish colonisation by joining the Navahos, who subsequently adopted much of Pueblo culture. This is reflected in the rock art, and in the continuing culture of the Navahos. Polychrome rock art occurs, as well as incised engravings. The rock art includes depictions of Spanish riders, as well as shield figures and numerous animals.

FREMONT - The Fremont Culture of Utah and some adjacent art forms of Nevada and Colorado date between A.D. 950 and 1200. The rock art is characterised by groups of often large, broad shouldered humans in frontal view, commonly adorned with horns, helmets and roundish ear pendants, necklaces and torso decoration. Eyes and mouuth are shown, but not noses, and limbs are not detailed. Usually found as petroglyphs, this style seems to continue as paintings in its southern distribution range.

BARRIER CANYON - These rock paintings are thought to be the southern extension of the Fremont human motifs, but an alternative theory has been proposed : that they are related to the Pecos River style. Barrier Canyon humans are of restricted distribution (south-eastern Utah). They are frequently very large, are painted mostly in red, have usually no limbs, broad shoulders, big eyes, internal geometric decoration, and they resemble mummies.

PECOS RIVER - This distinctive series of rock painting styles in western Texas is considered to be among the oldest in North America, and dating of charcoal pigment has recently produced an age of approximately 3800 years. The often polychrome art predates the introduction of bow and arrow, and consists of detailed depictions of often large human figures, together with various objects.

CHRONOLOGY - The chronology of the complex succession of the many rock art traditions of the south-western United States and some contiguous parts of Mexico has been determined by several means: the appearance of bow and arrow, the similarity of rock art motifs and pottery decoration, the proximity of settlements, in one case by direct dating of charcoal pigment, and in the more recent periods by historical data. However, much detail remains to be resolved still.

MEXICO

Rock art traditions from the Southwest of the U.S.A. continue into Baja California and the Sonora Desert. Other forms are found in lower Mexico, while on the Yucatan Peninsula, Mayan cave art is a notable feature at a limited number of sites.

BAJA CALIFORNIA - This is the long peninsula of California, a state of Mexico. The rugged and mountainous region is dissected by deep canyons. Many rock art sites have been found in them, some of them are of spectacular, large paintings on inaccessible rockshelter ceilings. The images depict groups of human figures as well as similarly large animal motifs.

SONORA - There are some large rock art complexes in this desert region, especially Cerro Blanco, near Caborca, and La Pintada, south of Hermosillo. The former is a group of petroglyph sites on dark-brown patinated rock. The latter is a group of painting sites in a steep canyon, which include unusually small painted figures that are often just two centimetres tall.

LOWER MEXICO - In the central and southern regions of Mexico, rock art is overshadowed by the attention given to the monumental carvings of the Aztec, Mayan and Oltec empires. These art forms, although executed in rock, are not considered under the rubric rock art.

YUCATAN - Rock art has been found in a small series of limestone caves on the Peninsula of Yucatan. It includes painted hieroglyphic inscriptions of the Mayas as well as detailed pictures of humans. A notable feature is the use of a blue mineral pigment which has resisted all scientific efforts to determine its manufacturing process, Maya blue.

MESOAMERICA

From the limited reports available it seems that rock art occurs in all the Mesoamerican countries. It is known to occur in Guatemala, Belize, Honduras and Costa Rica. There are also preliminary reports from Nicaragua and Panama, but knowledge about these traditions remains generally limited.

ANTILLES

Antillean rock art occurs on all large islands of the Caribbean. It is best known from Cuba and Hispaniola, where a notable component is the rock art in deep limestone caves. However, numerous rock art sites are also known from the Lesser Antilles. The chronology of these arts may be relevant to the islands' initial settlement history.

CUBA - Rock art occurs in at least fifty limestone caves on the island, in ten of them together with human burials. In seven of the sites, small numbers of petroglypys have been located, usually depicting faces. The remaining caves contain red or black paintings, figurative as well as non-figurative. The most elaborate of these is Cueva de Punto del Este I, with polychrome arrangements of concentric circles.

HISPANIOLA - Numerous rock art sites have been reported from various parts of the Dominican Republic, particularly from north-west of Santo Domingo and from the island's north coast. There are open sites, such as concentrations of petroglyphs on basalt boulders, and there are also many painted and carved art sites deep in limestone caves.

CAVE ART - At Bourbon and on the remote north coast of Hispaniola, concentrations of cave art sites are found. Their art consists entirely of paintings in black pigment and carved petroglyphs that usually depict fearsome human faces or humanoid figures. The caves on the north coast also contain large numbers of historical inscriptions by mariners and buccaneers who landed there in the search for freshwater.

LESSER ANTILLES- Petroglyphs have been recorded on at least eleven of the Lesser Antillean Islands, often on andesite, with the greatest concentration on Guadeloupe. Human figures and faces dominate, with smaller numbers of geometric figures and very few animals. There does not appear to be a discernible stylistic continuity with the rock art of the nearby South American coast, despite similarities in pottery.

CHRONOLOGY - The chronology of the Antillean rock art is related to the unresolved question of the islands' initial settlement. There is no clear archaeological evidence beyond 2000 years ago on Hispaniola, but on Cuba rock art has been suggested to be up to 5000 years old, at Cueva de los Cañones. The two principal theories are that settlement occurred first from South America via the Lesser Antilles, or that it was from North America via Florida and Cuba.

SOUTH AMERICA

Rock art is found widely in South America, occuring in all of the continent's countries. There is a great diversity of styles but there are also major consistencies. The greatest concentrations of rock art are found in Peru and Brazil. Some dating has been achieved, especially in Brazil. Rock art is probably best explored in Argentina, Bolivia, Peru and Brazil.

PERU

One of the world's great petroglyph concentrations is found in Peru, and rock paintings have been neglected in the country's rock art studies. The major concentrations are all in the coastal districts of the country, especially on the north coast, in the Lima and Ica Departemento and in Arequipa. The latter includes the important Toro Muerto Complex and other evidence of apparently narcotics - induced imagery.

NORTH COAST - This rock art concentration extends over Lambayeque, Cayamarca, La Libertad and the coast of Ancash. Motifs occur in complex arrangements and sophisticated artistic conventions, suggestive of intricate symbolisms. These involve combinations of human, animal and geometric forms and conform to few stylistic rules, and they are hardly ever repetitive.

LIMA AND ICA - The petroglyphs of these departmentos are less decipherable as figurative compositions, but they are often still based on figurative designs. Abstraction os more advanced, geometric patterns dominate, but the artistic sophistication of the general region prevails. Due to their extreme complexity and diversity, these art traditions are difficult to quantify.

AREQUIPA - This southern district offers one of the richest, most spectacular and sophisticated art traditions of the world. The valleys of the Rio Majes, Sihuas and Chili contain numerous sites, mostly of petroglyphs, but paintings and geoglyphs occur also. Some dense concentrations are found high on vertical cliffs of volcanic tuff. Motifs are dominated by figurative depictions of animals and humans.

TORO MUERTO COMPLEX - The largest rock art site in the Americas, it measures four kilometres, and is located in a desert side valley of the Rio Majes. Some 5000 large tuff blocks bear tens of thousands of petroglyphs. Human figures are common, apparently dancing under the influence of cultural narcotics, and the imagery includes many seemingly hallucinatory motifs.

NARCOTICS - Their cultural use was widespread in South America, including southern Peru, where ayahuasca was popular. Dancing humans with lines emanating from their eyes and heads, surrounded by probably drug-induced imagery and phosphene motifs make up much of the rock art at some Peruvian sites.

BOLIVIA

Bolivian rock art forms part of the major Andean traditions. Local features are the ancient petroglyphs in Toro Muerto Cave, distinctive painting styles, the frequent art of the Colonial Period, the continuing use of rock art sites by indigenes, and the evidence of Christian iconoclasm at some pre-Columbian sites. Rock art is often associated with sites of cultural significance.

TORO MUERTO CAVE- This site, located between Cochabamba and Santa Cruz, is a shallow cave in quartzite. It contains recent paintings and much older petroglyphs of several phases. The latter are non figurative and are separated by several events of rock exfoliation. Stone tools at the site are particularly archaic. The older of these art phases are therefore thought to be of considerable antiquity.

PAINTING STYLES - These include simple human figures, stylised tripartite motifs developed from them, and entirely geometric patterns. Animal figures such as cats are also found, and while in the altiplano, the high plateau, Andean styles occur, in the lowlands towards the Amazon basin, less stylised painting forms are found, besides some dense concentrations of vulva petroglyphs.

COLONIAL PERIOD - A frequent from of rock art in Bolivia is readily identified by the advent of Spanish influence, which is followed by the Colonial Period. Paintings from this time include depictions of settlements with church spires, crosses, horses with riders, and detailed human depictions with Spanish attire and weapons. This art also includes petroglyphs by the invaders.

INDIGENOUS USE - Recently it has been established that some indigenous use of rock art sites still continues in remote parts of Bolivia. This includes the ritual killing of animals such as oxen or chickens, blood sacrifice and the placement of gifts in stonelined burials. Ethnographic study of these practices seeks to elucidate the purposes of the rock art.

ICONOCLASM - The Spanish invaders decreed in 1567 an 'eardication policy of idolatry', and consequently some rock art sites were defaced by them. This was initially recognised at the site Pena Escrita, where red rock paintings have been damaged or partially obliterated, and Christian crosses were engraved with metal tools over painted figures. Rock art iconoclasm has occurred in many parts of the world, and on behalf of many religions.

BRAZIL

Petroglyphs have been reported from nearly all states of Brazil, and rock paintings are similarly widespread, especially in the north - east and the south. Rock art seems less common in the Amazon basin, but it still occurs there. Of particular importance are the sites in southern Piauf, where dating has been attempted, as well as those of the Mato Grosso.

AMAZON PETROGLYPHS - There are no petroglyphs along the lower Amazon, but they are found in numerous small occurrences along many of the tributaries, both north and south of the main river. Motifs are mostly ornamental, the only common figurative element being simple human figures. The rock art occurs usually on boulders along or near water courses, as these form the main traffic routes.

AMAZON PAINTINGS - Until recently, no rock paintings were thought to exist in the Amazon basin, but in 1986, a group of sites was discovered near Monte Alegre, Para state. Located in a limestone ridge, Serra da Lua, the paintings occur on cliffs as well as in deep caves. The age of the art is unknown, and its motif range consists of highly stylised faces, human figures, complex geometric mazes and other geometric arrangements.

MATO GROSSO - A series of sandstone rockshelters in this state contains numerous rock paintings, and some of these sites have been excavated in the hope of obtaining dating evidence for the rock art. Occupation evidence extends to just over 10,000 years ago in the site Santa Elina, which contains about 1000 paintings, and to 4600 years ago in Ferraz Egreja. The first site also produced evidence of megafauna associated with human occupation.

NORTH-EAST - The Nordeste includes parts of the states Maranhao, Piaui, Ceara, Pernambuco, Bahia, and four smaller states on the esternmost tip of the continent. The principal painting traditions are called Nordeste, Agreste and Geometrica. Petroglyphs also occur in the region and may predate the paintings, as some sites are extremely weathered and patinated. Of particular importance is the region of southern Piaui where research has been intensive.

PERNA I SITE - This painting site is a large sandstone shelter in the Parque Nacional da Serra da Capivara in southern Piaui. There are numerous painting motifs above ground, but a major excavation in 1986 exposed a further 100 or so below ground. As they extend down almost to a massive charcoal layer of about 10,000 years age, we know that this must be their minimum age. Perna I is the oldest dated rock art site in the Americas.

PEDRA FURADA - Another site in the same area, this large shelter contains supposed human occupation evidence dated up to 50,000 years ago, the oldest known in the Americas. The shelter also contains 1600 rock paintings, and it was attempted to provide dating from some spalls with paint traces found in the excavation. However, this dating attempt has not been accepted and the extant art is thought to be fairly recent.

ARGENTINA

Petroglyphs occur in all regions offering suitable rock surfaces, paintings are found where sheltered locations occur. The principal rock art regions are the north-western provinces, the Sierras Centrales, Cuyo, Neuquen and Patagonia. Rock art styles differ significantly between some of these regions, and they are of greatly differing antiquities. Climate and locations have often assisted preservation of the art.

NORTH-WEST- The states of Jujuy, Salta, Tucuman, Catamarca and La Rioja form Argentina's north-west. The sometimes polychrome geometric paintings in the shelters and caves of Jujuy and Salta resemble the rock art of nearby southern Bolivia. Petroglyphs on deeply paintated rock are also common, with large concentrations found in the region's south. Motifs are of very stylised figurative and non-figurative patterns.

SIERRAS CENTRALES - This region includes parts of Cordoba, Santiago del Estero and San Luis. The art is distinctive, with its sometimes deeply carved, complex abstract arrangements, as for instance in Para Yacu, Sierra de Sumampa. Deeply weathered geometric petroglyphs and much more recent simple paintings occur in the Cerro Colorado area, and also some semi-naturalistic animal paintings.

CUYO - Extending over the states San Juan and Mendoza, the Cuyana rock art region offers very dense concentrations of typically non-figurative petroglyphs, as well as highly stylised human faces and figures. Figurative and non-figurative elements are often beyond discrimination. Much of the art is found on rounded and painated boulders, or it occurs on cliffs.

NEUQUEN - An impressive corpus of ancient petroglyphs exists in the Norquin valley, at Cerro Morado and Cerro Pena Haichol, with vast numbers of entirely non-figurative motifs sometimes totally covering rock panels. Cupules and geometric linear marks dominate and are entirely repainated. Paintings occur at Cueva de Huenol, and at Colo-Michi-Co and El chacay, flat boulders are often densely covered with geometric petroglyph patterns.

PATAGONIA - This vast southern part of Argentina comprises some of the world's best preserved rock paintings. Sites such as Cueva de las Manos, with its large corpus of hand stencils, or Cueva Grande del Arroyo Feo occur on the Rio Pinturas. The latter cave has yielded occupation evidence of up to 9300 years. Early Patagonian petroglyphs are geometric, recent traditions include figurative elements and tracks.

OTHER SOUTH AMERICAN COUNTRIES

Rock art also occurs in the remaining countries of South America : in Chile, Ecuador, Colombia, Venezuela, Guyana, Surinam, French Guiana, Urguguay and Paraguay. With some exceptions, these rock art corpora are not well studied or well published, but they do indicate the universality of rock art in South America.

CHILE - Rock art occurs in all of the thirteen states of Chile, even on Terra del Fuego. Not only are there petroglyphs and rock paintings, geoglyphs are extremely common. In the northernmost region, continuing from Arequipa in Peru, well over 8000 geoglyphs have been recorded. Petroglyph motifs of felines and camelids are limited to northern Chile, with tracks and non-figurative motifs common in the south.

ECUADOR - Petroglyphs have been reported from ten of the twenty provinces of Ecuador. A major cluster occurs in the Rio Napo area, where twenty sites comprise over 1200 motifs include anthropomorphs, concentric circles, zigzags, double spirals, human foot prints, and some animal figures, such as frogs and camelids. Rock apintings occur also in Ecuador.

COLOMBIA - Rock art has been found in most of the country's departmentos. In regions forming part of the Amazon and Orinoco basins as well as in the Cordillera Oriental, motif spectra resemble those of the river basins themselves: human tracks, geometric symbols and stick figures. In the Sierra Nevada de Santa Marta, feline figures, framed crosses and human figures with headdresses occur.

VENEZUELA -Rock art has been observed and reported from at least seventeen of the twenty - one states, but is lacking in the Llanos and eastern Venezuela. Among the commonly mentioned motif types, human tracks, stick figures and a variety of geometric forms are foremost, the latter including concentric circles, framed crosses and double spirals. Less common are felines, faces with 'curled-up shoulders' and concentric circles with 'legs'.

GUYANA - Petroglyphs occur along the following rivers : Berbice, Essequibo and its tributory Potaro, Rupununi, Kwitaro, Kuyuwini, Kassikaityu and Ireng. They have also been found on the Rupununi savanna. Typical motifs are concentric circles with 'legs' birds with outstretched wings, stick figures, cupules, human tracks and various geometric patterns. Rock paintings occur at several sites, the best known being the spectacular Tramen Cliffs.

SURINAM - Petroglyphs have been reported from nine of Surinam's rivers as well the Sipaliwini savanna. The motif repertoire does not resemble that of neighbouring regions, consisting of concentric circles, 'frogs', stick figures, and faces with 'curled-up shoulders'. The art occurs frequently on granite or gneiss boulders along river banks, and is often quite deeply carved.

FRENCH GUIANA - Rock art motifs considered to typify this country's rock art include stick figures, 'frogs', zigzags, and the faces with 'curled-up shoulders'. About six rock art concentrations are known to exist in French Guiana, but the art is poorly explored. Most rock art is on granite or diabase rock.

URUGUAY - Rock art is not common, but petroglyphs are found in two departments, Artigas and Flores. In the former, they occur on the Rio Cuareim and in the Canon Nandubay, in the latter at the site Chamanga.

PARAGUAY - Five petroglyph concentrations have been reported from Paraguay:Tocumbu near Asuncion; from the Rio Paraguay near Rio Tapoti; from Paraguari, east of Asuncion; from the Alto Parana; and from the Sierra d'Ivytiruzu, east of Villa Rica. In the last - mentioned region, at Cerro Polilla, complex arrangements of entirely non-figurative petroglyphs have been recorded.

ASIA

The largest concentration of Asian rock art occurs in central India, consisting mainly of paintings. Other major traditions are found in China, central Siberia, the regions of central Asia, Sinai Desert and Arabia. Asian rock art includes the oldest known in the world, but the level of its exploration is very uneven among the many rock art regions of the continent.

AFRICA

While rock art probably occurs in most parts of Africa, the two main bodies and those best explored are found in the Sahara and in southern Africa. The former corpus extends across northern Africa, the latter from Zimbabwe to South Africa. Other bodies are much smaller, or less well known. Very early art evidence occurs in Namibia and South Africa.

DATING OF ROCK ART

Without some reliable information about the possible age of a rock art it cannot be related to archaeological data, and it remains of limited scientific use. Rock art dating is more difficult than archaeological dating, and for a long time only unreliable methods have been available in this field. In recent years, however, a series of new methods have been introduced.

HISTORY OF ROCK ART DATING

The subject of rock art antiquity has attracted interest since the beginnings of rock art studies. With the discovery of Palaeolithic rock art a century ago, the question attracted sustained interest and this led to archaeological dating methods for rock art. Recently, direct dating of rock art was developed, providing new directions in this field.

BEGINNINGS - The first published comments suggesting the use of patination for relative dating are from 1820, and relate to petroglyphs in Egypt. However, no progress in the area of reliable and testable rock art dating is discernible until the 1970s. During this intervening period, other currents of research dominated the dating of rock arts.

PALAEOLITHIC ART - The authenticity of the first Palaeolithic rock art reported (in Altamira) was rejected by archaeologists for decades, but it was finally accepted about the beginning of the 20th century. In the endeavours to date this art approximately for the purpose of its authentication lie the origins of archaeological dating of rock ant.

ARCHAEOLOGICAL DATING - In this methodology, traditional archaeology relates the rock art to some feature that is supposedly datable by some other means. For instance, the latter may be charcoal from a soil layer that has been found to cover rock art, and the charcoal is then dated via its radiocarbon content. The method is of limited applicability.

DIRECT DATING - This new methodology is by non-archaeological means, usually through geomorphology, geochemistry or paint analysis. It is subject to more rigorous logical and technical preconditions than archaeological dating, and provides usually less 'precise' but more reliable information about the rock art's antiquity. Direct dating is still in its infancy and will be developed considerably.

FUTURE DIRECTIONS - The developments in rock art dating, in the foreseeable future, are likely to include a significant expansion of direct dating methodology, and a continuing proliferation of new methods within this range. Methods will be developed for the many potential conditions that have so far resisted all attempts to provide quantifiable dating information for.

ARCHAEOLOGICAL DATING OF ROCK ART

In archaeological dating of rock art, an example of the art is in some way related to a feature that is supposedly datable by traditional archaeology. Methods include the excavation of rock art or exfoliated fragments of art, supposed topographical relation, inferred identification of depicted faunal elements and of antefacts that can be assigned an approximate age, and the tentative dating by stylistic means.

EXCAVATION OF ROCK ART - When petroglyphs are found covered beneath archaeological occupation layers, it is assumed that the lowest such stratum must be younger than the rock art, and that it provides a minimum age. This dating method relies on several interdependent deductions which are not always reliable. Also, the number of sites where such finds have been made is minute, and rock paintings are almost never found below sediment strata.

EXCAVATION OF EXFOLIATED ROCK ART - At a few sites of rock art, naturally exfoliated fragments of it may have fallen to the ground and become covered by sediments. Where these layers are supposedly datable by charcoal found in them, the radiocarbon age of the charcoal is thought to provide a minimum age for the rock art. The method depends on various deductions which cannot be tested.

TOPOGRAPHICAL RELATION - This applies usually only in enclosed sites such as caves: a floor or occupation site is thought to be related to the rock ant, sometimes even containing what appears to be the same pigment as used in the nearby rock paintings. The reliability of this method differs in each individual situation, but it is usually not very great.

IDENTIFICATION OF FAUNA - When pictures are thought to depict particular species that are assumed to mark specific periods they are thought to indicate the approximate age. This method is unreliable, for several reasons, and cannot be tested well. Identifications of pictures are often wrong, spectacular cases of misidentification are known. The method also relies on the validity of palaeontological assumptions.

IDENTIFICATION OF ARTEFACTS - Weapons, tools and ornaments are often depicted in rock art. Their subjective identification is thought to assist in determining the archaeologically perceived period from which such artefacts are known. The method can be very useful, but it can also be unreliable, and cannot be tested.

STYLISTIC DATING - This method is by subjective matching of what appear to be depictions of the same style. For instance, an archaeologically dated portable ant object may bear art of a style apparently matching the rock art. However, the portable art may be a much younger copy. The method is also quite subjective and unreliable because it relies on stylistic and untestable determinations.

DIRECT DATING OF ROCK ART

This must meet conditions of refutability, repeatability, and the physical relationship of the dated feature or substance to the rock art must be direct and irrefutable. The beginnings of this methodology related to mineral precipitates and rock varnish. Recently, organic paint components, paint recipes and microerosion dating were added as the most promising approaches of direct dating.

BEGINNINGS - After realizing the limitations of archaeological rock art dating during the 1 970s, some rock at researchers decided to engage scientific methods in the quest of determining the antiquity of rock art. The first method in this effort was applied in 1980 in Australia. In the subsequent ten years, many other methods were tried and developed.

PRECIPITATES - At numerous rock art sites, layers of art are covered or separated by layers of mineral deposits which were precipitated from solutions. Initially, carbonates were used in Australia, later oxalates. Both are datable by radiocarbon content and other methods. Other precipitates may also be used, such as silicas, which can contain organic residues.

ROCK VARNISH - Initially, it was attempted to date this dark-brown deposit of iron, manganese and other cations by cation-ratio dating, a method seeking to measure differential rates of leaching. This technique is unreliable and has been replaced by the determination of radiocarbon content of microscopic organic inclusions in the thin varnish cover. This provides only a minimum age for the art covered by the varnish.

ORGANIC PAINT COMPONENTS - Rock art paints may contain many types of organic substances, residues of which are all datable by their radiocarbon content. They include binders added intentionally to the paint, such as blood, plant juices and resins, fats, milk and others; as well as incidental inclusions, such as brush fibres, air-borne organic remains and other panticles.

PAINT RECIPES - The precise chemical composition of rock art paints has been used in France to demonstrate which paints were prepared at the same time, by matching these compositions. This information can also assist in dating the art when the same recipes are found on archaeologically datable portable objects.

MICROEROSION DATING - This Australian method was first tested only in 1990, in Russia. It uses the geometry of microscopic solution processes of features (edges of freshly fractured crystals) on centain rocks, and can only be used under certain favourable conditions. If all these are met, it may provide very reliable dating, but only for petroglyphs and only where suitable calibration conditions apply.

DATING PROJECTS

A review of some major or influential specific projects can provide an idea of the developments in rock art dating. It includes applications of archaeological dating, direct dating, and the use of laser-assisted combustion of organic remains, as well as a consideration of both currently proceeding and planned or potential rock art dating projects.

ARCHAEOLOGICAL DATING - Classical applications of archaeological dating methodology are those from Perna 1 in Brazil, Mud Portage in Canada, Early Man Shelter in Australia, Auditorium Cave in India, and at Laussel and La Ferrassie in France. In all these cases, minimum dating of rock art has been provided by archaeological deposits.

DIRECT DATING - The milestones in the recent development of direct dating techniques have been provided at the sites Malangine Cave (mineral precipitate), Judd's Cavern (blood binder), Wharton Hill (rock varnish) and Gnatalia Creek (charcoal pigment) in Australia; Pech Merle, Cougnac and Cosquer Cave in France (all charcoal pigment); and Besov Nos in Russia (microerosion).

LASER-ASSISTED COMBUSTION - In this new method, a laser beam is used to burn the organic content of mineral accretions covering petroglyphs, or the paints of rock paintings. The carbon dioxide so produced is collected and then processed for radiocarbon dating. The method provides precise control over sampling and eliminates contamination possibilities.

CURRENT DATING PROJECTS - Several direct rock art dating projects are proceeding at the time of preparing this text, in 1994. Among them are projects in Europe, southern Africa, Australia and U.S.A. Some will use new applications of current methods, others new methods. For instance, a current project in Kimberley, north-western Australia, will analyze wasp nest remains which have been found both over and under rock paints.

POTENTIAL PROJECTS - There are numerous potential new applications and new methods in rock art dating, and current methods can be introduced in many regions where they have not been used previously. There are further possibilities of cross-checking results of the various methods used, and of determining regional influences of climate and geology which apply to some methods.

RESOURCES - Information about current rock art dating methodology can be obtained from individual researchers in western Europe, Australia and U.S.A., from a few select universities in these regions, from rock art organizations and from the International Federation of Rock Art Organizations (IFRAO).

FUTURE METHODS

Direct dating of rock art has been developed so recently that only a few methods have so far found application. Many others are likely to be useful in the future, among them perhaps luminescence dating, the dating of various types of organic matter, palaeomagnetic dating, geomorphological studies, and perhaps even cosmogenic radiation products.

LUMINESCENCE DATING - Two methods, thermo-luminescence dating and optical luminescence dating, are in use in archaeology. They can determine the approximate time when a quartz grain was last exposed to intensive light. Not applied to rock art until 1994, these methods have considerable potential where suitable quartz grains can be found in paints or in wasp or termite nests.

ORGANIC MATTER - Various organic materials can be related to rock art, especially paintings. For instance, wasp nests or termite galleries often cover rock art, and sometimes the paint was applied over such features. They are datable by standard radiocarbon analysis. In the Arnhem and Kimberley rock art of northern Australia occur many pictures made of beeswax, which are currently being dated securely via their radiocarbon content.

PALAEOMAGNETISM - This method has long been used in archaeology, but not so far applied to rock art. Remnant magnetism in iron minerals are compared to known past magnetic orientations. Many rock art paints contain formerly heated iron pigments which should be susceptible to this method, and patination over petroglyphs usually has a high content of iron.

GEOMORPHOLOGY - The many geomorphological processes that have affected the rock surfaces on which the art is found should be particularly helpful in the case of petroglyph dating. They have hardly been explored so far, and offer great potential for future research. Among such processes are weathering by frost, water, wind, sun, glaciers, fire and biological factors.

COSMOGENIC RADIATION - This new technique measures the exposure of a rock surface to cosmogenic radiation from its isotopic products. Such radiation arrives from space. At present, this is not suitable for rock art dating because of the large sample sizes required for securing reasonable results. However, the method may be improved in the future. The technical aspects of rock art, apart from dating and conservation, cover such diverse subjects as its production, its study, its analysis, and particularly the questions of standardization. Without the latter, research work cannot be made globally compatible. The subject of rock art interpretation may also be considered here.

TECHNOLOGY OF ROCK ART

The technical aspects of rock art, apart from dating and conservation, cover such diverse subjects as its production, its study, its analysis, and particularly the questions of standardisation. Without the latter, research work cannot be made globally compatible. The subject of rock art interpretation may also be considered here.

ROCK ART PRODUCTION

Among the subjects to be considered in the area of rock art production are those of the fundamental division of rock art into petroglyphs and rock paintings, as well as more specific methods of production, such as sgraffiti petroglyphs, finger markings, other forms of rock art, and geoglyphs. Also, the topics of pigment sources and painting methods are relevant.

PETROGLYPHS - This main division of rock art was produced by a reductive process: something was removed from the rock surface. The process may have been by engraving, incising, abrading, drilling, hammering, pounding, pecking (chiselling), carving, finger marking or etching the surface. In general, petroglyphs are visible because of their colour contrast, their relief or both.

SGRAFFITI - In this form of petroglyph (singular: sgraffito), a distinctively coloured natural surface layer (patina) is removed to expose a very differently coloured layer beneath, thus creating an image. This method is also used in recent art, on building walls or ceramic surfaces, where differently coloured layers are first applied and images are then produced by exposing selected layers.

FINGER MARKINGS - Finger markings have been produced on the soft surfaces of carbonate precipitates in deep limestone caves, in France, Spain, Australia and Papua New Guinea. The soft deposit hardened upon desiccation or crystallization, and could then be preserved for long periods of time. Some of these traditions survived from the Ice Age.

ROCK PAINTINGS - The second main division of rock art, made by an additive process: a substance was added to the rock surface, usually of a pigment providing good colour contrast for visibility. This division includes wet-applied paintings, sprayed stencils and dry-pigment drawings.

PIGMENT SOURCES - Many substances have been used as the pigment component (the colouring agent) of rock paints. Some are minerals, especially ochres, kaolin or copper minerals; others are organic, including charcoal, cochineal and many more. In the case of mineral pigments, it may be possible to establish the quarry locations by chemical analysis.

PAINTING METHODS - The basic methods of producing rock paintings are painting with a brush, application with fingers, stencil production by spraying with mouth, and the application of dry pigment in crayon form. The stencil technique is often the most effective, and can also be used for creating line work, by spraying on a narrow space between two hands.

GEOGLYPHS - They are not true rock art, consisting of large stone arrangements, often measuring hundreds of metres. Positive and negative versions are distinguished: the former are arrangements of stones or rocks placed over an area to form an image; in the latter, the image is created by removing cobbles of a darkly patinated desert pavement to expose the lighter- coloured stones beneath.

OTHER FORMS - Other forms of rock art also exist, and there is no truly sharp division between rock art and other ant forms. For instance, the separation between rock ant and portable art can be blurred. In northern Australia, beeswax figures were produced by pressing small pieces of beeswax onto the rock. Taxonomically they would belong to paintings as the process is additive.

ROCK ART STUDIES

Despite its comparative long history, the discipline has only become well established in the last decade. At present, its main approaches are those based on archaeological studies, the history of art, semiotics, geomorphology and certain applications in epistemology. Recently, rock art conservation, preservation and site management have experienced rapid development.

HISTORY OF DISCIPLINE - Rock art studies as a discipline has a long history. The earliest known recordings of rock art, from China, are over 1500 years old. More work was published during recent centuries, and with the 19th century, concerted efforts began. During the present century, rock art was largely absorbed into archaeology, but emerged as a separate field in the 1 980s.

ARCHAEOLOGICAL STUDIES - Archaeology attempts to use rock art to acquire additional knowledge about specific societies of the past, particularly for 'cognitive archaeology'. To do this reliably, the approximate age of the rock art in question must be known. Sometimes archaeology can itself provide supplementary dating evidence for rock art.

HISTORY OF ART - The beginnings of art and its entire early development are recorded largely in rock art. The rock art traditions of the world are therefore the most important information source for the art historian who seeks to learn about past art systems and models of humanly perceived reality.

SEMIOTICS - The semiotician is concerned with systems of signs, meaning and communication through symbolism. The past meanings of rock art cannot be established usually, but semiotic analysis may provide some access to systems of symbols, their possible structures, and their geographical and chronological distribution.

GEOMORPHOLOGY - Rock art is always intimately related to the geomorphology and the geochemistry of the surface on which it occurs. Geomorphological processes and their traces are often physically related to rock ant, especially to petroglyphs. They provide a relative time frame for the art and thus help us in dating it. Geomorphology is also highly relevant to rock art conservation.

EPISTEMOLOGY - Rock art traditions document early ontologies of human societies, or the systems of understanding the physical and non-physical worlds people related to They therefore provide glimpses of these past models of reality, and in doing so remind us of the relativity of our own such system. This evidence is therefore important to epistemology.

ROCK ART ANALYSIS

Scientific techniques can help in determining many details of rock art production which may help in its study and interpretation. Pigment analysis and sourcing, or the analysis of paint stratigraphies at certain sites, assist in examining rock paintings. Microscopic and internal analyses are more appropriate for petroglyphs. Statistic approaches have been used, and computers have become a standard tool of research.

PIGMENT STUDIES - The study and analysis of rock art pigments can tell us about their sources, composition, the treatment they may have been subjected to (e.9. heat treatment to alter colour, or sedimentation to remove sand grains), paint preparation, additives such as binders and extenders, and they may result in the detection of residues or remains such as airborne matter, brush fibres and other incidental inclusions.

PIGMENT SOURCING - When rock art pigments are analyzed chemically, they can provide compositional 'finger-printing' details from trace elements and impurities. It is then possible to compare the composition with that of minerals from potential source sites or known prehistoric quarry sites, to determine where the paint came from. This can help in establishing ancient trading networks.

PAINT STRATIGRAPHIES - At Australian rock painting sites, many successive layers of paints have been discovered, often separated by layers of natural mineral deposits. Such sequences of art traditions can provide a wealth of information about the cultural archaeology of the region, and they may contain substances or residues which can be dated directly. Such stratigraphies are more reliable and culturally more relevant than those of archaeology.

MICROSCOPIC STUDIES - The use of the microscope is almost indispensable in scientific rock art studies. Microscopic investigation is necessary for the detection of small organic and other particles, for the study of minute surface striations, for microerosion studies and dating, for conservation studies, and for the application of 'internal analysis'.

INTERNAL ANALYSIS - This technique was originally developed to determine production details of cut marks and engravings on Upper Palaeolithic portable objects in western Europe. With it, direction of movement, sequence of markings, repeated use of the same tool, and even handedness of artist may be determined. The general technique is also used in rock art, especially on engravings in limestone caves.

STATISTICAL ANALYSIS - The use of various statistical methods to express characteristics of rock art bodies has been introduced from archaeology. However, it is of limited application in the case of rock art, and often it has only purely descriptive value. This is because many rock art bodies are cumulative rather than belonging to a single tradition and may include stylistic responses. Also, most rock art bodies have survived incompletely and their statistical characteristics are of little real value.

COMPUTER USES - The computer has become a very important tool in the study of rock art. For instance, it can be used to enhance poor colour contrast in faded paintings and so assist discrimination of individual figures; to standardize colour information from photographic records; to re-constitute original colour information from calibrated records; to store pictorial and written information; or for studies involving cross-referencing, for instance by keywording systems.

STANDARDIZATION OF RESEARCH

To facilitate international rock art studies and to make research results compatible, the standardization of practices and methods is essential. This applies to scientific terminology, dating and other analytical methodologies, colour calibration, as well as agreed recording standards. Specific practices, such as the recording of geomorphological topographies, are being made uniform, as are computerized archives. For this to be possible, effective information exchange is required.

TERMINOLOGY - The discipline of rock art studies is developing an internationally standardized terminology for scientific usage. This will replace the past practices which often differed significantly in various regions, and will remove many inconsistencies and ambiguities. Publishing and international co-operation will become correspondingly easier as this standardization progresses.

DATING METHODS - In the area of scientific rock art dating it is particularly important to introduce internationally compatible standards. Until recently, the methods of dating were haphazard, poorly defined and poorly understood in many parts of the world. Standardization will assist researchers to better compare results from different regions.

ANALYTICAL METHODS - The proliferation of new analytical methods in various areas of rock art research and their application around the world renders it essential that they be standardized. This is facilitated by international journals and specialist conferences, as well as by the exchange of visiting specialists.

COLOUR CALIBRATION - The recent global introduction of standardized colour calibration will greatly facilitate the study, archival storage, digitized manipulation and conservation of rock at. A colour calibration standard has been set by the International Federation of Rock Art Organizations (IFRAO) in 1994, through the IFRAO Standard Colour Scale which has been distributed to all rock art researchers of the world.

RECORDING STANDARDS - The reliability of rock art recordings varies enormously, both in terms of the quantity and quality of information found. In order to standardize at least the aspect of accuracy, a system has been suggested in which levels of accuracy are stated in each manual recording. It is suggested that they be defined on a range from 1 to 100, the highest number being impeccable recording of all detail.

GEOMORPHOLOGICAL TOPOGRAPHY - In order to improve the qualitative aspects of manual rock art recordings, such as tracings, a graphic symbol system has been suggested which provides information of the local geomorphological topography, particularly around petroglyphs, in addition to the recording of the art motif itself. This can include the presence of accretions, exfoliation or erosion as well as details of topographical relief. Such 'maps' provide superior scientific recordings.

COMPUTERIZED ARCHIVES - The establishment of a number of computerized archives of rock art is in progress or is planned in various parts of the world. Their purposes may differ, but computerized information is easy to transfer and such archives are expected to play a key role in creating a single global discipline of rock art research.

INFORMATION EXCHANGE - An extensive system of information exchange already exists in rock art studies, especially through the International Federation of Rock Art Organizations (IFRAO). There are numerous scientific journals around the world, specialized conferences and seminars on rock art, and the proliferation of computerized records, reference lists and information systems will facilitate this exchange further.

RESOURCES - The main initiatives in the area of global standardization of rock art studies are taken by the International Federation of Rock Art Organizations (IFRAO), and by the twenty-four national or regional rock art associations affiliated with this body. They operate around the world, providing a uniform scientific forum for the discipline.

ROCK ART INTERPRETATION

Rock art has been interpreted by humans for practically as long as it has been produced by them. Most of this interpretation was essentially iconographic. Many cultural responses to rock art have been documented, and rock art has been an important cultural determinant. Its meaning has occupied many people. The possibilities of archaeological interpretation are limited, whereas analytical interpretation proceeds on the basis of scientific data.

ICONOGRAPHIC INTERPRETATION - It is a natural human reaction to rock art to try recognizing motifs depicted in it. This is a subjective process; iconographic conventions can vary significantly from one society to another. Subjects depicted cannot be identified with scientific precision, nor are such subjective identifications, such as animal species, testable. They are therefore of limited relevance to the scientific study of rock art.

CULTURAL RESPONSES - Each human society may respond to earlier rock arts, and such responses differ according to belief system, cultural convention and social factors. Some cultures have engaged in the wholesale destruction of earlier rock art, some have adopted graphic elements or entire traditions into their own culture. Many more such cultural responses have been observed, including the modification of previous art.

MEANING OF ROCK ART - It has been a frequent preoccupation of people to ask questions concerning the meaning of rock art. For the arts of recent societies, we have a great deal of ethnographic information about this, and for some older arts, ethnographic extrapolation or analogy may help. However, the truly ancient rock arts of the world provide no scientific basis for establishing their meanings, only for endless and futile speculations about them.

ARCHAEOLOGICAL INTERPRETATION - Archaeologists have tried many interpretational approaches for rock art. In particular, the determination of motif categories and their tabulation for statistical analyses is popular. Archaeologists have also tried to use rock art to infer demographic patterns, social or cultural networks, and the extent of artistic traditions. Finally, there have been attempts to deduce ethnic information about prehistoric peoples from rock art.

ANALYTICAL INTERPRETATION - The interpretation of analytical data from rock art is much more reliable than archaeological interpretation. Technological information about the art helps in establishing methods of ant production, sequences of art traditions, the antiquity of rock art, and similar empirical deductions. Generally, this provides no information about meaning about the rock art, but it offers more reliable interpretations than other approaches.

CONSERVATION AND SITE MANAGEMENT

This field has developed rapidly in recent years, due to the realization that rock arts, which may have survived for very long periods, are coming under increasing threat of deterioration and destruction. Although natural factors do contribute to preservation threats, the main factors are attributable to human interference. Education, protective legislation and site management are important to the survival of rock art.

HISTORY OF ROCK ART CONSERVATION

Some methods of rock art conservation by tribal people have been recorded, and early conservation work is known. However, current practices were introduced comparatively recently. Future developments in rock art conservation are already being contemplated.

TRADITIONAL CONSERVATION - Some indigenous or tribal societies have traditionally conducted rock art conservation. For instance, the Aboriginal people of Australia have for a long time taken care of their rock art by placing rocks and grass above painted shelters to divert rain water. Also, they have for thousands of years re-painted rock paintings regularly whenever these became faint.

EARLY CONSERVATION - There have been attempts to preserve rock art for many decades, but this need became particularly pressing when it was observed that the rock art in some world- famous caves in Europe was deteriorating very fast. This led to the rapid development of the relevant technology within the last few decades.

CURRENT PRACTICE - Many of the current practices in rock art conservation have been developed in Australia in recent years. The general strategy is to not interfere with the rock art or the rock surface directly, but to create or maintain the natural conditions that have facilitated survival of the art in the past, or to rectify environmental imbalances. Conservation measures should be reversible.

FUTURE DEVELOPMENTS - Two main strategies are being pursued: the production of facsimiles of complete rock ant sites for exhibition purposes, to avoid visitor traffic at valuable sites; and the comPuterization of photoqraphic records with a standard colour scale, for permanent storage. The first method is in use already, the second will permit perpetual preservation of ant even if the original is destroyed.

CONSERVATION THREATS

Threats to rock art conservation can be divided into those of natural agents and human agents. The former are very diverse, and some of them remain beyond our control. Water, salt formation, dust deposition, weathering, exfoliation and biological agents are among the natural agents. Human agents are usually the greater threat to the rock art, but they can also be controlled more effectively.

WATER - The most common natural threat to rock art is water. It can be in the form of rain water, capillary moisture within the rock, condensation, run off, seepage or splash back. Each of these forms requires different treatment, but the effects of them can often be successfully mitigated. Damage by water can be very effective and destroy a site completely.

SALT FORMATION - When water travels within the rock, it may form a sub-cutaneous zone of salt deposition which with time will weaken to rock and cause spalling. Alternatively, water-soluble salts can precipitate on the rock surface and discolour or conceal the rock art. Salt crusts are also formed when vandalistic photographers wet rock paintings for better contrast.

DUST DEPOSITION - Dust is mostly caused by the feet of visitors of the site, be they human or animal visitors. This dust rises in the air and is then deposited on the rock surface. It may become cemented by a mineral precipitate, such as silica, rendering the unsightly covering difficult to remove.

WEATHERING - There are many forms of weathering, attributable to precipitation, frost, wild fire, running water, the wind, even the chemical products of weathering processes themselves. Mechanical and chemical weathering processes can be distinguished, and they are the basis of geomorphological changes to the rock.

EXFOLIATION - Exfoliation processes include those attributable to salt spalling, fire damage, insolation (radiation of the sun) or mechanical forces. Besides the exfoliation of layers or portions of rock, the process of exfoliation may also be active at the level of individual rock grains, particularly in sandstones. This is called granular exfoliation.

BIOLOGICAL AGENTS - These include lichens, fungi and microbiota, insects and birds, even mammals, and occasionally plants. Their effects are usually readily visible. Most can be controlled quite easily, although the respective methods of control differ significantly.

DAMAGE BY HUMAN VISITORS - The behaviour of tourists at rock at sites has been extensively studied in Australia during the 1980s. High risk groups have been identified, and the effectiveness of specific measures has been studied. Vandalism may be intentional or unintentional. Other forms of damage stem from the introduction of brganic materials to sensitive sites, or from walking on engraved rocks.

DAMAGE BY RESEARCHERS - Rock art researchers have been guilty of extensive damage to the rock art of the world, mostly through contaminating or damaging the surface in the course of recording activities. For instance, water applied to paintings has led to the deposition of soluble salts over the art, and badly executed casting attempts have left residues and altered the rock's patina. Chalk has been used, which has reduced the analytical potential of the rock art.

CONSERVATION METHODS - The main methods concern water control and dust suppression at the sites; salt removal from and stabilization of rock art panels; environmental control, including air conditioning of whole sites; the control of destructive insects and lichen, and the exclusion of large animals from rock art shelters.

WATER CONTROL - Rain water, run off and splash back can be remedied very easily. Artificial roofs, drip lines and gutters have been widely used. Seepage in the rock has been treated successfully by grouting of the entry points. Condensation has been treated by controlling atmospheric conditions. Only capillary moisture is usually problematic, and attempts at mitigation involve major changes to a site's hydrography.

DUST SUPPRESSION - This has been achieved by a number of means, including the establishment of walk ways of gravel, rock slabs or concrete; covering the ground with plastic matting; or the installation of wooden boardwalks. These methods also have the added advantage of protecting the archaeological floor deposit from erosion.

SALT REMOVAL - Salt can severely threaten rock art, in which case it can be removed by the repeated application of poultices. These are placed over the art, and they draw the salt out to the surface and deposit it in the poultice where they can be removed. This treatment can only be effected by experienced and trained rock art conservators.

STABILIZATION - Stabilization of rock surfaces has been attempted, but with very limited success. We possess no transparent miracle coating that can be applied over a rock surface to protect the art. Stabilization of disintegrating rock masses has also been attempted and has remained largely unsuccessful. It can only be arrested if the factor responsible for it is dealt with.

ENVIRONMENTAL CONTROL - This is a preferred conservation method and can take on many forms. Ideally, it is preceded by a painstaking study of the environmental conditions, to identify the atmospheric, hydrological or biological factors that cause deterioration. Once known they can be corrected for the benefit of the rock art, without directly interfering with the art.

AIR CONDITIONING - This is an extreme form of environmental control, in which the atmospheric conditions of a site are entirely controlled. Ambient air temperature and relative air humidity are set at ideal values and maintained by an air conditioning plant. This usually involves a limestone cave, but there is also an open rock art site at which this measure has been taken.

INSECT CONTROL - The insects most likely to cause rock art conservation problems are termites and mud-daubing wasps. The termites build covered tunnels over the rock surfaces, and the wasps construct complex nest structures made of mud. All termite nests within fifty metres need to be destroyed, and wasp nests can be carefully removed after wetting.

LICHEN CONTROL - Some lichen may have a corrosive effect on rock surfaces. To remove them, herbicides and other chemicals have been used. However, it must be remembered that any chemical treatment of the rock, for this or another reason, will always result in some contamination of the rock which reduces the scientific research potential.

ANIMAL EXCLUSION - Many animals have been found to damage rock art, including swallows which build nests in rockshelters, and a number of large mammals which roam in them or rub their bodies on the rock walls. This includes pigs, cattle, buffaloes and horses. They can be easily excluded by erecting fences around an exclusion zone.

SITE MANAGEMENT

Visitor control of some form is essential at rock art sites that are accessible to the public. Among the favoured measures are enclosures, raised boardwalks, visitor books, interpretation signs and barriers. In areas of very heavy tourist visitation, sacrificial sites may be selected for tourism. Supervision is essential at some sites, but the simplest measure is good protective legislation.

VISITOR CONTROL - The degree of visitor control necessary at a rock art site determines the types of measures most appropriate. At a highly sensitive and important site, visitors may be totally excluded by physical means. Public sites often have varying levels of visitor control, including barriers, boardwalks and enclosures.

ENCLOSURES - These are favoured at unsupervised sites close to urban regions. They usually consist of steel grids or cages enclosing the entire art panels, securely fixed to the rock, and strong enough to resist vandalistic damage. Such enclosures are found especially at Spanish and Australian sites.

RAISED BOARDWALKS - This measure is favoured for public sites with low supervision. Boardwalks are on stilts, and they have been constructed either from timber or steel. They protect the archaeological deposit from erosion, suppress dust, and restrain the visitor from reaching the rock art while gaining a good view of it.

VISITOR BOOKS - These serve to provide information to the site manager on the frequency of visits, and a visitation profile of the site can be extracted from the data provided by such books. Such information can help in planning site management practices, tourism policies and visitor facilities.

INTERPRETATION SIGNS - Most human damage at rock art sites is the result of a lack of information or the frustration of the visitor. This problem can be largely eliminated by good and informative interpretation signs. Such signs may also provide directions concerning visitor behaviour and make mention of the protection status of the site.

BARRIERS - Two types of barriers are in use at rock art sites: physical barriers and psychological barriers. The latter may be artificial features but may not be perceived as such, if they are well designed. Physical barriers may be counter-productive at unsupervised sites because they can be perceived as a challenge by the visitor.

SACRIFICIAL SITES - A favoured strategy is to select one site, or a small group of sites in a region, and sacrifice it to the public by making it available for visitation. In this way all public attention is focused on the selected site, while all other sites receive no attention and are much easier to protect. The eventual loss of the sacrificed site, through visitation damage, is an acceptable price to pay for the preservation of all other sites.

SUPERVISION - At sites that are very important but lack effective physical protection, or at sites of particularly high visitation levels, permanent supervision is usually essential. Such a level of protection has been established at many sites, especially in France and Australia.

LEGISLATION - Protective legislation of rock art exists in many countries, but it differs significantly from one region to another. In some countries, penalties for interfering with rock art are very severe, and as a consequence, the rock art in these countries is inevitably among the best preserved. There can be no doubt that effective legislative protection is required for all rock art in the world.

RESOURCES - There are several agencies around the world which can assist and advise on questions of rock art conservation. Among them are:
Department of Cultural Material Studies, University of Canberra, Australia
Getty Conservation Institute, Marina Del Rey, California, U.S.A.
ICOMOS, Paris, France
ICCROM, Rome, Italy
International Federation of Rock Art Organizations, Melbourne, Australia Australian Institute of Aboriginal and Torres Strait Islander Studies, Canberra, Australia

• INDEX •

INDEX